INTERNATIONAL RESPONSES TO GENDERED-BASED DOMESTIC VIOLENCE

This edited volume represents a joint effort by international experts to analyze the prevalence and nature of gender-based domestic violence across the globe and how it is dealt with at both national and international levels. With studies being conducted in 20 different countries and 4 distinct regions, the contributors to this volume shed light on the ways in which contextual particularities shape the practices and strategies of addressing the socio-cultural and legal problem of gender-based domestic violence in the countries or regions where they do research. Special attention is devoted to developing countries where there is a lack of a consistent legal definition of gender-based domestic violence and where violence against women is widely considered a private matter. The authors of the chapters share a common goal of raising public awareness of the significance in nuanced local experiences of women and other individuals from gender and sexual minority groups facing gender-based violence.

Furthermore, the authors attend, analytically, to the newly emerging, overlapping influences of COVID-19 and global warming. Their research findings acknowledge and provide a detailed account of how the two ecological and socio-economic crises can combine to produce economic devastation, disconnect victims from necessary social services and assistance, and create a large degree of panic and uncertainty. In addition, they intend to offer insights into next steps to not only adjust existing public policies, legislation, and social services to the ever-changing national and global contexts, but also to make new ones.

The book is intended for a wide range of scholars (both professors and students) and practitioners in a large number of areas, including but not limited to criminal justice, criminology, law, human rights, social justice, social work, nursing, sociology, and political or public affairs.

Dongling Zhang, PhD, is an Assistant Professor from the Department of Global Languages, Cultures and Societies Webster University, the United States of America. He earned his PhD degree in Justice Studies from Arizona State University. His research interests include university entrepreneurship education, micro-enterprise development program in China's urban areas, social capital theories, and feminist theories. His current research focuses on the power dynamics of entrepreneurship, exploring various forms of collective and interpersonal violence instigated by the overwhelming influences of entrepreneurial ethos. It specifically examines the institutions through which a social body—the entrepreneur—is continually structured and transformed. These institutions include the family, neighborhood, labor market, government, and more.

Diana Scharff Peterson, PhD, has nearly 20 years of experience in higher education teaching in the areas of research methods; comparative criminal justice systems; race, gender, class, and crime; statistics; criminology; sociology; and drugs and behavior at seven different institutions of higher education. She has been the chairperson of three different criminal justice programs over the past 20 years and has published in the areas of criminal justice, social work, higher education, sociology, business, and management. Her research interests include issues in policing (training and education) and community policing, assessment and leadership in higher education, family violence, evaluation research, and program development. She is the co-editor of *Domestic Violence in International Context* published by Routledge in 2017.

ADVANCES IN POLICE THEORY AND PRACTICE SERIES

Series Editor: Dilip K. Das

Honor-Based Violence: Policing and Prevention
Karl Anton Roberts, Gerry Campbell, and Glen Lloyd

Policing and the Mentally Ill: International Perspectives
Duncan Chappell

Security Governance, Policing, and Local Capacity
Jan Froestad and Clifford Shearing

Police Performance Appraisals: A Comparative Perspective
Serdar Kenan Gul and Paul O'Connell

Policing in France
Jacques de Maillard and Wesley G. Skogan

Women in Policing around the World: Doing Gender and Policing in a Gendered Organization
Venessa Garcia

Police Behavior, Hiring, and Crime Fighting: An International View
Edited by John A. Eterno, Ben Stickle, Diana Peterson, and Dilip K. Das

Translational Criminology in Policing
Edited by The George Mason Police Research Group with David Weisburd

Exploring Contemporary Policing Challenges: A Global Perspective
Sanja Kutnjak Ivković, Jon Maskály, Christopher M. Donner, Irena Cajner Mraović & Dilip Das

International Responses to Gendered-Based Domestic Violence
Gender-Specific and Socio-Cultural Approaches
Edited by Dongling Zhang and Diana Scharff Peterson

INTERNATIONAL RESPONSES TO GENDERED-BASED DOMESTIC VIOLENCE

Gender-Specific and Socio-Cultural Approaches

Edited by Dongling Zhang and Diana Scharff Peterson

Routledge
Taylor & Francis Group
NEW YORK AND LONDON

Designed cover image: © Getty Images / Klaus Vedfelt

First published 2023
by Routledge
605 Third Avenue, New York, NY 10158

and by Routledge
4 Park Square, Milton Park, Abingdon, Oxon, OX14 4RN

Routledge is an imprint of the Taylor & Francis Group, an informa business

ISBN: 978-1-032-20529-8 (hbk)
ISBN: 978-1-032-20530-4 (pbk)
ISBN: 978-1-003-26404-0 (ebk)

DOI: 10.4324/9781003264040

Typeset in Bembo
by Newgen Publishing UK

This is presented as a collection of gender-based domestic violence victims' and survivors' voices and dedicated to the UN and Women's UN Report Network who inspired this work.

CONTENTS

FIGURES

IMAGES

TABLES

CONTRIBUTORS

Alanoud AlSharekh, PhD, is the Director of Ibtkar Strategic Consultancy, leading the Empowering Kuwaiti Women in Politics training program, and has held senior consultative and teaching positions in academic, governmental, and non-governmental institutions in the Arabian Gulf and abroad. Her research won the Arab Prize for best publication in a foreign journal in 2014 and includes books such as *The Gulf Family* and *Popular Culture and Political Identity in the Arab Gulf States*, examining the persistent importance of family and tribe in modern Gulf politics and society. She was awarded the knighthood of the National Order of Merit by the French Government in 2016 for her dedication to improving women's rights in the region. She is currently an associate fellow at the Chatham House MENA Program and a research fellow at Arab Gulf States Institute in Washington. She has been named one of the 100 most influential and inspiring women in the world by the BBC for 2019.

Emily Acevedo, PhD, is an Associate Professor in Political Science at California State University, Los Angeles. Her research focuses on public security threats in Mexico, gender-based violence and femicide in Mexico, and institutional reform and strengthening democratic accountability and transparency.

Fikresus Amahazion, PhD, is an Assistant Professor at the National College of Arts and Social Sciences (Eritrea). His work focuses on Human Rights, Political Economy, and Development. His recent work, "Short-sighted Solutions: An Examination of Europe's Response to the Mediterranean Migration Crisis", is available in *Deadly Voyages: Migrant Journeys across the Mediterranean* (2019), published by Lexington Books.

Flor Avellaneda is currently a PhD candidate at the University of Houston Graduate College of Social Work. Her dissertation builds on her experiences with the intersectional challenges faced by minority women. Using a mixed-methods approach, her dissertation examines the relationship between migration (in-country vs. transnational), intimate partner violence, and health, in Mexican migrant women. She completed bachelor's and master's degrees in social work, and prior to her doctoral studies, she served as an advocate for victims of domestic violence at the Family Abuse Center, Executive Director of AVANCE, and faculty member of the Baylor University Diana

R. Garland School of Social Work, all in Waco, TX. Upon completion of her PhD, Flor will pursue a tenure-track faculty position at a Tier One research institution.

Nour AlMukhled is a Kuwaiti social activist focused on humanitarian issues with an emphasis on women's rights. She has been focusing on ending gender-based violence since 2017, a few months after earning her BA degrees from GUST, through managing Kuwaiti-based nonprofit Eithar, a civil society organization that advocates for women's rights and the prevention of violence against women. Meanwhile, Nour is the project manager of Abolish 153, a Kuwaiti-based NGO that aims to end honor killings, in collaboration with the Gibran Chair of the University of Maryland. In the course of the project, they have been working to fight against stereotypes against women as well as putting their efforts into aiding the state to increase the percentage of women in leadership positions.

Aneesa A. Baboolal, PhD, is an Assistant Professor in the Department of Crime and Justice Studies at the University of Massachusetts—Dartmouth. Her research interests include violence against women across intersecting identities, including race/ethnicity, immigrant, and religious minority status. She has conducted studies examining Caribbean women's experiences of intimate partner violence in ethnic enclave communities and her most recent work explores gendered and racialized violence against Muslims in the United States.

Arundhati Bhattacharyya, PhD, is an Associate Professor in the Department of Political Science at the University of Burdwan in West Bengal, India. She received her PhD from the University of Calcutta, India. She has been invited to the United Nations, Geneva, to present her research on Indian rural women and has authored two monographs.

Mostafa Boieblan, PhD, is an Associate Professor/a part-time instructor at the Polytechnic University of Madrid, and the Alfonso X el Sabio University, Spain. His research interests include issues in embodied cognition, discourse analysis, gender ideology, conceptual metaphor, and domestic violence against women. He is also a member of the organizing committee of Empirical Methods in Cognitive Linguistics workshops. He also worked as a research assistant at The Library of Social Science, New York City. He has published an article in a scientific journal "Dimensions of Coupling Source and Target Domains in Multimodality-Based and Orientational Metaphors".

Roksana Badruddoja, PhD, is a Professor of Sociology and Women's and Gender Studies at Manhattan College. She teaches courses on feminist research methods, women of color in the United States, feminist activism, race and resistance, codes of gender, social inequalities, and representations of women. Dr. Badruddoja's research in the areas of race and ethnicity, sexuality, gender, religion, and culture, and how these impact "South Asian" American women has been published in numerous peer-reviewed journals. These include the *National Women's Studies Association Journal*, the *International Journal of Sociology of the Family*, and the *International Review of Modern Sociology*. She is the author of *Eyes of the Storms: The Voices of South Asian-American Women* and the editor of *"New Maternalisms": Tales of Mother (Dislodging the Unthinkable)*.

Lindsay M. Cannon, MPH, MSW, is a PhD student in Sociology at the University of Wisconsin—Madison, and a demography trainee at the Center for Demography and Ecology. Her work focuses on the intersection between sexual and reproductive health, gender-based violence, and substance use. She has been involved with research in Ghana over the last three years, including facilitating the training of peer educators for a sexual violence prevention program.

Sarah D. Compton, PhD, MPH, is a Research Assistant Professor in the Department of Obstetrics and Gynecology at the University of Michigan Medical School. Dr. Compton has a background in public health where she has developed deep professional and research ties to Ghana, especially in the fields of sexual and reproductive health and emergency medicine.

Bahiyah Dato Haji Abd Hamid, PhD, is Associate Professor at the Centre for Literacy and Sociocultural Transformation, Faculty of Social Sciences and Humanities, Universiti Kebangsaan Malaysia. Her research interests are language and gender, gender issues, identity construction, code alternation and code choice, and discourse and semiotics analysis.

Eugene K. M. Darteh, PhD, MPhil, is an Associate Professor in the Department of Population and Health as well as the Dean of Students of the University of Cape Coast, Ghana. Dr. Darteh has worked as an academic and a researcher for the past 13 years. Over the last eight years, his research has focused on reproductive health issues among youth, aging, and the aged, and child and women's health. This work has been geared toward contributing to the discourse on making the world a better place and achieving some of the Millennium Development Goals (now Sustainable Development Goals).

Chuka Emezue, PhD, MPH, MPA, is a certified health education specialist and Assistant Professor at the Department of Women, Children, and Family Nursing at Rush University College of Nursing. Emezue earned a PhD in Nursing, a Master of Public Health (MPH), and a Master of Public Affairs (MPA) from the University of Missouri—Columbia. His research is focused on tailoring culturally relevant, gender- and age-responsive interventions for partner abusers and/or survivors of partner violence, with particular emphasis on male victims and abusers in immigrant and rural communities. His primary interests are the safety and well-being of male survivors of partner violence, early prevention of partner violence, and reducing post-intervention recidivism among recently rehabilitated partner abusers. He is currently adapting and disseminating mobile health interventions targeting dating violence among rural adolescent males to inform sexual, emotional, and reproductive health decisions among vulnerable or difficult-to-reach youth at the margins of traditional care.

Hiam Elgousi, PhD, gained her MSc in Development Training and Education from the University of Wolverhampton, United Kingdom. In her PhD research, she examined the role and influence of contemporary scholars (Ulma) on Arabian women's rights with a focus on Islamic women living in Egypt. She has over 15 years' experience in community development, training, and research in the Middle East and the UK. She has undertaken various consultancies and held several posts including the social mobilization officer with UNICEF—Sudan and was also a visiting lecturer with the Arab Academy for Science and Technology—Egypt—in cooperation with Virginia Tech University, the United States, between 2006 and 2008. Currently she is working as a consultant and research associate with several organizations in Egypt and the UK.

Tanya Grant, is an Assistant Professor at St. Mary's University, San Antonio, Texas. She holds a PhD in Criminal Justice from Capella University, an MS in Criminal Justice from the University of New Haven, and a BA in Psychology from Fairfield University. Dr. Grant's teaching interests include domestic and sexual violence and the intersection of pop culture, law enforcement's response to domestic violence, and domestic violence advocacy. Dr. Grant's field experience includes juvenile justice, corrections, and domestic violence advocacy. Dr. Grant is a member of the New England Council on Crime and Delinquency, The Northeastern Association of Criminal Justice Sciences, and Academy of Criminal Justice Sciences.

Verônica Alcântara Guerra holds a PhD in Anthropology. Her MSc thesis at the Federal University of Paraiba focused on transgender women in small towns of northeastern Brazil. In her doctoral dissertation, she did research with migrant transgender women focusing on the returning process to Brazil. Her actual research is on the political production of transfeminicide in Brazil.

Ruzy Suliza Hashim, PhD, is a Professor of Literature at the Centre for Literacy and Sociocultural Transformation, Faculty of Social Sciences and Humanities, Universiti Kebangsaan Malaysia (UKM). She currently serves as Director of Universiti Kebangsaan Malaysia Press.

Habibah Ismail, PhD, is a Lecturer at the Faculty of Major Language Studies, Universiti Sains Islam Malaysia. She has a doctoral degree in Linguistics (University of Sydney), focusing on gender issues in Malaysian sports news discourse based on media's examination of written and visual texts.

Mohd Muzhafar Idrus, PhD, is an Assistant Professor at Universiti Sains Islam Malaysia. His research interests include discourse analysis and literature. He is a reviewer for a number of Taylor & Francis' journals including *Critical Inquiry in Language Studies*, *Cogent Education*, and *Cogent Arts and Humanities*.

Sirin Knecht is a PhD candidate at the Max Planck Institute for Social Anthropology. Her current research focuses on the realization of transferred women's rights and empowerment claims NGOs are negotiating and practicing in their daily life as institutions and project implementation actors.

Tonny Kirabira is currently a Visiting Professional in the Office of Public Counsel for Victims at the International Criminal Court. He holds an LLM in International Human Rights Law from the University of Notre Dame (United States), and a bachelor of Laws degree from Uganda Christian University (Uganda). He has attained specialized training from the European University Institute (Italy), RFK Training Institute (Italy), and Lucerne Academy for Human Rights Implementation (Switzerland). He was a recipient of the VLIR-UOS scholarship under the Sustainable Development and Human Rights Law program at the University of Antwerp in Belgium. He was admitted to the Ugandan Bar in 2014 and practices as a Barrister and Solicitor in the High Court of Uganda and all courts of judicature. Tonny worked as a legal officer at Vision Group in Uganda. He has been involved in international human rights work, including participation in UN Human Rights Council sessions in Geneva (Switzerland). He is conducting research for a PhD in Law at the University of Portsmouth (United Kingdom), focusing on transitional justice and international criminal prosecution. He has teaching responsibilities which focus on criminal law and human rights at the undergraduate level.

Fiza Lee-Winter is a PhD candidate at the Institute of Development Research and Development Policy (IEE) at the Ruhr-Universität Bochum (RUB) in Germany where she is conducting her research project on the compatibilities of a human rights-based approach (HRBA) to refugee protection with Asian regionalism, using the Rohingya Refugee Crisis as a case study. Her research interests include international human rights law, transnational governance, refugee and forced migration studies, and gender-based violence. She is also a member of the Institute for International Law of Peace and Armed Conflict (IFHV) at the RUB, and an associate member of the SYLFF-Mikrokolleg on Forced Migration. Fiza Lee has obtained her Master of Arts in Human Rights and Democratization from EIUC/Global Campus of Human Rights and RUB, and a Bachelor of Arts in Criminal Justice from the University of Northern Colorado. She was recently awarded a PhD Research funding and support by the Konrad-Adenauer-Stiftung in Germany.

Alison Mc Letchie, PhD, is an Assistant Professor at South Carolina State University where she teaches anthropology and sociology in the Department of Social Sciences. She obtained her PhD in Sociology in 2013, an MA in Anthropology, and Certificate in Museum Management in 2003 from the University of South Carolina (USC). Her primary research interest includes race and ethnicity, economic inequality, music, and religion. Some of her current projects include investigations of Caribbean Carnivals in the Carolinas, behavioral and sexual health among Historically Black Colleges and Universities (HBCU) students, inclusion and diversity on HBCU campuses, and a study of Caribbean Catholic music.

Hiroaki Matsuura, PhD, is Provost and Vice President for Academic Affairs of Shoin University in Japan and a member of the World Committee of Tourism Ethics of the United Nations World Tourism Organization. He is an economist and demographer who is interested in the intersection between human rights and child health and welfare. Before joining Shoin, he was Lecturer at the University of Oxford's School of Interdisciplinary Area Studies. Hiroaki received his ScD in Global Health and Population from Harvard University. He is an editorial board member of the *Child Abuse Review* and international advisor of the *Sociology of Illness and Health* among others.

Michelle L. Munro-Kramer, PhD, CNM, FNP-BC, is an Assistant Professor, the Suzanne Bellinger Feetham Professor of Nursing, a Johnson & Johnson Nurse Innovation Fellow, and the Director of the Office of Global Affairs at the University of Michigan School of Nursing. She is trained as a family nurse practitioner and certified nurse midwife and has over a decade of research experience related to gender-based violence. For the last five years, she has been working extensively with colleagues in Ghana to explore interventions for gender-based violence prevention within the university setting.

Nancy Madera is a sociologist (Universidad de Buenos Aires) and a doctoral candidate in Political Science from the School of Government and Politics of the Universidad Nacional de San Martín (Argentina). Her dissertation thesis discusses the role of international human rights norms and its implementation on the paradigm shift regarding legislation on violence against women in Latin America. With publications on women's substantive representation, institutional mechanisms for the advancement of women, women's human rights agenda, and the feminist movement in Latin America, she is currently a member of the interdisciplinary research group "Gender, (In)equalities and rights in tension"—sponsored by the Consejo Latinoamericano de Ciencias Sociales (CLACSO)—and the Swiss School of Latin American Studies (SSLAS).

Daina Nathaniel, PhD, is a Professor of Communication, Media and Cultural Studies and Director of Undergraduate Programs in the Knight School of Communication at Queens University of Charlotte. A native of Trinidad and Tobago, her research interests center around culture, identity, nationhood, and digital inclusion. Most recently she has been exploring how the Caribbean diaspora use social media to create a sense of connection to their various homelands. Her primary research area is cultural studies which looks at the relationships between cultures within societies, marginalized communities, issues of power and domination, the postcolonial experience, issues of race and ethnicity between disparate groups, and all the attendant challenges that arise as people try to find a sense of place within their various environments: home, school, work, church, community, and online.

Pamela Neumann, PhD, is Assistant Professor of Sociology in the Department of Social Sciences at Texas A&M International University (Laredo, TX). Her research examines the politics of gender violence law, everyday state practices, feminist activism, and women's perceptions of laws and legal institutions in Nicaragua. Her work has been published in journals such as *Gender & Society, Social Forces, Law & Society Review*, and *Latin American Politics & Society*. She earned her PhD in Sociology from the University of Texas at Austin in 2016 and subsequently held a post-doctoral fellowship at Tulane University in the Stone Center for Latin American Studies (2016–2018) and a Visiting Assistant Professor position at Bucknell University (2018–2019). She also holds an MA in Latin American Studies (UT-Austin) and a BA in Political Science (Trinity University—San Antonio).

Anwar Ouassini, PhD, joined Delaware State University as an Assistant Professor of Sociology and Criminal Justice in Fall 2016. Dr. Ouassini earned his doctorate in Sociology from the University of New Mexico in 2013. His research interests include social movements, political sociology, and comparative criminal justice systems. He is currently working on projects that explore the intersection of race and religious identities in the Arab World, the relationship between civil society, social movements, and democratic development in West Africa, and Criminal Justice Reform in the Maghreb. Dr. Ouassini teaches courses in Sociological Theory, Complex Organizations, Contemporary Issues in Criminal Justice, and Sociology of Culture.

Nabil Ouassini, PhD, is an Assistant Professor at Prairie View A&M University in Texas. He received his PhD in Criminal Justice from Indiana University at Bloomington and his research interests include sociology, criminology, legitimation and legitimacy, and criminal justice reform in the Arab world.

Ruth Owusu-Antwi, MD, is a specialist psychiatrist in the Department of Psychiatry at Komfo Anokye Teaching Hospital as well as an adjunct lecturer at the Kwame Nkrumah University of Science and Technology in Kumasi, Ghana. As one of the few mental health professionals in Ghana, Dr. Owusu-Antwi has become acutely aware of the health effects of gender-based violence. She has recently developed the *Abuse Clinic* at Komfo Anokye Teaching Hospital in Kumasi, Ghana, to provide comprehensive care for the physical health, mental health, reproductive health, psychosocial, and legal needs of individuals who have experienced gender-based violence.

Thiago de Lima Oliveira is a doctoral student in Social Anthropology at the University of São Paulo and visiting researcher at the Vrije Universiteit Amsterdam. His current research is on gender and development projects in Amazon. He is also the author *Sobre o Desejo nômade*, a monography on sex and small towns in northeastern Brazil.

Luis R. Torres, PhD, is Associate Professor, Director of the Center for Drug and Social Policy Research, and Humana Endowed Chair for the Social Determinants of Health in the Graduate College of Social Work (GCSW) at the University of Houston. He is also Associate Professor of Behavioral and Social Sciences in the University of Houston College of Medicine. His research focuses on health disparities, social determinants of health, and co-occurring mental health, substance use, and medical disorders. Dr. Torres is also actively involved in research and community engagement initiatives aimed at building community resilience, with a focus on Hispanics, African Americans, and other minority communities. His work has been funded by SAMHSA, NIDA, ACF, and other federal and private funders. He has traveled and worked extensively in Latin America and has ongoing research collaborations in Mexico, El Salvador, and Puerto Rico.

Kiesha Warren-Gordon, PhD, is an Associate Professor of Criminal Justice/Criminology at Ball State University where she also serves as the Director of the African American Studies Program. Dr. Warren-Gordon's work centers on critical approaches of community engagement while working with marginalized communities. Her research explores the intersection of race, class, and gender as it relates to violence and intercultural conflict. Currently, Dr. Warren-Gordon is active in several research projects including critical pedagogical approaches to teaching positive community involvement outside of traditional criminal justice educational norms; violence against women of Belize. Dr. Warren-Gordon is also active in the criminal justice professional community. She currently serves as the Past President of the Midwest Criminal Justice Association. She is also Senior Faculty Fellow for Indiana Campus Compact.

FOREWORD

International Responses to Interpersonal Violence: Gender-Specific and Socio-Cultural Approaches

Lois A. Herman
Managing Director WUNRN
Women's UN Report Network
Https://orcid.org/0000-0002-3726-8081

ENDING VIOLENCE AGAINST WOMEN, INTERPRSONAL VIOLENCE—RHETORIC TO REALITY—DUE DILIGENCE

....

In today's complex and volatile world, tools and strategies to address interpersonal gender violence are even more urgent and serious than ever. This book uniquely reaches an expansive range of countries and cultures. In the recent past, we have seen shocking increases in violence against women and girls, interpersonal violence, due to the COVID-19 pandemic, guns and weapons from civil society to law enforcement, conflicts and wars and resulting migration, immigration, refugee status, and internal displacement. Political will and public will must be involved and accountable for addressing gender-based violence in all dimensions, throughout the world. Climate change and environmental challenges are increasing and can catalyze gender-based violence.

A major issue impacting gender violence is technology, and online violence. Online is the new front line for violence against women and girls, and it has increased exponentially during COVID-19 and the lockdowns. Online violence is an epicenter of risk, intersectional and intergenerational, and compounding multiple forms of violence against women and girls, including trafficking.

WHAT IS THE MOST RISKY, DANGEROUS HUMAN SITUATION IN THIS WORLD? TO BE A WOMAN

WHAT GROUP OF PEOPLE IN TODAY'S WORLD SUFFER THE MOST PERSECUTION? GIRLS

WHY IS VIOLENCE AGAINST WOMEN AND GIRLS SO GLOBALLY PREVALENT, YEAR AFTER YEAR, IN SPITE OF LAWS AND COUNTRY COMMITMENTS?

This book will explore new strategies, best practices, multisector engagement.

WHY IS THERE SUCH A BARRIER ON GENDER VIOLENCE BETWEEN THE PUBLIC AND PRIVATE SPHERES?

WHY DOES VIOLENCE AGAINST WOMEN CONTINUE TO BE A WEAPON OF WAR?

WHEN STATES HAVE AN OBLIGATION UNDER INTERNATIONAL HUMAN RIGHTS LAW TO INVESTIGATE AND PROSECUTE HUMAN RIGHTS VIOLATIONS AND PROVIDE REMEDY FOR VICTIMS, WHY SO OFTEN, PERVASIVELY, DOES THIS NOT HAPPEN? A former UN Special Rapporteur on the Independence of Judges and Lawyers:

> When crimes and human rights violations go unpunished, and assuredly those affecting women, then States should be held accountable for contributing to a culture of impunity and lawlessness. When certain types of crimes, such as honor crimes, affect disproportionately one gender, go UNPUNISHED, the State CAN, in addition, be held accountable for discriminatory treatment under the law.

YET, SPECIFIC MEMBER STATES, AS IN THIS AUDIENCE, HAVE TAKEN A LEADERSHIP POSITION ON VIOLENCE AGAINST WOMEN AND ARE CREATING LANDMARK EFFORTS FOR PREVENTION AND REDRESS ON VIOLENCE AGAINST WOMEN AND WILL BE INSTRUMENTAL IN FORMING OUR FRAMEWORK AND ACTION PLAN FORWARD.

WHY DO NEGATIVE GENDER STEREOTYPES EXACERBATE DISRESPECT, INEQUALITY, EVEN VIOLENCE AGAINST WOMEN AND GIRLS?

WHY IS THERE NO MECHANISM FOR FOLLOW-UP BY COUNTRIES AFTER THE REPORTS OF THE MISSION OF THE SPECIAL RAPPORTEUR ON VIOLENCE AGAINST WOMEN?

WHY HAS VIOLENCE AGAINST WOMEN AND GIRLS BECOME NORMALIZED IN SO MANY PARTS OF THIS WORLD?

WHY DO TRADITIONS AND CULTURAL PRACTICES THAT PERPETUATE VIOLENCE AGAINST WOMEN AND GIRLS CONTINUE WITHOUT REDRESS?

WHY DOES THE MEDIA GRAVITATE TO SENSATIONAL VIOLENCE AGAINST WOMEN AS ACID BURNING, FEMICIDE?

WHY ARE COUNTRY GENDER BUDGETS REPEATEDLY SHORTCHANGED AS FOR DATA, MONITORING, ENFORCING LAWS AND PROGRAMS ON GENDER VIOLENCE?

SO, WE HAVE THE CEDAW CONVENTION—No specific VAW component, but a General Recommendation.

WE HAVE CEDAW COMMITTEE REVIEWS OF COUNTRY REPORTS.

WE HAVE THE UPR—UNIVERSAL PERIODIC REVIEW—UPR Info:

> The issue of violence against women was by far the most prominent one on recommendations made by countries on women's rights.......Within violence, the issue that received the more attention was domestic violence...which was followed by Female Genital Mutilation and rape, and also sexual violence.

WE HAVE THE DECLARATION ON VIOLENCE AGAINST WOMEN—not an enforceable document.

WE HAVE THE BEIJING PLATFORM—AND +5, +10, +15, +20 +25 +

WE HAVE UN SECURITY COUNCIL RESOLUTION 1325 ON WOMEN, PEACE, AND SECURITY.

WE HAVE THE SUSTAINABLE DEVELOPMENT GOALS, AND INCLUDING SDG 5 ON GENDER EQUALITY

WE HAVE THE INTERNATIONAL DAY ON VIOLENCE AGAINST WOMEN—NOVEMBER 25.

WE HAVE THE UN SPECIAL RAPPORTEUR ON VIOLENCE AGAINST WOMEN

WE HAVE THE 16 DAYS CAMPAIGN ON VIOLENCE AGAINST WOMEN.

WE HAVE SO MANY RESOLUTIONS ON VIOLENCE AGAINST WOMEN AS AT THE UN HUMAN RIGHTS COUNCIL, THE COMMISSION ON THE STATUS OF WOMEN, AND THE GENERAL ASSEMBLY.

WE HAVE THE EUROPEAN UNION ISTANBUL CONVENTION ON DOMESTIC VIOLENCE.

WE HAVE THE SECRETARY-GENERAL'S ONGOING PROGRAM TO UNITE AGAINST VAW.

THERE ARE CONTINUED CONFERENCES, SEMINARS, COLLOQUIA ON VIOLENCE AGAINST WOMEN, BUT WE MUST BREAK THE IMPASSE WITH NEW FORCE, DUE DILIGENCE, CLOSING THE GAP!

NOW it is time to get serious with an **ACTION PLAN, BASED ON RESEARCH, ANALYSIS, LEGAL STRUCTURES, COMMITMENTS on VIOLENCE AGAINST WOMEN that can be specific, tangible, and monitored. It is time to move from rhetoric to reality for MEMBER STATE ENGAGEMENT and ACOUNTABILITY, for advocacy, with a well-strategized Framework for Action.**

THIS BOOK IS A VALUABLE TOOL TO EFFECTIVELY ADDRESS INTERPERONAL VIOLENCE, IN A MULTITUDE OF WAYS, AROUND THE WORLD, URBAN TO RURAL, INTERGENERATIONAL.

SERIES EDITOR'S PREFACE

While the literature on police and allied subjects is growing exponentially, its impact upon day-to-day policing remains small. The two worlds of research and practice of policing remain disconnected even though cooperation between the two is growing. A major reason is that the two groups speak in different languages. The research work is published in hard-to-access journals and presented in a manner that is difficult to comprehend for a layperson. On the other hand, the police practitioners tend not to mix with researchers and remain secretive about their work. Consequently, there is little dialog between the two and almost no attempt to learn from one another. Dialogs across the globe, among researchers and practitioners situated in different continents, are of course even more limited.

I attempted to address this problem by starting the IPES, www.ipes.info, where a common platform has brought the two together. IPES is now in its 31st year. The annual meetings which constitute the most major annual event of the organization have been hosted in all parts of the world. Several very impressive publications have come out of these deliberations and a new collaborative community of scholars and police officers has been created whose membership runs into several thousands.

Another attempt was to begin a new journal, aptly called *Police Practice and Research: An International Journal PPR*, that has opened the gate to practitioners to share their work and experiences. The journal focuses on issues that help give scholars and police officers a single platform. *PPR* has been edited under PES auspices from 2000 to 2020. It is certainly evidence of growing collaboration between police research and practice, given that *PPR* began with four issues a year, expanded into five issues in its fourth year, and it is now issued six times a year.

Clearly, these attempts, despite their success, remain limited. Conferences and journal publications do help create a body of knowledge and an association of police activists but cannot address substantial issues in depth. The limitations of time and space preclude larger discussions and more authoritative expositions that can provide stronger and broader linkages between the two worlds.

It is this realization of the increasing dialog between police research and practice that has encouraged many of us—my close colleagues and I connect closely with IPES and PPR across the world—to conceive and implement a new attempt in this direction. This led to the idea of a book series, Advances in Police Theory and Practice, that seeks to attract writers from all parts of the world. Further, the attempt is to find practitioner contributors. The objective is to make the series a serious contribution to our knowledge of the police as well as to improve police practices; the focus is not only on work that describes the best and most successful police practices but also challenges current paradigms and breaks new ground to prepare police for the 21st century. The series seeks comparative analysis that highlights achievements in distant parts of the world as well as one that encourages an in-depth examination of specific problems confronting a particular police force.

This book contributed to the Advances in Police Theory and Practice Series is an important addition to the studies of gender and violence. The chapters cover diverse topics and all continents with a galaxy of authors. This volume is a truly cooperative global enterprise in which scholars discuss gender-based domestic violence, its impact on different societies and contexts, and policies that must be followed to deal with these phenomena. The editors have done a great job in gathering researchers from different countries in order to understand the reasons for this kind of violence, and the potential solutions to reduce it. For these reasons, the themes analyze the impact of the laws promulgated to fight gender violence, and the contextual limitations to their enforcement. This is a contemporary and relevant topic because there is a growing movement to broaden the legal framework to protect women and other minorities. However, different elements interfere in this process such as poverty, culture, race, migrant populations, transgender abuse, elderly populations, the impact of COVID-19, and the fragilities of States in enforcing laws to curb domestic violence.

It has been an objective of IPES since its foundation to build bridges among academics and police practitioners. This book endorses this goal but goes beyond because it will build bridges among scholars, police officers, social workers, lawyers, judges, attorneys, public managers, and civil rights activists. For these reasons, this volume is a timely contribution to the field of gender studies and violence.

The global influence and service of IPES was recognized by the United Nations, and as a result, IPES is in Special Consultative Status with the United Nations. An account of the IPES meetings and publications is presented below.

Dilip K. Das, PhD, Professor

Founding President, International Police Executive Symposium, IPES, www.ipes.info

Founding Editor-in-Chief, *Police Practice and Research: An International Journal, PPR*, www.tandfonline.com/gppr (2000–2020)

Series Editor, Advances in Police Theory and Practice; Interviews with Global Leaders in Policing, Courts, and Prisons and Routledge IPES Co-publication

Professor of Criminal Justice, Coppin State University, Baltimore, Maryland

Vicente Riccio, PhD, Associate Professor, Federal University of Juiz de Fora (Brazil), IPES book editor.

ACKNOWLEDGMENTS

A book that takes several years to complete in such extraordinary circumstances of the COVID-19 pandemic owes much to others. We would like to gratefully acknowledge our intellectual debt to our family members, friends, colleagues, and institutions whose support and contributions are indispensable and, therefore, highly appreciated.

This work represents joint efforts by over 30 scholars, practitioners, and human rights activists across the globe to explore best practices to deal with and end historic cycles of gender-based domestic violence. Therefore, we would like to thank all authors and their families for their cooperation and contributions.

We are deeply debted to Ellen Boyne and Kate Taylor at Routledge who showed initial interest in this work and prepared it for publication with meticulous care and efficacy. We also gracefully acknowledge Drs. Dilip K. Das and Vicente Riccio's interest and eagerness to include our work in the book series titled "Advances in Police Theory and Practice". There is no way that we could have been able to complete this book without them guiding and supporting us through the entire long yet extremely rewarding process.

Heartful thanks go as well to the Global Languages, Cultures, and Societies Department at Webster University (St. Louis, USA) and the Program of Social Justice and Human Rights at Arizona State University—your help and support are of great importance to this final product.

On the personal side, we want to thank Qiao Ying Li, Bernessa Sum Zhang, Landon Peterson, Colten Peterson, Hayden Bruns, and Arolsen Bruns. Without all your support and understanding, we could not have done this.

INTRODUCTION

An Interfaces Approach to the Global Problems of Gender-Based Domestic Violence

Dongling Zhang and Diana Peterson

In this introduction, we elaborate on an interfaces approach to gender-based domestic violence (Wilcox et al., 2021) as an alternative to United Nations' and other Western-centric (notably individualist) interpretations. We suggest that an interfaces approach enables international academics, feminist activists, and policy/development specialists among others to employ gendered and sociologically informed understandings of the local and global contextual factors that necessarily shape individual experiences of abuse. The notion of interfaces, as it is explored by the authors whose works comprise this edited volume, raises a number of important research questions and these suggest a variety of next steps for academic researchers and social practitioners who wish to improve the safety and healing of individuals surviving or who have survived years of physical, emotional, and sexual abuse. Only by shedding light on the context-dependent particularities of gender-based domestic violence can researchers and activists hope to influence the legislators and policymakers who are best positioned to rapidly redefine legal and socio-cultural contexts to effectively address the often multi-generational cycles of abuse taking place within households, families, and intimate relationships around the world today.

The authors of the chapters that follow draw attention to the particularities of the contexts in which global quests to redress, prevent, and eradicate gender-based domestic violence occur. With research projects that are situated in 20 different countries and four distinct regions, they conducted their research with the shared goals of: first, better understanding domestic violence as a global phenomenon and; second, identifying best practices and strategies for breaking cycles of violence. After carrying out comprehensive examinations of the incidences and prevalences of gender-based domestic violence in the countries or regions in which they work, these authors composed detailed accounts of their findings, ones that render visible the ways in which local contexts can and do shape individual experiences of violence. Their conclusions reinforce pre-existing critiques of UN terminology (see, e.g., Schneider, 2000) and other dominant, Western-centric discourses, while also advancing the conceptualization/reconceptualization of the phenomenon of gender-based domestic violence.

Furthermore, their research has added another layer of analysis to gender-based domestic violence research by recognizing and exploring the impacts of social positions. Differences resulting from social positions—including those based upon gender identity, sexuality, class, race, ethnicity, indigeneity, immigration status, and the intersections thereof—all can influence the ways in which a personal story about violence is experienced and responded to by other individuals (Bhardwaj & Miller, 2021; Brassard et al., 2015; Crenshaw, 1991; Zhang & Zhao, 2018). At the edges of their

DOI: 10.4324/9781003264040-1

thinking, and especially timely, the contributors to this volume acknowledge that the COVID-19 pandemic and climate change have overly burdened those who were, already, disproportionately victimized by gender-based domestic violence.

Taken together, this edited volume demonstrates joint efforts by international scholars, practitioners, and activists to not only challenge the decontextualized, universal perspective that tends to see non-Western experiences of violence "...as extraneous to the experiences of violence" of Western victims (Carty & Mohanty, 2015, p. 9) but also expand the understanding by means of illuminating the multiplicity in experiences of abuse. Contingent on distinct local contexts and social positionality, survivor experiences can vary in terms of the survivor-perpetrator relationship, effects and risk factors of violence, types of violence, and responses from the authorities as well as other individual and organizational stakeholders.

In lack of a one-size-fits-all concept that can accurately capture all possible meanings and experiences of violence, we choose to use the term gender-based domestic violence to refer to harmful threats or acts disproportionately directed at women as well as other individuals from gender and sexuality minority groups. This contrasts with UN understandings of the term, in which domestic violence also gets called domestic abuse or intimate partner violence and generally refers to acts or threats of violence to exert power and control over a partner, child or children, parent(s), or other member(s) of a shared household (United Nations, n.d.). The term domestic violence has been widely recognized and used in international scholarship (see, e.g., Fulu & Miedema, 2015; Zhang, 2009), and keeping it as part of our term is good for clarity and consistency. Meanwhile, reaffirming and reconceptualizing domestic violence as a gendered experience highlights that such experience is fueled by hegemonic, heteronormative masculinity and sustains the normalcy of patriarchal society (Connell, 2005; Wilcox et al., 2021). In addition, "how violence is conceptualized and defined will determine what is visible and seen and known...and what is and is not done about it through policy and practice" (Itzin, 2000, p. 357). Hence, we choose not to give a clear-cut definition of the term because the overall goals of this edited volume are to: first, avoid a decontextualized, simplified understanding centering around one individual's threats or acts of violence against another; second, keep the concept open-ended so that it can accommodate and account for any possible incident of violence indicative of varied local contexts.

The term of our choice can enable research and praxis to respond to the transnational feminist scholars' call (see, e.g., Guthery et al., 2019; Nayak, 2003) to examine nuanced local experiences through the lens of various systemic forces. Good understandings of gender-based domestic violence are not necessarily gained through homogeneous experiences of violence but rather through distinct localized ones that exemplify various modes of domination and oppression. By providing these, researchers, practitioners, and feminist activists are able to develop a capacity to uncover and explicate victims' disparate traumatic realities of violence, and more importantly, the injustice of the system that consistently undermines their safety, freedoms, and well-being. The interfaces approach (Wilcox et al., 2021), which we will introduce and discuss in detail in the next section, comes to serve as a viable way to build the capacity to attend, analytically, to social positions, local particularities, transnational processes, and the intersections thereof. Also, adopting the approach will allow researchers and other investigators to open many new, and definitely important, lines of inquiry for social change and reform on the structural and institutional conditions sustaining the historical cycles of violence.

Thinking about Gender-Based Domestic Violence through Interfaces

Experiences of gender-based domestic violence cut across the divides of home/work, private/public, and individual/institution. Such intersectional injustice necessitates a gendered and sociologically informed understanding through which to not only problematize the status quote of victims' lived realities as individualistic and universal all the time, but also to offer new insights into public policies, laws, and social practices which engage all individual and organizational stakeholders in becoming aware of and responsible for social, and more specifically gender, justice. As suggested by Wilcox et al. (2021), the concept of interfaces can be seen and utilized as a heuristic tool—a useful means by which researchers, practitioners, and activists would be able to scrutinize how experiences of gender-based domestic violence span the divides and thereby illuminate the ways in which the dichotomous practices, ideas, and spaces connect and separate the experiences simultaneously. Thinking of interfaces invites us to (re-)theorize structured and institutionalized boundaries by considering "not only the boundaries that separate two fields but also that which connects them" (p. 704). Drawing up the idea of an interface, we can hold boundary and connectivity simultaneously by exploring "a whole range of general social processes present across a wide variety of…processes such as boundary-work, boundary crossing, boundaries shifting, and the territorialization, politicization, relocation, and institutionalization of boundaries" (Lamont & Molnar, 2002, p. 168).

Informed by the idea of interfaces, we lean to the conviction that special attention must be devoted to four interfaces that are essential to identifying and understanding the socio-legal phenomenon of gender-based domestic violence: home/work; business/society; men/women; and mind/body. A gendered examination of domestic and work spheres makes clear systemic gender inequalities—the patriarchal social structure in which work (public) sphere is naturally associated with men and, by contrast, home (private) sphere with women (Acker, 2004; Miller & Borgida, 2016). Furthermore, the home may not be safe for victims who experience gender-based domestic violence. In particular, the overlapping globalized socio-ecological crises of COVID-19 and climate change have caused major economic devastation, disconnected people from social resources and assistance systems, and created a great deal of uncertainty and panic. Scholars have found that such conditions very likely either worsened situations in families where violence had been a problem or stimulated violence in homes where there had been none before (see, e.g.,Sharma & Borah, 2022; Sultana, 2021).

In addition, the lines between domestic and work spheres have never stopped shifting, as both spheres continue to evolve. Many of these shifts happening in the domestic/work interface are gendered (Wilcox et al., 2021). Women's entry, en masse, into the labor force is a good case in point: despite a possibility of negotiating and redistributing responsibilities for childcare and housework between wives and husbands, many working mothers unfortunately come home to a second shift of unpaid work. Home and work spheres intrude on each other in these cases. As a result, it is pertinent to look at perceptions and experiences of these overlapping boundaries, and more significantly, how individual perceptions and experiences not only are shaped by but also shape global and local contexts. Researchers, activists, and practitioners should particularly be mindful of whether and in what ways this overlapping can amplify gender-based domestic violence and be responded to by victims.

Considering the interface between business and society requires us to be attentive to the globalized diffusion of neoliberal discourses featured by its emphasis on the value of free market competition as the most efficient way to allocate resources and its commitment to minimal state intervention in both economic and social affairs. Neoliberal agendas attempt to de-center the government's role toward providing public services for people in need and thereby shift the "responsibility for norm and standard setting from public institutions to private institutions, from state actors to local actors…[, wherein gender-based] domestic violence is no exception" (Wilcox et al., 2021, p. 708). In this process, as non-governmental organizations are "depoliticized, defunded, and forced to partner with corporate organizations", the public socio-legal issue of gender-based domestic violence is relocated to the private business area (p. 708). Indeed, neoliberal politics and accompanying strategies of privatizing responsibilities have been woven into the fabric of society. This poses another few significant research topics and questions that the contributors to this volume delve into and we believe future inquiry needs to address still further: what role should government and non-governmental organizations play in addressing the problem of gender-based domestic violence in particular and gendered social structure in general that supports it? What role does the government have in setting and maintaining conditions for non-governmental organizations' responses to gender-based domestic violence? What are victim perceptions and experiences of all these roles?

Feminist scholars have gradually come to a consensus that domestic violence is a form of patriarchal oppression that men exert against their intimate partners (Walby & Towers, 2018). Gendered power relations within intimate relationships and broader society are now understood to be essential to socio-cultural circumstances in which men's use of violence against women is tolerated and even facilitated (Harvie & Manzi, 2011). In the case of men/women interfaces, we suggest instead that we should view the phenomenon of gender-based domestic violence as a manifestation of structural and institutionalized gender power relations that reproduce unequal gendered hierarchies and reify the subordination of women and gender and sexuality minorities. In doing so, research on gender-based domestic violence can go beyond notions of individual determinants (i.e., individual characteristics of perpetrators and victims), instead focusing on gendered socio-cultural norms and structures where experiences of violence are normalized and enabled (Kuskoff & Parsell, 2021).

Moreover, bringing to the forefront and retheorizing the gendered nature of violence allows us to be attentive to intersections between gender-based domestic violence and other forms of socio-cultural inequalities (Wilcox et al., 2021). Violence against LGBTQ+ community members, which is often overlooked and under-researched, is a good case in point. This means the problems with notions of the gender binary must be noted. Importantly, in speaking of gender-based domestic violence, non-binary gender and sexuality identities should be taken into account so as to further recognize and investigate the multiplicity in experiences of violence. Drawing upon the idea of the men/women interface, the chapters included in this edited volume leverage a gender-focused, intersectional approach to promote an understanding of how multiple forms of gendered social relations can intersect in order to support the subordination of women and gender and sexuality minority groups, particularly in the form of gender-based domestic violence.

Throughout the world of traditional Western philosophy, the mind-body problem was often conceptualized from the male perspective (e.g., Gatens, 2003). The feminine perspective had been largely marginalized till Simone de Beauvoir published her seminal book, *The Second Sex* in 1953. Feminist scholars and activists since then have been engaged in a conflicting relationship with earlier philosophical ideas. In the book, de Beauvoir challenged explicitly the patriarchal social values and ordering that problematizes the female body as the othering of the male and therefore links it with body, emotion, instinct, and nature, as opposed to men who were thought of as the embodiment of intellectuality and rationality. In the case of women and other individuals from gender and sexual minority groups facing gender-based violence, the patriarchal subjugation of the feminine and the (related) mind/body duality reinforce the image of women (and gender and sexual minorities) being depicted as victims (Wilcox et al., 2021). That is to say, the multiplicity in women's life experiences is reduced to the one-dimensional daily reality of victimization.

The mind/body interface provides inspiration for calling into question the body-rationality dichotomy, and more specifically, institutionalized knowledge structures that privilege and normalize the association of masculinity with rationality at the cost of gender inequalities. The gender-aware and sociologically informed approaches that the authors in this volume collectively adopt can draw attention to victim's bruised bodies as a political body with great potentials to play an active role in negotiating with and even disrupting the social norms and values of patriarchal society (Wilcox et al., 2021). The feminine and emotional bodies, particularly their experiences of masculine violence, must be recognized as the centrality of multiplicity and be thought of as having agency for making social change.

This points to opportunities, available to victims and survivors of gender-based domestic violence, for agency—a concept that refers to "the meaning, motivation, and purpose people bring to their activities" (Kabeer, 1999, p. 438). This definition queries frequent assumptions that escaping violence is the only viable and best option for victims, and staying with perpetrators means lack of agency and victimhood. As a matter of fact, agency is not simply about observable acts of direct resistance but rather consists of a vast array of varyingly direct and subtle strategies, including "bargaining and negotiation, deception and manipulation, subversion and resistance, and more intangible, cognitive processes of reflection and analysis" (p. 438). From this perspective of agency, a victim's decision to stay with a perpetrator could be made through deliberately weighing up all available options and then willingly selecting the most expedient one serving the best interests of his/her own and other family members in extremely constrained situations. In these situations, the question for research on victims' and survivors' agency is how they could cope with restrictive and even oppressive contexts. In response to this question, the studies in this volume reveal how victims and survivors of gender-based domestic violence can and do negotiate with and transform the domestic, workplace, and societal arrangements that oppress and exploit them.

References

Acker, J. (2004). Gender, capitalism, and globalization. *Critical Sociology, 30* (1), 17–41. https://doi.org/10.1163/156916304322981668.

Bhardwaj, N., & Miller, J. (2021). Comparative cross-national analyses of domestic violence: Insights from South Asia. *Feminist Criminology, 16* (3), 351–365. https://doi.org/10.1177/1557085120987635.

Brassard, R., Montminy, L., Bergeron, A., & Sosa-Sanchez, I. (2015). Application of intersectional analysis to data on domestic violence against Aboriginal women living in remote communities in the province of Quebec. *Aboriginal Policy Studies, 4* (1), 3–23. https://doi.org/10.5663/aps.v4i1.20894.

Carty, L., & Mohanty, T. (2015). Mapping transnational feminist engagements: Neoliberalism and the politics of solidarity. In Baksh, R., & W. Harcourt (Eds.), *The Oxford handbook of transnational feminist movements* (pp. 82–115). Oxford University Press. Https://doi.org/10.1093/oxfordhb/9780199943494.013.010.

Connell, R. W. (2005). Change among the gatekeepers: Men, masculinities, and gender equality in the global arena. *Signs: Journal of Women in Culture and Society, 30* (3), 1801–1825. https://doi.org/10.1086/427525.

Crenshaw, K. (1991). Mapping the margins: Internationality, identity politics and violence against women of color. *Stanford Law Review, 43*, 1241–1299. http://dx.doi.org/10.2307/1229039.

De Beauvoir, S. (1953). *The second sex*. Knopf.

Fulu, E., & Miedema, S. (2015). Violence against women: Globalizing the integrated ecological model. *Violence Against Women, 21* (12), 1431–1455. https://doi.org/10.1177/1077801215596244.

Gatens, M. (2003). Towards a feminist philosophy of the body. In Cahill, A. J., & J. Hansen (Eds.), *Continental feminism reader* (pp. 275–286). Rowan and Littlefield.

Guthery, A., Jeffrey, N., Crann, S., & Schwab, E. (2019). Using transnational feminist theory to expand domestic violence understandings. In Collins, L. H., Machiza, W. A. S., & J. K. Rice (Eds.), *Transnational psychology of women: Expanding international and intersectional approaches* (pp. 165–183). American Psychological Association. https://doi.org/10.1037/0000148-008.

Harvie, P., & Manzi, T. (2011). Interpreting multi-agency partnerships: Ideology, discourse, and domestic violence. *Social & Legal Studies, 20* (1), 79–95. https://doi.org/10.1177/0964 663910384907.

Itzin, C. (2000). Gendering domestic violence: The influence of feminism on policy and practice. In Itzin C., & J. Hammer (Eds.), *Home truths about domestic violence: Feminist influences on policy and practice* (pp. 356–380). Routledge.

Kabeer, N. (1999). Resources, agency, achievements: Reflections on the measurement of women's empowerment. *Development and Change, 30* (3), 435–464. https://doi.org/10.1111/1467-7660.00125.

Kuskoff, E., & Parsell, C. (2021). Striving for gender equality: Representations of gender in "progress" domestic violence policy. *Violence Against Women, 27* (3–4), 470–488. https://doi.org/10.1177/1077801220909892.

Lamont, M., & Molnar, V. (2002). The study of boundaries in the social sciences. *Annual Review of Sociology, 28*, 167–195. https://doi.org/10.1146/annurev.soc.28.110601.141107.

Miller, A., & Borgida, E. (2016). The separate spheres model of gendered inequality. *PLoS One, 11*: e0147315. https://doi.org/10.1371/journal.pone.0147315.

Nayak, M. (2003). The struggle over gendered meanings in India: How Indian women's networks, the Hindu nationalist hegemonic project, and transnational feminists address gender violence. *Women & Politics, 25* (3), 71–96. https://doi.org/10.1300/J014v25n03_04.

Schneider, E. M. (2000). *Battered women and feminist lawmaking*. Yale University Press.

Sharma, A., & Borah, S. (2022). COVID-10 and domestic violence: An indirect path to social and economic crisis. *Journal of Family Violence, 37*, 759–765. https://doi.org/10.1007/s10896-020-00188-8.

Sultana, F. (2021). Climate change, COVID-19, and the co-production of injustices: A feminist reading of overlapping crises. *Social & Cultural Geography, 22* (4), 447–460. https://doi.org/10.1080/14649365.2021.1910994.

United Nations. (n.d.). *What is domestic abuse?* Retrieved June 21, 2022, from www.un.org/en/coronavirus/what-is-domestic-abuse.

Walby, S., & Towers, J. (2018). Untangling the concept of coercive control: Theorizing domestic violent crime. *Criminology & Criminal Justice, 18* (1), 7–28. https://doi.org/10.1177/1748895817743541.

Wilcox, T., Greenwood, M., Pullen, A., O'Leary Kelly, A., & Jones, D. (2021). Interfaces of domestic violence and organizations: Gendered violence and inequality. *Gender, Work & Organization, 28* (2), 701–721. https://doi.org/10.1111/gwao.12515.

Zhang, H., & Zhao, R. (2018). Empirical research on domestic violence in contemporary China: Continuity and advances. *International Journal of Offender Therapy and Comparative Criminology, 62* (16), 4879–4887. https://doi.org/10.1177/0306624X18801468.

Zhang, L. (2009). Domestic violence network in China: Translating the transnational concept of violence against women into local action. Women's Studies International Forum, *32* (3), 227–239. https://doi.org/10.1016/j.wsif.2009.05.017.

SECTION ONE

North and South America

1

THE MYTH OF THE UNIVERSAL WOMAN

The (White) Feminist Fantasy and the Invisibility of Violence against Women of Color

Roksana Badruddoja

The Mythical Declaration of Violence against Women of Color

Domestic violence (DV)—defined as physical, sexual, verbal, mental, and/or economic control perpetrated by spouse or extended kin—is a major health hazard for women globally. In the United States, Federal Bureau of Investigation (FBI) statistics tell us that every 12 minutes a woman is beaten by her intimate partner and 4 million women are physically abused by their husbands or live-in partners each year (underreported). In the past 50 years, DV activists, victim advocates, and feminist scholars successfully responded to the prevalence of DV in the United States by paving the way for an emerging movement and radical possibilities. By 1975, an industry of DV programs for both victims and offenders burgeoned, and research and evaluation activities were growing at a steady rate. The American feminist and battered women's movements solidly established much needed DV services, shelters, safe home programs, crisis centers, and hotlines. Shepard and Pence (1999) write "substantial reforms in the criminal justice system, greatly expanded shelter and advocacy services, an industry of domestic violence treatment programs for offenders, and steady growth in research and evaluations activities" (p. 3). Combined with the "initiation of community intervention projects to modify, coordinate, and monitor the response of community agencies" (Shepard & Pence, 1999, p. 3), the battered women's movement in the United States gained lively momentum and battered women's organizations aptly received recognition and accolades from the public and the government by the 1980s. However, while government and public policies placed DV as a priority issue on their agendas since the 1980s and 1990s in the United States, this attention has not been focused equally on all communities. The programs, services, projects, legal interventions, evaluations, and theories did not and do not adequately support researchers, advocates, and communities to grapple with different aspects, interventions, and DV prevention strategies as it impacts Women of Color (WoC) and im/migrant women. While the scholarship and advocacy work formed a robust pathway for the development of community-based reform and coordination with legal agencies, resulting in written policies and protocols, the strength of the American battered women's movement also manifested itself as a weakness and, frankly, a betrayal for WoC and im/migrant women in the United States. The (underreported) rates of prevalence of DV in the United States make it clear that DV crosses class, caste, nation, ethnicity, and several other borderlines and this means responding to heterogeneity is a critical factor in successfully handling DV cases (Abraham, 1995).

DOI: 10.4324/9781003264040-3

In this chapter, I engage with transnational intersectional feminist discourse to display the narrowness of normative feminism in the United States (read as "white" and non-im/migrant), and what I hope to demonstrate is that WoC and im/migrant women are a marginalized, invisible, and erased category in contemporary American feminism. I call out the troublesome cultural imaginations of feminism and representations of im/migrant and WoC—restricting definitions of marginalization and suffocating visions of what oppression looks like—and the desperate unschooling of Orientalism that is needed to answer a haunting question: *What does vulnerability really look like?* I draw on the power of the "black imagination" (hooks, 1992) to rupture the white gaze or the "white imagination" (hooks, 1992) and name our violent erasure and restore the realities of our lived experiences of systemic oppression, i.e., terror ("of whiteness") (hooks, 1992). I accomplish this by deploying Narayan's (1998) "gender essentialism" and "cultural essentialism" to stress the invisibility of the experiences of DV of immigrant WoC in the (white) feminist gaze and I turn to transnational intersectionality as a pathway to complicate our understanding of vulnerability, marginalization, and oppression.

The Violent Myth about Gender

I begin the exploration of vulnerabilities by returning to the 1980s and 1990s as a significant temporal nexus: The global struggles for gender equality shifted their focus to violence against women (VAW) and our sexual victimization. A critical moment in the American battered women's movement is the development and initiation of the *Domestic Abuse Intervention Project* (DAIP) in Duluth, Minnesota, in 1980 (Shepard & Pence, 1999): DAIP's intervention resulted in and solidified a standard practice of response to experiences of DV (Pence, 1983). In 1993, the United Nations General Assembly passed a *Declaration on Violence against Women*: The declaration recognized that VAW is a manifestation of historically "unequal power relations between men and women," which have led to domination over and discrimination against girls and women. The collective focus on VAW had important and beneficial consequences for women in the United States, like DV laws and funding for DV services through the Victims of Crime Act (VOCA) in 1984 and the 1994 Violence against Women Act (VAWA). However, while the women's right movement in the United States aptly focused on the rights of battered women with community-based reform intervention projects, successfully linking intervention practices to legal agencies and developing feminist theory offered service providers with an analysis of the experiences of victims of gender-based violence (GBV) (hooks, 1984), Narayan (1998) expressed serious trepidations around the claims for battered women's rights and empowerment in the United States. What was and is not fully recognized is the unequal power relation between white women and WoC in the United States. The battered women's movement, while a felicitous cause, was and is not a holistic one due to an exclusive reliance on what Narayan (1998) calls the fallacy of "gender essentialism" (and what Collins (1998) names as the "additive model of oppression").

Gender essentialism is the notion that all women are the same—that all women share a coherent group identity as women—and that we all experience oppression—namely the world view of sexism and the practices of misogyny—in homogenous monolithic ways or a "universal female identity" (Narayan, 1998). Intersectional theorists Crenshaw (1992) and Collins (1998) draw on the queer black goddesses who curated the *Combahee River Collective Statement* to ferociously point to the fallacy of essentialism: Such generalizations efface women's marginalization because of their class, race, religion, ethnicity, sexual orientation, culture, im/migration, etc. (The Combahee River Collective, 1997). The universal female identity is informed by the white liberal gaze of colorblind racism, one that serves to subtract our racial identities, among our other discursive identity work, from our experiences of marginalization and oppression as WoC. Succinctly, gender essentialism reduces all women to a homogenous group simply based on gender, which further fuels white solipsism and produces a homogenous category of sex where the struggles of white women represent the struggles of *all* women! (It is precisely within this logic of white feminist hegemonic thought that evades the specificities of gender, race, class, etc. to posit all women should have supported Hillary Clinton in the 2008 and 2016 Democratic presidential primaries.)

Our experiences of marginalization and oppression linked to our complex identity work as WoC teaches us the significant, poignant, and humane lesson of intersectionality: Race (white supremacy), class (predatory corporate capitalism), gender (patriarchy), and other identity variables work together to oppress and marginalize women, and the mosaic of our identities create differing forms and experiences of oppression and marginalization for different women. I am bitterly reminded of Rihanna's experience with intimate partner violence (IPV). McKenzie (2013), in *Black Girl Dangerous*, writes:

> I...find it interesting that the question of whether someone "chose" to be part of something that might be degrading to them and people like them only becomes important for (white) feminists when talking about black women and other women of color. (This is mostly because people don't see black women as victims, ever. We aren't ever innocent enough to be victims. We are always at fault, at least partly, for any violence or degradation perpetrated against us. That's why Rihanna was portrayed as an equal partner in the "hot mess" that was her relationship with Chris Brown, rather than a victim of violence). In all other cases, though, (white) feminists seem to understand that we live in a world that limits (white) women's choices.[1]

Crenshaw (1992) astutely points out the struggles of African American women are not the same as white American women. And Purkayastha (2012) pushes the boundaries of black feminist thought by aptly including transnational WoC (by naming the differing experiences of oppression between Ugandan Black immigrant women and Ugandan Indian immigrant women as a salient consideration). Race, class, gender, sex, ethnicity, culture, sexuality, religion, im/migration, able-body, citizenship, and nation cannot be understood as autonomous and mutually exclusive experiences. Crenshaw (1992) and Purkayastha (2012) teach us our everyday experiences of oppression and marginalization as WoC calls for a dialectical framework, where each identity variable feeds off one another other and bleed into each other as part of the interconnected mosaic of our lives. Collins (1998) calls this the "matrix of domination" or the "multiplicative model of oppression." Intersectionality prevents the reduction of a woman's experience as simply being "black" or simply being "woman" (Crenshaw, 1992). And Purkayastha (2012) vehemently asks us to consider the meanings of the set of social hierarchies that are involved in the American immigrant context, e.g., the relative positions of Blacks and Indians in differing historical circumstances, in South Africa and India or Uganda and India. An intersectional analysis allows one to recognize that women experience discrimination for numerous reasons because they lay on multiple identity axes simultaneously.

Clearly, race neutral, monolithic woman scholarship is simply unacceptable. I return here to DAIP's concrete standardized practice of response intervention to experiences of DV and IPV. While it was and is necessary to develop standards of response to DV victims to minimize the mishandling of cases (Pence, 1983), the signatures of white supremacy inform and result in standardized protocols to addressing family violence in women's lives. Crenshaw (1992) diligently points out mainstream service providers (read as "white" and "American") failed to include WoC and immigrant women who are victims of DV. And Dasgupta (1998a, 1998b, 1999) finds immigrant communities in the United States have escaped social watchfulness and, thus, suffer from lack of DV-related services and resources. The universal woman scholarship is dangerous; it not only serves to control images of us as WoC (Collins, 1991), but it also costs us our livelihood and, literally, our lives. We simply cannot and must not ignore studies of subordination and discrimination require an intersectional approach.

I concern myself with individual (versus institutional) advocacy here. Individual advocacy involves DV advocates assisting battered women to explain and evaluate their options and then, often, pursue a course of action within the legal system. The assumption underlying individual advocacy is that the advocate is trained to support a victim's decision even if the advocate does not agree with the choices the woman has made (Davis & Smith, 1995). While there is little disagreement about this discourse around battered women, and the battered women's movement did include discussions around "diversity" and "multiculturalism" (read as "WoC"), deep issues of "difference" were and remain ignored among and between women, further fueling the flames of white solipsism via the violent signatures of sexual racism. Shepard and Pence (1999) document sharp disagreement over the presence of police and courts in the lives of battered WoC and im/migrant women and white service providers, e.g., legal presence does not have the same meanings to Mexican American women compered to white American women. Dasgupta and Warrier (1997) write, "...these organizations have standardized training programs for their own counselors and service providers in various issues concerning domestic violence" (p. 1). I take this to mean WoC and im/migrant women were/are seen as tremendous challenge for established institutions; confronting "diversity" meant that WoC and im/migrant women were/are a problem to be managed, i.e., assimilation. Abraham (2000) argues that not all services are effectual and most practitioners and advocates in the United States base services on a one-size-fits-all service provision model. Dasgupta and Warrier (1997) staunchly argue standardized service provisions "...has alienated the majority of...minority groups...as evidenced by the infrequency of such individuals accessing the domestic violence intervention system" (p. 1). In other words, standardized services/ "one-size-fits-all" model deeply betrays WoC and im/migrant women.

Plainly, individual (and institutional) advocacy is intimately tethered to cultural, social, and institutional practices of colonial imperialism and sexual racism in the United States. Practitioners and agencies are unwilling to address the reality and the multi-layered nature of oppression in a contemporary transnational United States. Concerns relating to DV and its intersection with legal issues, such as an immigrant woman's residency status in the United States, were and continue to be ignored and silenced by the battered women's movement. Mainstream service providers and DV advocates continue to lack up-to-date information on laws affecting im/migrant victims of intimate and family abuse, advancements in research, and available resources that may help the victims and their families. Crenshaw (1992) documents the Marriage Fraud Act of 1986 was passed to reduce fraudulent marriages to either American citizens (USC) or legal permanent residence/green card holders (LPR). The Act requires a two-year conditional residency requirement on the non-resident spouse before they can become eligible for permanent residency status. Mainstream service providers are often unaware VAWA, signed into law on September 13, 1994, contains provisions that allow battered women to escape violent marriages without risking deportation.[2] Furthermore, the reauthorization of VAWA in 2013 included legislation for Lesbian, Gay, Bisexual, Transgender, and Queer (LGBTQ) individuals, Native Americans, and victims of human trafficking and expands protection for immigrant women through the U visa. The ubiquity of American immigration policies encourages and maintains abuse and victimization, silencing and erasing the experiences of im/migrant WoC.

Finally, Dasgupta and Warrier (1997) push us to think in deeper shades within intersectionality: They daringly point to not only the power differential between white women and WoC, but also to the power differential among women. They write with piercing clarity,

> [G]ender relations are influenced and structured by the interactions between members of the same sex. That is, the relationships between two women of the same household [are] affected by their relations to the men in the household and by the men's relationship to each other.
>
> *p. 7*

That is, gender relations are neither uniform nor historically static in any community. Within immigrant South Asian communities, this often translates into a tremendous unequal power dynamic between mother-in-law (son's mother) and a daughter-in-law (son's wife). This brings up for me how we continue to simply refuse to accommodate the multi-layered experiences of women, dangerously ignoring the codetermination of inequalities to produce complex configurations. Our approach to DV in the United States represents hegemonic notions of what vulnerability looks like.

The Violent Myth about Culture

I next turn your attention briefly to a rapidly growing community that chronically experiences lack of services and resources: "South Asian"[3] American women. Contrary to widespread belief, South Asian women's organizations in the United States expose DV as a serious problem in the community. Yet, there is little reliable statistical data on the incidence rate of intimate abuse in the South Asian American immigrant community, and this speaks volumes about the invisibility of the community. In general, "statistics on South Asian Americans are extremely hard to find as South Asians are often hidden under the categories of 'unknown' or 'other Asians'" (Hussain et al., 2020).[4] Compounding the intersection of gender and im/migration, mainstream DV advocates too quickly and comfortably link WoC and im/migrant women's experience with DV and IPV to passivity, deep repression, and denial. I point to the sister of gender essentialism here: "cultural essentialism" (Narayan, 1998). Briefly, cultural essentialism reduces WoC and im/migrant women to the status of structural dopes and victims of culture à la Orientalism. Common Orientalist stereotypes about South Asian women are passive-demure, dutiful-reserved, asexual-frigid, traditional-old fashioned, conservative-politically unaware, dependent-faithful, inarticulate-incompetent, loud-stupid, and slavish-subservient (Dasgupta & Warrier, 1996). Orientalist tropes about South Asian women have been internalized and they act as a filter to our experiences of battering. Mohanty (1988) pivots her work on the relationship between "Woman" a cultural and ideological composite Other constructed through diverse representational discourse—and "women"—real, material subjects and their collective herstories. My point is mainstream service providers interpret behaviors of individuals according to essentialist worldviews of "eastern"/"global south" women. The gratuitous connection between culture and violence is almost invariably brought up in relation to the "third world"—WoC and im/migrant women—or what Narayan (1998) calls "death by culture." Narayan demonstrates culture is frequently invoked to explain the kind of violence experienced by women in India, though it is not invoked in a similar way when discussing VAW in various "western"/"global north" contexts. Narayan argues cultural explanations deflect attention from the broader and more prevalent crime of DV and the many other reasons why women are beaten, abused, or killed in family violence situations. Such explanations reproduce the native subject of colonial discourse, leaving in place the distorted image of Indian women and other WoC and im/migrant women as both "exotic" and barbaric. This is cultural essentialism functioning at its best. Indeed, race, gender, and im/migration debates highlight the emblems of sexual racism posed by "western" feminist discourse. Then, the central trepidation against white feminist scholarship and the battered women's movement in America is the discursive colonization of heterogeneities of the lives of women (Mohanty, 1988). The reality is all women—*real* women—have multiple and contradictory loyalties (Naber, 2006).

Abraham (1995) challenges the stereotypes of South Asian women as passive and submissive, thereby implicating American feminist theory. The proliferation of organizations focusing on providing culture-specific DV services to WoC and im/migrant families in the mid-to-late 1980s in the United States is a response to the demands of WoC and im/migrant women who were victims of battering. Abraham (1995) points to the pivotal role South Asian American organizations continue to play in helping immigrant and WoC escape abusive relationships, which, in turn, demonstrates the strategic resistance of WoC to combat family violence.

COVID-19, Climate Change, and DV

Immigrant women are especially vulnerable to abuse due to immigration status, cultural assumptions, and stereotyping from mainstream society; unfamiliarity with American social, legal, economic, and other institutions; and the maintenance of the myth of model minority (Abraham, 1995, 2000). And the global pandemic has intimately intertwined with immigrant women and their experiences with DV in cataclysmic ways. Social pandemic-related distancing has resulted in a national (and global) spike in DV and accessing support and services has become even more challenging for WoC and im/migrant women. Simply put, women (and their children) have become vulnerable to family and intimate violence in unprecedented ways during the pandemic. As a result of COVID-19, DV calls from South Asian American immigrant women to South Asian American DV organizations, like *Manavi*, *Sakhi*, *Maitri*, and *Narika*, came to an abrupt halt soon after March 12, 2020 (Kam, 2020). South Asian American immigrant women with abusive partners found themselves unable to connect with DV advocates they were working with before the pandemic because women were trapped at home with their abusers. Kam (2020) writes, "Clients who had previously told them of abusive partners who choked them, struck them in the face or threw them [downstairs] were now saying: 'Don't call me. It's not safe.'"[5] The pandemic-related "lockdowns" not only made it more difficult for women to seek help and access services, but the abuse has also magnified (Hussain et al., 2020). Kam (2020) reports, "Not only were their partners watching them around the clock, but many took away their phones, cars and credit cards, making it harder for women to seek help or leave."[6] In addition, many immigrant women who called South Asian American DV organizations found themselves living in COVID hot spots, like Queens, NY. Coupled with limited English proficiency and lack of familial and friend support systems, many DV victims were left overwhelmingly dependent on their intimate partners during the "first" wave of the pandemic. In Silicon Valley, South Asian American women employed in the tech industry, who experience DV at the sophisticated intersection of family abuse and smart technology, exhibited a similar dynamic: The plethora of hotline calls from women abruptly declined during the "first" wave quarantine as abuse escalated. Mukherji (2020) documents how women struggled to make phone calls with their abusers at home, e.g., "One woman hid in her closet to make the call," and "A … *desi* woman … stopped receiving the spousal support … Her ex-husband used COVID-19 as an excuse … He is also … using the pandemic to keep her from seeing her children … ."[7] Bhatia (2020) writes, "The very conditions that are needed to battle the coronavirus – isolation, social distancing, restrictions on freedom of movement – are, perversely, the very conditions that feed into the hands of abusers who now find state-sanctioned circumstances tailor-made for unleashing abuse."[8] The silence was chilling for two months and as the "lockdowns" eased in May and June 2020, South Asian American DV organizations experienced a surge in calls as a response to the increase in abuse during the pandemic (Kam, 2020).

The pandemic coupled with climate change further aggravates the risk of DV against women. Climate change crises often displace women and their families and impact their economic well-being, particularly in rural areas in the United States. The loss of income renders women and their children economically vulnerable, increasing exposure to DV, and displaced women become even more vulnerable to sexual violence. The impacts of climate change from torrential floods to wildfires exacerbate the challenges women face in the home with abusive partners. Like the radio silence on South Asian American DV hotlines during the initial stages of the pandemic, crisis lines went dead immediately after the 2018 wildfires in California accompanied by an uptick in phone calls to shelters and domestic abuse hotlines three months after Camp Fire; shelter accommodation and restraining order requests were 300% higher (Zoledziowski, 2020). The stressors brought by climate change are intimately tied to increased domestic abuse, particularly for marginalized people like impoverished women and immigrant women on dependent immigration statuses. Climate change is not separate from the violence women experience in their lives every day.

I suspect the current infectious spike, the "second" wave, this winter, and climate change will continue to exacerbate the violence South Asian American women, and women in general, are facing at home and will continue to limit the ways in which women might seek for help. South Asian American DV organizations predict the subsequent rise in COVID cases, and the second cycle of "lockdowns" will prompt some women to flee their abusive intimate partnerships. Racism and im/migration limit the ways in which many women can seek help, and I am afraid the pandemic further heightens and seals the experiences of DV as women and their children are trapped at home with abusive partners under the "shelter in place" policy. And the effects of climate change-induced crises fuel the risks of VAW. It is critical for national governments to designate DV service providers as "essential workers" and the services they provide to victims of domestic abuse are categorized as "essential services" (Bhatia, 2020). Furthermore, "Effective service to the victims of domestic violence should be culture-specific and emanate from a close understanding of the client's background" (Dasgupta & Warrier, 1997, p. 1). Meaning, it is imperative for crisis counselors to assess DV with a heightened awareness of the client's understanding of the violence and acceptable ways of intervention to ameliorate family and intimate violence that is transnational, intersectional, and COVID—and climate change-informed. This is vital in providing effective services and feasible choices for victims of family abuse.

Stand under My Umbrella

In ending, I return to the question, what does vulnerability *really* look like? If the linchpin of a feminist model is to serve the *most* marginalized, then I am afraid we as a culture and community have fallen deeply short. Essentialism has serious implications for feminist strategies that are adopted to remedy the violence that women experience. Essentialism encourages "western"/ "global north" feminists to propose strategies within an imperial/colonial white signature, one that represents WoC and im/migrant women as victims of "backward" and "uncivilized" cultures or "death by culture." Narayan (1998) argues that such hegemonic generalizations represent the problems of privileged women, who are often white, "western," middle-class, and heterosexual. These generalizations are a part and parcel of white hegemonic feminist thought, producing a homogenous category of sex where the struggles of white women represent the struggles of all women, effacing the oppressions of marginalized women because of their class, race, religion, ethnicity, sexual orientation, etc. Narayan (1998) teaches me essentialism is ahistorical, it limits the possibilities of social reorganization, and it precludes a practical application of intersectional feminist theory. I take this to mean essentialism evades seriously exploring the moral practices of solidarity and what it means to provide services to the most marginalized. The mission of this chapter includes centralizing invisible, marginalized, and peripheral voices, and locating marginalized and peripheral voices inevitably raises questions about representation. I ask here: How are the dislocated silenced? How can we recover unrecognized or suppressed aspects of our experiences? And how can our silenced voices be located and inserted into a story in which we have a fuller role to play locally, nationally, and globally? It is imperative that we tease out the realities of oppression(s) to prevent the silencing and erasure of the most marginalized. "Now that it's raining more than ever," I invite you—as a WoC—to "stand under my umbrella" (Rihanna, 2007).

Notes

1 www.bgdblog.org/2013/11/easy-white-bitch-words-lily-allens-new-video/
2 The Act provides women with two forms of relief: (1) apply for suspension of deportation (effective as of September 13, 1994) and (2) self-petition for permanent resident status (effective as of January 1, 1995).
3 The population of Asian and Pacific Islanders in the United States increased 142% between 1970 and 1980. Between 1980 and 1990, the South Asian population increased 125% with Asian Indians comprising a large part of this group. According to the American Community Survey of the U.S. Census Bureau, the Asian Indian population in the United States grew from almost 1,679,000 in 2000 to 2,570,000 in 2007 (a growth rate of 53% or the highest for any Asian American community). Indian Americans are the third largest Asian American group (after Chinese Americans and Filipino Americans).
4 https://saalt.org/wp-content/uploads/2020/09/Unequal-Consequences_SAALT-2020.pdf?eType=EmailBlastContent&eId=faa50469-c2f7-4d40-b739-5b36773c7378
5 www.nbcnews.com/news/asian-america/why-domestic-violence-calls-are-surging-asian-american-women-amid-n1240663
6 www.nbcnews.com/news/asian-america/why-domestic-violence-calls-are-surging-asian-american-women-amid-n1240663
7 https://thewire.in/women/south-asian-domestic-violence-survivors-in-silicon-valley-grapple-with-covid-19-lockdown
8 www.unwomen.org/en/news/stories/2020/3/news-women-and-covid-19-governments-actions-by-ded-bhatia

References

Abraham, M. (1995). Ethnicity, gender, and marital violence: South Asian women's organizations in the United States. *Gender & Society, 9* (4), 450–468.
Abraham, M. (2000). *Speaking the unspeakable: Marital violence among South Asian immigrants in the U.S.* Rutgers University Press.
Bhatia, A. (2020). Women and COVID-19: Five things governments can do now. *UN Women.* www.unwomen.org/en/news/stories/2020/3/news-women-and-covid-19-governments-actions-by-ded-bhatia
Collins, P. H. (1991). *Black feminist thought: Knowledge, consciousness, and the politics of empowerment.* Routledge.
Collins, P. H. (1998). It's all in the family: Intersections of gender, race, and nation. *Hypatia, 13*, 62–82.
Crenshaw, K.W. (1992). Mapping the margins: Intersectionality, identity politics, and violence against women of color. *Stanford Law Review, 43* (6), 1241–1299.
Dasgupta, S. D. (1998a). Women's realities: Defining violence against women by immigration, race and class. In R. K. Bergen (Ed.), *Issues in intimate violence* (pp. 209–219). Sage publications.
Dasgupta, S. D. (1998b). Gender roles and cultural continuity in the Asian Indian community in the U.S. *Sex Roles, 38* (11/12), 953–974.
Dasgupta, S. D. (1999). Is all well with domestic violence work in the United States?. *SAMAR, 11* (Spring/Summer), 5–11.
Dasgupta, S. D., & Warrier, S. (1996). In the footsteps of 'Arundhati': Asian Indian women's experience of domestic violence in the U.S. *Violence against Women, 2* (3), 238–259.
Dasgupta, S. D., & Warrier, S. (1997). *In visible terms: Domestic violence in the Asian Indian context: A handbook for intervention* (2nd ed.). Manavi.
Davis, R. C., & Smith, B. (1995). Domestic violence reforms: Empty promises or fulfilled expectations?. *Crime & Delinquency, 41* (4), 541–552.
hooks, b. (1984). *Feminist theory: From margin to center.* South End Press.
hooks, b. (1992). *Black looks: Race and representation.* South End Press.

Hussain, M., Qureshi, S., Suryanarayanan, S., Sridaran, L., & Howard, R. (2020). Unequal consequences: The disparate impact of COVID-19 across South Asian American communities. *South Asian Americans Leading Together* (SAALT). https://saalt.org/wp-content/uploads/2020/09/Unequal-Consequences_SAALT-2020.pdf?eType=EmailBlastContent&eId=faa50469-c2f7-4d40-b739-5b36773c7378

Kam, K. (2020). Why domestic violence calls are surging for Asian American women amid the pandemic. *NBC News*. www.nbcnews.com/news/asian-america/why-domestic-violence-calls-are-surging-asian-american-women-amid-n1240663

McKenzie, M. (2013). Easy out there for a (White) bitch: A few words on Lily Allen and the continued use of Black women's bodies as props. *Black Girl Dangerous*. www.bgdblog.org/2013/11/easy-white-bitch-words-lily-allens-new-video/

Mohanty, C. T. (1988). Under western eyes: Feminist scholarship and colonial discourses. *Feminist Review, 30*, 65–88.

Mukherji, A. (2020). South Asian domestic violence survivors in Silicon Valley grapple with COVID-19 lockdown. *The Wire*. https://thewire.in/women/south-asian-domestic-violence-survivors-in-silicon-valley-grapple-with-covid-19-lockdown

Naber, N. (2006). Arab American femininities: Beyond Arab virgin/American (ized) whore. *Feminist Studies, 32* (1), 87–111.

Narayan, U. (1998). The essence of culture and a sense of history: A feminist critique of cultural essentialism. *Hypatia, 13* (2), 86–106.

Pence, E. L. (1983). *In our best interest: A process for personal and social change* (1st ed.). Minnesota Program Development Inc.

Purkayastha, B. (2012). Intersectionality in a transnational world. *Gender & Society, 26*, 55–66.

Rihanna. (2007). *Umbrella [Song]. On good girl gone bad: Reloaded* [Album]. Def Jam Recordings.

Shepard, M. F., & Pence, E. L. (1999). *Coordinating community responses to domestic violence: Lessons from Duluth and beyond*. Sage Publications.

The Combahee River Collective. (1997). A Black feminist statement. *Women's Studies Quarterly, 42* (3–4), 271–280.

Zoledziowski, A. (2020). Expect domestic violence to skyrocket after the California fires end. *Vice News*. www.vice.com/en/article/935pk7/expect-domestic-violence-to-skyrocket-after-the-california-fires-end

2

PARADIGM SHIFT IN LATIN AMERICAN LEGISLATION OVER TIME

From Domestic Violence Laws to Comprehensive Legislation on Gender-based Violence against Women (1990–2020)

Nancy Madera

Introduction

From the early 1990s, demands toward violence against women (VAW) that were historically promoted by feminist and women's movements around the world started to be institutionalized in the universal and regional human rights systems. In 1992, the Committee on the Elimination of Discrimination against Women (CEDAW) included violence within the scope of the 1979 Convention, recognizing it as a form of discrimination that inhibits women's ability to enjoy rights and freedoms on a basis of equality with men (CEDAW Committee, 1992, para. 1). The 1993 Declaration on the Elimination of Violence against Women (DEVAW) defined it as any physical, sexual, or psychological harm based on gender occurring both in public and private life (UN General Assembly, 1994, para. 1). The following year, the Inter-American Convention on the Prevention, Punishment and Eradication of VAW 'Convention Belem do Para' (BdPC) affirmed that VAW constitutes a violation of their human rights and fundamental freedoms, framed it as a manifestation of structural inequalities, and granted women a free-standing right to be free from gender-based violence (OAS, 1994, p. Preamble, para. 3). Later on, the Maputo Protocol and the Istanbul Convention stablished binding mandates to African and European member States regarding prevention, penalization, and eradication of VAW (Council of Europe 2011; African Union 2003).

More than 25 years after the emergence of this international normative consensus, only a handful of countries include its structural and gender sensitive approach toward violence in their legislation. As of 2020, 50 out of the 193 countries that are full members of the United Nations had adopted comprehensive laws and/or criminal reforms that specifically address VAW, domestic violence against women (DVAW), and/or gender-based violence in their legislation within a gender equality frame.[1] With 18 Latin American countries explaining a significant part of this figure, the region stands out as a remarkable case in the global context.

Toward mid-2000s, Latin American legislation shifted from a family oriented, mostly gender-neutral approach to violence toward a gendered and comprehensive interpretation of it, framed in human rights, gender inequality, and intersectionality perspectives. This emergent new generation of laws expanded the progress made during the previous decade reframing violence as a type of harm based on gender that takes place in domestic and public spaces, a form of discrimination that violates or limits women's human rights and that is rooted in social, cultural, and economic structural inequalities between men and women. Taken as a whole, these changes show

DOI: 10.4324/9781003264040-4

that, outside of a small number of previous national experiences around the world,[2] Latin America was the first region to converge in the adoption of a normative paradigm on VAW that highlights gender inequality as a structural root of violence and stablish the State responsibility to transform it (Galanti, 2013).

Through a qualitative comparison of domestic violence (DV), DVAW, and VAW laws enacted in 18 Latin American countries from the early 1990s until March 2020, this chapter provides an overview analysis of the changes in the regional legislative approach to gender-based violence, showing the emergence and consolidation of specific frameworks and definitions of the problem and its scope; various policy strategies to deal with it; and specific institutional reforms designed to increase the state's bureaucratic and social capacity to implement them. In the context of the COVID-19 pandemic, the chapter also focuses on the limitations of this legislation to address the specific vulnerabilities of women and girls in the context of humanitarian situations, natural disasters, and climate change and extends the empirical analysis beyond March 2020 to explore the specific legislative responses to the growing problem of gender-based violence during the first year of the pandemic in Latin America.

Theoretical and Analytical Approach

I study laws as institutionalized discourses that reflect the changing interpretations on VAW (Krook & True, 2012; Montoya, 2013). Dimensions and indicators used to compare the content of the laws include the recommendations of legislative and policy guides prepared by the universal and regional human rights systems (CIM & MESECVI, 2014; United Nations, 2009) and contributions from authors who studied legislative responses toward VAW (Den Boer & Ertan, 2017; Galanti, 2013; Galanti & Borzacchiello, 2013; Montoya, 2013; Ortiz-Barreda & Vives-Cases, 2013; Smulovitz, 2015).

The decision to look at legislative instruments rather than other types of policy is based on the culturally constitutive role of laws (Merry, 2006, pp. 89–90). Legislation on DV, DVAW, and VAW is the result of intense advocacy work from women's rights organizations and extensive social, political, and parliamentary debate. Thus, laws are privileged sites to observe a paradigm shift on VAW, a process that involves radical changes in objectives, instruments, and settings of a policy, accompanied by a substantive transformation in the discourses used to approach a problem and its causes (Hall, 1993, p. 284).

The comparison over time is structured according to empirical and theoretical reasons. The broad temporal scope allows to capture a policy shift that started in the early 1990s as a result of feminist mobilization and norm diffusion (Galanti, 2013; Galanti & Borzacchiello, 2013; Htun & Weldon, 2012, 2018).[3] The two time periods follow the work of Galanti (2013) and Galanti and Borzachiello (2013), who identified 2006 as the year when the paradigm shift started in the region with the adoption of the *Maria da Pelhna* Law in Brazil. Finally, to identify the specific legislatives responses during the COVID-19 crisis, I analyze all provisions oriented to tackle gender-based VAW adopted in Latin American Legislatures from March to December 2020.

Data Collection

The dataset for this study was the result of a systematic search for national legislation oriented toward DV, DVAW, and VAW enacted up to March 2020 using three main sources: the UN Global Database on VAW (ONU Mujeres, 2016), country profiles developed by the OECD Gender Index (OECD, 2020), and the law database of the Gender Equality Observatory for Latin America and the Caribbean (CEPAL, 2019). This information was complemented with legislation accessible online, global and regional reports (CEPAL, 2014; Garita Vílchez, S/f; LOC, 2020; UNDP & UN Women, 2017; United Nations, 2009), and academic work (Chibán, 2013; Galanti, 2013; Klugman, 2017; Ortiz-Barreda & Vives-Cases, 2013; Richards & Haglund, 2015).

To signal the particularities of the Latin American case in the global context, I consider a universe of the 193 countries that are full members of the United Nations (United Nations, 2020), among which I identify a total of 176 laws directed at VAW, GBV, and/or DVAW, adopted from 1990 until March 2020 in 57 countries. The regional analysis focuses on the 119 laws on VAW and DVAW identified in Latin America, and the 64 laws on DV adopted in the 18 countries from which that specific legislation on gender-based violence emerges.[4] The final cluster of 183 laws, from which 53 were adopted up to 2005 and 130 from 2006 on, includes current and repealed legislation, as well as law amendments.[5]

Finally, to explore legislative efforts during COVID, I resorted to information provided by the COVID-19 Global Gender Response Tracker (UNDP, 2021), the COVID-19 Observatory in Latin America and the Caribbean (CEPAL, 2021), and the CIM/MESECVI report VAW and the Measures to Contain the Spread of COVID-19 (CIM & MESECVI, 2020). I complemented this data with publications from national women/gender policy agencies, other official institutions, documents from women's organizations, and news outlets.

Legislative Instruments to Address VAW

Three types of legislative instruments to address VAW emerge from both global and regional data: comprehensive legislation on VAW, DVAW, or DV; criminal reforms; and provisions on specific aspects of the issue. Comprehensive legislation includes a variety of different strategies to address the problem. Penal Code reforms focus on penalization while offering a distinctive definition of violence. Specific provisions address key topics such as shelters, protection measures, procedural rights, and support for complainers and survivors but rarely contain extended framing and/or concrete definitions of violence. Figure 2.1 shows that along with the trend toward a broader focus on violence, after 2005 comprehensive legislation and specific provisions gained prominence over criminal reforms.

Before 2006, comprehensive legislation on VAW corresponds with DV laws that focus on women as a specific group to be protected.[6] The only Penal Code reform including VAW as a specific crime was the Dominican Republic Law 24–97. All DV laws adopted after 2005 were amendments of legislation from the previous period. From 2006 on, 15 comprehensive laws on VAW, DVAW, and/or GBV were adopted in Latin America. Two of them addressed VAW in the domestic and/or family context[7] and the rest broaden the scope to cover public as well as private settings.[8] Eleven of these fifteen laws were later amended.

Frames and Definitions of VAW in Latin American Legislation

Human Rights, Gender Inequality, and Intersectional Framings on VAW

Discursive framings capture how legislation interprets the nature and causes of VAW. Montoya (2013) identifies three basic feminist frames on this issue: as a human rights violation, a manifestation of gender inequality, and a problem that requires an intersectional approach (Montoya, 2013, pp. 14–20). As these views were institutionalized in both CEDAW and the BdPC, I draw upon the standards set by these conventions to analyze their presence and strength over time and in relation with the evolution of a gender-neutral and family-oriented interpretation of violence. Figure 2.2 shows the evolution of these discursive framings in Latin American legislation over time.

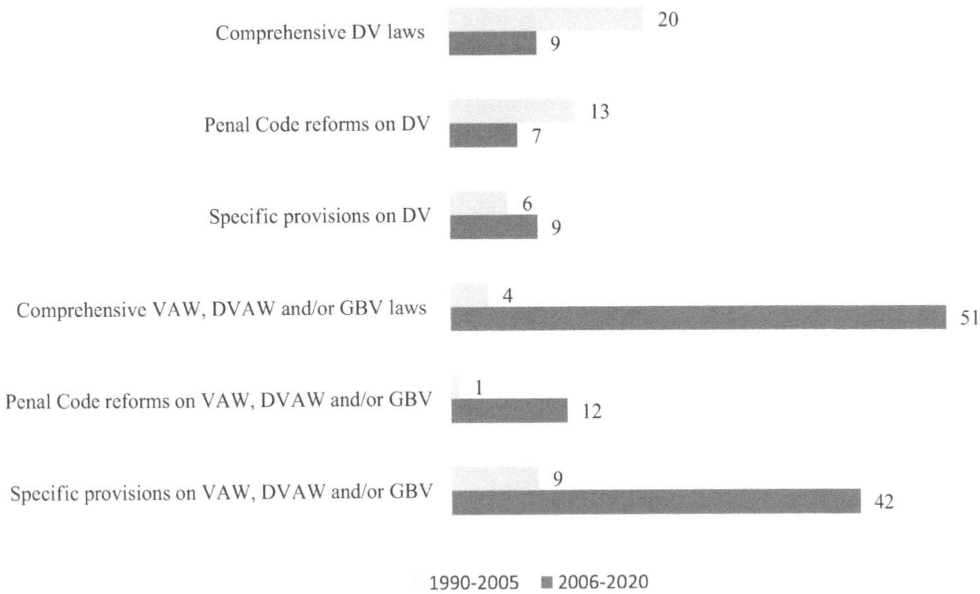

FIGURE 2.1 Legislative instruments used to address violence against women in Latin America. Own elaboration based on the regional cluster of 183 laws.

Figure 2.2 shows that is more likely to find a human rights approach, a gender perspective on VAW, and an intersectional approach in legislation adopted after 2005. The intersectional approach, which address the differing vulnerabilities of women regarding gender-based violence (Montoya 2013, p.19) appears only in two laws before 2006 and shows a lower presence overall. Reversely, the gender-neutral approach based on family values is present mostly in DV legislation enacted before 2006.

Changes in the way VAW is framed in the legislation consolidate over time with the inclusion of specific provisions recommended by international and regional instruments. The women's right to a life free from gender-based violence, which reinforces the protection of life and personal integrity established by international law, was included in 14 laws, all comprehensive legislation on VAW.[9] The 'due diligence' principle, addressing the State duty to prevent, protect, investigate, penalize, and provide compensation for acts of violence and discrimination committed by private actors against women (CIM & MESECVI, 2014; United Nations, 2009), was internalized in the first period as a procedural principle, with laws committing States to secure speedy and effective protection and legal procedures in DV cases, or a mandate for state agents to act diligently when attending or witnessing an act of violence. After 2005, 10 out of the 28 laws that included the 'due diligence' principle expanded its effects transversally across the State, including prevention as well as support and assistance for complainants/survivors as part of State obligations toward VAW.[10]

The inclusion of 'transformational' duties regarding gender inequalities, meaning the State's responsibility to promote social and cultural transformation of the social roles and patterns that promote or legitimize VAW (Galanti, 2013, p. 184, 192), emerged mostly in laws adopted from 2006 on. Likewise, all but five of the laws with provisions targeting vulnerable groups of women appear in the second period. This legislation identifies the risks for indigenous and rural women, women in detention and from different ethnic background, sexual orientation, and gender identity as well as vulnerabilities associated with situations such as motherhood, pregnancy, disability, age,

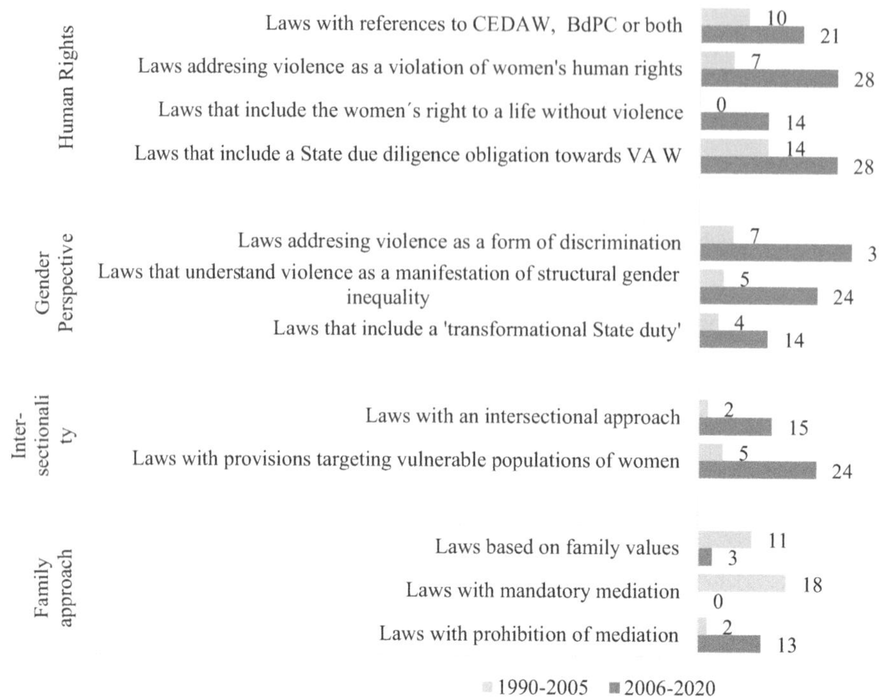

FIGURE 2.2 Discursive framing in Latin American legislation on VAW, DVAW, GBV, and DV. Own elaboration based on the regional cluster of 183 laws.

illiteracy, and socio-economic situation. The Uruguayan comprehensive legislation on VAW is the only one explicitly including trans women into its provisions. Of the 17 laws that incorporated an intersectional approach, 10 also included provisions for one or more of these vulnerable groups, all but one of which were adopted after 2005.[11]

Mediation between victim and aggressor, a common strategy in DV cases aimed to restored 'lost harmony' among family members,[12] was not directly discussed in the first international norms on VAW and was still a matter for debate until the mid-2000s (United Nations & Centre for Social Development and Humanitarian Affairs, 1993; United Nations Secretary-General, 2006). Later on, however, its prohibition became a consensual recommendation across the human rights systems (CEDAW Committee, 2015, 2017; MESECVI, 2008, 2014; United Nations, 2009). As shown in Figure 2.2, this normative development was clearly reflected in Latin American legislation. Most laws that included mandatory conciliation and/or confrontation with the aggressor were adopted before 2006[13] and, reversely, laws that explicitly prohibited were mostly enacted from that year on.

Definition and Scope of VAW

The definition of VAW in international law encompasses four elements: it identifies women as the subject toward whom this violence is directed; characterizes violence as gender-based; includes forms of physical, psychological, and sexual harm; and establishes that these forms are manifested in both the private and public spheres (Edwards, 2011, pp. 20–25). Figure 2.3 shows how these four elements were included in Latin American legislation over time.

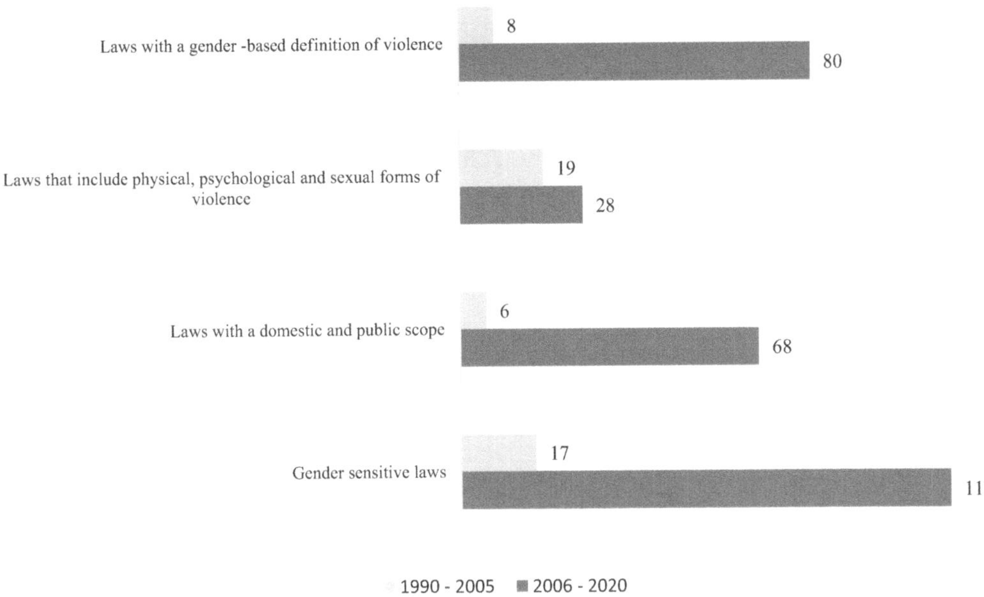

FIGURE 2.3 Definitions of violence in Latin American VAW, DVAW, GBV and DV legislation. Own elaboration based on the regional cluster of 183 laws.

Out of the 129 laws identified as gender sensitive,[14] 119 included women in the definition of violence, and another 10 included women through specific provisions. Only 17 of these laws were adopted before 2006. The majority of the 88 laws that explicitly include a definition of violence motivated by gender, women's status, discrimination, and/or unequal power relations were also adopted in the second period. A similar trend emerges from laws that cover violence both in private and public settings, with an overwhelming majority being enacted from 2006 on. The only element showing a more stable presence over time is a definition that includes physical, psychological, and sexual forms of violence. A definition of violence that includes all four elements can be found in 28 laws. Among them, there are 13 comprehensive laws on VAW, two amendments that reinforce their definition of violence,[15] and one comprehensive law on femicide.[16] There are also seven Penal Code reforms and five specific provisions explicitly directed at VAW.[17] All but two of these 28 laws were adopted after 2005.

For a deeper look into the scope of this legislation, I explore which personal relationships are covered under DV definitions and how this scope expanded over time[18] (Figure 2.4).

An explicit definition of the type of personal relationships protected by legislative provisions on DV was found in 61 laws. Figure 2.4 shows that these laws have a broad coverage in the type of relationships included, with the wider range of protection consolidating in legislation adopted after 2005. This pattern of inclusiveness is replicated in every national trajectory except for Costa Rica, where the comprehensive VAW law of 2007 reduced the coverage of the 1996 DV law[19] by not explicitly considering past relationships. Peru and Chile's original femicide/feminicide laws only covered personal relationships (excluding non-cohabitational ones) and were later modified to broaden this scope to include all gender-based killing of women.[20]

FIGURE 2.4 Scope of personal relations covered under domestic violence definitions in Latin American legislation. Own elaboration based on the 61 laws with the most up-to-date definition of domestic violence.

Policy Strategies: Presence and Strength of a Comprehensive Approach toward VAW in Latin American Legislation

The international normative paradigm on VAW propose a comprehensive policy approach, broadly defined as a multidisciplinary response to all forms of violence that encompass ' (…) issues of prevention, protection, survivor empowerment and support (health, economic, social, psychological), as well as adequate punishment of perpetrators and availability of remedies for survivors' (United Nations, 2009, p. 14). Even though a comprehensive strategy toward VAW started to be included as a fundamental principle in laws enacted after 2005, a deeper analysis shows that this principle was not always translated into policy provisions. In order to observe how the policy approach toward gender-based violence evolved over time in Latin America legislation, I analyze the inclusion of five strategies and two key indicators for each based on international and regional recommendations (CIM & MESECVI, 2014; United Nations, 2009) (Table 2.1).

Based on the features synthetized in Table 2.1, I elaborate a two-dimensional measure to capture both the presence of different strategies in the legislation (1 point for each strategy mentioned in the law) and the strength of each strategy (1 point for each indicator covered by the law). Strength levels allows to discriminate between a nominal and a substantive presence of the comprehensive approach in the legislation, with scores lower than 5 indicating a nominal presence, with less than one key provision per strategy, and scores above 5 indicating a more substantive presence of each strategy. There are 22 laws with provisions covering all five policy strategies.[21] There is no significant variation among them over time or across legislative instruments nor are there differences in their perspective or scope: there are neutral as well as gender-sensitive laws, laws limited to a domestic scope, and others covering both domestic and public settings. Variation does emerge when adding to the analysis the strength level of the comprehensive policy approach (Figure 2.5).

TABLE 2.1 Comprehensive policy approach toward VAW

Strategies	*Indicator 1*	*Indicator 2*
Prevention	Awareness-raising activities regarding women's human rights, gender equality, and the right of women to be free from violence, including the sensibilization of the media	Use of use of educational curricula to modify discriminatory social and cultural patterns of behavior, as well as derogatory gender stereotypes
Protection	Protection orders for survivors of violence against women	Sanctions for violations of protection orders
Access to justice and investigation	Due diligence in police response	Free legal assistance for complainants/survivors
Penalization	Explicit prohibition of mediation in all cases of VAW, both before and during legal proceedings	Penal sanctions for violence against women
Support and assistance to complainants/survivors and family	Shelters for survivors	Social policies directed at survivors and their family, including financial assistance, employment protection, housing rights, and other support measures

Source: Own elaboration based on United Nations (2009) and CIM & MESECVI (2014).

First, if we consider that the average strength of the comprehensive approach in legislation adopted before 2006 was 5 out of 10, Figure 2.5 shows that the Brazilian 2006 *Maria da Pehna* law, with a strength level of 9, represents a clear shift in this process. From 2006 on, the average strength of legislation was 8 out of 10. Higher scores (8 to 10) only emerged in the second period. Overall, scores below 6 correspond with DV laws adopted in the first period, with the only exception of Guatemala comprehensive VAW law of 2008.

If we analyze law amendments that modified the policy approach of original legislation, we find a trend toward further comprehensiveness and increase strength. First, the only two comprehensive laws on VAW that did not show the presence of all five policy strategies in their original text – Costa Rica Law 8589/2007 (Score 2) and the Colombian Law 1257/2008 (Score 4) – were later complemented with laws containing specific provisions that improved each country's overall legislative approach toward VAW (Costa Rica Law 8688/2008 and Colombia Laws 1542/2012 and 1761/2015). Second, out of the six law amendments that modified the original legislation policy approach, five of them increased its level of strength, with Nicaragua being the only country in the region with legislation that reduced the strength of its policy approach over time[22] (Figure 2.6).

Institutional Reforms and State Capacity toward VAW

Institutional Reforms

Institutional reforms that strengthen State coordination and monitoring capacities play a fundamental role in a comprehensive policy approach toward VAW (Htun & Weldon, 2012, 2018; United Nations, 2009; Weldon, 2002). I explore this dimension by identifying the creation and characteristics of agencies designed to coordinate VAW policies, the presence of coordinating mechanisms such as a national plan or strategy, and the development of specialized agencies to monitor and evaluate policy implementation (Figure 2.7).

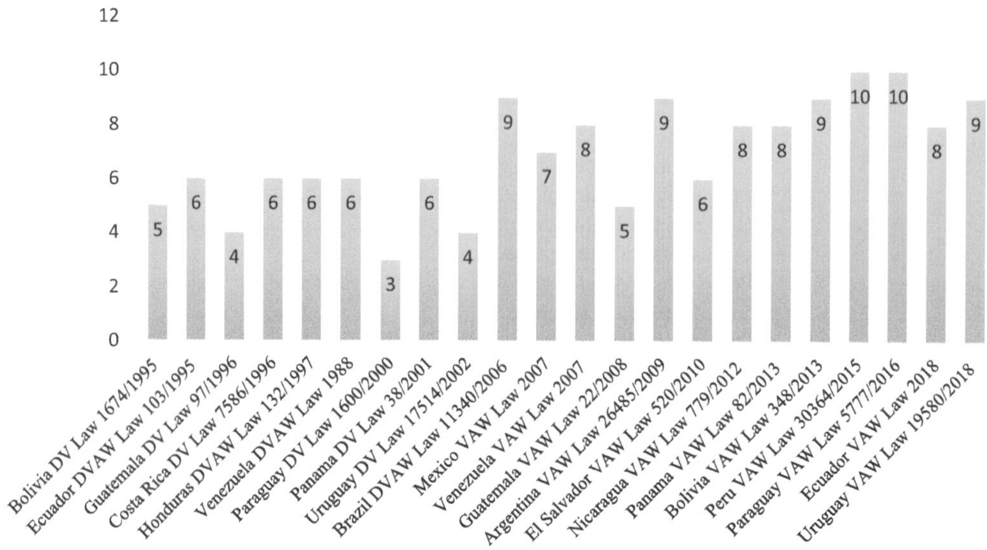

FIGURE 2.5 Strength of the policy approach in VAW, DVAW, and DV laws in Latin America over time (1990–2020). Own elaboration based on the 22 laws with provisions covering all five policy strategies included in Table 2.1.

A specific provision on agencies responsible of coordinate implementation of VAW policies was found in 45 laws. Figure 2.7 shows that the appointment of existing women's policy agencies[23] to fulfill this role is a stable provision across both periods and that the creation of specialized agencies to perform this task emerges only after 2005.[24] Coordinating mechanisms also gain presence over time. The majority of the 22 laws that mandate the formulation of a national policy/plan to implement its provisions were adopted in the second period while all 12 laws that contemplate the creation of coordination mechanisms, with representatives from different ministries within the Executive Power as well as from other branches and levels of government, emerge only after 2005.[25] In three of these general coordination systems, 'alert mechanisms' were set up with special measures in cases when an emergency on VAW, such as an increased number of femicides/ feminicides, is identified at a local or national level.[26] Two other laws, both adopted after 2005, specifically mandate the creation of alert mechanisms on VAW in the context of a natural disaster and/or special risk situations[27] or for the immediate search of missing women.[28]

The creation of institutions designed to monitor and evaluate implementation consolidated in the second period, with more laws including government only[29] as well as mixed monitoring commissions with stable participation of social organizations.[30] Seven laws also stablished the creation of observatories on VAW, specialized agencies designed to collect data, produce reports, and propose policy on this issue.[31]

State Bureaucratic and Social Capacity-Building Provisions

A comprehensive approach toward VAW also increases the demand for strong bureaucratic and social capacities across the State. Provisions such as funding, data collection, and training of public officials, as well as institutionalized participation of non-governmental and civil organizations, are of fundamental importance to aspire to an effective and socially accountable implementation of policies to tackle and eradicate VAW (CIM & MESECVI, 2014; United Nations, 2009).

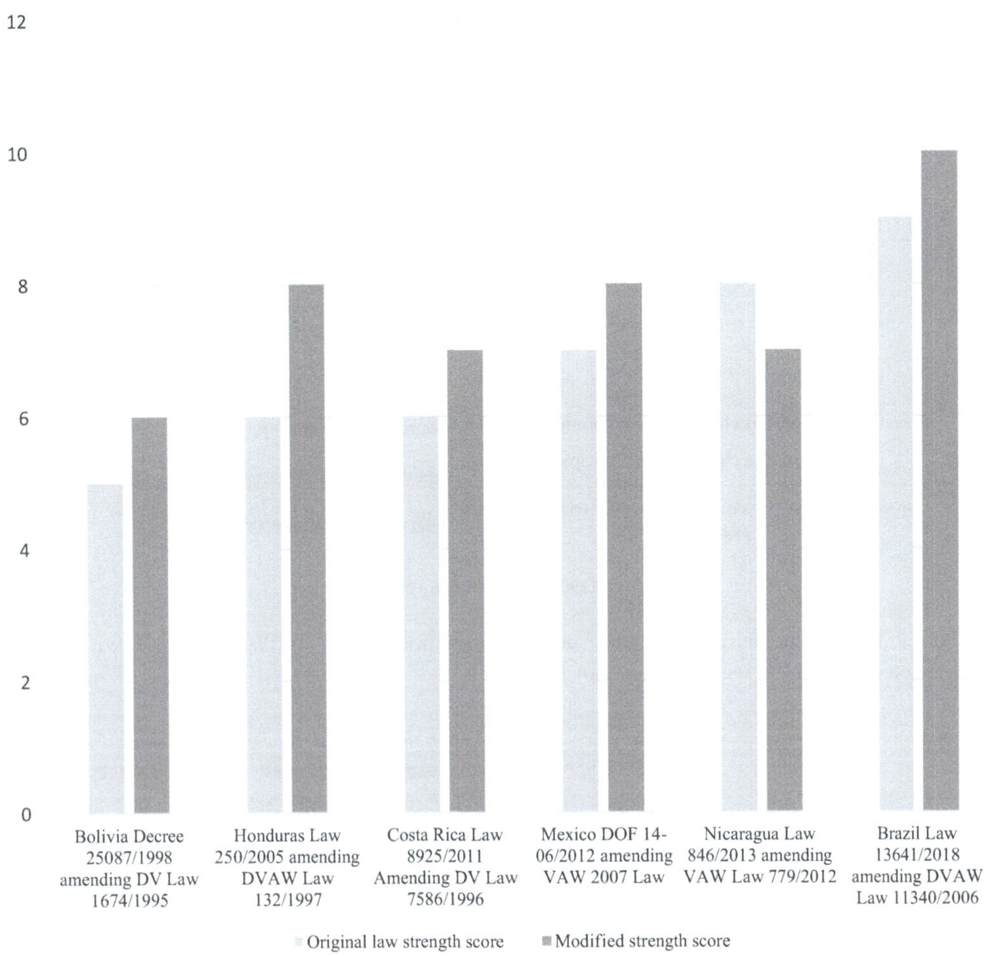

FIGURE 2.6 Laws that modified the strength of the comprehensive policy approach to violence in Latin American legislation (1990–2020). Own elaboration based on the 6 laws that modified the strength of its comprehensive policy approach over time.

Figure 2.8 shows that while there is a clear increase in specific budgetary provisions from 2006 on, other measures show a more stable presence through both periods. However, differences emerge when we differentiate specific characteristics of these capacity-building measures.

Social participation in law implementation was included in an even way in both periods, but legislation adopted after 2005 strengthened these provisions, extending them beyond specific processes (such as providing legal support or shelter) to incorporate a more transversal view of societal participation rights and duties regarding VAW.[32] The inclusion of training for public officials shows an even and primarily nominal presence in VAW laws over time, with provisions aimed at personnel directly linked with implementation, to change to a more substantive and transversal approach in legislation adopted from 2006 on, with laws promoting training programs in gender and human rights perspective across the State.[33]

Regarding research and production of data, laws enacted after 2005 went beyond demanding the elaboration of gender-based violence indicators and started promoting the creation of specialized systems of data collection on VAW.[34] In nine laws, all adopted in the second period, provisions on

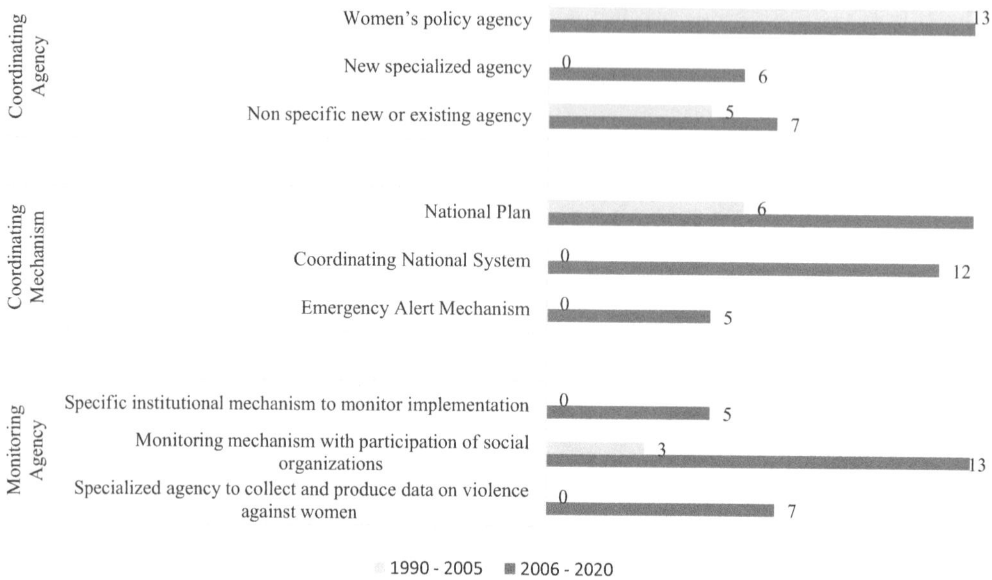

FIGURE 2.7 Institutional reforms in Latin American legislation on DV, DVAW, and VAW. Own elaboration based on the regional cluster of 183 laws.

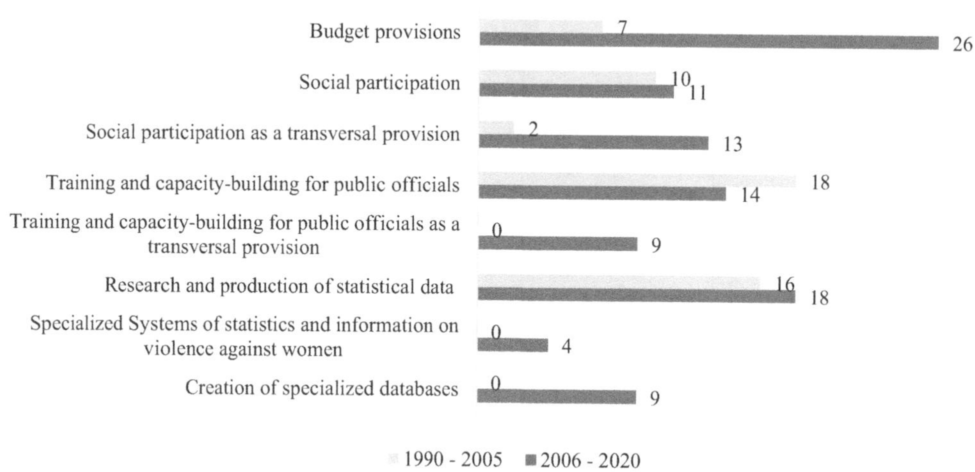

FIGURE 2.8 State capacity provisions in Latin American legislation on DV, DVAW, and VAW. Own elaboration based on the regional cluster of 183 laws.

building specialized databases, such as legal cases on VAW,[35] records on victims and aggressors – including sex offenders – [36] and missing women[37] were included.

Provisions to Address Gender-Based Violence in the Event of Disasters and Climate Change in Latin American Legislation

Since mid-2000s there has been a growing concern regarding the disproportioned effect of natural and humanitarian disasters and climate change on women, particularly the increase of gender-based violence in situations of economic insecurity, breakdown of societal infrastructure, and services and mobility restrictions (Peterman et al., 2020). International and regional organizations specialized in women's rights address this agenda through declarations and special recommendations, with calls to governments to prevent, mitigate, and remedy the gender-related impacts of a diverse types of high-risk situations (CEDAW Committee 2018; CIM 2008, Human Rights Watch 2016).

Latin American comprehensive legislation on VAW scarcely includes this topic into its provisions, with only two exceptions for this regional legislative gap. One is El Salvador's Special Comprehensive Law for a Life Free of Violence (Law 520/2010) which gives the WPA the mandate to 'define strategies and manage a national or local emergency situation, in order to prevent and detect acts of violence against women' (para. 13d) and stablishes a state duty to incorporate protection of the different modalities of VAW in the occurrence of risks and disasters that increase women's vulnerability (para.22b). The second is Ecuador's Comprehensive Organic Law to Prevent and Eradicate VAW (Registro Oficial No. 175/2018). This norm includes violence in emergencies and humanitarian situations as one specific context in which gender-based violence can occur, defining them as 'situations that promote inequalities between men and women and increase the risk of women, girls, and older adults of suffer physical, psychological, and sexual violence' (para.12, 10).

Legislative Responses toward VAW in the Wake of the COVID-19 Pandemic in Latin America

In the wake of the COVID-19 pandemic, in March 2020, Latin American countries, with the only exception of Nicaragua and Brazil,[38] imposed different degrees of movement restrictions that included school closures and scaling down public and private services considered non-essential. The restrictions varied from strict lockdowns as in Argentina, Peru, and Colombia to more flexible arrangements under a sanitary emergency context as in Mexico and Uruguay. Most countries started reopening activities between May and June (AS/COA, 2020).

Early in this process, state reports, news outlets, and women's organizations showed a significant rise in calls to DV helplines and shelters across the world (Mittal & Singh, 2020; Special Rapporteur on Violence against Women, 2020). A similar pattern was identified in VAW helplines calls across Latin American countries (López-Calva, 2020; Werth, 2020), next to an alarming number of intimate femicides perpetrated during the restrictions (CIM & MESECVI, 2020; Muñoz Lima, 2020). Since the beginning of the pandemic, international and regional organizations called for States to address the specific risks that reduced mobility represented for women's safety (CEDAW Committee, 2020; CIDH, 2020; Comité de Expertas MESECVI, 2020; UN Secretary-General, 2020a, 2020b; UN Women, 2020).

In this scenario, legislatives responses toward the intersection between COVID containment policies and DV against women in Latin America were varied. With most of the parliaments reorganizing their own work during the pandemic (IPU, 2021), it is not surprising that the majority of the measures adopted were originated in the Executive Power. From the analysis of the 52 measures adopted by Legislatures or that included legislative actors/institutions, three distinctive strategies emerge: (1) adoption of laws and formulation of bills proposing a comprehensive approach toward VAW during the sanitary emergency; (2) creation of institutional spaces inside the Legislatures to promote women's rights affected by the pandemic; and (3) interactive spaces to exchange experiences with legislators across the region as well as domestic, regional, and international stakeholders.

Legislation and Bills

Three laws address VAW under the pandemic in Latin America during 2020. In April, Peru enacted a decree elaborated under the delegation of legislative capacity on the Executive Power (Peru

Legislative Decree 1470/2020). In July, Brazil adopted Law 14022/2020 to establish measures to combat domestic and family VAW during the public health emergency and that same month the Decree 99/2020 passed in the Honduran Congress, with provisions for the prevention and attention of VAW and to guarantee gender equality throughout the sanitary crisis.

All laws contemplate the launching of campaigns about gender-based violence using different tools, such as social media advertising, hashtags, SMS, and WhatsApp messages, to raise awareness and/or disseminate information about the availability first response, legal and support services for women. Legislation also declares essential all services designed to support women affected by gender-based violence and looked to guarantee a variety of different mechanism to access information and counseling through government helplines. Peru and Honduras laws specifically address the provision of health services for victims, with Honduras legislation including access to sexual and reproductive health (para.10).[39] This law also expanded its scope beyond the essential services to include provisions oriented enhance the economic autonomy of survivors of gender-based violence (para.7, 11 and 12).

Brazil and Peru legislation contemplate provisions to ensure a diligent response toward violence from the police and the judicial systems, including the possibility of virtual communication and hearings and outlining a simplified procedure to issue protective orders. To secure the safety of members of social organizations working on the ground with gender-based violence victims, Honduran law extends the exception to the mobility restrictions granted to survivors of violence and their companions to women's rights activist, including shelter workers (para.5). It also promotes the creation of an institutional coordination space between government agencies and women's organizations to address issues related to VAW and girls during the COVID-19 pandemic (para.3).

Law initiatives aimed at protecting women from violence during the pandemic were presented in Argentina, Chile, and Mexico. Women deputies from the Argentinian Congress presented a project to incorporate the gender perspective in crisis committees (Iglesias, 2020) and another initiative looked to declare gender-based violence as a public social emergency for a period of two years, including a monthly financial allowance for victims (Secretaría Internacional de ParlAmericas, 2020). In Chile, during a special session in which senators analyzed the impact of the pandemic on gender-based-VAW, there was an agreement to speed up the approval of a bill to incorporate a special precautionary measure in favor of victims of DV and empower courts to control its compliance through electronic monitoring (Senado de la República de Chile, 2020c).

In the Mexican Congress, one bill proposed to include in the comprehensive law on VAW a specific State duty to guarantee the right of women to live free from violence in emergency isolation contexts and another one promoted the immediate separation of aggressors from their victims during mobility restrictions (Gómez Macfarland & Sánchez Ramírez, 2020). Mexican legislators also made 18 proposals with points of agreement[40] related to family and intrafamily violence in times of COVID and directed them to federal and local governments (Gómez Macfarland & Sánchez Ramírez, 2020, pp. 27–28).

Institutional Innovations

Next to legislation, the creation of coordination spaces to address gender-based violence during the sanitary crisis was identified in Chile, Honduras, and Peru. In Chile, the Presidency of the Senate established the 'Gender Table and COVID-19', with participation of feminist organizations and international human rights agencies, to analyze and make proposals for responding to the crisis with a gender focus. It adopted 13 urgent measures, with emphasis on sub-national coordination and implementation, access to justice by women survivors of violence, and a special focus on women with disabilities (Senado de la República de Chile, 2020a; UNDP, 2021).

The Gender Commission of the Honduran National Congress formed the 'Gender and Equity Table', in which they worked together with feminist organizations to address problems faced by women as a consequence of the pandemic (INAM, 2020). In Peru, the Woman and Family commission, with the support of all political parties, promoted a special session called '*Pleno Mujer*', with its first meeting in September 2020 dedicated to discuss violence against women VAW, among other topics (Andina Agencia Peruana de Noticias, 2020). During this session, the Minister of Women and Vulnerable populations presented to deputies the work of the ministry under the COVID-19 emergency (Ministerio de la Mujer y Poblaciones Vulnerables, 2020).

Actions of Legislative Gender Institutions: Gender Commissions and Women Caucuses

Women/gender commissions and women's caucuses play an important role in developing a woman's human rights agenda in Latin American parliaments (Rodríguez Gustá & Madera, 2014, 2017). This role was expressed during the pandemic through different actions. In Ecuador, the women's caucus *Grupo Parlamentario por los Derechos de las Mujeres* organized the virtual conversation 'Domestic violence in times of COVID-19', with the participation of other policy agencies and women's rights organizations (Secretaría de Derechos Humanos, 2020). The Commission for Social Equity and Gender of Paraguay's Lower Chamber received from the Ministry of Women a report on all the actions undertaken to address VAW during the sanitary emergency (Ministerio de la Mujer, 2020; MMGyD, 2020). In Chile, in a virtual reunion regarding legislation on VAW in the region, the Women and Gender Equality Commission of the Senate discussed the impact of the pandemic on gender-based violence with representatives of UN WOMEN (Senado de la República de Chile, 2020b). In the virtual event 'Legislative actions to prevent violence against women in the framework of the COVID-19 pandemic' organized by Parlamericas, representatives of 15 Latin American Legislatures shared experiences on the actions carried out to prevent and alleviate the effects of the pandemic on VAW during the sanitary crisis (Secretaría Internacional de ParlAmericas, 2020).

This brief analysis of the legislative responses toward VAW during the COVID-19 pandemic in Latin America shows that in addition to enacting/proposing a comprehensive set of laws on this issue, parliaments were active in creating institutions to define an agenda across political parties, coordinate actions with the Executive Power, and interact with local, regional, and global stakeholders engaged in a wider advocacy network of woman human rights. The continuous challenges posed by a global health emergency – which in many countries of the region is intertwined with economic, social, and political crises – will demand the consolidation of these actions as well as the development of new strategies to promote a progressive agenda for gender equality and a life free from violence.

Conclusions

This chapter describes Latin America's legislative shift on VAW through a qualitative comparative analysis of legislation adopted in 18 countries during the last three decades. Following Galanti (2013) characterization of this process as a paradigm shift, I use the emergent data from law content analysis to show the marginalization over time of a gender-blind approach directed at the family and restricted to the domestic sphere and the increasing consolidation of a gender-sensitive approach that acknowledges the structural bases of violence and women's specific experience of it in both private and public settings.

Although this shift is primarily driven by comprehensive legislation on VAW and legislation on femicide/feminized adopted in the region from 2006, the analysis shows that the standards promoted by women's and feminist movements and human rights instruments are also found in DV laws, reforms of the Penal Code, and legislation with specific provisions regarding gender-based violence. Overall, law content reveals a regional trend toward more thorough definitions of VAW, a strengthening of the comprehensive policy approach to address the structural and individual aspects of this problem and more specialized and transversal institutional reforms designed to increase the effectiveness of the implementation process.

Despite this progress and the pioneer role of Latin American legislation worldwide, its objectives of protecting women and eradicating gender-based violence are far from being achieved. A new wave of social mobilizations across the region (Friedman & Tabbush, 2016) and recent international recommendations (CEDAW Committee, 2017; CIDH, 2019; MESECVI, 2017) expose the gap between legal commitments and policy implementation, showing that without economic and political resources, and robust State capacities, comprehensive legislative action is not sufficient to transform structural inequalities and guarantee the women's right to a life without violence.

Notes

1 In 50 countries, specific laws on VAW, DVAW, and/or gender violence were identified: 19 countries are from the Americas (USA 1994, Honduras 1997, Brazil 2006, Costa Rica 2007, México 2007, Venezuela 2007, Colombia 2008, Guatemala 2008, Argentina 2009, El Salvador 2010, Nicaragua 2012, Bolivia 2013, Panamá 2013, Dominican Republic 2014, Perú 2015, Paraguay 2016, Uruguay 2017, Ecuador 2018, Chile 2020); 13 from Africa (Central African Republic 2006, Zimbabwe 2007, Rwanda 2008, Mozambique 2009, Cape Verde 2011, Zambia 2011, Benin 2012, Comoros 2014, Burkina Faso 2015, Togo 2015, Burundi 2016, Tunisia 2017, Morocco 2018); 8 from Asia (Bangladesh 2000, the Philippines 2004, Indonesia 2004, India 2005, Afghanistan 2009, Turkey 2012, Laos 2015, Georgia 2017); and 10 from Europe (Portugal 1991, Sweden 1997, Spain 2004, San Marino 2008, France 2010, Monaco 2011, Italy 2013, Andorra 2015, France 2010, Malta 2018). In three of these countries, VAW laws include discriminatory provisions toward women (Afghanistan Law on the Elimination of Violence against Women, Edition No. 989/2009; Mozambique Law 29/2009 Domestic Violence against Women; and the Central African Republic Law on Protection of Women against Violence 06.032/2006).

2 Sweden (Bill 1997/98:55 Kvinnofrid), USA (VAW Act 1994, 2005), and Spain (Law 121-000002/2004) were pioneers in adopting legislation addressing violence against women specifically. The Honduran Domestic Violence Law 132/1997 represents an early example, although limited, of a gender sensitive approach toward domestic violence in Latin America.

3 Out of the 183 laws identified for this study, only three were adopted before the emergence of international norms on VAW: The Costa Rican Law 7142/1990 and the Peruvian Penal Code Law 635/1991 were adopted before CEDAW General Recommendation No. 19 in 1992 and the Peruvian Law 26260/1993 was adopted before the adoption of the Belém do Para Convention in 1994.

4 Argentina, Bolivia, Brazil, Colombia, Costa Rica, Chile, Ecuador, El Salvador, the Dominican Republic, Guatemala, Honduras, Nicaragua, Mexico, Panama, Peru, Paraguay, Uruguay, and Venezuela.

5 Law amendments are only visible in the frequency analysis if they changed the original norm in one indicator and/or dimension. This data processing criterion was not applied on two indicators: all laws, including amendments, were classified as gender sensitive or gender neutral; and in all cases in which mandatory conciliation was identified in the original law, the attribute was extended to all amendments unless they specifically modified it.

6 Ecuador Law 103/1995; Honduras Law 132/1997 and its amendment in 2005; and Venezuela Law on violence against women and the family of 1998.

7 Brazil Law 11340/2006 and Costa Rica Law 8589/2007.

8 Mexico General Law of Women's Access to a Life Free of Violence (DOF 01-02-2007); Venezuela Organic Law on the Right of Women to a Life Free of Violence (Gaceta Oficial 38668/2007); Colombia Law 1257/2008; Guatemala Law 22/2008; Argentina Law 26485/2009; El Salvador Law 520/2010;

Nicaragua Law 779/2012; Bolivia Law 348/2013; Panama Law 82/2013; Peru Law 30364/2015; Paraguay Law 5777/2016; Uruguay Law 19580/2017; and Ecuador Organic Law to Prevent and Eradicate VAW (Registro Oficial Suplemento 175, 05-feb.-2018).

9 The only comprehensive law not including this right is the Costa Rica Law 8589/2007.

10 In the first previous period the only law including this more transversal mandate was Guatemalan Law 7/99.

11 In the first period, the only law including an intersectional approach and provisions for vulnerable groups of women was Panama Law 4/1999.

12 Colombia Law 294/1996, para. 3.g.

13 The two laws adopted after 2005 were amendments of a previous DV law that maintained the original provision of confrontation with the aggressor but added the possibility for the hearing to take place without the alleged aggressor being present (Costa Rica laws 8925/2011 and 9692/2019).

14 Laws that explicitly include women in their definition of violence and/or in their specific provisions toward the issue.

15 Mexico DOF 13-04-2020 includes a gender-based definition of political violence against women; and Peru Law 1323/2017 strengthens the fight against feminicide, family violence, and gender-based violence.

16 Colombia Law 1761/2015.

17 Argentina Law 27234/2015 Education with equality: Prevention and Eradication of Gender-based Violence; Law 10778/2003 Mandatory notification in cases of violence against women; Costa Rica Law 9063/2012 Psychological support to aggressors in all cases of violence; Ecuador Law 67/2006 Organic Health; and Nicaragua Law 648/2008 de Equality of Rights and Opportunities.

18 For this analysis, I apply an adapted version of the 'protected groups' category developed by Smulovitz (2015).

19 Costa Rica Law 7586/1996.

20 Perú Law 29819/2011 and its amendment 30068/2013; and Chile Law 20480/2010 and its amendment 21212/2020.

21 All original legislation except for Panama Domestic Violence Law 38/2001, which amended the Domestic Violence Law of 1995 to include a protection strategy to its original four strategy approach.

22 The 2013 amendment reintroduced the possibility of mediation for certain cases of VAW, which was prohibited in the original law.

23 Women policy agencies are government institutions whose main purpose is to promote the status of women (Htun & Weldon, 2018, p. 59).

24 The creation of specialized agencies was included in Guatemala LD 22/2008, Nicaragua Law 779/2012, Panamá Law 82/2013, and Costa Rica Law 8688/2008 (which complements the Law 2007). Is also the case of Argentina Law 27210/2015, with a coordination agency for the implementation of a public and free legal aid for victims of gender-based violence; and Guatemala LD 22/2008Law 9/2016, which creates a National Coordination Agency for the immediate search of missing women.

25 Mexico DOF 02-08/2006 and DOF 01-02-2007; Costa Rica Law 8688/2008; Bolivia Law 348/2013; Peru Laws 30364/2015, 1368/2018, 30823/2018, 1408/2018, and 30926/2019; Paraguay Law 5777/2016; Ecuador ROS 175/2018; and Uruguay Law 19580/2018.

26 Mexico DOF 01-02-2007; Bolivia Law 348/2013; and Ecuador ROS 175/2018.

27 El Salvador Law 520/2010.

28 Guatemala Law 9/2016.

29 Costa Rica Law 8688/2008; Colombia Law 1959/2019 (amendment to DV Law 299/2000); Panama Executive Decree 100/2017; and Peru Laws 30862/2018 and 1368/2018.

30 The only laws enacted before 2006 that included mixed monitoring agencies into their policy provisions were Honduras Law 132/1997, Uruguay Law 17514/2002 2002, and Dominican Republic Law 88/03.

31 Colombia Law 1257/2008; Argentina Law 26485/2009; Peru Laws 30364/2015 and 1408/2018; Paraguay Law 5777/2016 2016; Ecuador RO 175/2018; and Uruguay Law 19580/2018.

32 Except for Venezuela 1998 Law on Domestic Violence against Women and the Family and Panamá Law 38/2001 amendment the Domestic Violence law of 1995, legislation that included a transversal participation of social organizations in the implementation of the VAW provisions was adopted from 2006 on.

33 An example of this provision is the Argentinian Law 27499/2019, which established mandatory gender training for all public official at the Executive, Judicial and Legislative branches of the State.

34 Guatemala LD 22/2008; El Salvador LD 520/2010; Colombia Law 1761/2015; and Panama ED 100/2017.
35 Mexico DOF 01-02/2007.
36 Peru Laws 30364/2015, 3090/2018 and 30862/2018; Guatemala Laws 9/2016 and 22/2017; Ecuador ROS 175/2018; and Panama Executive Decree 100/2017.
37 Mexico DOF 14-06/2012 and Guatemala LD 9/2016.
38 In Brazil, the only national policy was the suspension of schools, on March 26, while other regulations depended on states and municipalities (AS/COA, 2020).
39 Honduras has one of the most restrictive norms regarding abortion in Latin America, as it is forbidden in any case since 1983 (CEPAL, 2021). In January 2021, in a clear step back for women´s rights in the country, the Congress approved a constitutional reform that reinforced this prohibition by elevating the majority necessary to modify it (DW, 2021).
40 Mechanism by which legislators can request information on the management in any branch of the public administration, summoning an official of the federation to appear, or urging them to comply with any provision or expedite any government action (SIL, n.d.).

Bibliography

African Union. (2003). *Protocol to the African Charter on Human and Peoples' Rights on the Rights of Women in Africa.* https://au.int/sites/default/files/treaties/37077-treaty-charter_on_rights_of_women_in_africa.pdf.

Agüero, J. M. (2020). *COVID-19 and the Rise of Intimate Partner Violence.* University of Connecticut. Department of Economics Working Paper Series, *Working Paper 2020–05R May 2020, Revised September 2020.* https://ideas.repec.org/p/uct/uconnp/2020-05.html

Andina Agencia Peruana de Noticias. (2020, September 5). *Congreso realiza hoy primer pleno mujer.* https://andina.pe/agencia/noticia-congreso-realiza-hoy-primer-pleno-mujer-812617.aspx

AS/COA. (2020). *The Coronavirus in Latin America.* AS/COA. Americas Society. Council of the Americas. www.as-coa.org/articles/coronavirus-latin-america

CEDAW Committee. (1992). *Recomendación General Nro. 19. La violencia contra la mujer.* United Nations. https://tbinternet.ohchr.org/_layouts/15/treatybodyexternal/Download.aspx?symbolno=INT/CEDAW/GEC/3731&Lang=en

CEDAW Committee. (2015). *Recomendación general Nro. 33. Sobre el acceso de las mujeres a la justicia* (CEDAW/C/GC/33). United Nations. https://tbinternet.ohchr.org/_layouts/15/treatybodyexternal/Download.aspx?symbolno=CEDAW/C/GC/33&Lang=en

CEDAW Committee. (2017). *Recomendación general Nro. 35 sobre la violencia por razón de género contra la mujer, por la que se actualiza la recomendación general Nro. 19* (CEDAW/C/GC/35). United Nations. https://tbinternet.ohchr.org/_layouts/15/treatybodyexternal/Download.aspx?symbolno=INT/CEDAW/GEC/3731&Lang=en

CEDAW Committee (2018). General Recommendation No. 37 (2018) on the Gender-related Dimensions of Disaster risk Reduction in the Context of Climate Change (CEDAW/C/GC/37). United Nations. https://documents-dds-ny.un.org/doc/UNDOC/GEN/N18/068/98/PDF/N1806898.pdf?OpenElement

CEDAW Committee. (2020). *Guidance Note on CEDAW and COVID-19.* https://www.ohchr.org/Documents/HRBodies/TB/COVID19/Guidance_Note.docx

Comisión Económica para América Latina y el Caribe (CEPAL). (2014). Informe anual 2013-2014. El enfrentamiento de la violencia contra las mujeres en América Latina y el Caribe. Naciones Unidas. https://repositorio.cepal.org/bitstream/handle/11362/37185/S1500499_es.pdf?sequence=4&isAllowed=y

Comisión Económica para América Latina y el Caribe (CEPAL) (2019) (2019). *Leyes de violencia.* Observatorio de Igualdad de Género de América Latina y el Caribe. https://oig.cepal.org/es/leyes/leyes-de-violencia

Comisión Económica para América Latina y el Caribe (CEPAL). (2021). *Observatorio de Igualdad de Género de América Latina y el Caribe. Leyes. Leyes sobre aborto.* Retrieved February 1, 2021, from https://oig.cepal.org/es/leyes/leyes-sobre-aborto

Comisión Económica para América Latina y el Caribe (CEPAL) (2021). Observatorio COVID-19 en América Latina y el Caribe Impacto económico y social. *CEPAL COVID-19 RESPUESTA.* www.cepal.org/es/temas/covid-19

Council of Europe (2011). *Council of Europe Convention on Preventing and Combating Violence against Women and Domestic Violence.* Council of Europe Treaty Series – No. 210. https://rm.coe.int/168008482e.

Chibán, A. L. (2013). *Violencia de género y reformas penales en América Latina: La regulación de la acción penal en los delitos sexuales* [Tesis de Abogacía, Universidad de San Andrés. Departamento de Derecho]. http://hdl.handle.net/10908/2467

Comisión Interamericana de Derechos Humanos (CIDH). (2020). *La CIDH hace un llamado a los Estados a incorporar la perspectiva de género en la respuesta a la pandemia del COVID-19 y a combatir la violencia sexual e intrafamiliar en este contexto.* www.oas.org/es/cidh/prensa/comunicados/2020/074.asp

Comisión Interamericana de las Mujeres (CIM) (2008). Integración de la perspectiva de género en las políticas hemisféricas y en la Cumbre de las Américas. CIM/RES. 248 (XXXIV-O/08). Organization American States.

Comisión Interamericana de Derechos Humanos (CIDH) (2019). *Violencia y discriminación contra mujeres, niñas y adolescentes* (Informe temático OEA/Ser.L/V/II. Doc. 233 14 noviembre 2019 Original: Inglés; Human rights--. 2. --. I. Title. II. Series.). Organización de Estados Americanos. www.oas.org/es/cidh/informes/pdfs/ViolenciaMujeresNNA.pdf

Comisión Interamericana de la Mujer (CIM) y Mecanismo de Seguimiento de la Convención de Belém do Pará (MESECVI). (2014). Guía para la aplicación de la Convención Interamericana para Prevenir, Sancionar y Erradicar la Violencia contra la Mujer (Convención de Belém do Pará). *Organización de Estados Americanos.* www.oas.org/es/mesecvi/docs/BdP-GuiaAplicacion-Web-ES.pdf

Comisión Interamericana de la Mujer (CIM) y Mecanismo de Seguimiento de la Convención de Belém do Pará (MESECVI). (2020). *Violence Against Women and the Measures to Contain the Spread of COVID-19* (OAS. Documentos oficiales; OEA/Ser.L/II.6.26; p. 25). Organización de Estados Americanos. www.oas.org/en/cim/docs/COVID-19-RespuestasViolencia-EN.pdf

Comité de Expertas MESECVI. (2020). *Comité de Expertas solicita la incorporación de la perspectiva de género en las medidas que se tomen para la mitigación del COVID-19 y el reforzamiento de acciones para la prevención y atención de la violencia de género.* www.oas.org/es/mesecvi/docs/CEVI-ComunicadoCOVID-2020-ES.pdf

Demirdjian, S. (2020, June 11). Violencia de género durante la pandemia: Una puesta a punto de la respuesta del Estado. *Periódico La Diaria.* https://ladiaria.com.uy/feminismos/articulo/2020/6/violencia-de-genero-durante-la-pandemia-una-puesta-a-punto-de-la-respuesta-del-estado/

Den Boer, A., & Ertan, S. (2017, June 8). Explaining Cross-National Variation in Domestic Violence Legislation. European Conference on Politics and Gender, Lausanne, Switzerland. https://ecpr.eu/Events/Event/PaperDetails/33696

DW. (2021, January 22). Honduras blinda la prohibición total del aborto. *Deutsche Welle (DW) en español.* www.dw.com/es/honduras-blinda-la-prohibición-total-del-aborto/a-56311291

Edwards, A. (2011). *Violence against women under international human rights law* (2013th ed.). Cambridge University Press.

Friedman, E. J., & Tabbush, C. (2016). #NiUnaMenos: Not One Woman Less, Not One More Death! *The North American Congress on Latin America (NACLA).* https://nacla.org/news/2016/11/01/niunamenos-not-one-woman-less-not-one-more-death

Galanti, V. (2013). *Conditions for plausibility of Women's Conventions: Internalising the paradigm shift in the Inter – American System of Human Rights. Analysing a comparable experience for the Istanbul Convention* [PhD Program in Political Systems and Institutional Change XXIV Cycle, IMT Institute for Advanced Studies]. http://e-theses.imtlucca.it/121/1/Galanti_phdthesis.pdf

Galanti, V., & Borzacchiello, E. (2013). IACrtHR's Influence on the Convergence of National Legislations on Women's Rights: Legitimation through Permeability. *International Journal of Social Sciences, II* (1), 7–27.

Garita Vílchez, A. I. (S/f). La regulación del delito de Femicidio/Feminicidio en América Latina y el Caribe. *Secretariado de la Campaña del Secretario General de las Naciones Unidas ÚNETE para poner fin a la violencia contra las mujeres.* https://periodicooficial.jalisco.gob.mx/sites/periodicooficial.jalisco.gob.mx/files/la_regulacion_del_delito_de_femicidio_feminicidio_en_america_latina_y_el_caribe-_ana_isabel_garita_vilchez.pdf

Gómez Macfarland, C. A., & Sánchez Ramírez, M. C. (2020). Violencia familiar en tiempos de Covid. *Mirada Legislativa, Instituto Belisario Domínguez, Senado de la República, No. 187.* http://bibliodigitalibd.senado.gob.mx/bitstream/handle/123456789/4891/ML_187.pdf?sequence=1&isAllowed=y

Hall, P. (1993). Policy Paradigms, Social Learning, and the State: The Case of Economic Policymaking in Britain. *Comparative Politics, 25* (3), 275–296.

Htun, M., & Weldon, L. (2012). The Civic Origins of Progressive Policy Change: Combating Violence against Women in Global Perspective, 1975–2005. *The American Political Science Review, 106* (3), 548–569.

Htun, M., & Weldon, L. (2018). *The logics of gender justice: State action on women's rights around the world.* Cambridge University Press.

Human Rights Watch. (2016). Submission to the Committee on the Elimination of Discrimination against Women on "Gender-related dimensions of disaster risk reduction and climate change". https://www.ohchr.org/sites/default/files/Documents/HRBodies/CEDAW/ClimateChange/HumanRightsWatch.doc

Iglesias, M. (2020, April 23). Coronavirus en Argentina: Diputadas presentan un proyecto para que participen mujeres en el comité de crisis de la pandemia. *Periódico Clarín.* www.clarin.com/sociedad/coronavirus-argentina-diputadas-presentan-proyecto-participen-mujeres-comite-crisis-pandemia_0_BkWeyA5If.html

Instituto Nacional de la Mujer de Honduras (INAM). (2020). *Boletín Especial COVID-19 y Género (Julio 2020).* www.inam.gob.hn/index.php?option=com_phocadownload&view=file&id=162:boletin-inam-julio-2020&Itemid=110

Inter-Parliamentary Union (IPU) (2021). *Country compilation of parliamentary responses to the pandemic.* Inter-Parliamentary Union. www.ipu.org/country-compilation-parliamentary-responses-pandemic

Klugman, J. (2017). Gender Based Violence and the Law. World Development Report Background Paper. *World Bank.* https://openknowledge.worldbank.org/handle/10986/26198

Krook, M. L., & True, J. (2012). Rethinking the Life Cycles of International Norms: The United Nations and the Global Promotion of Gender Equality. *European Journal of International Relations, 18* (1), 103–127.

Library of Congress (LOC) (2020). *Legal Provisions on Gender Equality Arab Countries. Israel. Iran* (LL File No. 2020-018615). The Law Library of Congress (LOC), Global Legal Research Directorate. www.loc.gov/law/help/gender-equality/legal-provisions-gender-equality.pdf

López-Calva, L. F. (2020, November 3). ¿No hay lugar más seguro que el hogar?: El aumento en la violencia doméstica y de género durante los confinamientos por COVID-19 en ALC. *Blog del Director Graph For Thought. PNUD. América Latina y el Caribe.* www.latinamerica.undp.org/content/rblac/es/home/presscenter/director-s-graph-for-thought/no-safer-place-than-home---the-increase-in-domestic-and-gender-b.html

Martin, N., & Mayorga, C. (2020). Abused in Lockdown. *Violentadas en Cuarentena.* https://violentadasencuarentena.distintaslatitudes.net/abused-in-lockdown/

Merry, S. E. (2006). *Human rights and gender violence: Translating international law into local justice.* The University of Chicago Press.

Mecanismo de Seguimiento de la Convención de Belém do Pará (MESECVI) (2008). *Primera Ronda de Evaluación Multilateral: Segunda Conferencia de Estados Parte. Informe Hemisférico. Decisiones, Conclusiones y Acuerdos.* (Informes hemisféricos sobre la Implementación de la Convención de Belém do Pará Primer Informe Hemisférico). Organización de Estados Americanos. https://www.oas.org/es/mesecvi/docs/InformeHemisferico2008-SP.pdf

Mecanismo de Seguimiento de la Convención de Belém do Pará (MESECVI) (2014). (2014). *Segundo Informe de Seguimiento a la Implementación de las Recomendaciones del Comité de Expertas del MESECVI* (p. 122) [Seguimiento]. Organización de Estados Americanos. www.oas.org/es/mesecvi/docs/MESECVI-SegundoInformeSeguimiento-ES.pdf

Mecanismo de Seguimiento de la Convención de Belém do Pará (MESECVI) (2017). *Tercer Informe Hemisférico sobre la Implementación de la Convención de Belém do Pará. Prevención de la Violencia contra las Mujeres en las Américas. Caminos por Recorrer.* (p. 228) [Seguimiento]. Organización de Estados Americanos. www.oas.org/es/mesecvi/docs/TercerInformeHemisferico-ES.pdf

Ministerio de la Mujer. (2020, September 1). *Se presentó a Diputada informe sobre acciones contra la violencia. Ministerio de la Mujer. República del Paraguay.* www.mujer.gov.py/index.php/noticias/ministra-de-la-mujer-presento-diputada-un-informe-sobre-acciones-emprendidas-contra-la-violencia

Ministerio de la Mujer y Poblaciones Vulnerables. (2020, September 5). Ministra Sasieta expresó compromiso del Ejecutivo en respaldar iniciativas del Legislativo a favor de las mujeres, niñas y adolescentes. *Perú – Ministerio de la Mujer y Poblaciones Vulnerables.* www.gob.pe/institucion/mimp/noticias/300611-ministra-sasieta-expreso-compromiso-del-ejecutivo-en-respaldar-iniciativas-del-legislativo-a-favor-de-las-mujeres-ninas-y-adolescentes

Mittal, S., & Singh, T. (2020, September 8). Gender-Based Violence during COVID-19 Pandemic: A Mini-Review. *Frontiers in Global Womens Health.* www.frontiersin.org/articles/10.3389/fgwh.2020.00004/full

Ministerio de las Mujeres, Géneros y Diversidad Argentina (MMGyD) (2020) Medidas en materia de género y diversidad en el marco de la emergencia sanitaria. https://www.argentina.gob.ar/generos/medidas-en-materia-de-genero-y-diversidad-en-el-marco-de-la-emergencia-sanitaria

Montoya, C. (2013). *From global to grassroots: The European Union, transnational advocacy, and combating violence against women*. Oxford University Press.

Muñoz Lima, R. (2020, July 28). COVID-19: ¿qué ha hecho América Latina para evitar más feminicidios? *Deutsche Welle (DW) en español*. www.dw.com/es/covid-19-qué-ha-hecho-américa-latina-para-evitar-más-feminicidios/a-54356170

OAS, O. of A. S. (1994). *Convención Interamericana para Prevenir, Sancionar y Erradicar la Violencia contra la Mujer 'Convención Belém do Pará'*. www.oas.org/juridico/spanish/tratados/a-61.html

OECD. (2020). *Social Institutions & Gender Index. Country profiles*. OECD Development Centre's Social Institutions and Gender Index (SIGI). www.genderindex.org/country-profiles/

ONU Mujeres. (2016). *Global Database on Violence against Women*. http://evaw-global-database.unwomen.org/en

Ortiz-Barreda, G., & Vives-Cases, C. (2013). Legislation on Violence against Women: Overview of Key Components. *Pan American Journal of Public Health, 33* (1), 61–72.

Peterman, A., Potts, A., O'Donnell, M., Thomposon, K., Shah, N., Oertelt-Prigione, S., & van Gelder, N. (2020, April 1). Pandemics and Violence against Women and Children. *Center for Global Development, Working Paper 528 April 2020*. www.cgdev.org/sites/default/files/pandemics-and-vawg-april2.pdf

Richards, D. L., & Haglund, J. (2015). *Violence against women and the law* (2016th ed.). Routledge.

Rodríguez Gustá, A. L., & Madera, N. (2014). Dimensiones colectivas, relacionales y supranacionales en la construcción de una agenda legislativa de derechos humanos de mujeres en América latina. *Revista Uruguaya de Ciencia Política, 3* (2), 37–64.

Rodríguez Gustá, A. L., & Madera, N. (2017). Organizational Repertoires for Advancing Women's Rights: An Analysis of Structures, Groups and Policies in National Legislatures in Latin America and the Caribbean. In *Women, Politics, and Democracy in Latin America* (pp. 89–105). Palgrave MacMillan.

Secretaría de Derechos Humanos. (2020, August 12). *Secretaría de Derechos Humanos participa en diálogo sobre «Violencia intrafamiliar en tiempos de COVID-19» organizado por el Grupo Parlamentario por los Derechos de las Mujeres*. https://www.derechoshumanos.gob.ec/secretaria-de-derechos-humanos-participa-en-dialogo-sobre-violencia-intrafamiliar-en-tiempos-de-covid-19-organizado-por-el-grupo-parlamentario-por-los-derechos-de-las-mujeres/

Secretaría Internacional de ParlAmericas. (2020). *Acciones legislativas para prevenir la violencia contra las mujeres en el marco de la pandemia COVID-19*. http://parlamericas.org/uploads/documents/VAW_webinar_report_SPA.pdf

Secretariado Ejecutivo del Sistema Naciona de Seguridad Pública. (2021, January 25). Información sobre violencia contra las mujeres (Incidencia delictiva y llamadas de emergencia 9-1-1), diciembre 2020. *Secretariado Ejecutivo del Sistema Nacional de Seguridad Pública*. www.gob.mx/sesnsp/articulos/informacion-sobre-violencia-contra-las-mujeres-incidencia-delictiva-y-llamadas-de-emergencia-9-1-1-febrero-2019

Senado de la República de Chile. (2020a, May 8). *Crean Mesa de Género Covid 19 que busca visibilizar la situación de la mujer en la pandemia*. Senado República de Chile. www.senado.cl/crean-mesa-de-genero-covid-19-que-busca-visibilizar-la-situacion-de-la/senado/2020-05-08/144156.html

Senado de la República de Chile. (2020b, June 2). *ONU mujeres para América Latina y el Caribe expuso sobre panorama regional de la legislación sobre violencia contra la mujer*. Senado República de Chile. www.senado.cl/onu-mujeres-para-america-latina-y-el-caribe-expuso-sobre-panorama/senado/2020-06-02/124611.html

Senado de la República de Chile. (2020c, August 20). *Aumento de violencia de género: Acuerdan oficios para agilizar proyectos para protección de víctimas y de apoyo*. Senado República de Chile. www.senado.cl/aumento-de-violencia-de-genero-acuerdan-oficios-para-agilizar-proyectos/senado/2020-08-20/123332.html

Sistema de Información Legislativa (SIL) (2021). *Proposición con punto de acuerdo* [Sistema de Información Legislativa]. Retrieved January 31, 2021, from http://sil.gobernacion.gob.mx/Glosario/definicionpop.php?ID=194

Smulovitz, C. (2015). Legal Inequality and Federalism: Domestic Violence Laws in the Argentine Provinces. *Latin America Politics and Society, 57* (3), 1–26.

Special Rapporteur on Violence against Women. (2020). *Report of the Special Rapporteur on violence against women, its causes and consequences, Dubravka Šimonović. Intersection between the coronavirus disease (COVID-19) pandemic and the pandemic of gender-based violence against women, with a focus on domestic violence and the "peace in the home" initiative* (A/75/144; p. 24). UN. Human Rights Council. https://documents-dds-ny.un.org/doc/UNDOC/GEN/N20/193/96/PDF/N2019396.pdf?OpenElement

UN General Assembly. (1994). *Declaration on the Elimination of Violence against Women*. www.un.org/en/genocideprevention/documents/atrocity-crimes/Doc.21_declaration%20elimination%20vaw.pdf

UN Secretary-General. (2020a). *Policy Brief: The Impact of COVID-19 on Women*. www.unwomen.org/en/digital-library/publications/2020/04/policy-brief-the-impact-of-covid-19-on-women

UN Secretary-General. (2020b). *COVID-19 and human rights: We are all in this together*. www.un.org/en/un-coronavirus-communications-team/we-are-all-together-human-rights-and-covid-19-response-and

United Nations Development Programme (UNDP). (2021). *COVID-19 Global Gender Response Tracker*. UNPD COVID-19 Data Futures Platform. https://data.undp.org/gendertracker/

United Nations Development Programme (UNDP) & UN Women. (2017). *From Commitment to Action: Policies to End Violence against Women in Latin America and the Caribbean. Regional Analysis Document*. United Nations Development Programme, UNDP Regional Center for Latin America and the Caribbean. www.undp.org/content/dam/rblac/docs/Research%20and%20Publications/Empoderamiento%20de%20la%20Mujer/UNDP-RBLAC-ReportVCMEnglish.pdf

United Nations. (2009). *Handbook for Legislation on Violence against Women*. www.un.org/womenwatch/daw/vaw/handbook/Handbook%20for%20legislation%20on%20violence%20against%20women.pdf

United Nations. (2020). Naciones Unidas. Asamblea General. Estado Miembro. *Naciones Unidas*. www.un.org/es/member-states/index.html

United Nations & Centre for Social Development and Humanitarian Affairs. (1993). *Strategies for confronting domestic violence: A resource manual* (ST/CSDHA/20). United Nations. https://www.unodc.org/pdf/youthnet/tools_strategy_english_domestic_violence.pdf

United Nations Secretary-General. (2006). *Estudio a fondo sobre todas las formas de violencia contra la mujer. Informe del Secretario General* (A/61/122/Add.1). United Nations. www.acnur.org/fileadmin/Documentos/BDL/2016/10742.pdf

UN Women. (2020). *Policy Brief: Strategies for the prevention of violence against women in the context of COVID-19 in Latin America and the Caribbean*. www2.unwomen.org/-/media/field%20office%20americas/documentos/publicaciones/2020/05/un%20women%20violence%20prevention%20brief%20ingles.pdf?la=en&vs=251

Weldon, L. (2002). *Protest, policy and the problem of violence against women: A cross-national comparison*. University of Pittsburgh Press.

Werth, B. (2020, June 29). The Perils of Quédate en Casa: COVID-19 and Gender Violence in Latin America. *AULA BLOG. Center for Latin American & Latino Studies. American University. Washington DC*. https://aulablog.net/2020/06/29/the-perils-of-quedate-en-casa-covid-19-and-gender-violence-in-latin-america/

3

GENDER-BASED VIOLENCE AND FEMICIDE IN MEXICO

Why Is the Law Failing to Protect Mexico's Women?

Emily Acevedo

Femicide is an extreme form of gender-based violence (GBV), defined as the deliberate killing of a woman or girl because of her gender. The term femicide was first used in Mexico in the 1990s to describe the murders of young girls and women in Chihuahua. From 1993 to early 2000, an estimated 370 murdered women and 137 were sexually assaulted in Chihuahua City and Ciudad Juárez (Camacho, 2005, p. 259). These murders fueled mobilization efforts for many civil society organizations to seek justice for those women. In response to the pressure exerted by mobilization efforts, Mexico's Congress adopted the 2007 Law on Women's Access to a Life Free of Violence (LGAMVLV) that coordinates efforts at all levels of government to prevent, punish, and eradicate violence against women. While this legislation was a step in the right direction, much work remains to be done, as evidenced by rising femicide rates.

In early January 2018, Mexican authorities updated the official homicide total for 2017, revealing a staggering 72% rise in femicides over the previous two years, with approximately 2,585 women killed in 2017 (Deschamps, 2018). In 2020, Mexico registered 3,723 killings, but only 940 were investigated as femicides (Agren, 2021). Why have femicide rates climbed in recent years when significant legislative action has been taken? This chapter will examine the current state of GBV in Mexico and explain why federal and state efforts are failing to curb this violence. First, I will explore the shifting climate from Ciudad Juárez to the present that has contributed to violence against women as a prominent issue in the Mexican human rights discourse. Next, the chapter will examine efforts to combat GBV in Mexico by exploring the legislation and criminal justice responses at the federal and state levels. Lastly, this chapter will discuss the shifting political, social, and economic realities in Mexico that account for the failure to reduce violence against women, including contributing factors that result in the escalation of femicide, concluding with future research that could address these shifting realities.

The Persistence of Femicide

Despite appearances that the Mexican government is directing its resources to combat violence against women, there is evident institutional inertia. The persistence of GBV and femicide reflects the failure to confront internalized behavioral patterns and remedy social practices directed toward women. For instance, until 1974, women were not legally permitted to work after dark. While the laws have changed, the gendered beliefs about women out after dark remain deeply engrained.

DOI: 10.4324/9781003264040-5

When women fall victim to GBV and potentially death, the perception then and even now is that the woman is unchaste and must not come from a good home (Haney, 2012). These machismo beliefs prevent adequate acceptance and enforcement of the laws that contribute to widespread impunity.

Scholars contend that femicides can only be understood by placing this issue within the broader understanding of GBV. Femicide is the final outcome, but the daily occurrences of GBV serve as the necessary preconditions for the occurrence of femicide (Koutsoyannis, 2011). Feminicide, a term often used in Latin America, goes beyond the social context of femicide and includes the political context of judicial and political structures that normalize the crime (Joseph, 2017).

Bovarnick (2007) shows in her comparative analysis of rape, how violence is constituted in Mexico and Pakistan, revealing how culturally specific manifestations of violence against women are allowed, and at times justified, as part of the subordination of women in a patriarchal society. In her fieldwork, Bovarnick noted that "women's rights and access to the legal system are not exclusively determined by the law" (p. 66). In other words, what may account for why women do not discuss, much less report violence, particularly within a marriage, has more to do with the importance of social and cultural norms. The rights a woman enjoys are contingent on how influential "traditional customary discourses are in the context she lives in" (p. 67).

Liu and Fullerton Jr. (2015) investigate whether a women's relative social status determines lethal and nonlethal violence against women. Their study examines female homicidal data from 2002 through 2010 for all of Mexico. Their study found that females with higher social standings experienced lower homicide rates and lower intimate partner violence rates. Furthermore, homicides committed in the home are often by people familiar with the woman versus homicides committed outside the home.

Mexico's cultural machismo attitude is an underlying reason behind GBV and femicide. However, what is critical is understanding how this cultural attitude influences and shapes Mexico's formal and informal institutions. In addition to institutional explanations, there are three contributing explanations for the persistence of GBV and femicide. First, a major driving force behind these deaths is a result of the drug war. In 2006, former president Felipe Calderón launched a military offensive against drug trafficking organizations. From 1985 to 2016, there were 52,210 recorded killings of women, with a third of those killings occurring in those last six years, coinciding with the military campaign that devastated the country as they fought one another for control of drug supply routes and territory. Second is the global COVID-19 pandemic. GBV and femicide have intensified, not just in Mexico but worldwide, as countries issued stay-at-home orders to halt the spread of COVID-19. UN Women references a "shadow pandemic" to describe how stay-at-home orders subject women and young girls to remain in confinement with their aggressors due to the global pandemic, putting them at higher risk of GBV. Finally, emerging scholarship highlights the gender-related dimensions of disasters in the context of climate change that links gender inequality and violence against women (Vithanage, 2021). Combined, each of these factors helps situate how GBV stems from "long-standing, deeply entrenched discriminatory norms that treat gender inequality with permissibility and further embed these inequalities within societal structures and institutions" (Castañeda Carney et al., 2020).

Human Rights Discourse on Women

Significant advances have been made to address GBV at the international, regional, and national levels. Internationally, the United Nations (UN) has been at the forefront of establishing norms and guidelines to end violence against women. In 1979, the Convention on the Elimination of all Forms of Discrimination against Women (CEDAW) was passed. States who have signed onto

CEDAW, such as Mexico, commit themselves to undertake a series of measures to end discrimination against women in all of its forms. By 1992, CEDAW included GBV with General Assembly Recommendations No. 19, which recognized that violence against women serves as a form of discrimination against women since this act either impairs or nullifies the ability of women to enjoy human rights (CEDAW/C/GC/35).

The 1993 Declaration on the Elimination of Violence against Women provided a framework for national and international action and defined violence against women as

> any act of gender-based violence that results in, or is likely to result in, physical, sexual or psychological harm or suffering to women, including threats of such acts, coercion or arbitrary deprivation of liberty, whether occurring in public or in private life.
>
> *A/RES/48/104*

Notably, these efforts paved the way for action at the regional level, with the passage of the Inter-American Convention on the Prevention, Punishment, and Eradication of Violence against Women (also known as the Convention of Belém Do Pará) by the Organization of American States in 1995. The Convention condemns all forms of violence against women, and states agree to policies to prevent, punish, and eradicate such violence (Convention of Belém Do Pará, Article 7). More importantly, states agree to work toward specific measures, including programs that "modify social and cultural patterns of conduct", "promote education and training of all those involved in the administration of justice", and "provide specialized services for women who have been subjected to violence" (Convention of Belém Do Pará, Article 8).

Legal and Institutional Frameworks

The National Survey on the Dynamics of Household Relationships (ENDIREH) administered by the National Institute for Women (INMUJERES) and the National Institute of Statistics and Geography (INEGI) was the first national survey on violence against women, conducted in Mexico in 2003. The second was the National Survey on Violence against Women (ENVIM) undertaken by the Ministry of Health and the National Institute of Public Health. Each survey revealed that violence against women was not a private problem but rather a public problem that affected a large number of women and required coordinated efforts by the government to remedy it. Shortly after, Mexico began to align its legislation to comply with international human rights standards on gender equality and the prevention and punishment of violence against women with the passage of two legal frameworks.

The first legal framework, Norma Oficial Mexicana 046 (NOM-046-SSA2-2005) on family and sexual violence against women, establishes criteria for medical personnel in the public health system. Medical personnel must notify the prosecutor's office whenever a case of domestic or sexual abuse is suspected. The prosecutor's office is then responsible for investigating these suspected cases of abuse.

The second legal framework is the 2007 General Law on Women's Access to a Life Free of Violence (Ley General de Acceso de las Mujeres a una Vida Libre de Violencia, LGAMVLV), which includes much of the above-mentioned legal framework. LGAMVLV provides measures for protecting, preventing, and punishing all violence against women. To that end, this federal law obligates each state to harmonize legislative content and adopt state Law on Women's Access to a Life Free of Violence. LGAMVLV identifies six types of violence, psychological, physical, patrimonial, economic, sexual, and violence against the woman's dignity, integrity, or freedom (Article 6), as well as identifies patterns of violence that women confront, such as in the home (Article 7), in the workplace and educational institutions (Article 10), in the community (Article 16), and femicide violence (Article 21). Article 18 also recognizes institutional violence perpetrated on women by government officials' actions or blatant omission to investigate, punish, and eradicate violence against women. The LGAMVLV also provides access to women's shelters for women who are victims of violence. These shelters offer comprehensive support that addresses various needs ranging from housing, clothing, medical and psychological care, access to legal services, educational programs, and job training (Article 56).

The National Commission to Prevent and Eradicate Violence against Women (CONAVIM) supports these legal frameworks. CONAVIM was created in 2009 to craft national policy, to coordinate efforts at the federal, state, and municipal levels, as well as to ensure Mexico's compliance with international agreements, to prevent, punish, and eradicate violence against women, and to guarantee women's access to a life free of violence (Article 5). CONAVIM is responsible for issuing gender violence alerts as defined in Article 22 of LGAMVLV, which creates a formal process for civil society organizations to request activation for a gender violence alert and seek assistance from the federal government to monitor state efforts to combat violence against women. When a gender violence alert is issued, emergency measures are implemented, in compliance with Articles 35 and 36 of LGAMVLV, at the federal, state, and municipal levels. The objective is to combat violence by directing government resources to ensure women receive legal, medical, and/or psychological assistance, and unsolved cases get prioritized for investigation.

One Step Forward, Two Steps Back

Mexico has a legal framework designed to protect women against violence, yet, rather than witness a decrease in femicide, the acts have grown more brazen and wanton. This section will first focus on four interrelated institutional factors that undermine the legal and institutional frameworks, hinder the judicial process, and contribute to a culture of corruption and impunity.

First, misogynistic attitudes remain deeply embedded in society despite launching various educational campaigns to raise awareness and broaden women's rights. Htun and Jensenius (2020) analyze the 2011 ENDIREH survey results of 150,000 women across Mexico on their experiences with violence and interaction with the state institutions to evaluate compliance with LGAMVLV (pp. 142–143). Htun and Jensenius found that several "women (19%) say they did not report because the incident was 'not important,' a response indicative of the cultural normalization of violence" (pp. 157–158). Social and cultural norms heavily influence the realization of women's rights and access to the legal system (Bovarnick, 2007).

Second, misogynistic attitudes contribute to the poor enforcement of laws that promotes a culture of impunity. When women seek assistance from state institutions, such as police, health and social services, and the justice system, the response is often inadequate. Of the 3,892 femicides identified in 2012 and 2013, Bautista (2017) noted that authorities investigated only 24% of cases and 1.6% sentenced. Law enforcement authorities often are dismissive of intimate partner violence and either fail to take the claims seriously or women are encouraged to resolve the conflict by having sex with their partner, irrespective of whether that is what the woman wants (Htun and Jensenius, 2020).

Sadly, victims of femicide are often re-victimized in their death by government officials charged with enforcing the laws to protect women. On May 3, 2017, Lesvy Berlin Rivera Osorio was found dead with a telephone cord wrapped around her neck at the National Autonomous University of Mexico (UNAM). Her death was ruled a suicide despite video evidence provided by UNAM that showed her boyfriend, Jorge Luis González, beating Rivera minutes before she died. Bautista (2017) noted that Mexico City's public prosecutor ruled Rivera's death a suicide, and her boyfriend was charged with homicide by negligence for failing to prevent her death. Mexico City's Attorney General's Office (PGR) shifted attention to Rivera a day after her death. The PGR disparaged her character with several tweets saying that she used drugs, was a high school drop-out, and not a UNAM student. Several women responded to the PGR's tweets with the hashtag #SiMeMatan (#IfTheyKillMe). Women used this hashtag to shed light on the PGR's attempt to blame Rivera for her death and list how newspapers would classify their death.

It was not until November 2005 that Mexico's Supreme Court ruled marital rape as a crime. This ruling overturned a 1994 decision that rejected the notion of marital rape, arguing that since the purpose of marriage is to procreate, forced sexual relations were simply a man exercising his conjugal rights (Malkin & Thomspon, 2005). These examples demonstrate that gender inequality is well entrenched in institutions, which explains the failure to prevent GBV.

Educational campaigns and programs designed to thwart misogynistic attitudes must coincide with government actions ranging from law enforcement officers who treat a woman's complaints, prosecutors willing to charge the offender (often an intimate partner), and judges who uphold the rule of law. Yet, this training should also extend to the treatment of women in the workforce. In Querétaro, female officers reported discrimination by their male superiors, who evaluated them based on their appearance rather than competency. Female officers went on strike, calling for the removal of the police chief, Hidalgo Eddy, for a sexualized work environment. In his previous role as police chief in Aguascalientes, Eddy formed an all-female unit of attractive officers whose uniform consisted of wearing high-heeled boots, tight clothes, and lots of lipstick (Agren, 2016).

Third, the inability to collect and process data further inhibits progress on women's issues. Part of the problem is that while femicide is now part of the criminal code for all states, the definition varies by state. In the absence of a uniform definition, it is challenging to compare states or determine the severity of femicide at the national level. Even if a consistent definition did exist, a more significant challenge lay in recording murders at the time of death.

Lastly, the lack of data is directly tied to inadequate funding for law enforcement to effectively collect evidence and assist the prosecutor's office in building a case. Local law enforcement remains understaffed, underpaid, lacking criminal investigative techniques, including gathering evidence, and facilities are in desperate need of basic infrastructure. Vice News (2015) documentary "Femicide Crisis in the State of Mexico" uncovered the poor conditions of the morgue. Many facilities lacked space for the number of bodies, so multiple bodies shared a space designed for one body. Once no room was left, bodies were left outside to decompose. Forensic science is a central component of law enforcement. Without the proper collection and preservation of evidence, cases remain unsolved. Criminals continue to walk the streets, and impunity reigns.

The Drug War and GBV

Corruption and impunity are further linked to Mexico's criminal landscape, which has changed dramatically since the late 1990s. The ever-growing threats to public security no longer stem from drug trafficking organizations but now include mid-level groups and local gang activity (Beittel 2019). Mexico's criminal landscape is an unintended consequence of President Calderón's militarized campaign against drug trafficking organizations from 2006 through 2012 that focused on targeting cartel leadership. Variation in femicide rates across Mexico seems driven primarily by drug trafficking organizations and the military campaigns to combat DTOs.

Justice in Mexico compiled data on organized crime-related homicides collected by year and by state from 2007 to 2016 as reported by Mexico City-based newspaper *Milenio* (Heinle, Rodríguez Ferreira & Shirk, 2016). What becomes increasingly evident is that a relationship exists between the presence of organized crime groups and homicide rates. These homicide rates support the findings from an April 2016 report titled "Violent Femicide in Mexico: Approximations and Tendencies 1985–2014" (*La Violencia Feminicida en México: Aproximaciones y Tendencias 1985–2014*) by Mexico's Ministry of the Interior, the National Women's Institute, and UN Women (SEGOB, Inmujeres, UN Women, 2016). Before the drug war,

> the annual femicide rate was 3.8 per 100,000 women in 1985 before it began a steady decline to 1.9 in 2007. From there it rose sharply to peak at 4.6 per 100,000 in 2012, tapering off in the following years and then rising again last year to 4.4. Of the 52,210 killings of women recorded over the 32-year period, nearly a third took place in the last six years.
>
> *Orsi, 2017*

While more data and research are needed to explore this relationship fully, initial data suggests that the increased violence perpetrated by organized crime groups has contributed to a climate of public insecurity for Mexicans, exacerbating the femicide crisis in Mexico.

Global Pandemic and GBV

COVID-19 and stay-at-home orders have fueled GBV and femicide as more women continue to live in precarious situations with their aggressors. Only three weeks into the stay-at-home order, the number of emergency calls to 911 increased by 60%, and federal authorities estimated that violence against women had gone up between 30% and 100% based on the number of emergency calls (*El Universal*, April 9, 2020). In March 2020, shortly after implementing the stay-at-home order, a record number of 26,171 emergency calls were made, and the following month, there were 21,722 calls (Gallón, 2020). President López Obrador, also known by his initials AMLO, countered that 90% of those calls were false, but his response fails to acknowledge that several calls were cut short and, in many cases, law enforcement failed to follow up and resolve those calls.

AMLO has minimized GBV, and his responses often demonstrate a poor comprehension of the day-to-day challenges confronting women. How are women expected to call for help when confined at home with their aggressors? During a global pandemic, what shelters are available that are safe from exposure to COVID-19? This disconnect is evident in a government-aired public service announcement directed at preventing domestic violence at home. The video showed several images of stressful moments and tension building for the family. The advice was for everyone to count to ten to calm down, then pull out a white flag of peace. The last image showed family members smiling and waving small flags (Gallón, 2020).

Climate Change and GBV

Several studies outline the gender trends within the broader climate change literature that identify patterns of vulnerability to climate change. Carr and Thompson (2014) note that research on gender and climate change fails to consider the structural inequities and gendered power relations, particularly among poor and rural populations. Buechler (2009) explores how climate change affects the sustainability of gendered agricultural activity. Similarly, Castañeda Carney et al. (2020) explore linkages between land tenure and women's poverty and exclusion. Vithanage (2021) notes that gender inequality is both a cause and a consequence of GBV. To understand GBV and environmental linkages better, one must first understand how gender-differentiated roles may put women further at risk. Le Masson et al. (2019) contend that resilience-based development must acknowledge the factors that sustain the exclusion of a particular group that prevents them from fully engaging in decisions that could potentially affect their lives.

The CEDAW General Recommendation 37 (2018) acknowledges the increasing number of severe weather and climate hazards and the risks to life and livelihood. While climate change affects everyone, specific groups are more vulnerable to these effects, such as those living in poverty, indigenous, and women. General Recommendation 37 seeks to "underscore the urgency of mitigating climate change" and identify ways that states can move toward gender equality, which will "reinforce the resilience of individuals and communities globally in the context of climate change and disasters" (CEDAW/C/GC/37).

Initial research linking GBV to climate change proves promising. As states work toward sustainable development goals, such as gender equality, affordable clean energy, and clean water and sanitation, empowering more vulnerable groups through inclusion in disaster risk reduction can minimize risk for those most vulnerable populations.

Shifting Realities

By early 2018, frustrated Mexicans voiced their growing discontent over three different presidential administrations (Vicente Fox, Felipe Calderón, and Enrique Peña Nieto 2012–2018) failure to tackle the ever-increasing public security threats. As a presidential candidate, López Obrador, spoke about representing those who have been traditionally ignored, such as the poor and indigenous groups that disproportionately include women. During his campaign, he acknowledged the challenges women confront, particularly those who suffer from domestic abuse by intimate partners. Many were hopeful that he would be a champion for women's issues. Despite his campaign promises, his actions revealed that women were not a priority for his administration. In his first 100 days in office, López Obrador slashed funding for two programs: daycare and women's shelters, as part of his austerity program.

The daycare program Estancias Infantiles was created by the Ministry of Social Development (SEDESOL) in 2007 to support parents or guardians living in poverty who also work or study. Program care is available five days a week for eight hours a day for children between one and three years. Estancias Infantiles was a nationwide program that included education, health care, and nutrition (Pérez-Escamilla, 2017). In February 2019, the government halted the distribution of roughly 900 pesos per child, which led to several protests and demonstrations. López Obrador argued that rather than subsidizing the daycare center at 900 pesos per child, he would directly pay parents or guardians 1,600 pesos bimonthly.

In a similar vein, López Obrador cut funding for women's shelters, arguing that victims of domestic abuse would directly be compensated (Agren, 2019). He also implemented a series of budget cuts, including a "75% budget cut for the federal women's institute and state funding for non-for-profit women shelters" (Thomas, 2020), to counter the pressure that lockdowns had on Mexico's economy. The plans for the 2021 budget will cut an additional 10–20%, including money toward Indigenous and Afro-Mexican Women's Shelters. These shelters are in remote areas, highly regarded by the UN for providing culturally respectful services. The UN issued a statement that Mexico is at risk of reneging on its international agreements, and budget cuts undermine efforts to end discrimination and violence against women (Jiménez-Santiago, 2020).

These budget cuts undermine one of the levels of protection stipulated in the LGAMVLV, ensuring victims of violence have a safe haven. Between 2012 and 2016, the number of women stabbed or strangled at home increased by 54% (Gómez Romero and Iribarne González, 2019). This level of violence against women corresponds to the findings of a nationwide telephone survey conducted by Mexican daily newspaper *El Universal* that surveyed 800 women aged 16 and over on intimidating partner violence. Of those surveyed, 11% of women reported having sex against their will, 9% are in fear of being attacked or abused, 9% said that their partners threatened to take away their children or remove them from home, and 7% reported being locked up or prohibited from leaving home (*El Universal*, 8 March 2017).

Furthermore, it reveals that specific laws and initiatives have done little to change the "cultural patterns that devalue women and consider them disposable, allowing for a social permissiveness in the face of violence and its ultimate expression, femicide" (Orsi, 2017). Ingrid Escamilla is the most recent victim of femicide who was brutally killed by her boyfriend on February 9, 2020, in Mexico City. Some newspapers in Mexico published graphic photos of her mutilated corpse and on social media. *Pásala* newspaper blamed cupid for Escamilla's brutal death with the headline "It was Cupid's fault" (McDonnell and Sanchez, 2020). Ingrid's senseless death and re-victimization by the press and social media sparked outrage among many Mexicans, leading to a Valentine's Day demonstration march to the Presidential Palace.

The thoughtless response of López Obrador's administration to the increase in GBV fueled a surge of protests throughout Mexico. López Obrador stated that femicide continues to persist because of the neoliberal policies put in place by previous presidents. As the number of femicide cases increased throughout 2020, there were a series of demonstrations despite the global pandemic. On March 8, 2020, International Women's Day, women worldwide demonstrated to raise awareness about GBV and femicide. Roughly 80,000 women participated in this demonstration to protest the government's failure to respond to the growing femicide crisis. The following day, women participated in a "Day without Us" strike. López Obrador claimed that political opponents were behind the strike trying to remove him from office by disguising themselves as feminists (*Washington Post*, 6 March 2020).

In September 2020, a group of activists seized control of Mexico's National Human Rights Commission office, and the occupation continues during this pandemic and has become a sanctuary for women. This year's Día de los Muertos (Day of the Dead) witnessed a surge in *ofrendas* (altars) to call attention to the plight of women. Most notably, one *ofrenda* situated at the aqueduct in the city of Querétaro showed 489 gravestones bearing the names of femicide victims. This figure represented the number of femicides recorded in Mexico between January and October 2020 (Aguilar, 2020).

This past March 8, 2021, women again took to the streets to protest López Obrador's support of Felix Salgado Macedonio, despite rape accusations, in his run for governor of Guerrero. Despite public outcry, both by women's groups and female members of his National Regeneration Movement (Morena) party, López Obrador said these were politically driven accusations by those who opposed him. The National Electoral Institute ultimately blocked Salgado Macedonio's candidacy on a technicality, failure to submit the requisite pre-campaign expense reports. In the run-up to the March 8th demonstration this year, López Obrador's administration erected 10-foot barriers to deny demonstrators access to the presidential palace. These barriers could be interpreted as his apathy toward the plight of women but soon were painted with slogans and the names of murdered women (Berger, 2021).

President López Obrador is halfway through his six-year term. Mexicans remain critical of his performance in addressing the myriad of problems confronting Mexico, including the COVID-19 pandemic, the economy, climate change, public security threats, and escalating GBV. The June 2021 midterm election had 500 congressional seats in contention, and gubernatorial races in 15 states, not including local races throughout Mexico, where public security threats have persisted and drug trafficking organizations have taken over parts of the country. While Morena managed to secure a majority, it was not the resounding qualified majority López Obrador sought to make constitutional changes to renationalize the energy sector.

Conclusion

Mexico has a robust legal and institutional framework in place, which is an essential first step, but the mere existence of laws and statutes does not assure its implementation. So far, there is little evidence that these laws and initiatives have done much to change the "cultural patterns that devalue women and consider them disposable, allowing for a social permissiveness in the face of violence and its ultimate expression, femicide" (Orsi 2017, paras. 15).

Mexico became the third Latin American country to participate in the joint European Union and UN effort called "Spotlight Initiative" to eliminate all violence against women. The program launched in May 2019 and is operational in the three states with the highest femicide rates: the State of Mexico, Chihuahua, and Guerrero (UN Women: Mexico). While civil society organizations found the timing of this program suspect, in light of the growing criticism building against President López Obrador, this program still has the potential to improve policies and raise awareness in these states. Spotlight Initiative launched a media campaign, #NoEstásSola, focused on the prevention of violence against women. The video seeks to give women a message of hope that they are not alone.

In December 2020, Spotlight provided safe hotel accommodations in six municipalities. This plan offers temporary, secure, and free accommodation to women experiencing violence and their children for one week. Afterward, women worked with justice centers and other women's organizations (National Institute of Women, 2020). Programs such as these are needed, but in light of budget cuts to daycare centers and women's shelters, and a president who does not seem to emphasize the plight of women, women will continue to suffer unnecessarily.

Moreover, Mexico is grappling with the effects of climate change, exacerbated by López Obrador's decision to roll back clean energy measures to curb global warming. Felbab-Brown and Norio (2020) contend that global warming has contributed to an increase in wildfires, as the Mexican National Forestry Commission registered 5,583 wildfires throughout Mexico from January through September 2020. Contrary to efforts to move toward green energy, López Obrador has moved away from solar and wind farms claiming that they do not contribute to the national electricity system, preventing some companies from connecting to the national grid. Mexico's Energy Regulatory Commission countered that "private energy companies generate 46% of the nation's electricity … at a cost up to 85% less" than the Federal Electricity Commission (Hernández, 2020).

Mexico has experienced several disasters in 2020 and 2021 as a consequence of climate change. On June 23, 2020, an earthquake registering 7.4 struck Oaxaca, destroying homes and killing ten people. Later, a tsunami warning was issued for Mexico and Central America. On August 8, 2021, Hurricane Grace brought heavy rain in Xalapa, Veracruz, and left eight people dead due to collapsed buildings caused by widespread flooding and mudslides. On September 7, 2021, an earthquake registering 7.0 magnitude near Acapulco killed one person, damaged infrastructure, and lost power. On that same day, more than 30,000 people in towns across the state were affected by the floods due to torrential rains that caused the river to burst its banks (Reuters, 2021).

Mexico is also experiencing a surge of migration from Central American countries, escaping similar problems at home due to climate change. In November 2020, Hurricane Eta and Iota tore through the region, destroying crops and infrastructure, resulting in more than 200 deaths, displacing approximately half a million people (Marsh and Menchu, 2020). Global warming has contributed to an intensification of natural disasters that bear a high human and financial cost, further deepening the suffering of those living in poverty.

In conclusion, Mexico has the legal framework in place to tackle GBV and femicide effectively, but both the state and federal governments need to work to address the structural weaknesses that currently undermine these frameworks. Media campaigns, such as #NoEstásSola, are a step in the right direction, but more campaigns should focus on raising awareness and challenging negative stereotypes. Additionally, the government should focus on promoting gender equality by tackling gender norms and attitudes. Programs must engage both sexes at all ages. Targeting young boys and girls is particularly useful before negative gendered values become deeply engrained. Chile's Cultura Salud is an example of an educational workshop targeting young men in public schools and health centers. The workshop's focus was on the prevention of violence against women. Participants in these educational workshops reported an increased use of contraceptives, more awareness in the different forms of violence, and increases the likelihood that they were less likely to engage in abusive behavior toward women (Gruebel, 2012).

Lastly, Mexico can promote gender equity through investing in safety net programs, such as women's shelter and domestic abuse centers, and advocate for women's economic empowerment, such as microcredit financing. Minimizing gender inequities also builds adaptive capacity to mitigate the effects of climate change. Although the López Obrador administration has not signaled a shift in tactics, the women's movements in Mexico continue to pressure his administration. The push toward gender equity is a step in the right direction.

References

Agren, D. (2016). Female police officers subjected to 'attractiveness' inspections in Mexico. *The Guardian.* April 8, 2016. www.theguardian.com/world/2016/apr/08/female-police-officers-mexico-attractiveness-inspections-complains-queretaro

______. (2019). Mexico slashes funding for women's shelters. *The Guardian.* March 5, 2019. www.theguardian.com/world/2019/mar/05/mexico-funding-cuts-womens-shelters-domestic-violence

______. (2021, September 20). Ten women and girls killed every day in Mexico, Amnesty report says. *The Guardian.* www.theguardian.com/global-development/2021/sep/20/mexico-femicide-women-girls-amnesty-international-report

Aguilar, M. (2020, November 3). *Femicides given higher prominence around Mexico with day of the Dead ofrendas.* Mexico News Daily. https://mexiconewsdaily.com/news/femicides-given-higher-prominence-around-mexico/

Bautista, Nidia. (2017). "Justice for Lesvy: Indifference and outrage in response to gender violence in Mexico City." *The North American Congress on Latin America (NACLA).* July 31, 2017.

BBC. (2020, February 11). Ingrid Escamilla murder: Mexico outraged over brutal stabbing. *BBC.* www.bbc.com/news/world-latin-america-51458949

Beittel, J. S. (2019). *Mexico: Organized crime and drug trafficking organizations.* Retrieved from Congressional Research Service Report for Congress website: https://crsreports.congress.gov/product/pdf/R/R41576/40

Berger, M. (2021, March 9). Women in Mexico are protesting femicide. Police have responded with force. *Washington Post.* www.washingtonpost.com/world/2021/03/09/womens-day-protests-amlo-mexico

Bovarnick, S. (2007). Universal human rights and non-Western normative systems: A comparative analysis of violence against women in Mexico and Pakistan. *Review of International Studies, 33* (1), 59–74. https://doi.org/10.1017/S0260210507007309

Buechler, S. (2009). Gender, water, and climate change in Sonora, Mexico: Implications for policies and programmes on agricultural income-generation. *Gender and Development,* 17 (1), 51–66. https://doi.org/10.1080/13552070802696912

Camacho, A. S. (2005). Ciudadana X: Gender violence and the denationalization of women's rights in Ciudad Juárez, Mexico. *CR (East Lansing, Michigan),* 5 (1), 255–292. https://doi.org/10.1353/ncr.2005.0030

Carr, E. R., & Thompson, M. C. (2014). Gender and climate change adaptation in agrarian settings: Current thinking, new directions, and research frontiers: Gender and climate change adaptation in agrarian settings. *Geography Compass,* 8 (3), 182–197. https://doi.org/10.1111/gec3.12121

Castañeda Carney et al. (2020). "Gender-Based Violence and Environment Linkage" (Gland, Switzerland: IUCN Global Programme on Governance and Rights (GPGR), https://portals.iucn.org/library/node/48969

Deschamps, M. (2018, January 31). Mexico's first 'Seduction School,' rape culture and femicide. *Telesur.* Retrieved from https://mronline.org/2018/01/31/mexicos-first-seduction-school-rape-culture-and-femicides/

Felbab-Brown, V., & Norio, E. (2020, September 26). Global warming, fires & crime in Mexico & beyond. *Mexico Today*. https://mexicotoday.com/2020/09/26/opinion-global-warming-fires-crime-in-mexico-beyond/

Gallón, N. C. (2020, July 16). Women are being killed in Mexico at record rates, but the president says most abuse calls are "false." CNN. https://edition.cnn.com/2020/06/05/americas/mexico-femicide-coronavirus-lopez-obrador-intl/index.html

Gómez Romero, L., & Iribarne González, M. (2019). Mexican women are angry about rape, murder and government neglect – and they want the world to know. University of Wollongong Australia. https://www.uow.edu.au/media/2019/mexican-women-are-angry-about-rape-murder-and-government-neglect--and-they-want-the-world-to-know.php

Gruebel, L. (2012). Engaging men to prevent gender-based violence: A multi-country intervention and impact evaluation study. *Instituto Promundo*. https://resourcecentre.savethechildren.net/library/engaging-men-prevent-gender-based-violence-multi-country-intervention-and-impact-evaluation

Haney, C. (2012). Imperiled femininity: The dismembering of citizenship in Northern Mexico. *The Journal of Latin American and Caribbean Anthropology, 17* (2), 238–256. http://dx.doi.org/10.1111/j.1935-4940.2012.01224.x

Heinle, K., Rodríguez Ferreira, O., & Shirk, D.A. (2016 April). Drug Violence in Mexico. Justice in Mexico. https://justiceinmexico.org/wp-content/uploads/2016/04/DrugViolenceinMexico-Final-2015.pdf

Hernández, M. (2020, May 7). Generan luz barata... y AMLO desdeña. *Reforma*. www.reforma.com/aplicaciones/articulo/default.aspx?id=1937041&referer=--7d616165662f3a3a78706d7c767a7b70626671747c796c3b767a783a--

Htun, M., & Jensenius, F. (2020). Aspirational laws as weak institutions: Legislation to combat violence against women in Mexico. In D. Brinks, S. Levitsky, & M. Murillo (Eds.), *The Politics of Institutional Weakness in Latin America* (pp. 141–160). Cambridge: Cambridge University Press. doi:10.1017/9781108776608.006

Jiménez-Santiago, B. (2020, November 16). Mexico's cuts to services put women at risk. Fair Observer. www.fairobserver.com/region/latin_america/barbara-jimenez-santiago-mexico-gender-violence-inequality-pandemic-budget-cuts-womens-rights-news-16821/

Joseph, J. (2017). Victims of femicide in Latin America: Legal and criminal justice responses. *Temida*, 20 (1), 3–21. https://doi.org/10.2298/TEM1701003J

Koutsoyannis, S. (2011). Background paper Femicide in Ciudad Juárez: Ever-Present and Worsening, 1–24. http://peacebuild.ca/Koutsoyannis%20final.pdf

Liu, Y., & Fullerton, T. (2015). Evidence from Mexico on social status and violence against women. *Applied Economics*, 1–15.

Malkin, E., & Thompson, G. (2005, November 17). Mexican Court says sex attack by a husband is still a Rape. *New York Times*. www.nytimes.com/2005/11/17/world/americas/mexican-court-says-sex-attack-by-a-husband-is-still-a-rape.html

Marsh, S., & Menchu, S. (2020, December 3). Storms that slammed Central America in 2020 just a preview, climate change experts say. *Reuters*. www.reuters.com/article/us-climate-change-hurricanes/storms-that-slammed-central-america-in-2020-just-a-preview-climate-change-experts-say-idUSKBN28D2V6

McDonnell, P.J., & Sanchez, C. (2020, February 14). In Mexico, a grisly killing inflames debate about femicide. *Los Angeles Times*. https://www.latimes.com/world-nation/story/2020-02-14/in-mexico-case-of-murdered-women-inflames-debate-about-femicide

National Institute of Women. (2020, March 28). # NoEstásSola, campaign against violence against women in the home [Press release]. www.apa.org/news/press/releases/2020/11/anxiety-depression-treatment

Orsi, P. (2017, December 13). Spike in murders of women erases decades of gains in Mexico. *The Chicago Tribune*. Retrieved from www.chicagotribune.com/sns-bc-lt--mexico-killings-of-women-20171213-story.html

Pérez-Escamilla, R. (2017). Estancias infantiles y desarrollo infantil en México: avances y retos. *Boletín Médico Del Hospital Infantil de México*, 74 (2), 84–85. https://doi.org/10.1016/j.bmhimx.2017.01.005

Reuters. (2021, September 7). Seventeen people, most with COVID-19, die in flooding of Mexican hospital. Reuters. www.reuters.com/world/americas/17-people-die-mexican-hospital-due-severe-flooding-2021-09-07/

SEGOB, Inmujeres, UN Women (2016), La Violencia Feminicida en México: Aproximaciones y Tendencias 1985–2014, UN Women, www2.unwomen.org/~/media/field%20office%20mexico/documentos/publicaciones/2016/02/violencia%20feminicida%20en%20méxico%20aproximaciones%20y%20tendencias%201985_2014.pdf?v=1&d=20160418T214527

Thomas, B. (2020, November 17). *Violence against Women Protesters Met with Police Gunfire*. The Organization for World Peace. https://theowp.org/violence-against-women-protesters-met-with-police-gunfire/

UN Committee on the Elimination of Discrimination Against Women (CEDAW), (2018). *CEDAW General Recommendations Nos. 19 and 20, adopted at the Eleventh Session, 1992 (contained in Document A/47/38)*, 1992, A/47/38. https://www.refworld.org/docid/453882a422.html

Vice News. (2015, June 23). The Femicide Crisis in the Staste of Mexico [Video file]. Retrieved from www.youtube.com/watch?v=UB69VbhxmUk

Vithanage, A. C. (2021). Addressing correlations between gender-based violence and climate change: An expanded role for international climate change law and education for sustainable development. *Pace Environmental Law Review*, 38 (2), 327–382.

4

VIOLENCE AGAINST WOMEN IN MEXICO CITY

A Cry for Change

Flor Avellaneda

Luis R. Torres

Introduction

Intimate partner violence (IPV) is a significant public health concern that transcends borders, with approximately 30% of women worldwide reporting lifetime IPV (WHO, 2017). Violence against women in Mexico remains a significant and growing public health and human rights crisis, with rates exceeding the worldwide average. Two-thirds (66.1%) of females ages 15 and older report experiencing at least one lifetime incident of violence. Over 4 in 10, 43.9%, report experiencing violence by a current or past partner, and over a third, 34.3%, report experiencing sexual violence in a public setting (INEGI, 2017). Since March 2020, government-mandated lockdowns and overwhelming health and financial stressors due to the COVID-19 pandemic have further worsened an already dire situation.

These persistently high IPV rates have given rise to protests throughout Mexico, and especially in Mexico City. In early 2020, just before the start of the COVID-19 pandemic, women of all ages took to the streets to protest, raise awareness, and demand action by the government, in the wake of the gruesome deaths of 25-year-old Ingrid Escamilla and 7-year-old Fatima Aldrighett (Semple & Villegas, 2020). While the COVID-19 pandemic has curtailed protests, efforts continue—especially by women—to bring the severity of IPV to the attention of national, state, and local Mexican governments and the international community. Clearly, women want change: policies that protect women of all ages, prevent violence, and punish the perpetrators to the full extent of the law. We also need changes in cultural and social norms that may be tied to IPV.

Cultural attitudes and rigid, socially constructed gender roles operating in some sectors of Mexican society may override safety concerns, making it harder for women to leave abusive relationships. IPV can be a taboo topic, often difficult to talk about, limiting their ability to seek help. Furthermore, growing financial independence, lack of knowledge of women's rights in IPV situations, and limited access to resources may perpetuate the cycle of violence. Mexican migrant women, whether in transit within Mexico or transnationally, may be at even higher risk of IPV and the dynamics of migration can make it even more difficult to seek help and leave.

Multiple factors highlight the need to examine the link between migration, IPV, and health. These include continued migration from rural to urban areas in Mexico, especially to Mexico City, and between Mexico and the U.S.; the rising costs of healthcare; and growing calls for gender equality in all areas. Our research has examined the relationship between in-country migration, IPV, physical and mental health, and substance use, in Mexican migrant women in Mexico City.

DOI: 10.4324/9781003264040-6

This chapter reports on our work and highlights recommendations to promote social change and help break the cycle of violence toward women. A more thorough understanding of the complex relationship between IPV and health in Mexican migrant women can inform best practices, policy, and research efforts.

Mexican women make up over half of the Mexican population, at 0.96 males per female (Central Intelligence Agency, 2020). Over 43% of Mexican women are actively engaged in the labor force (INEGI, 2017) and contribute to their family's finances. However, gender inequality in Mexico remains pervasive, negatively impacting women's lives, especially those migrating within the country. Many Mexican migrant women work as domestic workers, in "mercados" (one-stop-shopping markets), and other low-income jobs, often without benefits. They earn less than men, even for comparable positions, and have less power in society. These inequities can increase the risk of IPV. Violence against women is a pervasive public health concern that affects millions of Mexican women. Many die at the hands of their perpetrators through strangulation, hanging, and drowning, among other forms of murder. In 2019, Mexico ranked first among countries in Latin America in feminicides (Angulo Lopez, 2019).

Violence against women in Mexico is a result of structural violence, which includes environmental factors that place migrant women at risk of IPV (Sajnani & Nadeau, 2006). These factors fall under the larger umbrella of sexism, racism, and classism, all systemic issues that continue to afflict modern-day Mexico. Some factors may specifically contribute to violence against internal migrant Mexican women residing in Metropolitan areas, like Mexico City. These include lack of access to formal education, healthcare, legal rights, or employment; lack of community and familial support; and even the stigma of being considered an immigrant in your own country (Soriano, 2017). Embedded within the fabric of society, these barriers make it challenging for women to deal with and overcome IPV. Deeply ingrained gender norms within the culture further perpetuate the cycle of violence. In the following section, we discuss how cultural values may influence violence against internal migrant women in Mexico.

Cultural Values and IPV

Mexico is a multicultural society with rich cultures dating back hundreds of years. Pre-Hispanic and Spanish influences are still evident throughout Mexican society. Most men and women continue to conform to traditional gender roles, especially in lower socioeconomic groups. These rigid gender roles are tied to traditional Mexican values such as *familismo, respeto, fatalismo, machismo, and marianismo*. These values can serve as protective factors within the family and they may also be potential risk factors for IPV (Paat, Hope, Mangadu, Núñez-Michiri, & Chavez-Baray, 2017; Roditti, Schultz, Gillette, & de la Rosa, 2010). Of course, these cultural values are not unique to Mexicans and may be shared by many traditional cultures (e.g., filial piety among Asian cultures). Moreover, not all Mexican individuals subscribe to these cultural values, and those who do subscribe to them may do so to different degrees. As such, it would be a mistake to state that these values "cause" or even contribute to IPV (Frías & Angel, 2012). Like most human phenomena, IPV has multiple determinants. However, the fact is that these values do exist in Mexican society, to varying degrees, and their role in family dynamics and multiple outcomes has been the subject of study for decades. As such, it is important that we consider their role in IPV.

Familismo. Family is central to Mexican society, and a core cultural value is *familismo*, defined as a multidimensional construct that includes strong ties and support among family members; behaviors and attitudes related to the primacy of family; and preference for family honor and obligation (Marrs Fuchsel, 2013). Beyond the nuclear family, which is the core of more individually focused, non-traditional societies, for Mexican families, the extended family can be a source of support as well, especially in times of hardship (Umaña-Taylor, Updegraff, & Gonzales-Backen, 2011). Family often plays a crucial role in the decision-making process when it comes to raising children, making medical decisions, and even in the selection of romantic partners (Calzada, Fernandez, & Cortes, 2010; Muñoz-Laboy, 2008). *Familismo* is undoubtedly a strength in Mexican culture, yet it may also negatively influence a woman's decision to disclose an abusive relationship to family members. Marrs Fuchsel (2013) found that immigrant Mexican women experiencing IPV had a desire to disclose their abuse to immediate family members but were less likely to do so due to feeling ashamed or for fear of their families' negative reactions. Pressure to maintain the family intact can often override a woman's decision to disclose or leave an abusive relationship (Alcalde, 2010).

Respeto. Mexican parents teach *respeto* to their children at an early age, including obeying authority, behaving in a socially appropriate manner, and showing reverence to older family members (Calzada, Fernandez, & Cortes, 2010). It is common for immediate and extended family, including aunts, uncles, and grandparents, to share the same household, with each adult modeling *respeto* and behavior toward authority figures for the children. However, this may impose challenges on women experiencing IPV. *Respeto* may mean not questioning a male's actions, whether the male is her father or her husband, because men are viewed as having power and authority over the household. As young girls, they may be taught to show respect for authority figures, and in most cases these authority figures are men. This may make it harder for them to disclose their abuse to family or report it to the authorities, to avoid jeopardizing their partners. Thus, reverence toward authority figures can be harmful in cases where the distinction between *respeto* and safety (or the lack thereof) is ambiguous.

Fatalismo is the belief that a person's fate is inevitable because it's not within her/his control, but determined by a higher power or by destiny (Rosales & Calvo, 2017). This belief contributes to underutilization of mental health services (González, Vega, Williams, Tarraf, West, & Neighbors, 2010). In addition to lack of knowledge about services or adequate resources (e.g., health insurance, transportation, availability of culturally and linguistically competent services), *fatalismo* may keep individuals mired in hopelessness, hindering them from getting the help they need (Espinosa de Los Monteros & Gallo, 2013). *Fatalismo* may also play a role in preventing women from seeking IPV services.

Gender roles. The family unit is the cornerstone of Mexican culture, with males and females playing different, sometimes rigid roles. Mexican women are key to maintaining the family structure and often seen as nurturing caretakers, while men are viewed as the primary breadwinners (DiGirolamo, & Salgado de Snyder, 2008). Acceptance of rigid gender roles can hinder a woman's human, economic, and social development (Hietanen & Pick, 2015). The terms *machismo* and *marianismo* describe rigid gender roles that can often perpetuate IPV, especially in a conventionally patriarchal society like Mexico. Many Mexican states are adopting more progressive views that recognize the detrimental effects of these rigid gender norms. However, these traditional norms continue to be widespread. *Machismo* depicts Mexican men as protectors of their families (Cianelli, Villegas, Lawson, Ferrer, Kaelber, Peragallo, & Yaya, 2013). It can have both positive aspects, such as male courage and responsibility, and negative aspects, such as domineering and aggressive behavior (Torres, Solberg, & Carlstrom, 2002). Traditional *machismo* is thus described "aggressive, sexist, chauvinistic, and hypermasculine", what today we would refer to as "toxic masculinity" (Connell, 2002). *Caballerismo* (i.e., chivalry or gentlemanliness) is associated with being "nurturing, family centered, and chivalrous" (Arciniega et al., 2008). Negative aspects of *machismo* are often associated with antagonistic male traits that influence men's actions toward women, leading to higher IPV risks. *Marianismo* (derived from the name *Maria* or Mary, the mother of the biblical Jesus) depicts Mexican women as submissive, nurturing, and self-sacrificing (Da Silva, Verdejo, Dillon, Ertl, & De La Rosa, 2021). Although more research is needed on this topic, women who adhere to the traditional aspects of *marianismo* may be more likely to experience, and less likely to disclose, IPV. Mexican women, especially internal migrants to Mexico City, can be susceptible to IPV if they subscribe to these traditional gender norms.

IPV, Internal Migration, and Health

Internal migration has consistently been a driving force for Mexico's economic growth (Perez-Campuzano, Ramirez, & Perez, 2018). Individuals migrate to reunite with family members, for political reasons, or to seek safety, but the primary motive continues to be economic opportunity (Quintana & Salgado, 2016). Thriving markets with higher per capita GDP (gross domestic product), such as those in medium-sized cities to metropolitan areas, lure people living in regions with lower per capita GDP with higher salaries (Quintana & Salgado, 2016). Internal migrants usually leave states facing economic crises such as Puebla, Morelos, Tlaxcala, Veracruz, Chiapas, Oaxaca, and Tabasco (Pérez Oseguera, Coppe Gorozpe, Pérez Petrone, & Trujillo Viruega, 2008). A struggling economy is one of the major factors impacting large internal migration of men and women from rural areas to Mexico City and other large cities, especially in the industrial north of the country (e.g., Monterrey). Indeed, Mexican women tend to migrate internally at higher rates, when compared to males, who typically migrate to the U.S. in larger numbers. Migration can also adversely affect the health and well-being of women.

IPV adversely impacts the physical and mental health of women (Campbell, 2002; Campbell et al., 2002). Physical violence often requires going to the hospital for treatment (Muelleman, Lenaghan, & Pakiesser, 1996). Women exposed to IPV also experience chronic conditions such as traumatic brain injury, gynecological disorders, sexually transmitted diseases, and chronic pain syndromes, which significantly reduce their quality of life (Wong & Mellor, 2014). Along with worsened physical health, women may also experience adverse mental health outcomes such as depression, post-traumatic stress disorder, and substance use, among many others (Campbell, 2002). The need for accessible and equitable health services is critical to help these women face the health consequences of IPV.

Women who experience IPV are also at a higher risk of substance use. Some may resort to drug use to cope with the violence they are experiencing (Poole, Greaves, Jategaonkar, McCullough, & Chabot, 2008). Some are coerced into using a substance by a substance-using partner and may become dependent on their partner to provide them with illicit drugs. Stigma may also limit their ability to seek help (Bennett and Bland, 2008). Women's overall well-being can be negatively impacted if they don't get the help they need, which can further exacerbate the cycle of violence, and many women lack the support and resources to seek help for addiction. Understanding their complex needs is essential to connecting them with the appropriate resources.

The Impact of COVID-19

The COVID-19 pandemic has further exacerbated the grave pandemic of violence against women, who are experiencing some of the most significant rates of IPV in decades. During the pandemic, women are staying home due to government-enforced lockdowns, job losses, and social distancing requirements (Caivano, Lalinde, & Ordóñez, 2020). While home, they may find themselves doing the majority of the household work; caring for children and other family members; helping children with schoolwork; and possibly still keeping a job in the formal or informal sector (Marinque De Lara & Medina Arellano, 2020). The disproportionate impact of COVID-19 on women has left them extremely vulnerable: not only are they isolated from the rest of society, but they may also be trapped at home with their abusers.

In Mexico, a country with one of the highest rates of female homicides, COVID-19 quarantines have contributed to a steep increase in IPV cases. Since the quarantine began in March 2020, emergency 911 calls have significantly increased, based on data from the Consejo Ciudadano para la Seguridad y Justicia de CDMX (Citizen Council for Security and Justice of CDMX) (Pérez, 2020). In Mexico City alone, there was a 24.5% increase in reports of IPV since March 2020, including physical violence (66%), emotional violence (22%), and economic violence (3.5%) (Cervantes, 2020). Clearly, the pandemic has made a terrible situation even worse.

Moving Forward: Recommendations to Promote Social Change

Mexico remains one of the countries with the highest rates of violence toward women, with stories of women being murdered by an intimate partner common in news outlets. Although this significant public health and human rights issue remains pervasive, there are strides being made to bring awareness to and end violence against women. Mexican women and allies have been actively involved in bringing attention to the hundreds of women murdered in Mexico each year. On March 9, 2020, women across Mexico participated in "Un Día Sin Nosotras" (A Day without Us), a national protest that encouraged women to stay home as a way to bring attention to the inequalities they face in modern-day Mexican society. Many women were absent from their workplaces, schools, and public spaces. Many businesses, universities, public officials, church leaders, and celebrities offered their support to the cause. This national strike was expected to cost the Mexican economy $1.37 million in losses (Semple & Villegas, 2020), providing a small glimpse of how vital women's contributions are to the Mexican economy, and more importantly, highlighting the seriousness of protecting women's lives.

Feminist and women's rights activism efforts have only gotten stronger and will not cease until justice for all women is served. In June 2020, activists, academics, researchers, artists, and politicians came together to form a network to combat the alarming increase—believed to be growing due to COVID-19 conditions—of violence toward women. This coalition, which goes by the name, "Red Nosotras Tenemos Otros Datos" ("We Have Other Data" Network), aims to pressure government officials to pass policies that protect and ensure the equal treatment of Mexican women (Carina, 2020).

Equitable access to services is critical to the well-being of Mexican women. Social services for women who experience IPV exist, although they may be scarce. Migrant women who may be new to an area, however, may not know how to access services. Therefore, outreach and enhancing visibility of services is important so that victims know where to seek help. For some women, mental health treatment may be a new approach to help, but stigma about seeking mental health services may deter them. Providers need to be equipped with culturally tailored trauma interventions that will meet clients' needs and advertise their services in culturally relevant, stigma-reducing ways. Furthermore, service providers across sectors (e.g., social services, health, legal) must have knowledge of essential resources that they can connect clients to, including legal, healthcare, housing, childcare, and other services, so that there is no wrong door into services. Providers should also be at the forefront of policy advocacy and add their voices to the voices of women with lived experience of IPV and their millions of allies who are seeking change. Knowledge of clients' IPV challenges and experiences must be considered when making policies that directly affect victims and their families. IPV has been a serious public health crisis in Mexico for hundreds of years, and most recently exacerbated by the COVID-19 pandemic. Women, primarily, continue to experience the severe consequences. Women activists and allies must not lose momentum in their efforts and progress made thus far. Every woman deserves to live a life free of violence, and Mexico has the opportunity to lead in creating a just and fair society for all women.

References

Alcalde, M.C. (2010). Violence across borders: Familism, hegemonic masculinity, and self – sacrificing femininity in the lives of Mexican and Peruvian migrants. *Latino Studies, 8*, 48–68.

Angulo, G.A. (2019). Femicide and gender violence in Mexico: Elements for a systemic approach. *The Age of Human Rights Journal,* 12, 158–183.

Arciniega, G.M., Anderson, T.C., Tovar-Blank, Z.G., & Tracey, T.J.G. (2008). Toward a fuller conception of machismo: Development of a traditional machismo and caballerismo scale. *Journal of Counseling Psychology, 55* (1), 19–33.

Bennett, L., & Bland, P. (2008, May). *Substance abuse and intimate partner violence*. Retrieved from https://vawnet.org/sites/default/files/materials/files/2016–09/AR_SubstanceRevised.pdf

Caivano, J., Lalinde, S., & Ordóñez, M. (2020, June 16). La violencia doméstica en tiempos de COVID-19: Respuestas estatales y alianzas en América Latina. The Dialogue: Leadership for the Americas. Retrieved from www.thedialogue.org/blogs/2020/06/la-violencia-domestica-en-tiempos-de-covid-19-respuestas-estatales-y-alianzas-en-america-latina/?lang=es

Calzada, E.J., Fernandez, Y., & Cortes, D.E. (2010). Incorporating the cultural value of respeto into a framework of Latino parenting. *Cultural Diversity and Ethnic Minority Psychology, 16* (1), 77–86.

Campbell, J.C. (2002). Health consequences of intimate partner violence. *The Lancet, 359* (9314), 1331–1336.

Campbell, J., Jones, A.S., Dienemann, J., Kub, J., Schollenberger, J., O'Campo, P., Gielen, A.C., & Wynne, C. (2002). Intimate partner violence and physical health consequences. *Archives of Internal Medicine, 162* (10), 1157–1163.

Carina, G. (2020, January 6). Ante violencia de género, activistas crean la Red Nosotras Tenemos Otros Datos. El Universal, Retrieved from www.eluniversal.com.mx/nacion/ante-violencia-de-genero-activistas-crean-la-red-nosotras-tenemos-otros-datos

Central Intelligence Agency. (2020). Mexico. *In the World Factbook*. Retrieved from www.cia.gov/library/publications/the-world-factbook/

Cervantes, M. (2020, 2 de abril). En aislamiento aumentan de 60 a 160 las denuncias por violencia intrafamiliar. RadioFórmula [online]. Disponible en: www.radioformula.com.mx/breaking-news/2020/4/2/en-aislamiento-aumentan-de-60-160-las-denuncias-por-violencia-intrafamiliar-443705.html

Cianelli, R., Villegas, N., Lawson, S., Ferrer, L., Kaelber, L., Peragallo, N., & Yaya, A. (2013). Unique factors that place older Hispanic women at risk of HIV: Intimate partner violence, machismo, and marianismo. *Journal of the Association of Nurses in AIDS Care, 24* (4), 341–354.

Connell, R.W. (2002). On hegemonic masculinity and violence: Response to Jefferson and Hall. *Theoretical Criminology, 6* (1), 89–99.

Da Silva, N., Verdejo, T.R., Dillon, F.R., Ertl, M.M., & De La Rosa, M. (2021). Marianismo beliefs, intimate partner violence, and psychological distress among recently immigrated, young adult Latinas. *Journal of Interpersonal Violence*, 36 (7–8), 3755–3777.

DiGirolamo, A.M., & Salgado de Snyder, N. (2008). Women as primary caregivers in Mexico: Challenges to well-being. *Salud Publica Mexico, 50* (6), 516–522.

Espinosa de los Monteros, K., & Gallo, L.C. (2013). Fatalism and cardio-metabolic dysfunction in Mexican-American women. *International Journal of Behavioral Science, 20* (4), 487–494.

Frías, S.M., & Angel, R.J. (2012). Beyond borders: A comparative qualitative research on partner violence in the United States and Mexico. *Violence against Women, 18* (1), 5–29.

Gonzalez, H.M., Vega, W.A., Williams, D.R., Tarraf, W., West, B.T., & Neighbors, H.W. (2010). Depression care in the United States too little for too few. *Arch Gen Psychiatry, 67* (1), 37–46.

Instituto Nacional De Estadistica y Geografia. (2017). Resultados de la Encuesta Nacional sobre la dinamica de las relaciones en los hogares. *Ciudad de Mexico*, MX.

Marinque De Lara, A. & Medina Arellano, M. (2020). The COVID-19 Pandemic and ethics in Mexico through a gender lens. *Journal of Bioethical Inquiry, 17* (4), 613–617.

Marrs Fuchsel, C.L. (2013). Familism, sexual abuse, and domestic violence among immigrant Mexican women. *Journal of women and social work, 28* (4), 379–290.

Muelleman, R.L., Lenaghan, P.A., & Pakiesser, R.A., (1996). Battered women: Injury locations and type. *Annals of Emergency Medicine, 28* (5), 486–492.

Muñoz-Laboy, M.A. (2008). Familism and sexual regulation among bisexual Latino men. *Archives of Sexual Behavior, 37* (5), 773–782.

Paat, Y.-F., Hope, T.L., Mangadu, T., Nunez-Michiri, G.G., & Chavez-Baray, S.M. (2017). Family – and community-related determinants of intimate partner violence among Mexican and Puerto Rican origin mothers in fragile families. *Women's Studies International Forum, 6*, 136–147.

Pérez, M. (2020, 26 de abril). Llamadas por violencia, al alza. El Economista. Retrieved from www.eleconomista.com.mx/politica/Llamadas-por-violencia-al-alza-20200426-0096.html

Perez-Campuzano, E., Ramirez G.C., & Perez, M.C.G. (2018). Internal migration in Mexico: Consolidation of urban-urban mobility, 2000–2015. *Growth and Change, 49* (1), 223–240.

Pérez Oseguera, M.L., Coppe Gorozpe, L., Pérez Petrone, T., & Trujillo Viruega, T. (2008). Mujeres migrantes y violencia. *Revista Internacional de Ciencias Sociales, 18* (1), 229–250.

Poole, N., Greaves, L., Jategaonkar, N., McCullough, & Chabot, C. (2008). Substance use by women using domestic violence shelters. *Substance Use and Misuse, 43* (8–9), 1129–1150.

Quintana, L., & Salgado, U. (2016). Internal migration in Mexico from 1990–2010: A new economic geography approach. *Problemas del Desarollo, 47* (184), 137–162.

Roditti, M., Schultz, P., Gillette, M., & de la Rosa, I. (2010). Resiliency and social support networks in a population of Mexican American intimate partner violence survivors. *Families in Society, 91* (3), 248–256.

Rosales, R., & Calvo, R. (2017). "Si Dios Quiere": Fatalismo and use of mental health services among Latinos with a history of depression. *Social Work in Health Care, 56*, 748–764.

Sajnani, N., & Nadeau, D. (2006). Creating safer spaces for immigrant women of color: Performing the politics of possibility. *Canadian Woman Studies, 25*, 45–52.

Semple, K., & Villegas, P. The grisly deaths of a woman and a girl shock Mexico and test its president (2020, February 19). *The New York Times*, Retrieved from: www.nytimes.com/2020/02/19/world/americas/mexico-violence-women.html

Soriano, L. (2017). *Ethics implications in use of the word "immigrant" for the case of indigenous peoples and their rights to mobility*. Paper presented at the 2nd Binational Mexico–U.S. Conference on Social Work, Migration and Human Rights, November 15 & 16.

Suarez-Orozco, M, Paez, M. (2002). *Latinos*. 1st ed. Berkeley: University of California Press.

Torres, J. B., Solberg, V.S.H., & Carlstrom, A.H. (2002). The myth of sameness among Latino men and their machismo. *American Journal of Orthopsychiatry, 72* (2), 163–181.

Umaña-Taylor, A.J., Updegraff, K.A., & Gonzales-Backen, M.A. (2011). Mexican-origin adolescent mothers' stressors and psychosocial functioning: Examining ethnic identity affirmation and familism as moderators. *Journal of Youth and Adolescence, 40*, 140–157.

Wong, J., & Mellor, D. (2014). Intimate partner violence and women's health and wellbeing: Impacts, risk factors and responses. *Contemporary Nurse, 46* (2), 170–179.

World Health Organization. (2017). Violence Against Women [Fact sheet]. Retrieved from www.who.int/mediacentre/factsheets/fs239/en

5

SEVERE LICKING

Calypso Considers Domestic Violence

Alison Mc Letchie and Daina Nathaniel

According to a 2021 report by the then Minister of Social Development and Family Services, Senator Donna Cox, in 2017 Trinidad and Tobago 30% "of partnered women experienced physical and/or sexual violence by an intimate partner in their lifetime" (Government of Trinidad and Tobago, 2021). The report claimed that COVID-19 and the resulting economic instability has contributed to the vulnerability of women and girls. One year before the publication of this report, at press conference, the Commissioner of Police, Gary Griffith (2018–2021), indicated that there was a "rise in domestic violence cases from 232 in 2019 to 558 in 2020" (Mendes-Franco, 2020), one of the contributing factors for this rise, according to the Commissioner, was the establishment of Gender-Based Violence Unit in January 2020. The Minster's and the Commissioner's reports highlighted what was an open secret in the nation: domestic violence is widespread and there has been little effort to systemically address its causes, develop interventions, support victims, or deal with perpetrators.

The growing number of murders and attacks reported in the Trinidad and Tobago media on a daily basis are of grave concern to both the government and the citizens. This concern is made even more intense given that a significant percentage of these cases have been traced to domestic violence. While the Domestic Violence Act of 1999 was instituted specifically to protect the rights of victims and to lay down defined parameters for how domestic violence perpetrators are to be dealt with, the reality of what is happening on the ground remains the same: women are kept silent, women are made to believe they have no choice, women receive sometimes little or no family support for leaving the abusive situation, which has resulted in women being attacked and killed. This Act was amended in 2020 and sought to identify those who can apply for Protection Orders, provide for Emergency Protection Orders, and to establish the National Domestic Violence Register for Domestic Violence Complaints (Government of Trinidad and Tobago, 1999).

These formal attempts to address the problem of domestic violence are one indication that this is a serious social problem. This chapter suggests that in the context of the Caribbean in general, and Trinidad and Tobago in particular, popular songs – calypsos – are another indicator of pressing social concerns. The themes addressed in calypsos often raise social issues, sometimes even before the national political leadership. Significantly as well is that these songs and their singers draw from a tradition that recognizes them as the voice of the people. Historically, many of these songwriters were working-class and had little formal education but used their art form to call attention to concerns of the marginalized communities of which they are members.

DOI: 10.4324/9781003264040-7

The exact origins of calypso are difficult to pinpoint since they are a combination of various cultural backgrounds (Mason, 1998). Scholars of the art form generally agree, however, that the earliest roots of this genre can be traced to the African *griot* and French *chantwell* (Dudley, 2004; Regis, 1999; and Warner, 1982). In the Caribbean, these traditions merged with various Aboriginal practices and the many subsequent immigrant groups from Africa, Europe, India, the Middle East, China, and other parts of the Caribbean and Latin America that settled in the region to create calypso (Cowley, 1996). Over time, various forms of calypso and its derivative, soca, have emerged and the music is often thought of as the musical accompaniment for Carnival because of its infectious rhythms; the songs' lyrical content is also important. Often characterized as speaking truth to power, many songs address significant political and social issues, sometimes using humor or double entendre, while others are more direct and forceful.

Interestingly, while Caribbean scholars have long recognized the significance of calypso and other folk art as an important recorder of social history, Western scholars, according to Loseke (2009), have only recently begun to use narratives as an academic resource. Loseke points out that one reason for this interest is the acknowledgement "that narratives are important to study because they are a *pervasive* feature of social life" (p. 1) and they are both socially and personally consequential. As a social institution, calypso serves as an important indicator of social trend and reflection of popular culture. Warner (1982) suggests that because the majority of calypsos is written and performed by men, the male ego is ever present in these songs, and it is important to remember that calypsonians use "their material to illustrate prevailing attitudes with the Trinidad society, even when these were the result of myth and stereotype" (p. 105).

Warner's reminder is important because the purpose here is to examine the public discourse about domestic violence articulated in calypsos. The songs analyzed span a time period from the 1940s up to the 1980s and cover a number of themes including the descriptions of wife-beating, alternatives to violence, and suggestions for female liberation and in some instances revenge. For the purposes of this discussion, domestic violence is limited to physical aggression between adults involved in an intimate relationship, dating or marriage (common law or legal). Sometimes as a bystander or active participant, the calypsonians in these songs address domestic violence from a variety of worldviews that mirror both the complexity and development of Trinbagonian[1] society. Along with the various themes addressed in the songs, the paper includes calypsos sung by both male and female performers to ensure a more comprehensive public dialogue that reflects a range of perspectives.

Defining domestic violence, intimate partner abuse, or family violence is problematic. Many scholars, according to DeKeseredy and Schwartz (2000), have debated just how to define domestic violence. DeKeseredy and Schwartz agree with Ellis that the research decisions, particularly methodological approaches, are informed by the definition used. They contend that broad definitions often include rape or sexual cruelty, physical battering, psychological and emotional abuse, while narrow definitions are limited to specific instances or behaviors frequently found in criminal law. Traditionally, domestic violence has been a well-accepted, if not endorsed, behavior in Trinidad and Tobago and perhaps other parts of the Caribbean. The practice may have stemmed from the days when women were considered property to be controlled. Perhaps it stemmed from the Judeo-Christian idea that men are the head of the household and the women are expected to love, honor, and obey. Or perhaps, according to a Caribbean Court of Justice report,

> the rationale for this form of violence is rooted in the historical philosophy of women's subordination and inferiority to men. Women were, and many still are, conditioned to believe in the superiority of their male partners in any relationship; further, they regard everything which occurs within the four walls of a home as being private and not to be disclosed to

> anyone no matter how devastating. This has resulted in under-reporting of incidents of family violence.
>
> *Bernard, 2007*

Wherever the sentiment was born, it fed a belief system that that which occurred between husbands and wives was not only sanctioned but was to be left alone as a matter of course.

Moreover, according to the Caribbean Court of Justice report,

> Women in the main are ambivalent about violence perpetrated by family members. Apart from the private nature of such violence, many women suffer from feelings of guilt believing that they deserve the beatings because of some wrong committed by them. Others refrain from speaking out about the violence because of fear of further abuse or shame and embarrassment, threats of financial deprivation or lack of options. In marital and common law relationships wives convince themselves that their vows or conjugal duties include occasional corporal punishment from their spouses or partners, as frequently glorified in calypsos and dance hall music.
>
> *Bernard, 2007*

This means that women rarely find solace in family, far less in the law, which caused many to continue to suffer in silence and others lose their lives in one way or another.

Man Talk

Beginning with Bomber's Domestic Violence; Hawk's Husband and Wife; and Attila's Philosophy/Treat dem Rough, the practice of wife beating, as portrayed in these calypsos, is seen as normative. These songs remind the listener that the man is the head of the house; a woman's duty is to serve her man; and domestic arrangements are private and should not be the concern of the wider society. Writing about the historical roots of wife abuse in the West, Brown and Hendricks (1998) point out that the idea a man has the right to hit his wife is rooted in English common law which "made it permissible to strike one's wife as long as the rod or stick was no thicker than the husband's thumb" (p. 120) – the rule of thumb. Coupled with the patriarchy informed by Judo-Christianity culture and the physical and psychological violence of the plantation, these songs exemplify the traditional values of Trinbagonian civilization. Hodge (1974) maintains that "Caribbean society was born out of brutality, destructiveness, rape" (p. 111) and this cruelty has been internalized and is reflected in all relationships.

Attila's "Philosophy" and Shorty's "Sixteen Commandments" go beyond just reinforcing traditional patriarchal domestic arrangements. These songs also absolve men of any personal responsibility for their behavior. The perpetrators in these songs display the classical characteristics of batterers that Vaselle-Augenstein and Ehrlich (1992) list as "dependence, depression, anxiety, low self-esteem, paranoia, dissociation from their own feelings, poor impulse control, antisocial tendencies, and hostility towards women" (p. 139). The calypsos remind women that they must not only expect regular beatings, but they also must provide financial support for themselves and their male partners while passively accepting the fact that their men will cheat, although they, the women, must remain faithful. This contradiction speaks to the *saga boy* image of the Trinbagonian male. He offers his body and charm to women as a prize but seeks to limit his emotional and financial commitment to the household. Hodge (1974) argues this role is a direct outcome of African slavery where "the function of fatherhood was limited to fertilizing the female. Gone was the status of head of the family, for there was no family, no living in a unit with wife and children" (p. 115).

Attila in "Philosophy" claims that he knows how to keep a home happy. According to him, the best way to keep a woman is to:

> every now and then knock dem down,
> dey love you long and dey love you strong.

Both these songs are of particular interest because the writers invoke philosophical and religious authorities. Shorty mirrors the Hebrew bible in Sixteen Commandments while Philosophy claims the same intellectual tradition as Socrates and Plato. Writing about occurrences of abuse in American minority groups, Casanova Oats (1998) claims that "value placed on religious beliefs and the role that the church plays in family life might impact a victim's reactions to an incident of intimate violence" (p. 237). The authoritative nature of the relationship these calypsonians sing about indicates a reliance on Old Testament interpretations of the marital home.

This group of songs suggests that wife beatings are necessary to establish a man's "maleness." In "Philosophy" we hear,

> don't be fooled with sentimentality,
> or dey tell their friends you are a sissy.

Male strength is displayed not simply in the violence of the beating, but also in the very willingness to beat. True men beat, weak men coddle. In these songs, women are viewed in part as children to be controlled and managed. Their ability to act as independent free thinkers is belittled. The male partner demands power and authority over the woman. Calypsonians in these songs encourage men to subscribe to the biblical tenet "spare the rod and spoil the child."

The female body itself and its ownership and control is another subject addressed in these songs. The singers maintain that men must establish and retain possession both physically, by restricting her movement, and sexually. In fact, women are not allowed to deny men sexual access as Lord Kitchener sings in Pillow Fight and Sparrow in Wine Back. For Kitchener, Doreen's refusal to be intimate with him is grounds for a beating. This, even though he acknowledges that he had an inappropriate encounter with a *winer girl* earlier. Doreen, however, is not prepared to take Kitchener's demands "lying down"; she tells him:

> you cyar get de bam bam tonight

Zandolee's "Man Family" goes beyond demanding physical control to include social relationships. Kurst-Swanger and Petcosky (2003) write that "the goal of threatening or harming a partner is ultimately to get the partner to 'behave' in certain ways. Abusers, for whatever reason … have a need to dominate and control their partners' every move" (p. 110).

In "Sixteen Commandments," for example, Shorty explains that as a consequence of his many beatings, Angela's face is no longer beautiful and that she is required to ask permission to speak and use the bathroom. At the core of this need to manage her is the fact that the woman's sexuality is seen as a threat to the man. Her partner must not only train her to fulfill his carnal needs but also teach her to use her sexual skills only with him or for his benefit. If, however, a man is able to train his woman, she will in fact use her skills to support her partner. Sparrow sings in Wine Back that for his lover to get any financial support from him she must

> Wine back, if you want mey currency
> Wine back, whether you tired or you sleepy

Wine back, you got to dingolay, kafa and karay
Wine back, and when you dancing, break away
Wine back, and ah shame to tell you so
Wine back, otherwise you got to go

He is displeased with her sexual abilities in spite of what he acknowledges are her excellent housekeeping skills and emotional support. Female sexuality is seen as a method by which women might be controlled by men. We hear again from Sparrow in Rose how pleased he is with her, even though according to him, her deception should result in blows; she is his "everything." This song, along with Kitchener's "Pillow Fight" and "Take dat" by Funny, illustrates an emerging trend in calypsos and the wider society. Women appear to be taking ownership of their bodies and relationships. Men, therefore, are encountering resistance to their beatings ("Pillow Fight" and "Severe Licking") from women. But, more significantly, men are also beginning to acknowledge the error of their ways. There is an examination of the right of men to beat or at the least consideration of the effects of wife beating on the household and intimate relationships ("Rose").

One song that best expresses this tension between the traditional and the modern is Brynner's Soul in she Soul. In this calypso, Brynner complains that his woman has become a fan of soul music. For him, this is a problem not only because of the financial strain that comes from the purchase of the many records but also because in her enjoyment she neglects her household responsibilities. Brynner, therefore, beats her in an attempt to re-establish order in the home. Weissman (2009) suggests that domestic violence might be a possible manifestation of the stress produced by political, economic, and social transitions. The "Americanization" of the national community is the issue addressed by the song. For Brynner, soul music and America has a different set of values and norms that he does not want in his home. On a more practical level, soul music is a direct threat to his ability as a calypsonian to earn a living. This song, therefore, not only demonstrates a shifting of values but also exposes the vulnerability of the local economy to the global market.

Hawk warns that even when witnessing violence in the public space between spouses, bystanders should not act. This runs counter to the tradition of *gayap*, or community, common in the Caribbean. Instead, failure to intercede mirrors the society's convention that for a long time gave subtle permission to men to hit their wives. Even the police and wider legal system was not seen as a resource. Buzawa and Hirschel (2009) write that inaction "was not understood as a failure on the part of the police, but merely as reflecting the unspoken assumption that internal family disputes largely fell outside their area of responsibility" (p. 69). Lazarus-Black (2001 & 2003) indicates that it was not until 1991 that the courts in Trinidad and Tobago could grant an order of protection because of domestic abuse. This right and its enforcement are very significant especially given the number of spousal murders in Trinidad and Tobago. This trend reflects the failure of both the legal services and the wider community to protect victims. Baron sings in "Severe Licking"

People form a circle, then came a constable
And he tried to put a stop to de trouble
Mama yo, Shorty find a heat,
De police nearly get beat
It was real bacchanal on Charlotte Street
De girl say "Constable, have care
Dis is my man lickin' me here
And if he feel to lick me
He can lick me damn it
Doh interfere!"

Both Baron and Hawk maintain that intervening results in the couple turning against the assistant. This view illustrates the belief that the abused "like it" and is summarized by the local saying, "if he eh beat meh, he doh love meh." Intervention is viewed as problematic because of the likelihood of women returning to their partners; the lack of formal institutional services; and common law principle that the government should have limited powers in private household.

Just as the society has various views, there are a number of songs that contend domestic violence is wrong. "Think about the Children" by Merchant; Brown Boy's "Domestic Violence"; Young Unknown's "No More Domestic Violence"; "That Kind of Love" by Explainer; and Brigo's "Do So Eh Like So" are some examples. In these songs, the men remind the listener that violence is not an appropriate solution for marital strife. In fact, Brown Boy offers a new interpretation for domestic violence and uses violent-sounding words and phrases to describe the act of passionate love making:

> You have to hold she round she waist
> Bust kiss on she face
> Throw she on de bed
> Start to rub she leg
> And when she feeling sleepy
> Start to scratch she and bite she
> And when you want to have your fun
> You have to roll she on de ground
> This is my consequence
> Love for domestic violence

Brown and Hendricks (1998) suggest there are a number of interventions for battering. They may be informal (crisis hot-lines and shelters) or formal (criminal or family court; counseling programs; and mediation programs). Saunders (2009) examined programs for male abusers and found that these curricula attempt to move the definition of abuse beyond simply the physical; encourage men to take ownership of their behavior; and introduce them to more suitable ways of dealing with aggression. These songs propose a new understanding of marital relationships.

Brother Resistance's "Homegrown" goes further by openly challenging Attila's "Philosophy." Resistance dismisses Attila's thesis, the social norms that permit domestic violence and the legal system that fail to protect women. Specifically, Resistance confronts men by asking them to consider the purpose of the home and their relationships with all the women in their life. Poser in "No Man Eh Own No Woman," like Resistance, promotes the idea of individual agency, recognizing the need for sex role re-socialization. This group of songs reveals a transformation in social arrangements but there are some that also demonstrate changes in the views of calypsonians. In "Respect Woman" and "Treat She Nice," Shorty and Sparrow both advocate for men to reform. Sparrow offers that

> bareback and love don't agree

and that affection produces martial harmony. Similarly, Shorty tells men when they get a woman they

> must give her respect and honor,
> treat her like a queen, never abuse her.

Shorty and Sparrow both offer interesting examples of the complexity of the male-female relationship and social norms. Both men in their music, particularly with regard to the theme discussed here, move from a traditional to more and more enlightened position. Examining Sparrow's larger body of work, one could argue that a great many of his songs objectify women. But in the songs analyzed in this study ("Rose," "Brenda," and "Treat She Nice"), Sparrow transforms from a wife beater, to acknowledging the consequences of his abuse, and finally to admonishing other men for battering. Shorty also has a similar conversion, but in "Severe Licking" by Baron, listeners learn that while Shorty abused his partner, she fought back.

> Bomber tell me de fight was great,
> Shorty lick out de girl plate
> She get vex and decided to retaliate
> Dey say dis girl was really tough, she make out of real hard stuff
> Because she stand up dere and take 'bout 25 cuff
> Shorty get mad and he pelt a kick
> De gyal bob and weave under it
> And she hold on to it till he sweetness and start squeezin' it
> Oh god she squeeze it, oh Jesus she squeeze it
> Shorty start to shout, she say "Shut your damn mouth"
> She squeeze it till she squeeze it out
> And she squeeze it, she squeeze it

Maybe it was the public humiliation that causes Shorty to change. Or perhaps it could be the pain of the experience, but when we hear from Shorty in "Respect Woman," it is a duet sung with a woman and much of the song is in Hindi. Shorty is known for experimenting with Indian rhythms in his music but, arguably in this song, he is also speaking directly to the East Indian population.

Baron's use of double entendre in "Severe Licking" suggests two events. Firstly, he describes the physical altercation between Shorty and his wife. Additionally, Baron's decision to refer to the beating as a licking is a not-so subtle allusion to oral sex. In this song, Baron forces the listener to consider the proximity of violence and sex in relationships. The nation was forced to address this association in 1986 with the debate of the Sexual Offences Bill and its "Clause 4" (Mohammed, 1991) which acknowledged rape within a marriage as possible, many years after this song was written. According to Baron, Shorty's wife is the victor on this occasion because as:

> Shorty start to shout, she say, "Shut your damn mouth"
> She squeeze it "till she squeeze it out"

But this is not necessarily so because as Mahoney, Williams and West (2000) note,

> many women are pressured to engage in sex directly after being beaten, to "make up." A woman who has been physically assaulted by her partner in the past – particularly when that assault has occurred in the context of a sexual act – may choose to submit to unwanted sex acts out of fear, hopelessness, exhaustion, the desire to minimize injury to herself or others or simply the hope that doing so will end the whole episode.
>
> *p. 150*

There are some songs that address ideas of retaliation. Ebony's "Two Round Things"; Brigo's "Do So Eh Like So"; and Ras Kommanda's "Gramazone in de Curry" all consider the possibilities when women react to abuse. Ebony describes the pain he experienced when his wife grabbed his testicles when he attempted to beat her. This song not only warns men of a likely consequence of their actions but also instructs women on how to deal with abusers. Although he does not offer detailed lessons to women on dealing with violence, Brigo tells men that their wives are entitled to engage in the same neglectful behavior as the men. He suggests that the men "remember she's your woman, not a child."

"Gramazone in de Curry" offers very specific recipes for dealing with difficult husbands. Ras Kommanda cautions men that there is no excuse for abuse and reminds them that they are vulnerable particularly in traditional households where women are responsible for the cooking. His admonition resembles the suggestion that in some instances a person may have to "sleep with one eye open" to avoid harm. Common to these types of songs is the presentation of a more equitable male/female relationship as well as the sanctioning of female retribution.

Woman Talk

As illustrated by the songs above, many calypso singers over the years have performed lyrics that have celebrated domestic violence as legitimate behavior for anything from infidelity to keeping women "in line." Simultaneously, however, predominantly female calypso singers have sung out against this violence and have used the artform to advocate for resilience, retaliation, and revenge from women. This section of the paper is an attempt to trace female advocacy in calypso by highlighting songs that seek to empower women. This subset of calypso shines the light on the ways that women can find agency in an atmosphere of domestic violence, and thereby transform themselves from victims to victors. While many calypsos over the years that have addressed female advocacy with respect to domestic violence, three specific works will be considered here: "Run Away" by Singing Francine, "Ah Fightin" Back' by Leslie Ann Ellis and "I Am A Woman" by Karen Eccles. It is important for the reader to remember that although these songs were performed by women, they were not necessarily written by them. Run Away was written by Ronald Howard but as Munro (2016) citing Rohler (1990) and Dikobe (2003) reminds us, "*[r]*egardless of who composed a particular song, the calypsonian is accepted at face value as the author of the song's message" (62).

Arguably Singing Francine was the first female calypsonian to urge the woman to simply leave an intimate partner relationship. In the chorus of Run Away she says:

> Chile does run away,
> Fowl does run away,
> Woman, cat does run away when man treating dem bad.
> Cow does run away,
> Dog does run away,
> What happen to you?
> Woman you could run away too. Get out!

In these lyrics, the message is clear – at all cost the woman must flee. By relating to the woman directly, Francine became the lone voice in the 1970s to reassure women that they deserve a better life and that it was theirs for the taking. This one voice stood against the many others that discouraged women from breaking marital vows and destroying family life for children. After all, the prevailing sentiment was that to have two warring parents was better than having only one. Not only did Francine open the discussion of appropriate female action when faced with domestic violence, but she also made the topic less taboo, thereby making it possible for other singers after her to continue the same call.

Furthermore, what Francine does in this song is suggest that to be abused is to be relegated to a level less than an animal. And that even animals have the good sense to flee a situation where the treatment is less than desirable. She gives the woman another perspective of her abusive situation, a perspective that she is due more respect and regard than is being meted out to her. That she is not a lesser species but an equal who can claim her right to a life free from fear. In *Run Away*, Francine speaks to victims, "as individuals who are entitled to freedom of choice and basic human rights, exhorting them to see themselves as individuals with power over their destinies, and cajoling – if not beseeching – them to take control of their lives" (Mahabir, 2001).

But female singers who came after Francine did not always encourage the woman to simply leave. Some, like Leslie-Ann Ellis in her song "Ah Fighting Back," encourages the woman instead to take control of the situation and stand up for herself. While much of this song has metaphoric overtures about actually killing the husband with the possibility of the wife losing her own life in the process, what it clearly does is purges the woman of all that she has been through. It gives her voice by allowing her to speak her mind. This would be her revenge as illustrated in the third verse:

> Gave you the best years of my life.
> God knows in good and bad, I am a devoted wife.
> When yuh sick I am yuh doctor, yuh nurse, yuh psychologist, yuh sexual healer.
> Never once hungry and food not ready but yuh still use yuh foot on me.
> Once I took 12 stiches behind meh neck because you push me down the step.
> Serve you like a god, like Prince ah Wales, treat you like a king
> But tonight ah tek off meh wedding ring.
> Fed up being brutalized and kicked and smacked,
> Tonight boy ah fighting back.
> Doh mind how ah hide, yuh finding meh tracks,
> Tonight boy ah fighting back.
> Before you kill me in some brutal act,
> Tonight boy ah fighting back.
> Doh feel you could run and lock down de shack,
> Tonight boy ah fighting back.

Too often, domestic violence victims remain silent even after they are out of the violent situation. What this song does instead is provides an outlet for the woman in the course of her taking control to say what she needs to say. She calls out her abuser on all that he has done to her physically and mentally, while reminding him of her own devotion and strength through it all. This type of lyric has the power to translate into the society as it strikes a chord with the audience with respect to the oppressive nature of domestic violence. This song, in its specifics about what the abuser has done, brings a new level of awareness to the audience. The very term "domestic violence" is vague, which causes people often to wonder what it really involves. By itemizing the egregious actions directed at the woman, the audience is left with little doubt that the situation is one that needs serious attention.

The Karen Eccles song "I am a woman" takes a further step than the other two songs. Not only does she speaks directly to the abused woman but also embodies the victimized woman, who has found a new sense of self. It is here that the resilience of women becomes the major message. The abused speaks directly to her abuser in this song, which ends in a testimonial from Eccles who stands as an example of one who has bounced back from that dark situation. She says:

> I appeal to all women who suffer silently
> Is time to come out please and talk to somebody.

Healing time is now, so receive all yuh healing.
You are a victor and no longer girl, ah victim.
I complained to his family
They turn around and start blaming me
So I stand boldly; ah speaking out now for you and me.

The repeated invocation of "I am a woman" serves to elevate the status of women, as listeners journey through the song. It is as though as the singer comes to the realization upon each repetition that to be a woman to be something great, something important, something sacred. This song departs from the others in the way that it injects a sense of legitimacy in woman-ness. The woman does not necessarily have to run nor become violent herself, but simply remember who she rightfully is and that she can claim that space with confidence. To be out of that violent place is to claim that space.

Conclusion

All the songs examined for this paper reveal the pervasiveness of domestic violence in Trinidad and Tobago. If the conventional role of the calypsonian is to be acknowledged, then, as these songs illustrate, the transition from a traditional to modern society has been problematic in the marital/intimate partnership sphere. The men in these songs demonstrate the conflicts that all men confront as they attempt to reconcile their role as "head of the house" with that of intimate partner. For some, violence seems to be the best answer while others look for alternatives. With few exceptions, these songs are men singing to other men and the conversations, frank and painful. Over time, these songs move from reinforcing the practice of battering to calling for a re-ordering of male/female relationships. The male singers, and hopefully the wider society, also appear to be transformed and more enlightened.

The small collection of female voiced calypsos reminds society that women have options in terms of getting out of domestic violence situations. It is not that these options were previously lacking but that there was little social and legal support for victims. Female calypsonians have opened a way for domestic violence to be discussed in the socio-political arena that is calypso. They have brought increased awareness of the issue, which, when added to the strides being made in the establishment of government and non-government programs and safe houses, perhaps we will begin to see fewer and fewer victims.

The COVID-19 pandemic and the related quarantines reminded many citizens of the danger that many victims of intimate partner violence confront in their daily lives. Starting in 2020, there were a number of high profile murders of women by their partners, relatives, and stalkers, who had increased access to women because they were confined to their homes. One report claims there was a 44%[2] increase in domestic violence in 2020. Because of the lock-down/stay home orders, the general population became more aware of the vulnerability of women and children to issues of violence, rape, incest, and sexual assault. There have even been discussions about the unreported and often unacknowledged problem of intimate partner violence where men are the victims. Given the responsiveness of calypsonians to current events, it will be interesting to see if they continue to address this topic in their songs going forward.

Calypsos Referenced

Ah Fighting Back – Leslie-Ann Ellis
Brenda – Slinger Francisco (Mighty Sparrow)

Do So Eh Like So – Samuel Abraham (Lord Brigo)
Domestic Violence – Clifton Ryan (The Mighty Bomber)
Domestic Violence – Knolly Brown (Brown Boy)
Gramazone in the Curry – Steve Pascall (Ras Kommanda)
Home Grown Violence – Roy Lewis aka Lutalo Masimba (Brother Resistance)
Husband and Wife – Andrew Heywood (Hawk)
I am a Woman – Karen Eccles
Man Family – Sylvester Anthony (Mighty Zandolee)
No Man Eh Own No Woman – Sylvester Lockhart (Poser)
No more Domestic Violence – Young Unknown
Philosophy/Treat dem rough – Raymond Quevedo (Atilla the Hun)
Pillow Fight – Aldwyn Roberts (Lord Kitchener)
Respect Woman – Garfield Blackman (Shorty aka Ras Shorty I)
Rose – Slinger Francisco (Mighty Sparrow)
Run Away – Singing Francine
Severe Licking – Timothy Watkins (Baron)
Sixteen Commandments – Garfield Blackman (Shorty aka Ras Shorty I)
Soul in she Soul – Kade Smion (Lord Brynner)
Take Dat – Donric Williamson (Lord Funny)
That Kind of Love – Winston Henry (Explainer)
Think about de Children – Dennis Franklyn Williams (Merchant)
Treat she nice – Slinger Francisco (Mighty Sparrow)
Two Round Things – Fitzroy Joseph (Brother Ebony)
Wine Back – Slinger Francisco (Mighty Sparrow)

Acknowledgment

The authors would like to thank Zeno Obi Constance for sharing his collection of songs used in this paper.

Notes

1 Trinbagonian, a colloquial shortened form of Trinidadian and Tobagonian.
2 https://blogs.worldbank.org/latinamerica/casting-light-shadow-pandemic-caribbean-violence-against-women

Works Cited

Bernard, Desiree. (2007). Confronting Gender-Based Violence in the Caribbean. In Kenneth O. Hall and Myrtle Chuck-A-Sang (Eds.) *The Caribbean Integration Process: A People-Centered Approach*, Ian Randle Publishers: Jamaica.

Brown, Michael P. Brown & Hendricks, James E. (1998). Wife Abuse. In Ali Jackson and Casanova Oates (Eds.) *Violence in Intimate Relationships: Examining Sociological and Psychological Issues*, Butterworth-Heinemann: Boston, MA.

Buzawa, Eve S. & Hirschel, David (2009). Evolution of the Police Response to Domestic Violence. In Evan Stark and Eve S. Buzawa (Eds) *Violence against Women in Families and Relationships*, Praeger: CA.

Casanova Oates, Gisele (1998) Cultural Perspectives on Intimate Violence. In Ali Jackson and Casanova Oates (Eds.) *Violence in Intimate Relationships: Examining Sociological and Psychological Issues*, Butterworth-Heinemann: Boston, MA.

Cowley, John (1996) *Carnival, Canboulaly and Calypso: Traditions in the making,* Cambridge University Press: Cambridge.
DeKeseredy, Walter S. & Schwartz, Martin D. (2000) Definitional Issues. In Renzetti, Edleson and Kennedy Bergen (Eds.) *Sourcebook on Violence Against Women,* Sage Publications: London.
Dudley, Shannon (2004). *Carnival Music in Trinidad: Experiencing Music, Expressing Culture,* Oxford University Press: Oxford.
Government of Trinidad and Tobago. (1999) The Domestic Violence Act http://www.ttparliament.org/legislations/a1999-27.pdf
Government of Trinidad and Tobago. (2021) *Incidence of Violent Crimes against Women and Girls.* Retrieved from www.social.gov.tt/wp-content/uploads/2021/04/Statement-on-Violent-Crimes-Against-Women-and-Girls-April-27th-2021.pdf
Hodge, Merle (1974). The Shadow of the Whip. In Orde Coombs (Ed.) *Is Massa Day Dead? Black Moods in the Caribbean,* Doubleday: New York.
Kurst-Swanger, Karel & Petcosky, Jacqueline L. (2003). *Violence in the Home: Multidisciplinary Perspectives,* Oxford University Press: Oxford.
Lazarus-Black, Mindie (2001). Law and the Pragmatics of Inclusion: Governing Domestic Violence in Trinidad and Tobago. *American Ethnologist,* Vol. 28 (2), 388–416.
Lazarus-Black, Mindie (2003). The (Heterosexual) Regendering of a Modern State: Criminalizing and Implementing Domestic Violence Law in Trinidad. *Law and Social Inquiry,* Vol. 28 (4), 979–1009.
Loseke, Donileen R. (2009). Public and Personal Stories of Wife Abuse. In Evan Stark and Eve S. Buzawa (Eds.) *Violence against Women in Families and Relationships* Praeger: California.
Mahabir, Cynthia (2001). The Rise of Calypso Feminism: Gender and the Musical Politics in the Calypso. *Popular Music,* Vol. 20 (3), 409–430.
Mahoney, Patricia, Williams, Linda M. & West, Carolyn M. (2000). Violence against Women by Intimate Relationship Partners. In Claire Renzetti, Jeffery L. Edleson and Raquel Kennedy Bergen (Eds.) *Sourcebook on Violence Against Women,* Sage Publications: London.
Mason, Peter. (1998). *Bacchanal! The Carnival Culture of Trinidad,* Latin American Bureau Ltd: London.
Mendes-Franco, J (2020, April 10). Stay-at-home orders accompanied by rise domestic violence in Trinidad & Tobago. *Global Voices* Stay-at-home orders accompanied by rise in domestic violence in Trinidad & Tobago Global Voices.
Mohammed, Patricia (1991). Reflections on the Women's Movement in Trinidad: Calypsos, Changes and Sexual Violence. *Feminist Review,* Vol. 38, 33–47.
Munro, Hope (2016). *What She Go Do: Women in Afro-Trinidad Music,* The University of Mississippi Press: Jackson, MS.
Regis, Louis (1999). *The Political Calypso: True Opposition in Trinidad and Tobago: 1962–1987,* The Press University of the West Indies: Barbados.
Saunders, Hilary (2009). Securing Safety for Abused Women and Children in the Family Courts. In Evan Stark and Eve S. Buzawa (Eds.) *Violence against Women in Families and Relationships,* Praeger: California.
Vaselle-Augenstein, Renata and Ehrlich, Annette (1992). Male Batterers: Evidence for Psychopathology. In Emilio C. Viano (Ed.) *Intimate Violence: Interdisciplinary Perspectives,* Hemisphere Publishing Corporation: London.
Warner, Keith (1982). *Kaiso! The Trinidad Calypso: A Study of the Calypso as Oral Literature,* Three Continents Press: Washington, DC.
Weissman, Deborah (2009). Domestic Violence and the Postindustrial Household. In Evan Stark and Eve S. Buzawa (Eds.) *Violence against Women in Families and Relationships,* Praeger: California.

6

GENDER-BASED VIOLENCE IN THE ENGLISH-SPEAKING CARIBBEAN

Chronicling Guyana's Progress

Aneesa A. Baboolal

Country Profile

Guyana ("Land of Many Waters"), formerly British Guiana, is located in northern South America bordered by the Atlantic Ocean and situated between Suriname, Venezuela, and Brazil.

Originally inhabited by indigenous Carib and Arawak tribes, Guyana became a seventeenth-century Dutch colony and was subsequently held as a slave-holding British colony by 1815. Guyana remains the only English-speaking nation in South America after establishing independence in 1966. The population is estimated to be around 750,000. Guyana's colonial history continues to foster persistent ethno-cultural divisions and politics and legacies of violence (Henry, 2019). The two largest ethnic groups are Indo-Guyanese, descendants of 240,000 East Indian indentured laborers imported to work on sugar plantations between 1838 and 1917, and Afro-Guyanese, descended from formerly enslaved Africans (The World Factbook - Central Intelligence Agency [CIA], 2020).

Overview of Gender Inequality in Guyana

Guyana has a progressive legal framework that prohibits discrimination based on gender, race, disability, language, social status, religion, or national origin. Yet, societal gender inequalities[1] persist due to inadequate social services and weak infrastructures which engender high levels of poverty and female unemployment, few jobs for women, and out-migration as a survival strategy[2] (Trotz, 2004). According to the Bureau of Democracy, Human Rights and Labor (United States Department of State, 2007), Guyana faces several human rights issues including government corruption, sexual and intimate partner violence against women, abuse of minors, and discriminatory laws against marginalized gender and sexual minorities including lesbian, gay, bisexual, and transgender (LGBTQ+) persons. Employed women occupy significant roles as farmers, market vendors, teachers, nurses, civil servants, and clerks. Even though outnumbered by men, women are more often the head of household due to limited job opportunities and more often live in poverty, a risk factor for domestic violence.

Interpersonal Partner Violence in Guyanese Society

Two-thirds of all Guyanese women experience intimate partner violence during their lifetime; the most prevalent form of interpersonal violence in the country (Parekh, Russ, Amsalem, Rambaran,

DOI: 10.4324/9781003264040-8

Langston, & Wright, 2012). Guyana has legislation addressing women's rights including the Domestic Violence Act of 1996 that has provisions to protect survivors of violence including verbal, physical, sexual, and psychological abuse within the household (UN Women, 2010). However, progress on the social front has been hindered partly due to sociocultural perceptions of violence against women, as well as limited data regarding the prevalence of intimate partner violence in the nation. Rape[3] (including spousal rape) and domestic violence are criminalized yet, incidents largely go unreported to law enforcement, are seldom prosecuted by authorities, while both stigma and retribution of further violence persist (Help and Shelter, n.d.). Survivors frequently do not pursue charges due to a lack of confidence in the courts and inadequate sentences.

According to Guyana Human Rights Association (GHRA), domestic violence emerges from cultural underpinnings that marginalize women, thus, changes in various social sectors including employment and religious institutions, along with legislative advances are critical to addressing gender-based violence while alleviating socio-economic pressures. Recent global-scale research indicates that violence against women and girls in the Caribbean emerging from unequal power dynamics results in controlling and aggressive behaviors that are exacerbated by traumatic childhood histories of violence for both victims and perpetrators (Sayed & Bland, 2020). These cultural underpinnings also inadvertently contribute to forms of legitimized violence, rooted in historical gender inequities further exacerbated by patriarchal traditions and colonial legacies which can be observed amongst immigrant Guyanese communities in the US (Baboolal, 2016).

In 2019, Guyana conducted its first national survey on gender-based violence and found that 1 in every 2 women experienced intimate partner violence (IPV) in their lifetime; with at least 55 percent of all women experiencing at least one form of gender-based violence. The Guyana Women's Health and Life Experiences Survey (GWHLES) also found extensive violence against women beyond partner-based abuse including sexual violence, rape, and harassment (UN Women, 2019a). A health study also indicated a high prevalence of women presenting with traumatic physical injuries related to IPV (Parekh et al, 2012). According to UNIFEM (United Nations Development Fund for Women, now UN Women), a total of 28 women were murder victims of domestic violence in 2004 alone. Guyana also has the second-highest HIV/AIDS rate in the Caribbean, and it is suspected this is linked to the high rates of intimate partner violence (World Health Organization, 2005).

According to the Guyana Report on Human Rights Practices (United States Department of State, 2007), intimate partner violence against women and children remain pervasive issues within the nation. In a study of 360 Guyanese women, four out of every five respondents perceived violence in the family to be very common (76.8 percent), while one in three knew a survivor currently experiencing domestic violence (35.5 percent). Eighty-three percent of women viewed domestic violence as physically violent behavior (defined as fighting, beating, or hitting) that occurred on a daily basis. Only 50 percent of the respondents regarded verbal abuse such as curses, threats, and humiliation as a form of interpersonal violence (Nelson & Peake, 2000).

In regard to legislation combating domestic violence in Guyana, more than 65 percent of women were unaware of the Domestic Violence Act. According to Help and Shelter (n.d.), the number of reported cases of intimate partner violence by victims increased from 2,145 in 2001 to 2,769 by 2005. Help and Shelter reported a total of 6,414 clients from February 1998 to May 1996. According to their records, during this same time period, 2,969 cases were of spousal physical abuse, over 1,300 cases regarded non-physical spousal abuse, 35 cases of spousal sexual abuse, and 774 cases of spousal abuse that was alcohol or drug-related.[4]

While violence against women occurs across race and socioeconomic status, legal prohibitions provide women the right to seek protection, including penalties for violating order of protections from abusers; however, legislation regarding domestic violence is infrequently enforced.

Furthermore, vanishing domestic violence complaints are high throughout the Caribbean region (Lazarus-Black, 2008).[5]

In Guyana, survey data indicates that over 80 percent of women believe that intimate partner violence is endemic to Guyanese society and more than 30 percent of women have experienced partner violence in their adult lives (Trotz, 2004). A study of Trinidadian and Guyanese immigrants to the US found that women also viewed gender-based violence in comparable ways to their homelands (Baboolal, 2016). Specifically, in Guyana where legislation remains loosely enforced due to social and legal tolerance surrounding violence against women and girls, gender hierarchies and cultures of reconciliation work against the institutionalized forces of law that reflect patriarchal norms that keep women out of legal processes.[6]

Domestic Violence Law in Guyana

More than 65 percent of women were unfamiliar with the Domestic Violence Act[7] and 77 percent were unaware that the law was intended for their protection. The Domestic Violence Act of 1996 was largely the result of the work of the National Women's Rights Campaign, led by women lawyers and activists. Women's initiatives also fostered the emergence of non-governmental organizations such as Help and Shelter (established in 1995) a counseling service and shelter for survivors of violence, as well as groups like Red Thread, Men Against Violence Against Women, and Mothers in Black (Trotz, 2004).[8] Women's organizations, various government agencies, and non-governmental organizations have conducted initiatives independently and collaboratively in Guyana to address IPV through policy and programing; however, IPV-specific research has only emerged in recent years (DeShong & Haynes, 2016).

In 1998, Red Thread conducted a survey developed by the Caribbean Association for Feminist Research and Action (CAFRA) which explored the attitudes of women pertaining to domestic violence regarding female behavior and knowledge of sexual/reproductive health. Findings indicated that 77 percent of Guyanese women were unaware of the legislation pertaining to their own protection and only 15 percent knew what it provided for (Nelson & Peake, 2000).[9]

Furthermore, domestic violence laws are not strictly enforced due to silence surrounding the issue and perceptions of gender-based violence as private familial matters, perhaps rooted in cultures of reconciliation[10] (Baboolal, 2016; Lazarus-Black, 2007). While there has been some success with legal mechanisms to address domestic violence, those responsible for implementing the law including court staff, magistrates, and law enforcement are sometimes insensitive to the issue.

Help and Shelter notes that further training of court staff is needed, as well as a specialized Family Court. Additionally, sexual violence, including spousal rape, remains infrequently reported and prosecuted. Even though there are increasing numbers of victim reports, survivors remain socially stigmatized in Guyanese society. There is also a lack of sensitivity toward survivors of domestic violence (as well as sexual abuse) and a sense of tolerance toward perpetrators (United States Department of State, 2007). Social tolerance, inadequate law enforcement measures and legal shortcomings of the court system including ingrained tactics of subordination, intimidation, imposed legalization, humiliation, objectification, lacking professional support, and judicial discretion favoring the men's rights, fosters a climate of impunity for gender-based violence in Caribbean nations (Lazarus-Black, 2007).

Guyana's Shadow Pandemic: Domestic Violence and COVID-19

During the early phase of the pandemic outbreak in the Caribbean region, more women were impacted by COVID-19 (BMJ Global Health, 2020). While these findings were during the early stages of the pandemic and included small samples from various Caribbean nations, given women's occupations in service and health-care fields, as well as the gendered nature of household labor, women had more exposure to the virus in their daily activities by accompanying children to school or caring for elderly relatives. Human Rights Watch (2020) notes that the pandemic has decreased women's access to private internet and mobile phones to obtain resources, while elderly women, and those working within the home, are at an increased risk but remain invisible to policymakers. As of October 2021 (more than a year after the previous statistics were collected), Guyana had over 68,500 total infections, with 1,264 coronavirus-related deaths but cases were on the decline as almost 40 percent of the population was vaccinated at that point (Reuters COVID-19 Tracker, 2022).

COVID-19 also resulted in a shadow pandemic of violence as it worsened financial strain contributing to joblessness and exacerbating mental illness in a society already plagued by stigma surrounding mental health. According to The World Bank Blog, domestic violence rates, including physical, sexual, economic, and emotional violence in the Caribbean, further underscore the urgency of empowering women and girls to end such acts of discriminatory violence (Sayed & Bland, 2020). The Gender & COVID-19 Working Group (2020) noted that staying at home has become increasingly dangerous for survivors of intimate partner violence as the pandemic magnified isolation, increased interaction with abusers, limited support systems, and compounded caregiving burdens (both emotional and physical) within the household, thus changing relationship dynamics. The COVID-19 pandemic has further shed light on inadequate service resources available to survivors, especially in rural areas like Guyana's hinterland. Thus, it continues to be critical to consider responses to domestic violence at the intersection of health-care policy and racial/ethnic identity that have varying effects on women's experiences of intimate partner violence. Additionally, centering marginalized victims by taking into account social class and ability, and can result in more inclusive resources for survivors.

Enforcement of COVID-19 measures in Guyana remains critical given concerns surrounding lacking preventative measures that increase virus exposure and transmission within households for partners, children, and other relatives in extended households, already experiencing trauma (Help & Shelter, 2020). Given societal perceptions and norms regarding links between alcoholism and intimate partner violence in Guyana (Baboolal, 2016), Help and Shelter, a Guyana-based non-governmental organization working toward eliminating violence against women and children, also called for stricter enforcement of COVID-19 restrictions, such as administering fines for rum shops and bars, in an attempt to reduce the potential for violence.

Response from Law Enforcement

In 1992, the Guyana Police Force (GPF) began increasing the awareness of domestic violence among police ranks. Domestic violence training was also implemented in the curriculum of the Police Training College. In March 2000, the United Nations Human Rights Committee critiqued Guyana's inability to produce information concerning the effectiveness of the Domestic Violence Act. The country has not been able to reduce the level of violence perpetrated against women even with legal measures in place and therefore the United Nations Human Rights Committee encouraged police training and other enforcers of the law to become active in ensuring the rights and protection of women. A two-week training initiative was later put in place for the police force and in 2001 the first local non-governmental organization aiming to target domestic violence and promote awareness evolved. Help and Shelter (H&S) dedicated itself to combating domestic violence by focusing on the reeducation of society in order to create sensitivity among the public to the issue of domestic violence. Tolerance of gender-based violence is also apparent within the legal system as non-governmental organizations report that police officers and magistrates are influenced by bribes to disregard cases of domestic violence (United States Department of State, 2007).

However, despite these efforts to foster sensitivity and understanding of the plight of survivors, reports of interpersonal violence are often treated as less serious with women reporting seeking protection and assistance, only to be met with unsympathetic and sometimes hostile treatment (Help & Shelter, n.d.). Respondents commonly experience police officers that either fail to respond to calls for help or abusers are warned or referred to counseling agencies where partners are encouraged to "work it out." This can partially be attributed to lack of implementation of the Domestic Violence Act, but even in cases where officers are aware of the law, domestic violence is still considered a private matter. Victims who file reports sometimes request no action be taken, thus, police officers may also be hesitant to offer protection thus, contributing to a larger misunderstanding of the complexity of power, control, and victimization, in cases of intimate partner violence. Ultimately, discriminatory attitudes, behaviors, and actions limit women's access to legal support services as it mars their interactions with both law enforcement and the overall legal system. Red Thread (established in Guyana in 1986 and focuses on issues in the country regarding race, gender and poverty) further notes that the majority of domestic violence-related police complaints never reach the courts (Help and Shelter, n.d.).

Despite these hindrances, the Guyana Police Force (GPF) has been legally mandated to improve record-keeping (Nelson & Peake, 2000). According to the GPF, 2,000 warnings were given to men guilty of domestic violence in 2005, up from a little over 1,000 in 2001; however, charges against perpetrators of the crime have held steady at approximately 500 for a period of five years with only slight fluctuations. An improvement in the way police have been dealing with domestic violence cases is evident at some stations, particularly with regard to collaboration with non-governmental organizations (NGOs) and other agencies.

Civil Society Response

While legislation aids victims of violence through practical support programs for housing and training in income-generating skills, challenges surrounding violence against women persist. Non-governmental organizations have been critical in these advances, including in the passing of laws, training of police, and providing social support services. Non-profit organizations have implemented public service announcements, as well as trained health-care providers, teachers, agricultural workers, religious groups, and clinics to disseminate information regarding domestic violence and sensitize society on the critical issues surrounding gender-based violence. Additionally, there is a Task Force on Violence against Women whose membership includes representatives from NGOs, law enforcement, youth, and health-care providers. The Task Force gathers data in preparation for drafting national policy on domestic violence.

Measuring domestic violence in Guyana remains difficult as many victims do not seek help outside of their friends and family. Social stigmatization deters women from sharing experiences of violence as they fear community ostracization. Help and Shelter reports that traditions about "wife beating" are enforced in Guyana and thus it is a prevalent private affair and as such complaints to police are generally viewed as disloyalty. Despite these hindrances, the GPF has been legally mandated to improve record keeping and non-governmental organizations such as Red Thread has increased efforts to maintain records of domestic violence (Nelson & Peake, 2000).

Addressing Domestic Violence in Guyana

On the international level, the critique of Caribbean nations' inability to produce information concerning the effectiveness of domestic violence legislation to reduce gender-based violence via legal measures has resulted in culturally insensitive recommendations to increase police training to ensure the protection of women (United Nations Human Rights Committee, 2020. These solutions do not address the social stigmatization of victimization where attitudes regarding abuse as a "private family affair" and police complaints are viewed as disloyalty.[11] Yet, the United Nations Committee on the Elimination of Discrimination against Women (CEDAW, 2005) indicated that there have been positive changes in regard to gender-based violence such as the creation of a national task force and the inclusion of social workers to support survivors in court. Furthermore, the limited capacity of social service organizations, along with inconsistent research regarding gender-based violence, continues to pose a hindrance to adequately addressing violence against women (Barberet & Baboolal, 2020). Domestic violence responses are informed by institutional challenges at the government level (including partisan politics), placing overwhelming responsibility for addressing gender-based violence on under-funded non-governmental organizations, and narratives surrounding survivors, thus, identifying gaps in state responses, promoting gender sensitivity, and examinations of social power and biases are critical measures that need to be implemented (DeShong & Haynes, 2016). The Guyana Bureau of Statistics conducted its first national survey of gender-based violence in 2019 in collaboration with various international organizations (UN Women, UNDP – United Nations Development Program, USAID – United States Agency for International Development), the Inter-American Development Bank [IADB]) to examine the magnitude of violence against women. These results serve as a foundation for educational programing and community-based initiatives to address violence prevention; however, it is clear that such data-gathering efforts and extensive research programing cannot be conducted without additional support from international institutions.

While addressing domestic violence has a variety of direct costs related to prevention including offering treatment, and penalizing offenders, specifically in relation to court fees, medical care, counseling, housing, and social services, the benefits outweigh the social cost which includes mental and physical health costs (homicide/suicide, drug abuse, and psychological issues), as well as an overall decrease in economic participation (reduced productivity, absenteeism, lower earnings, etc.) (Buvinic, Morrison, & Shifter, 1999). In a report on Violence in Latin American and the Caribbean, The IADB notes several prevention strategies in terms of the education, health, and justice sector. Some of these recommended solutions include prevention and intervention programs that address social and cultural determinants of violence via policy. Guyanese society would benefit from policy options that address contributing factors of violence including substance abuse (alcoholism, for example), poverty, and gender inequality. This can begin in schools via educational programing or community organizations, media campaigns that target alcohol/drug consumption, treatment services for addiction and anger management, increasing women's participation in the workforce as a means to balance familial power and foster economic autonomy (Buvinic et al, 1999).

In order to uphold policies and progressive programing, further information is needed to evaluate and assess current circumstances as intimate partner violence continues to be an understudied issue in Guyana. Help and Shelter has addressed this gap by conducting surveys and producing various reports addressing domestic violence. In 2005, an informal survey of 20 police stations by Help and Shelter found 12 that had one police officer trained in domestic violence issues, 7 with designated spaces where persons reporting domestic violence could be interviewed privately, and understood the need for privacy. These efforts underscore the importance of developing sustained, collaborative, and long-term approaches that recognize the complexity of domestic violence issues.

To combat domestic violence in Guyana, a critical step would be a national survey that can assess the extent of domestic violence within the nation, including among all of the ethnic groups (coastal Afro-Caribbeans and Indo-Caribbeans, as well as indigenous Amerindians in the hinterland). Limited national and government-based data is scarce, crime and police data can be unreliable, thus, published reports from social service organizations still serve as a critical tool in measuring and ultimately, addressing gender-based violence within Guyana. Gender inequality remains woven into cultural norms that influence societal views of abuse as "normal," thus, bias must also be recognized to address entrenched and widespread views of inequality (Parekh et al, 2012). Gender-based violence in the Caribbean is linked to patriarchal values, and legacies of colonialism, that exacerbate intergenerational trauma for men and women (Henry, 2019). It remains important to disseminate information regarding domestic violence as it pertains to social norms, rights afforded by legislation like the Domestic Violence Act of 1996, and publicity of support services available to normalize discussions around abuse, as well as addressing the stigma surrounding it.

High rates of violence are also linked to poverty; therefore, local campaigns regarding domestic violence awareness should include addressing the health and economic impact of abuse, normalize ideologies that support gender equality, and acknowledge the risk to familial safety and children's welfare that violence poses. Such initiatives address societal attitudes about conflict via non-violent alternatives and provide health awareness (that can also combat the spread of HIV/AIDS as Guyana has the second-highest infection rate in the Caribbean[12]). Combating domestic violence in the Caribbean requires more extensive data collection and internal societal change; however, community organization efforts, including via non-governmental organizations, have demonstrated unity as a national strategy that can ultimately eradicate gender-based violence in Guyana but requires further social and financial support.

Guyana's shadow pandemic of intimate partner violence during COVID-19 lockdowns further emphasizes the importance of enforcing legislation to protect women, allocating funds to social service organizations to continue the important work of eradicating gender-based violence, and providing social education about the intergenerational and intra-family harm of domestic violence for partners, children, and family members. Lockdown measures during COVID-19 not only confined women and girls to homes where heightened risks to physical, emotional, and sexual violence were present, but such measures also cut off already limited access to education, employment, social networks, and vital social service protections (Bobbili & Rodney, 2020; Plan-International, 2020; UN Women, 2020). The IADB indicated that many shelters and counseling centers in Guyana remain understaffed, thus, further exacerbating vulnerability especially to those in rural areas with limited transportation and access to communication services (internet, phones, and mobiles). In addition to this ongoing problem, either the victim or the perpetrator must leave the household which is difficult, if not impossible for some, thus, difficulties under quarantine persist and further strategizing is required such as being able to report via code words at pharmacies or supermarkets (as implemented in France) or allocating government funds toward transportation and shelter (Telson, 2020).

The United Nations Special Rapporteur on violence against women, Dubravka Simonovic, noted that COVID-19 measures across the globe relied on a gender-blind framework thus exposing pre-existing shortcomings in gender-based violence prevention. These measures ultimately result in less intervention by law enforcement, closure of courts, further reduction in already limited access to support services, helplines, and shelter accommodations that ultimately emboldened perpetrators as they faced little to no consequences for violent acts (United Nations Human Rights: Office of the Higher Commissioner, 2020). As subsequent waves of the pandemic continue, it remains critically important that governments take into account women's lives while formulating protective health-care measures. This includes allocating additional financial resources to social service support for survivors, spreading awareness of the increased risk of violence, as well as upholding measures to address patriarchal ideology within the society to curtail and eventually eradicate gender-based violence.

Notes

1 Guyana ranked 117 on the Gender Inequality Index, which measures maternal mortality, birth rates, labor force participation, education, and seats in parliament held by women (United Nations Development Programme, 2013; UN Women Global Database on Violence against Women, 2016).

2 Guyanese women have engaged in high levels of out-migration as a strategic means of survival in the face of their increasing unemployment, thus, remittances largely support Guyana's economy (Trotz, 2004).

3 The legal age of marriage is eighteen; however, both boys and girls can marry at age 16 with parental consent. While there has been a decrease in child marriages in recent years, UNICEF reports that 23 percent of marriages have taken place when the bride was under the age of 18 (2013).

4 Help and Shelter (n.d.) also kept records on clients that were perpetrators of domestic violence from May 1996 to 1999. The cumulative numbers of clients stood at 5,087, with 1,912 persons committing physical spousal abuse and almost 900 perpetrating non-physical abuse, 36 in spousal sexual abuse. A total of 761 committed these acts while under the influence of drugs or alcohol. In urban areas, there were 2,093 perpetrators of abuse and in rural areas there were over 2,300. (Help and Shelter, n.d.).

5 For example, a sample of 8,297 applications for protection orders from 11 magistrates' courts in Trinidad and Tobago from August 1991 to April 1993 found that only 3,248 applications resulted in some form of action. A later study in 1997 and 1998 found that over 75 percent of cases were withdrawn or dismissed.

6 Mindie Lazarus-Black examines trends of domestic violence in the English-speaking Caribbean (See *Everyday Harm: Domestic Violence, Court Rites, and Cultures of Reconciliation)*. She has identified the court system of Trinidad to be one of a "culture of reconciliation" where local practices are in opposition to the law but influences the decisions people make regarding violence in their personal lives.

7 The act provided women with the right to seek protection orders, occupation, and tenancy orders that prohibit abusers from being near the victim's home, workplace, or school and violations resulted in a fine of $54US ($10,000G) and imprisonment up to a year.

8 Red Thread has also been involved in anti-violence public education and advocacy over the years, including conducting a radio series and community-based workshops on domestic violence; criminal justice interventions, as well as, producing and disseminating information regarding the Domestic Violence Act of 1996. Furthermore, Red Thread also conducted a survey and published report that included recommendations for addressing institutional and cultural transformation related to women's health and domestic violence in the nation (Trotz, 2004).

9 Forty percent of women surveyed who were experiencing domestic violence sought help from the police, relatives (34 percent), a friend (15 percent), a neighbor (5 percent), a priest (less than 3 percent), or to a counselor (less than 3 percent) (Nelson & Peake, 2000). As a result of this outreach for help, their partners received a warning (40 percent), nothing changed (over 30 percent) or the abuse continued. In 20 percent of the cases, violence decreased as a result of seeking help. Thirteen women who were surveyed went to the police regarding family violence and only seven of their partners were given a warning. Almost 80 percent of women indicated that they did not report their case to the police, and more than 50 percent noted that they had knowledge of where abused women could receive help (almost 60 percent).

10 Gender hierarchy in cultures of reconciliation is shaped by colonialism, slavery and indentureship and is successful in keeping victims out of court systems. This practice of reconciliation is rooted in learned violence for men and gender, as violence is seen as an integral part of Caribbean masculinity (in direct opposition to femininity). Lazarus-Black (2007; 2008) identifies 12 rites of domination that are ingrained within the court system in countries like Trinidad, Jamaica, and Antigua that hinders the implementation of domestic violence legislation allowing victim complaints to simply vanish. Rites of domination are defined as customary or formal actions that occur within and around the legal process that influence the behaviors of survivors of violence.

11 Furthermore, the Guyana Police Force gave 2,000 warnings to men guilty of domestic violence in 2005, up from a little over 1,000 in 2001; however, charges against perpetrators of the crime have held steady at approximately 500 for a period of five years with only slight fluctuations.

12 Given the detrimental impact of domestic violence on health outcomes, medical researchers recommend focused efforts on health provider education and training addressing gender-based violence (Parekh et al, 2012).

References

Baboolal, A. (2016). Indo-Caribbean Immigrant Perspectives on Intimate Partner Violence. *International Journal of Criminal Justice Sciences, 11* (2), 159–176.

Barberet, R. & Baboolal, A. (2020) "The Global Femicide Problem: Issues and Prospects" in *Research Handbook on Gender, Sexuality and the Law*, edited by Chris Ashford and Alexander Maine. Edward Elgar Law and Society Series.

BMJ Global Health. (2020). COVID-19 in the Caribbean region: Indications of gendered nature. https://blogs.bmj.com/bmjgh/2020/03/29/covid-19-in-the-caribbean-region-early-indications-of-gendered-nature/?utm_campaign=shareaholic&utm_medium=twitter&utm_source=socialnetwork

Bobbili, S. & Rodney, R. (April 2020). Violence against women and COVID-19. *Starbroek News*. https://www.stabroeknews.com/2020/04/14/features/in-thediaspora/violence-against-women-and-covid-19/

Buvinic, M., Morrison, A., & Shifter, M. (1999). Violence in Latin America and the Caribbean: A framework for action. *Inter-American Development Bank*. https://publications.iadb.org/publications/english/document/Violence-in-Latin-America and-the-Caribbean-A-Framework-for-Action.pdf

CEDAW (2005). Women's anti-discrimination committee takes up Guyana's periodic report: Strengthening gender equality bodies, combating violence among issues. *UN Press Release WOM/1513*. www.un.org/News/Press/docs/2005/wom1513.doc.htm

Central Intelligence Agency (CIA). (2020). The World Factbook: South America: Guyana. www.cia.gov/library/publications/the-world-factbook/geos/gy.html

DeShong, H. A. F., & Haynes, T. (2016). Intimate partner violence in the Caribbean: State, activist and media responses. *Global Public Health, 11* (1–2), 82–94.

Gender & COVID-19 Working Group. (2020). When home is not a safe place: COVID-19 and domestic violence. www.genderandcovid-19.org/webinar/when-home-is-not-a-safe-place-covid-19-and-domestic-violence/

Help and Shelter. (n.d.). Domestic violence in Guyana. www.hands.org.gy/files/dvguyana.pdf

Help and Shelter (2020, October 3). Help and Shelter concerned about increasing COVID-19 cases and domestic violence. *Kaieteur News*. www.kaieteurnewsonline.com/2020/10/03/help-and-shelter-concerned-about-increasing-covid-19-cases-and-domestic-violence/

Henry, D.E. (2019). More than 50 years since independence, colonial violence plagues Guyana and its diaspora. *Pulitzer Center*. https://pulitzercenter.org/stories/more-50-years-independence-colonial-violence-plagues-guyana-and-its-diaspora

Human Rights Watch. (2020). Women face rising risk of violence during COVID-19. www.hrw.org/news/2020/07/03/women-face-rising-risk-violence-during-covid-19#

Lazarus-Black, M. (2007). *Everyday harm: Domestic violence, court rites and cultures of reconciliation*. Champaign, IL: University of Illinois Press.

Lazarus-Black, M. (2008). Vanishing complainants: The place of violence in family, gender, work and law. *Caribbean Studies, 36* (1), 25–51.

Nelson, C. & Peake, L. (2000) Women researching women: Study on issues of reproductive and sexual health and of domestic violence against women in Guyana. *Red Thread*. www.hands.org.gy/download/wom_surv.htm

Parekh, K., Russ, P., Amsalem, S., Rambaran, D., Langston, A., & Wright, N. (2012). Prevalence of intimate partner violence in patients presenting with traumatic injuries to Guyanese emergency department. *International Journal of Emergency Medicine, 5* (1), 1 5.

Plan-International. (2020). Shadow pandemic unfolding as girls' health rights and freedoms erode. https://plan-international.org/news/2020/05/27/shadowpandemic-unfolding-as-girls-health-rights-and-freedoms-erode/

Reuters COVID-19 Tracker (2022). Latin America and the Caribbean: Guyana. https://graphics.reuters.com/world-coronavirus-tracker-and-maps/countriesand-territories/guyana/

Sayed, T. & Bland, E.B. (2020) Casting light onto the shadow pandemic in the Caribbean: Violence against women. World Bank Blogs: Latin America & the Caribbean https://blogs.worldbank.org/latinamerica/casting-light-shadow-pandemic-caribbean-violence-against-women

Telson, L. (2020). Home not so sweet in times of COVID-19. *Inter-American Development Bank Blog*. https://blogs.iadb.org/caribbean-dev-trends/en/home-not-so-sweet-in-times-of-covid19/

The NGO Caribbean Development Foundation (2009). *Help & Shelter.* https://www.ngocaribbean.org/help-shelter/

Trotz, A.D. (2004). Between despair and hope: Women and violence in contemporary Guyana. *Small Axe: A Caribbean Journal of Criticism, 8* (1), 1–20.

United Nations Development Programme (UNDP). (2013). *Human Development Report: Guyana 2013.* http://hdr.undp.org

United Nations Women (UN Women) (2000). *Committee on the Elimination of Discrimination against Women: Concluding Comments* www.un.org/womenwatch/daw/cedaw/cedaw25years/content/english/CONCLUD NG_COMMENTS/Guyana/Guyana-CO-2.pdf

United Nations Women (UN Women). (2010). *Global Database on Violence against Women.* https://evaw-global-database.unwomen.org/fr/countries/americas/guyana/1996/domestic violence-act-1996

UN Women Global Database on Violence against Women (2016). Ending Violence Against Women. https://evaw-global-database.unwomen.org/en

United Nations Women (UN Women). (2019a). 1 in every 2 women in Guyana will experience Intimate Partner Violence: Guyana's first national survey on gender-based violence Launched. https://caribbean.unwomen.org/en/news-and-events/stories/2019/11/1-in-every-2-women-in-guyana-will-experience-intimate-partner-violence#:~:text=1%20in%20every%202%20women%20in%20Guyana%20will%20experience%20Intimate%20Partner%20Violence,-Guyana's%20First%20National&text=Georgetown%2C%20Guyana%3A%201%20in%20every, (IPV)%20in%20their%20lifetime.

United Nations Women (UN Women). (2019b). *Guyana.* https://evaw-global database.unwomen.org/fr/countries/americas/guyana#2

UN Women COVID-19 Response. (2020). Policy Brief #7: COVID-19 and violence against women and girls: Addressing the shadow pandemic. https://www.unwomen.org/sites/default/files/Headquarters/Attachments/Sectins/Library/Publications/2020/Policy-brief-COVID-19-and-violence-againstwomen-and-girls-en.pdf

United Nations Human Rights: Office of the Higher Commissioner. (2020). COVID-19 measures are gender-blind; increase risk of violence against women, says UN expert. www.ohchr.org/EN/NewsEvents/Pages/DisplayNews.aspx?NewsID=26369&LangID=E

United States Department of State (USDS). (2007). Bureau of Democracy, Human Rights, and Labor Country Reports on Human Rights Practices 2006: Guyana. https://2001-2009.state.gov/g/drl/rls/hrrpt/2006/78894.htm

World Health Organization (WHO). (2005). Guyana Summary Country Profile for HIV/AIDS Treatment Scale-Up. www.who.int/hiv/HIVCP_GUY.pdf

7

INTERSECTIONALITY AS A MEANS TO UNDERSTANDING VIOLENCE AGAINST WOMEN IN BELIZE

Kiesha Warren-Gordon

Belize is a small, English-speaking country located on the northeastern coast of Central America. Boarded by Mexico, Guatemala, and the Caribbean Sea, the country's location, with its year-round warm weather, Mayan temples, and scenic landscapes, makes it a major tourist destination. Although known as one of the most ethnically diverse countries in Central American, with a population made up of seven ethnic groups, each with its unique language and cultural customs, the strong push toward nationalism has created a national identity of being Belizean (McClaurin, 1996). Tourism and agriculture make up major parts of the economic base of the developing country, which has a young parliamentary democracy that consists of legislative, executive, and judicial branches to create, interpret, and enact the laws.

Belize, like other countries throughout the world, struggles with the issue of violence against women, although it has been proactive in attempting to address the problem. In 1992, the Belize Domestic Violence Act was passed, and it was re-enacted in 2007. The re-enacted law extended protection orders for longer periods of time, broadened the category of people who could apply for an order of protection, and included the option to add the requirement of child support. It also included the requirement that the police confiscate any weapon used in a domestic violence incident and required more severe penalties for violating protective orders. The Women's Commission has been instrumental in working to make changes to the laws, as well as to change how people understand violence against women. As a result, they changed the definition of domestic violence to include financial abuse (Canada: Immigration and Refugee Board of Canada, 2012). Changes continued in 2010, when a domestic violence protocol for police officers was developed by the Women's Commission, with the goal of improving the effectiveness of police investigative practices in addressing violence against women. The new protocol included sections such as guiding principles, police response procedures, court orders, and directives on their enforcement, risk assessment, and procedures to submit complaints concerning inadequate police response (Canada: Immigration and Refugee Board of Canada, 2012).

Although the country has enacted laws to combat violence against women and worked to change the way police response to the problem, it continues to be a major social problem in Belize. According to the report 2019 A Glimpse into Gender Issues in Belize by the Women's Commission, in 2018 there were 2,061 domestic violence calls to the police, with 78% of those calls made by women, and there were 143 murders, of which 124 were women.

DOI: 10.4324/9781003264040-9

The vast amount of studies focusing on violence against women in Belize are situated within an anthropological approach (Beske, 2009, 2014; McClaurin, 1996; McClusky, 2001). Although these studies have provided some insight into understanding violence against women in Belize, there is still a lack of understanding how this phenomena occurs, and how law enforcement and other governmental agencies respond, especially in rural communities, from an intersectional perspective.

Intersectionality is a concept rooted within the earliest examinations of black women's marginalization within broader society, and given the label by critical legal scholar Kimberlee Crenshaw (1989, 1991). Crenshaw's (1991) work around intersectionality recognizes that an individual's identity is not based on one singular identity, but on multiple identities, and that those identities often overlap by race, gender, and class disparities. Crenshaw (1989, 1991) identifies three ways in which intersectionality presents itself:

- *Structural intersectionality*, which posits that women of color who live in lower socioeconomic status communities have limited financial resource preventing them from escaping abuse.
- *Political intersectionality*, where existing laws and policies do not recognize the disparities in women's experiences as victims of crime.
- *Representational intersectionality*, the lack of cultural representation in the analysis of violence against women.

Intersectionality has been expounded upon by leading Black feminist scholars such as Patricia Hill-Collins (2015) and Jennifer Nash (2018) as a way to continue to develop an understanding of the ways in which black women are "othered" within feminist discourse. The usage of the term intersectionality has also evolved to examine the multidimensionality that exists within marginalized groups in a society.

This theoretical framework creates an opportunity to understand how the multidimensionality of Belizean women shapes structural, political, and representational aspects of violence, and to provide a robust understanding of Belizean women as victims of violence. Crenshaw's (1991) original analysis focused on Black women in the United States; however, she recognized that intersectionality can be applied to any marginalized group of individuals.

Methodology

This study was part of a larger research project that explored the lived experiences of Belizean women who had been victims of intimate partner abuse. Interviews took place during August 2019 and February 2020, and 12 women who participated in the larger project were the focus of this study. All 12 women had been victims of intimate partner violence and had received support from one of the two support centers in San Ignacio, Belize, with one woman receiving support while still living with her abusive partner. The two centers provide different services. One provides emergency housing and support services for women who are victim of abuse, and the other provides skill training and a supplemental food assistance for children and women. Prior to conducting interviews, I spent significant time with the directors of both programs discussing the services they provide to gain an understanding of the intricacies of each program.

Participants/Interviews

All of the women who participated in the interviews were invited to participate by the directors of the centers. Deferring to the director of each center to identify women who may want to participate helped to ensure that the women were emotionally prepared to share their lived experience.

All of the women described being in long-term relationship with their abusers that began in their teenage years, developed into marriage, and led to between four to ten children. The women's ages were between 26 and 47 years.

Each interview took 90–120 minutes. It was important to me that I spent time with the women having meaningful conversation prior to the interview, so before the start of the semi-formal interview, I spent time with each woman in general conversation. We talked about things such as the weather, hairstyles, parenting, sharing pictures of our children, discussing parts of Belize that I had visited, and parts of the United States. The point of these conversations was to connect with the women in ways that went beyond the interviews. All interviews were conducted in rooms at one of the two centers that provided privacy and would allow for no interruption. All of the women were given Institutional Review Board (IRB) approved consent forms in both English and Spanish. Although it was written on the form, it was also reiterated to the women that choosing to participate or not in the interviews was not related to their ability to receive support services from the center that referred them to me. Along with having consent forms that did not require signatures, I also gave the women the opportunity to not take the consent form with them, recognizing the cultural stigma that exist in Belize around discussing such personal topics. A series of open-ended questions had been established for semi-structured interviews as part of the IRB protocol. However, the intent was to meet with the women and allow for the conversations to develop organically, only using the question protocol if needed. A subset of questions from the larger study addressed issues of intersectionality and was posed using broad, open-ended queries to gain an understanding of the multidimensionality of women who have been victims of intimate partner violence.

Data/Analysis

Each interview was audio recorded and transcribed immediately after the interview. All interviews took place in English, and when the women would code switch into Spanish or Creole clarification was requested. The transcriptions were read over by a Belizean who speaks English, Creole, and Spanish to ensure accuracy. Fearing causing unnecessary harm to the women in having to relive their stories again, I did not ask them to review the transcripts. However, women were offered the opportunity to review the final draft of this chapter for accuracies. The transcriptions were then screened for themes using Berg's (2004) outline for conducting qualitative content analysis. First, transcriptions were screened for themes based on the literature review, research questions, and review of the transcripts. This was followed by developing systematic selection of data chunks, sorting the data chunks in categories, and seeking out patterns based on the various categories. Based on the analysis, there were two themes that emerged: women lacking financial resources, and women lacking trust of judicial system supporting them as abuse victims, with the analytic categories based on the multidimensionality of the participants.

Women Lacking Financial Resources

Financial resources preventing them from escaping abuse was represented in many of the women's shared experiences. All of the women interviewed discussed limited job opportunities affecting their ability to leave the abusive relationships at various points in time. None of the women who participated in this study had completed higher education or vocational training. One participant stated:

> He would lock the door and we could not get out. If we tried to open the door he could tell. I didn't work and he would not give me money. We would look out the window and

> our neighbor would see us. Sometimes she would give us food through the window. I had nothing. [inaudible] my kids would cry.

Another participant conveyed a similar sentiment in regards to lacking financial resources to support herself and her children, and having to make the conscience decision to leave her children with her abusive spouse due to the lack of financial resources. She stated:

> I don't have a job so I just left. I took a bag of clothes and left by myself. He took the kids to his sister. She is good with them and I see them every day. I walk them to school and walk them to his sister's house after school. My house is only one room and I sleep on the floor at his sister's house they have beds.

Another participant stated:

> I had no money and he would not give me any. He bought our food and said I could not have money. We just stayed locked in the house. He would let me take to kids to school and pick them up. With no money, I had nothing.

Women Lacking Trust of Judicial System Supporting Them as Abuse Victims

Some of the participants discussed the lack of trust in police and judicial support regarding seeking support to address their abuse. One participant stated, "I would call the police and tell them that there was a women and children locked in a house and screaming for help. The police never came no matter how many times I called." Other women expressed their distrust for the police by stating, "I will never call the police," and "You call them they do nothing." Another participant discussed her experience with the police resulting in her arrest. She stated, "When they [police] came they took us both. I will never call them again." With regards to seeking support from other judicial branches, only one of the women mentioned getting a restraining order/protection order. She stated, "I went to the police station to have it served and it cost too much. I waited until he was drunk and served him myself." Other women expressed indifference or frustration with the idea of getting a restraining/protective order. For example, "Why get one it won't do anything."

Intersectionality and Violence against Women in Belize

Crenshaw (1991) recognizes that intersectionality can be applied to a marginalized group, and, as a result, the ways in which it presents itself may vary based on the marginalized group and the cultural context in which the group resides. Women lacking the financial resources to make decisions regarding their abuse is a clear indication of their marginalization. Lack of employment opportunities, or other means of financial support, is a clear indicator of women being marginalized in society. All of the women interviewed in this study indicated that they did not work, and, up until they left, they had been financially dependent on their abusers. The lack of financial opportunities for women can also be attributed to the cultural expectation of gender roles, which traditionally frowned upon women working outside of the home. Some of the women who participated in this study also spoke in terms of gender roles contributing to the abuse and expressed understanding that they were expected to maintain the household as part of their responsibility. Although divisions of labor within the household is universal point of discord in countries like Belize where job opportunities are limited, giving women the opportunity to work outside the home can provide much needed income. At the same time, however, it can cause strain in the household due to the women's inability to both maintain the household and work outside the home.

Within this study, women lacking trust in the judicial system to support them as abuse victims is the result of the historical lack of responding to abuse in ways that did not result in revictimization. Although the Belizean government has implemented stricter laws to protect women from being victims of intimate partner violence, a lack of trust continues as there are few women working within the police and the judicial branch of the government. The lack of representation lends to a continuation of distrust in the judicial system for support by this marginalized group. This is also manifested in the lack of support services for women who are victims of intimate partner violence. There are only two shelters in Belize that offer long-term support and shelter for women wanting to escape their abuse. Both located in more populous areas in Belize, one in Belize City and the other in San Ignacio. A country with a population of 396,212, for whom the leading cause of death for women is homicide, must pay extensive attention to women who are victims of intimate partner violence. With 54.28% of the population living in rural communities (IndexMundi, n.d.), outreach and support for women who live in these communities is sparse at best.

Final Thoughts

Being of low social socioeconomic status while being female clearly limits the ability of women to navigate leaving their abusive mates. Belize is a patriarchal society, and men working and being the financial leader in the household is part of the gendered norms of the country. The intersection of being a woman and of low socioeconomic status limits a woman's ability to make a decision. Seeking legal support to withdraw from the abusive mates is difficult to navigate due to the lack of trust in police and limited available resources. Belize is a sparsely populated country, and women living in rural villages do not have access to support for leaving their abusive relationships. While Belize has worked to train some of their police officers on how to deal with intimate partner violence, there is still much work that needs to be done. Not all police receive the training, and for women, who live in rural villages, not only is there limited access to the police, but also very few of those officers have received the intimate partner violence training.

Although this study provides an initial understanding of intersectionality and violence against women in Belize, a larger sample size will provide a more robust understanding of the areas of intersectionality and women in Belize. Within this study, I also attempted to understand if ethnic differences contribute to responses to intimate partner violence. When I asked about the women's race and ethnicity, most of the women responded by stating "Belizean." After reframing the question all of the women respond with their ethnicity, confirming the idea of nationalism, and that many of the women look at their primary identity as Belizean. Future studies should continue to explore the aspect to Belizean culture and expand research questions to address issues of colorism.

Addendum

March 5, 2020, I took a flight from Belize City to Indianapolis, Indiana, after spending time working with survivors of intimate partner violence and those who are working to change the lives of women in Belize. We said our goodbyes and we scheduled dates for my return in May and August. Neither I nor did anyone knew that our lives would change in ways that we had not anticipated and that I would not be making those trips back to Belize. When my plane touched down, I was inundated with news of Covid-19. While in Belize, I had watched a few news stories about the virus but had not paid it much attention. Instead, focusing on my work in the country. Since leaving the country, my contact with my Belizean collaborators have been limited to conversation over WhatsApp, Zoom, and email. I have not had any contact with any of the women who participated in this original study.

Like countries around the world, Covid-19 has impacted every aspect of life in Belize. Belize closed all of its boarders April 8, 2020, and reopened for air travel only on October 1 and has maintained a curfew from 8pm to 5am. Many schools have moved to virtual learning. For women who are living in homes where they are victims of intimate partner violence being confined in a home with their abuser having few options to escape even if temporarily by going to visit friends, family, just being outside, or going to work has increased the rates of abuse. According to López-Calva (2020, November 3), various quarantine lockdown policies such as stay at home orders may not only keep people safe from the virus but also contribute to domestic and gender-based violence. López-Calva (2020, November 3) states,

> Higher levels of social and economic stresses due to the pandemic combined with restricted mobility outside of the home and reduced access to services have created a pressure cooker for potential abuse. In Latin America and the Caribbean, where gender-based violence was already widespread prior to the pandemic and where stringent stay at home orders have been prolonged, this potential is particularly concerning (par 2).

As we continue to understand the impact that Covid-19 is having on various aspects of life, we must continue to develop strategies to support individuals who are living in abusive households. International data suggest that there has been a significant increase in the number of calls into domestic violence hotlines. Future research should look at whether that increase is represented in Belize. Future research should also explore the lived experiences of women who are victims of intimate partner violence while living through a pandemic.

References

Berg, B. L. (2004). *Qualitative research methods for the social sciences* (5th ed.). Pearson.

Beske, M. A. (2009). Applying international human rights laws to promote wellness within the community: On diminishing intimate partner violence in the context of western Belize. *Global Public Health, 4* (5), 490–499. https://doi.org/10.1080/17441690902815447

Beske, M. A. (2014). An Analysis of the Collaborative Endeavors to Lessen Gender-Based Intimate Partner Violence in Cayo, Belize, and a Case for Anthropological Engagement. Gendered Perspectives on International Development Working Papers, 304, 16.

Canada: Immigration and Refugee Board of Canada. (2012, November 21). *Belize: Domestic violence, including state protection*. Retrieved February 29, 2020, from www.refworld.org/docid/53ecbfe34.html

Collins, P. H. (2015). Intersectionality's definitional dilemmas. *Annual Review of Sociology, 41* (1), 1–20. https://doi.org/10.1146/annurev-soc-073014-112142

Crenshaw, K. (1989). Demarginalizing the intersection of race and sex. A Black feminist critique of antidiscrimination doctrine, feminist theory and antiracist politics. *University of Chicago Legal Forum, 1989*, 139–167.

Crenshaw, K. (1991). Mapping the Margins: Intersectionality identity politics, and violence against women of color. *Stanford Law Review, 43* (6), 1241. https://doi.org/10.2307/1229039

IndexMundi. (n.d.). *Belize – Rural population (% of total population)*. Retrieved February 29, 2020, from www.indexmundi.com/facts/belize/indicator/SP.RUR.TOTL.ZS

López-Calva, L. (2020, November 3). *No safer place than home?: The increase in domestic and gender-based violence during COVID-19 lockdowns in LAC*. UNDP. www.latinamerica.undp.org/content/rblac/en/home/presscenter/director-s-graph-for-thought/no-safer-place-than-home---the-increase-in-domestic-and-gender-b.html

McClaurin, I. (1996). *Women of Belize: Gender and change in Central America*. Rutgers University Press.

McClusky, L. J. (2001). *"Here, our culture is hard": Stories of domestic violence from a Mayan community in Belize*. University of Texas Press.

Nash, J. C. (2018). *Black feminism reimagined: After intersectionality*. Duke University Press.

8

THE DANGERS OF BEING A WOMAN IN NICARAGUA

Pamela Neumann

Introduction

Recent statistics show that the Latin American continent is one of the most dangerous for women (Small Arms Survey 2016). In Nicaragua, current scholarly estimates suggest that approximately one out of every three women has experienced some form of physical or sexual violence during her lifetime (Ellsberg et al 2020). Although documented rates of femicide in Nicaragua are lower than its Central American neighbors, the problem of gender-based violence remains quite serious, particularly in terms of the rape and sexual abuse of adolescent girls and women, as well different forms of psychological violence, such as threats and intimidation. Drawing on ethnographic and archival research, in this chapter, I begin by reviewing key aspects of Nicaragua's social and political context, followed by an analysis of existing government data on domestic violence. I then highlight recent political struggles over the country's gender violence laws to show how the Nicaraguan government symbolically and sporadically makes commitments to protect women's rights while simultaneously normalizing and invisibilizing acts of violence against women. In doing so, I also address how government repression in the aftermath of a massive citizen uprising in April 2018 has impacted women's efforts to hold the state accountable for its failure to protect women's right to a life free of violence. Finally, I highlight the impact of two worldwide crises with implications for gender inequality and violence against women: the COVID-19 pandemic and climate change. I discuss the risks that these unfolding social, epidemiological, and environmental disasters pose for the safety and well-being of women and girls in Nicaragua.

Nicaragua's Social and Political Context

Like much of Central America, Nicaragua suffers from high poverty rates and substantial out-migration. Unlike Guatemala, Honduras, and El Salvador, however, Nicaragua has not experienced high levels of criminal and gang violence, nor the same rates of femicide as its northern neighbors. Space does not permit a full analysis of these differences, but it bears noting that Nicaragua is the only country in Central America to have gone through a successful socialist revolution (the 1979 Sandinista Revolution) which led to a number of radical reforms to reduce class and gender inequality in the country during the 1980s.

Throughout the 1990s and early 2000s, Nicaragua was governed by a series of neoliberal administrations focused primarily on reducing Nicaragua's foreign debt by promoting foreign

DOI: 10.4324/9781003264040-10

investment and reducing state funding for health care and education (Babb 2001). It was also during this time (1992) that Nicaragua's first law addressing domestic violence was passed and when women's police stations were first established (1997) (Jubb et al 2008). These latter actions were part of the first region-wide wave of legal and institutional changes to address violence against women that occurred in response to pressure by transnational feminist advocacy networks and the expansion of the human rights framework to include women's rights (Friedman 2009).

The Frente Sandinista de Liberación Nacional (FSLN) returned to power in 2007 under the leadership of President Daniel Ortega, who also had governed the country during the 1980s. However, in the intervening years, Ortega and the FSLN had changed dramatically (Kampwirth 2008). Two of the most important developments with direct relevance to women's rights and gender violence were: (1) Ortega's step-daughter accusing him of sexual abuse in 1998 and the subsequent break between many local women's organizations and the FSLN, and (2) the alliance Ortega developed with the Catholic Church. Since regaining power, Ortega and his wife Rosario Murillo (Vice President since 2016) have utilized a religiously inflected discourse that strongly emphasizes family unity/harmony. In practice, this discourse has led to the marginalization of gender-based violence as a social problem in Nicaragua, one that state officials argue is best resolved through practices like mediation and family counseling (Neumann 2018).

Statistical Snapshot of Gender-Based Violence in Nicaragua

Data on violence against women in early 21st century Nicaragua is highly fragmented. The lack of consistency and transparency in government reports on domestic violence and other crimes against women prevent a clear and comprehensive analysis of domestic violence, either within or across years. For example, the Nicaraguan National Police report the number of femicides (the murder of women on the basis of their gender), rape, aggravated rape, and intimidation/threats against women. The Institute of Legal Medicine (*Instituto de Medicina Legal*, or IML in Spanish) reports the number of forensic evaluations completed for cases of "intrafamily violence" without distinguishing whether the perpetrator is the woman's partner or other family member. The Public Prosecutors' Office [*Ministerio Público*] in their annual reports provides information about the total number of accusations made in "gender-based violence" cases and sometimes reports a total of "major offenses" (e.g. rape, sexual assault) and "minor offenses" (e.g. intimidation, threats, psychological violence) but not always. The Specialized Gender Violence Courts [*Juzgados Especializados en Violencia de Género*] established in 2013 report the total number of cases that enter their docket every year, the number resolved, and the number pending, but no additional information about the characteristics of those cases. Despite these limitations, this section presents the available data on gender-based violence in Nicaragua, with an emphasis on the 2013–2017 period. This period was chosen because it falls neatly between the passage of a key piece of legislation concerning gender-based violence in 2012 (Law 779) and a nationwide civic uprising in 2018 which substantially altered the social and political context of Nicaragua. Subsequent sections discuss both of these bookending events.

Police data on violence against women in Nicaragua is confined to specific crimes: femicide, rape, aggravated rape, and intimidation/threats against women (see Table 8.1). Importantly, no data on intimidation/threats against women was collected prior to 2012 when new legislation expanded the definition of violence against women to more explicitly include these acts of psychological violence. Table 8.1 summarizes the available police data from 2013 to 2018 concerning these crimes against adult women. Sexual abuse against children and youth is also a significant problem in Nicaragua but is beyond the scope of this chapter.

TABLE 8.1 Crimes against adult women in Nicaragua

	2013	*2014*	*2015*	*2016*	*2017*	*2018*
Femicide	31	26	16	11	25	23
Rape	646	550	469	468	396	275
Aggravated rape	480	473	411	346	301	244
Intimidation/threats	6291	6131	3561	2042	2123	1505

Source: Nicaraguan National Police.

There are two noteworthy aspects of the data reported by the Nicaraguan police. The first is the substantial decline in reported cases of intimidation and threats against women beginning in 2015. The stunning drop in such cases (from 6131 to 3561 in 2015) is no doubt in part due to changes in how state institutions dealt with so-called minor offenses beginning in mid-2014. As outlined in more detail below, beginning in August 2014, women reporting minor offenses were often encouraged to engage in mediation or referred to family counseling facilitated by neighborhood leaders or representatives of the Ministry of the Family. Hence, these cases were likely not reported by the police. Moreover, it is possible that as public awareness of these changes grew, fewer women chose to report incidents of psychological violence in the first place. Women's reticence to report was further exacerbated by declining trust in the police following the state's violent repression of mass protests that began in April 2018.

The second important element of the data presented in Table 8.1 concerns the crime of femicide. Since 2014, local women's organizations have disputed the state's official reporting on femicide, arguing that the actual rates of women's deaths is significantly higher (at least double and sometimes triple what the state reports) but the government has limited its count to those cases which involve a pre-existing affective relationship and take place in the private sphere (the home), counting all other murders of women as homicides or parricides (Vásquez 2014). Complicating matters further, the Nicaraguan Supreme Court's reports do not always match the femicide data reported by police. For example, the Supreme Court reported 41 femicides brought to trial in 2014, compared to the 26 reported by the police (Vásquez 2016).

A slightly expanded picture of domestic violence in Nicaragua can be found by examining data compiled by the Institute of Legal Medicine (see Table 8.2), which conducts forensic evaluations of crime victims.

Consistent with research across the world, the data provided by IML demonstrates that women are overwhelmingly the primary victims of domestic violence in Nicaragua. Notably, it also shows that domestic violence by intimate partners comprises approximately 60% of all reported intra-family violence in Nicaragua. Not all women are equally susceptible to such violence, however. Data from the IML consistently highlights that women with lower levels of income and education (particularly those who do not work outside the home) are more likely to experience domestic violence.

Data from Nicaragua's public prosecutors' office (*Ministerio Público*) provides some insight into how domestic violence cases may or may not advance through the legal system (see Table 8.3). However, the MP's annual reports lack comparable figures beyond 2015 for basic measures of interest, such as number of formal charges made. The MP's 2014 report states that the most common *major* offenses are sexual abuse and rape of minors, and the most common *minor* offenses are failure to pay child support, intimidation and threats against women, and psychological violence. Cases involving the failure to pay alimony are the ones most commonly resolved with mediation. MP reports for other years did not include data on most common offenses.

TABLE 8.2 Forensic evaluations in domestic violence cases in Nicaragua

	2014	*2015*	*2016*	*2017*	*2018*
Intra-family violence [total cases]	9067	8823	8047	8531	7629
Intra-family violence [couple only]	5394	5282	4960	4985	4581
Women victims of couple violence	4947	4740	4355	4470	4096
	[91.7%]	[89.7%]	[87.8%]	[89.7%]	[89.4%]

Source: Nicaraguan Institute of Legal Medicine.

TABLE 8.3 Formal charges in domestic violence cases in Nicaragua

	2013	*2014*	*2015*
Charges made in DV cases	8,450	10,310	11,291
Total DV cases	18,919	19,669	14,296
Percentage of DV cases in which charges made	45%	52%	79%

Source: Ministerio Público, Nicaragua.

TABLE 8.4 Court resolution of domestic violence cases in Nicaragua

Year	*Intake (Docket)*	*Resolved from calendar year*	*Resolved from prior years backlog*	*Total resolved*
2014	5440	1112	433	1545
2015	5859	1825	1212	3037
2016	5273	1202	1706	2908
2017	7349	1464	n/a	1464

Source: Poder Judicial de Nicaragua (2014–2017).

The most common reasons why cases do not advance to the stage of formal charges or further, to trial, are due to lack of evidence or witnesses, or because some form of mediation is pursued prior to that step in the judicial process. For example, the MP (2015) reports that in 2015, 2,395 cases were resolved with mediation during the judicial process; in 2016, more than 5,000 cases of gender violence were resolved with mediation (Ministerio Público 2016). Another reason for the relatively low percentage of cases that move beyond the evidentiary stage has to do with the inadequate number of prosecutors needed to represent victims effectively. As of 2015, only 65 out of 153 municipalities in Nicaragua had a dedicated prosecutor's office (Ministerio Público 2015). As of 2016, there were a total of 335 prosecutors for a country of 6 million people (Ministerio Público 2016). This may also partially explain why, even though the MP reports that charges were filed in 11,291 cases in 2015, only 1,994 trials occurred.

The judicial process in Nicaragua moves at an extremely slow pace, creating a substantial backlog of cases, including in the courts specifically dedicated to gender violence cases. A review of annual reports from the Judicial Branch [*Poder Judicial*] shows that the gender violence courts [*Juzgados Especializados de Violencia*] received an average of 5,980 new cases per year between 2013 and 2017 and resolved an average of 1,400 from the same calendar year, or about 23% (see Table 8.4). Gender violence courts hear a number of different kinds of cases, not only related to violence against women, but also cases involving child sexual abuse, for example. However, government reports do not specify the number of each kind of case resolved, nor the type of resolution (e.g. guilty verdicts, sentencing). Nevertheless, one important factor contributing to the low resolution rate is that as of 2016, there were just 17 specialized gender violence courts across the country (Poder Judicial 2016). In provinces or municipalities without a specialized court, local judges hear all criminal cases, including domestic violence cases. These judges may or may not have received specialized training on gender-based violence.

Struggles for Legal Justice: The Fight over Law 779 and Women's Police Stations

Nicaragua passed its first domestic violence law in 1992 and established specialized women's police stations known as *comisarías de la mujer* in 1997 (Delgado, 2003; Jubb et al 2008). Women's police stations were specifically designed to receive domestic violence cases and were comprised not only of police investigators, but also psychologists, social workers, and legal advocates. By 2014, according to the government, every municipality in Nicaragua had its own *comisaría*.

Despite the existence of these institutions, many local women's organizations and activists remained deeply troubled by the ongoing problem of gender-based violence and the impunity with which such crimes were treated. Inspired by similar efforts across Latin America, Nicaraguan women's organizations mounted an extensive campaign to pass a new law that would more comprehensively address both the prevention and punishment of gender-based violence in the country (Neumann 2018). In 2012, following an arduous advocacy campaign, Nicaragua passed its most comprehensive legislation addressing violence against women to date, Law 779 [*Ley Integral Contra La Violencia Hacia Las Mujeres*]. Law 779 was notable for a number of reasons. It criminalized femicide, expanded the definition of violence toward women to include psychological violence and the destruction of women's property, and established specialized prosecutors and courts for gender-based violence cases. One of the law's most important provisions was the elimination of nonbinding mediation agreements, a practice commonly used by Nicaraguan police to settle domestic violence cases but which often put the lives of women at greater risk. Law 779 also radically altered the language of previous statutes, which had referred to crimes against women in terms of "domestic violence" or "intrafamily violence." Under the new law, such crimes were defined as "gender-based violence" or "violence against women." This language recognized the violence to which women are subjected on the basis of their gender, regardless of marital or family status.

Disappointingly for its proponents, the passage of Law 779 in 2012 did not include any additional funding for comisarías, new state prosecutors, or courts specializing in gender violence. Moreover, the law's ban on mediation sparked an immediate backlash from conservatives, religious leaders, and some local attorneys who filed a formal legal challenge to Law 779 with the Nicaraguan Supreme Court. The Supreme Court ultimately upheld Law 779 as constitutional but ordered the National Assembly to revise the prohibition on mediation. The National Assembly soon passed a modified law that permitted mediation under five conditions: (1) the accused has no prior legal offenses, (2) the alleged crime was classified as a "minor offense" with a carceral penalty of five years or less, (3) the women agrees of her own volition to mediate, (4) no previous mediation has occurred between the two parties, and (5) mediation is conducted and documented by the attorney general's office or a judge (Carranza 2013).

In late July 2014, President Ortega issued a special decree setting forth new regulations for the implementation of Law 779 (Decree 42–2014). First, the decree redefined the objective of Law 779 as "to strengthen Nicaraguan families … [and] a culture of familial harmony." Second, it reduced the crime of femicide (originally encompassing the killing of women in either the public or private sphere) to include only the killings of women committed in the home in the context of a pre-existing relationship. Third, it shifted the responsibility for implementing Law 779 from an interinstitutional commission to the Ministry of the Family. The decree stated that women victims would need to engage in neighborhood-based counseling to resolve "family conflict" prior to placing a legal complaint with the police. If neighborhood level mediation was unsuccessful, the case would be referred to the Ministry of the Family and then to the police once all other remedies were exhausted (Romero and Vásquez, 2014).

In October 2014, I attended the inauguration ceremony for the Ministry of the Family's new counseling office at one comisaría in Managua. The comisaría had been freshly painted and decorated with balloons for the event. One wall featured a large bulletin board with several posters. One poster said, "A family united in the love of Christ lasts forever. Give God control of your family today and always." Another featured a black and white drawing likening the ideal relationship between parents and children to the Father, the Son, and the Holy Spirit, known in Christian theology as the Holy Trinity. By the end of 2015, family counseling offices had been established in most municipalities in the country, while women's police stations were on the verge of being shut down completely. Between 2016 and 2019, local media and feminist organizations reported that although there were still some staff working at the comisarias in some places, for all practical purposes, they were unavailable to victims of gender-based violence. The all-encompassing discourse about the importance of "the family" had effectively sidelined women's individual needs and safety.

April 2018 and Its Aftermath: Implications for Gender-Based Violence

In April 2018, a small group of university students and elderly residents gathered in Managua to protest a series of proposed pension reforms announced by the Ortega government which would have increased worker and employer payments but reduced future benefits (Morris 2018). These protests quickly spread across the nation and were met with an unprecedented level of state repression, which included extra-judicial killings, torture, kidnappings, obstruction of medical care, and sexual violence. At least 350 people have died, 2,000 have been injured, and hundreds more have been detained, disappeared, or imprisoned as of this writing (IACHR 2018).

Local women's organizations, which have been openly critical or the Ortega government since 2008, were also integral participants in these demonstrations (Lacombe 2013). Their visible role as dissidents has made them a frequent target of threats, intimidation, and physical violence by police and para-police actors (CIDH 2018). Since the civic uprising of 2018, there is also some evidence that newer kinds of violence have been increasing. For example, a 2019 study found that digital harassment against women in Nicaragua had increased from 57.6% to 73.1% since the crisis began (FUNIDES 2018). In this environment, in which protest has been criminalized and many women's organizations legal status has been eliminated, dozens of feminist activists fled the country in fear for their safety (Regidor 2019; Villavivencio 2018).

For women still living in Nicaragua, the documented role of the police in the violent repression of 2018 raises a number of questions and concerns about the institution's ability to effectively serve women victims of gender-based violence. Even before the April 2018 uprising, police frequently treated women victims with skepticism, condescension, and even outright hostility, expecting them to shoulder many of the burdens of investigating the crimes committed against them (Neumann 2017). Now, as one woman put it, "It's going to take a long time to trust in the National Police. And where are you going to denounce [the crime] if the person who abused you is an officer?" (Fernández 2019). In February 2020, with great fanfare, the government suddenly announced it was "relaunching" the comisarias; every week, one new re-opened comisaria is featured on the government's main media platforms (*El 19 Digital* 2020). However, it remains to be seen whether women will once again seek help from the comisarias and if these institutions will provide women with the assistance they need.

The Gendered Penal Regime in Nicaragua

One of the most common concerns expressed during the political struggle over the scope and application of gender violence law in Nicaragua was the country's lack of prison capacity. More specifically, opponents of the law saw its provisions as so draconian that the number of men who would likely end up behind bars if prosecuted would overwhelm Nicaragua's prison system. Indeed, Nicaragua's prison population nearly tripled over the course of a decade, from 5,610 prisoners in 2007 to 13,007 prisoners in 2016 (World Prison Brief 2016). This figure continued to rise, exacerbated by the detention of hundreds of political prisoners during 2018 (CIDH 2018; Romero 2016).

The overcrowding and other inhumane conditions in Nicaragua's prisons are a significant concern. However, the manner in which such concerns are articulated demonstrates a clear hierarchy in terms of which crimes are "worthy" of imprisonment – or which individuals "deserve" to be behind bars – and which do not. For example, young men involved in neighborhood gangs, petty theft or small-scale drug-dealing have long been disproportionately targeted by Nicaragua's criminal justice system (Weegels 2018); more recently, political dissidents have also been constructed as criminals to justify their arrest or detention (Álvarez 2020). Yet simultaneously, gender-based violence is constructed not as a problem that urgently threatens the security and well-being of women throughout Nicaraguan society, but rather as an issue that merely requires counseling or "working it out," as one police woman I met at a comisaría in Managua put it. These dynamics are indicative of what I call a gendered penal regime, one in which the state minimizes the importance and visibility of crimes against women, thereby justifying and normalizing gender-based violence.

Although the Nicaraguan government has taken the important step of slowly re-opening the comisarías as of February 2020, this is just one step in what will surely be a long process of regaining the trust of women victims of domestic violence. Beyond merely opening the door to a repainted building, it remains to be seen whether the everyday practices of police and other state actors will change in such a way that women victims will feel comfortable seeking out their assistance in the future. Moreover, the government's lack of transparency in reporting violent crimes against women and how they are handled will make assessing its progress difficult. Overall, the criminal justice system in Nicaragua has a long way to go in guaranteeing women victims of violence real access to legal justice.

Domestic Violence in the Era of COVID-19

The COVID-19 pandemic, which began to spread worldwide in March 2020, has had an undeniable effect on the situation of women and girls in Nicaragua. Although official government data is sparse and unreliable, concerning both the spread of the virus and the incidence of violence against women, multiple citizen observatories have continued to document the public health situation with regard to the pandemic as well as gender-based violence. This section briefly summarizes the Nicaraguan government's response to the pandemic since March 2020, publicly available data on violent crimes against women during this period, and the responses of local women's rights groups.

The problem of domestic violence – so often hidden behind closed doors – has become even less visible or harder to detect in places that implemented strict lockdown policies throughout the pandemic. Most of Latin America followed this pattern: closing borders, shutting down businesses, moving schooling online, and enforcing curfews. Nicaragua, however, argued that such measures would jeopardize its already highly precarious economic position. The country has faced an ongoing economic crisis since April 2018 when citizens began protesting proposed reforms to the country's pension system; severe government repression led to a nationwide escalation of demonstrations not only against specific policies but also against the Ortega government itself, which has been in power since 2007. President Ortega justified the government's position rejecting a nationwide quarantine in this way: "We have not stopped working because if we stop working, the country dies, and if the country dies, the people die." (Baltodano 2020a).

The Nicaraguan government projected confidence, arguing that its health care sector was well equipped to deal with any potential outbreaks. However, recent research suggests that this is an overly optimistic assessment of its capacities. For example, Nicaragua has 0.9 hospital beds per 1000 inhabitants (compared to 2.2 for the Latin American region as a whole) and just 160 ventilators, according to estimates by local medical professionals (Miranda Aburto 2020). Throughout the spring and summer of 2020, the Nicaraguan government insisted that COVID-19 cases were minimal and the situation was well under control (Pearson et al 2020). As late as December 2020, the Ministry of Health (MINSA) declared there were just 6,046 cases and 165 deaths in the country (Baltodano 2020b). However, data collected by an independent citizens' observatory (https://observatorioni.org) suggests that actual COVID-19 cases are far higher than MINSA has publicly acknowledged. In a bulletin dated January 15, 2021, the citizens' COVID-19 observatory group reported a total of 12,404 suspected cases and 2,908 deaths due to the virus. This latter number is more consistent with reported cases in neighboring countries like Costa Rica, which reported 12,070 cases as of January 21,2021. Meanwhile, MINSA's own data is no longer accessible online since their databases were hacked during the summer of 2020 (Kincaid 2020).

Violent crimes against women have continued unabated during the pandemic in Nicaragua. Although comprehensive police data for 2020 was not yet publicly available online at the time of this writing, as of August 2020, the Nicaraguan police reported the following statistics:

- 1,166 cases of threats or intimidation against women
- 532 cases of rape
- 505 cases of psychological violence
- 474 cases of sexual abuse
- 102 cases of statutory rape
- 74 cases of severe physical violence
- 11 femicides
- 100 "other crimes" (unspecified) (Policia Nacional Nicaragüense 2020)

The women's police stations also reported that of 7,900 cases sent to the public prosecutor's office, 6,320 were resolved through mediation rather than through criminal proceedings. As noted previously, women's organizations in Nicaragua have been highly critical of the practice of mediation, since it frequently leads to escalations in domestic violence and even femicide. Statistics reported by the Institute of Legal Medicine (IML) also show a slight increase in the total number of forensic evaluations conducted for intrafamily violence in 2020 compared to 2019.

As we know, however, government data can only tell part of the story. In particular, this is because the government's definition of femicide is more limited than the original Law 779 specified. Using the broader definition outlined earlier in this chapter, the Nicaraguan chapter of Catholics for the Right to Decide (CDD) documented 71 femicides during 2020, 39 of which took place in the home and 32 of which occurred outside the home. This total represents eight more murders of women in 2020 than in 2019 and ten more than 2018. CDD also reported a substantial increase in the numbers of *attempted* femicide (115 total), 43 more than in 2019 and 39 more than in 2018.

Many women living with an abusive relationship may not seek help from authorities at all, depending on their circumstances, preferring instead to approach more trusted allies like the Nicaraguan Women's Network against Violence (RMCV). The RMCV reported a 30% increase in the numbers of women seeking help at one of the 29 affiliated centers across the country during 2020.

The pandemic has demanded creativity and flexibility on the part of women's organizations across the country. One of the new steps that these organizations took was to organize a telephone hotline to support women who are not able to leave their homes or do not feel safe doing so in the middle of the expanding pandemic. Through this hotline, women have received both emotional and legal assistance – not only for those women who wish to press criminal charges, but also for those who prefer to pursue child support claims in family court. Feminist organizations have also started a new advocacy campaign to draw attention to the ongoing plight of women, with the tagline "Machismo is a pandemic" (Shiffman 2020).

Domestic Violence and Climate Change: A Dangerous Combination

In addition to the epidemiological crisis presented by the COVID-19 pandemic, women and girls across the world are facing increasing risks to their physical health, safety, and livelihoods due to the unfolding climate change crisis. Rising global temperatures, driven by fossil fuel emissions, have unleashed a broad spectrum of extreme weather events (heat waves, wildfires, hurricanes, cyclones, droughts, etc.), as well as seemingly small shifts in rainfall patterns which are negative impacting both rural and urban areas across Latin America, including Nicaragua (Radel, Schmook, Carte, and Mardero 2018; Reyer, Adams, Albrecht et al 2017). These climate impacts are not distributed evenly, however; they disproportionately fall on already precariously situated communities and social groups – specifically women and girls, especially those living in rural areas (Islam and Winkel 2017). Research suggests that women and girls living in rural areas may be more vulnerable to some of the consequences of climate change because of the "unequal gendered power relations that limit women's access to and control over resources" (Bradshaw 2015; but see Andersen et al 2017).

In terms of extreme weather events, in November 2020, Nicaragua and much of Central America was devastated by two consecutive hurricanes (Eta and Iota). Hurricane Iota (a category 5 storm) was particularly destructive, causing severe damage to local infrastructure as well as agricultural production (including grains, fruits, and vegetables). Nicaragua's national business council (COSEP) estimated that up to 70% of the expected bean harvest could be lost due to the storm (Olivares 2020). These kinds of losses exacerbate food insecurity and economic stress in already struggling households, which can trigger acts of violence against women and girls due to their more vulnerable social and economic position (Camey et al 2020). In many instances, women's vulnerability to domestic violence is linked to their economic dependence on men for survival (Wonders and Danner 2015).

Desai and Mandal (2021: 138) emphasize that women are at high risk of gender-based violence during social and environmental crises because of the ways that such crises contribute to the "sudden breakdown of family and community structures," including access to social services and other kids of community support that previously provided some modicum of protection. Research also shows that women's economic and political rights are less likely to be respected during a natural disaster situation (Detraz and Peksen 2017). Because of the Nicaraguan government's general lack of transparency and accountability, we do not have a comprehensive picture of how natural disasters such as hurricanes may have directly impacted domestic violence rates across the country over the last several years. Based on existing research, however, we would expect to find higher rates of domestic violence in rural and impoverished areas of the country, and/or those most impacted by hurricanes and other climate-related events (OHCHR 2012).

Urban areas are not exempt from the potential negative impacts of climate change. One of the most immediate consequences of climate change for city-dwellers is rising food prices when crop production is reduced due to extreme weather events, or even small changes in the amount and timing of rainfall. The lack of access to adequate amounts of affordable nutritious food can contribute to economic stress for households in these more densely populated areas as well and increase the risk of violence or conflict in the home. At the same time, in many areas of Managua, the capital of Nicaragua, families live in flood-prone areas in structures built with materials (e.g. heavy duty plastic, unsealed wood, sheet metal) that will not withstand severe storm winds or heavy rain. When families are left without adequate shelter (whether or not because of an extreme weather event), this lack of privacy increases the risk of sexual and gender-based violence.

When climate change make already precariously situated people's livelihoods unsustainable, migration levels from those affected countries and regions are likely to increase. In 2019, 3.78 million people from Central America, a region already dealing with high levels of poverty, gang violence, and state corruption, migrated to the United States (Babich and Batalova 2021). A survey by the Food and Agriculture Organization and World Food Program found that a significant number of families said they planned to migrate from the "Dry Corridor" of Central America due to the environmental hardships they were facing (Pons 2021). These numbers are likely to continue to rise as the environmental impacts of climate changes grow more severe, particularly given the small amount of international aid available to assist small farmers in the region with climate-related disruptions (Pons 2021). Migration itself poses grave risks to the safety and integrity of women and girls, who face the possibility not only of robbery, but also sexual assault and/or rape at the hands of cartels, human traffickers, and police (Fernandez 2019; Hallock, Ruiz Soto, and Fix 2018). These risks are heightened when women and girls are forced to live in environments like tents or other outdoor spaces, as thousands of Central American migrants have been forced to over the last several years at the U.S.-Mexico border (Desai and Mandal 2021; Diaz and Dwyer 2021).

Nicaraguans comprise a relatively small percentage of migration to the United States. In 2019, for example, Nicaraguans comprised just 6.8% of total Central American migration to the U.S. (Babich and Batalova 2021). However, thousands of Nicaraguans have fled to other destination countries like Costa Rica and Spain, particularly since the citizen uprising of 2018 (Murillo 2021). Although gangs and cartels do not pose the same threat in Nicaragua as they do to their Central American neighbors, fears of political persecution, ongoing gender and sexual violence, and the search for economic opportunity continues to drive out-migration from Nicaragua. As sea levels rise and extreme weather events become more common, these trends will undoubtedly continue.

Works Cited

Álvarez, Leonor. (2020). "Nicaragüenses siguen en las cárceles por manifestarse contra el regimen de Daniel Ortega." *La Prensa*, 6 May. Online. www.laprensa.com.ni/2020/05/06/politica/2670805-86-nicaraguenses-siguen-en-las – carceles-por-manifestarse-contra-el-regimen-de-daniel-ortega

Andersen, Lykke E., Verner, Dorte, and Wiebelt, Manfred. (2017). Gender and Climate Change in Latin America: An Analysis of Vulnerability, Adaptation and Resilience Based on Household Surveys. *Journal of International Development* 29 (7): 857–876. https://doi.org/10.1002/jid.3259

Babb, Florence. (2001). *After Revolution: Mapping Gender and Cultural Politics in Nicaragua*. Austin: University of Texas Press.

Babich, Erin and Batalova, Jeanne. (2021). "Central American Immigrants in the United States." *Migration Policy Institute*. www.migrationpolicy.org/article/central-american-immigrants-united-states

Baltodano, Isela and Navas, Lucía. (2020a). Daniel Ortega: "No se ha dejado de trabajar, porque si se deja de trabajar el país se muere". 2020. *La Prensa*, Nicaragua. www.laprensa.com.ni/2020/04/15/politica/2662221-daniel-ortega-reaparece- publicamente

Baltodano, Isela (2020b). "MINSA asegura que COVID-19 ha dejado 6046 casos y 165 muertos en Nicaragua." *La Prensa*, 29 December. Nicaragua. Available: www.laprensa.com.ni/2020/12/29/nacionales/2765412-minsa-asegura-que-covid-19-ha-dejado-6046-casos-y-165-muertes-en-nicaragua

Bradshaw, Sarah (2015). "Engendering Development and Disasters." *Disasters* 39: 54–75. DOI: 10.1111/disa.12111

Camey, Itzá C., Sabater, Laura, Owren, Cate, and Boyer, A. Emmett (2020). Gender-based violence and environment linkages. The violence of inequality. *IUCN, Gland, Switzerland*. https://portals.iucn.org/library/sites/library/files/documents/2020-002-En.pdf

Carranza, Miguel. (2013). "Mujeres a mediar tras aprobación de reforma" *El Nuevo Diario*, 25 September 2013. Online: www.elnuevodiario.com.ni/nacionales/297642-mujeres- mediar-aprobacion-reforma/

Comisión Interamericana de Derechos Humanos (CIDH) (2018). "Graves violaciones a los derechos humanos en el marco de las protestas sociales en Nicaragua." Online. www.oas.org/es/cidh/informes/pdfs/Nicaragua2018-es.pdf

Delgado, Violeta. (2003). "The Experiences and Achievements of the Women's Network against Violence." *Envio Magazine*. Online. www.envio.org.ni/articulo/2083

Desai, Bharat and Mandal, Moumita (2021). "Role of Climate Change in Exacerbating Sexual and Gender – Based Violence against Women: A New Challenge for International Law." *Environmental Policy and Law* 51: 137–157.

Detraz, Nicole and Peksen, Dursen (2017). In the Aftermath of Earth, Wind, and Fire: Natural Disasters and Respect for Women's Rights. *Human Rights Review* 18: 151–170. https://doi.org/10.1007/s12142-016-0440-4

Diaz, Lizbeth and Dwyer, Mimi. (2021). "Migrant Camps Swell in Mexican Border Towns as Central American Families Flee." *Reuters*. www.reuters.com/article/us-usa-immigration-mexico/migrant-camps-swell-in-mexican-border-towns-as-central-american-families-flee-idUSKBN2BH3K4

Ellsberg Mary, Ugarte William, and Ovince Junior, et al. (2020). "Long-Term Change in the Prevalence of Intimate Partner Violence: A 20-year Follow-up Study in León, Nicaragua, 1995–2016". *BMJ Global Health* 2020 (5): e002339.

Fernández, June. (2019). "Red Feminista por Nicaragua: 'Nuestro violador es Daniel Ortega'". *Pikara Magazine*. Online. www.pikaramagazine.com/2020/02/red-feminista-por- nicaragua-nuestro-violador-es-daniel-ortega/

Fernandez, Manny. (2019). "'You Have to Pay With Your Body': The Hidden Nightmare of Sexual Violence on the Border." *New York Times*, 3 March. www.nytimes.com/2019/03/03/us/border-rapes-migrant-women.html

Friedman, Elisabeth. (2009). "Re (gion)alizing Women's Human Rights in Latin America." *Politics & Gender* 5 (3): 349–375.

Fundación Nicaragüense para el Desarrollo Económico y Social (FUNIDES). (2018). Violencia de Género a través de la Tecnología. Online. https://funides.com/publicaciones/violencia-de- genero-tecnologia/

Hallock, Jeffrey, Ruiz Soto, Ariel G. and Fix, Michael. (2018). "In Search of Safety, Growing Numbers of Women Flee Central America." www.migrationpolicy.org/article/search-safety-growing-numbers-women-flee-central-america

Inter-American Commission on Human Rights (IACHR). (2018). "Gross Human Rights Violations in the Context of Social Protests in Nicaragua." Organization of American States: Washington, D.C. https://www.oas.org/en/iachr/reports/pdfs/Nicaragua2018-en.pdf

Islam, S. Nazrul and Winkel, John (2017). "Climate Change and Social Inequality", UN Department of Economic and Social Affairs (DESA) Working Papers, No. 152, UN, New York, https://doi.org/10.18356/2c62335d-en

Jubb, Nadine, et al. (2008). "Acceso a la justicia para mujeres en situación de violencia: Estudio comparativo de las Comisarías de la Mujer en América Latina." Quito: CEPLAES.

Kampwirth, Karen. (2008). "Abortion, Antifeminism, and the Return of Daniel Ortega in Nicaragua: Leftist Politics?" *Latin American Perspectives* 35 (6): 122–136.

Kincaid, Jake. (2020). "Anonymous Hack Exposes Nicaraguan Government Secret COVID-19 Data." *Miami Herald*, 28 August. Available: www.miamiherald.com/news/nation-world/world/americas/article245303525.html

Lacombe, Delphine. (2013). "Struggling Against the 'Worst-Case Scenario'? Strategic Conflicts and Realignments of the Feminist Movement in the Context of the 2006 Nicaraguan Elections." *Bulletin of Latin American Research* 33 (3): 274–288.

Miranda Aburto, Wilfredo. (2020). "Hospitales tienen menos de 160 ventiladores para pacientes de covid-19." *Confidencial*, 21 March. Nicaragua. Available: https://confidencial.com.ni/nacion/hospitales-sin-ventiladores-suficientes-pacientes-criticos-por-covid-19/

Morris, Courtney D. (2018). "Unexpected Uprising: The Crisis of Democracy in Nicaragua." NACLA. https://nacla.org/news/2018/07/11/unexpected-uprising-crisis-democracy-nicaragua

Murillo, Alvaro (2021). "Soaring Number of Nicaraguans Seek Refuge in Costa Rica amid Domestic Crackdown." *Reuters*. www.reuters.com/world/americas/soaring-number-nicaraguans-seek-refuge-costa-rica-amid-domestic-crackdown-2021-08-11/

Neumann, Pamela. (2017). "When Laws are Not Enough: Violence against Women and Bureaucratic Practice in Nicaragua." *Social Forces* 95 (3): 1105–1125.

Neumann, Pamela. (2018). "Gender-Based Violence and the Patrimonial State in Nicaragua: The Rise and Fall of Ley 779." *Cahiers des Amériques latines*, 87: 69–90. https://journals.openedition.org/cal/8515?lang=en

OHCHR (2012). "Women and Right to Adequate Housing." United Nations. www.ohchr.org/Documents/publications/WomenHousing_HR.PUB.11.2.pdf

Olivares, Iván (2020). Iota deja más de 1200 kilómetros de caminos destruidos y zonas de cultivos inundadas. *Confidencial*, 22 November. https://www.confidencial.digital/economia/iota-deja-mas-de-1200-kilometros-de-caminos-destruidos-y-zonas-de-cultivos-inundadas/

Pearson, Andy A., Prado, Andrea M., and Colburn, Forrest D. (2020). "Nicaragua's Surprising Response to COVID-19." *Journal of global health*, 10 (1): 010371.

Policia Nacional Nicaragüense. (2020). "Mujeres Nicaragüenses sienten respaldo de nuestro gobierno" www.policia.gob.ni/?p=54736

Pons, Diego. (2021). "Climate Extremes, Food Insecurity, and Migration in Central America: A Complicated Nexus" *Migration Policy Institute*. www.migrationpolicy.org/article/climate-food-insecurity-migration-central-america- guatemala

Radel, Claudia, Schmook, Birgit., Carte, Lindsey, and Mardero, Sofia (2018). Toward a Political Ecology of Migration: Land, Labor Migration, and Climate Change in Northwestern Nicaragua. *World Development*, 108: 263–273. https://doi.org/10.1016/j.worlddev.2017.04.023

Regidor, Cindy. (2019). "Nicaraguan Feminists in Exile: 'While Ortega Remains in Power, Nobody will be Safe.'" *Confidencial*, 5 April. Online. https://confidencial.com.ni/english- nicaraguan-feminists-in-exile/

Reyer, Christopher, Adams, Sophie, and Albrecht, Torsten et al. (2017). Climate Change Impacts in Latin America and the Caribbean and Their Implications for Development. *Reg Environ Change* 17: 1601–1621. https://doi.org/10.1007/s10113-015-0854-6

Romero, Elizabeth. (2016). "Casi 15 mil presos en cárceles de Nicaragua." *La Prensa*, 25 October. Online. www.laprensa.com.ni/2016/10/25/nacionales/2122877-casi-quince- mil-presos-en-carceles-de-nicaragua

Romero, Elizabeth and Martha Vasquez. (2014). "Gabinetes de la familia son 'consejeros'." *La Prensa*, 7 August. https://www.laprensani.com/2014/08/07/nacionales/206623-gabinetes-de-la-familia-son-consejeros

Shiffman, Geovanny. (2020). "El machismo es pandemia: nueva campaña virtual de colectivos feministas." *La Prensa*, 22 September. Available: www.laprensa.com.ni/2020/09/22/nacionales/2723512-colectivos-feministas-lanzan-campana-virtual-el-machismo-es-pandemia

Small Arms Survey (2016). Annual Report. Online. www.smallarmssurvey.org/fileadmin/docs/M-files/SAS-Annual-Report-2016.pdf

Vásquez, Martha. (2016). "Odio es la causa de los femicidios en Nicaragua." *La Prensa*, 29 December. https://www.laprensani.com/2016/12/29/nacionales/2157255-odio-es-la-causa-de-los-femicidios

Vásquez, Martha. (2014). "Si no hay relación de pareja, no tiene porqué ser femicidio." *La Prensa*, 15 July. https://www.laprensani.com/2014/07/15/nacionales/203384-si-no-hay-relacion-de-pareja-no-tiene-porque-ser-femicidio

Weegels, Julienne. (2018). "Implementing Social Policy through the Criminal Justice System: Youth, Prisons, and Community-Oriented Policing in Nicaragua." *Oxford Development Studies* 46 (1): 57–70.

Wonders, Nancy and Danner, Mona J. E. (2015). "Gendering Climate Change: A Feminist Criminological Perspective." *Critical Criminology* 23: 401–416.
World Prison Brief (2016). "Nicaragua." Online. www.prisonstudies.org/country/nicaragua

Government Reports

Instituto de Medicina Legal de Nicaragua (2013–2017). Anuarios. Online. www.poderjudicial.gob.ni/iml/anuarios.asp
Ministerio Público de Nicaragua (2013–2016). Informes Anuales. Online. https://ministeriopublico.gob.ni/informe-anual-2/
Poder Judicial de Nicaragua (2014–2017). Anuarios. Online. www.poderjudicial.gob.ni/die/anuarios.asp
Policía Nacional de Nicaragua (2013–2018). Anuarios Estadísticos. Online. www.policia.gob.ni/cedoc/sector/estd/fich.htm

SECTION TWO

Asia and Oceania

9

RESPONSE TO DOMESTIC VIOLENCE

India

Arundhati Bhattacharyya

I Introduction

Home is a place where a person needs to be the safest as the people residing there are the near and dear ones. But, when they face violence within the four walls of the house, it is very scary. The harm done is at the deeper level. Violence has far-reaching impact on the physical and the psychological arena. It severely strains the emotional plane as their trust level is hit the most. It affects all their inter-personal relationships and their interactions with the outside world. It has adverse effect on the health. The United Nations Declaration on the Elimination of Violence against Women has defined violence against women as physical, sexual or psychological acts or threats of such acts in the public and the private sphere. (Krantz, Garcia-Moreno, 2005) Domestic violence in India is mostly male-to-female violence in India. The Global Gender Gap Report of 2020 held that India ranks 112 among the 153 countries (Dutta, 2020). It is a worst kind of social evil which is committed by the near and dear ones of the victim. National Family Health Survey-4, published by Union Health Ministry in 2018, revealed that every third woman from the age of 15 faced different forms of violence. Physical abuse was reported in 29% and 23% in rural and urban areas, respectively. The perpetrator of the crime for married women, in 83% cases, is present husband. For unmarried women, the perpetrators of physical violence are mother or step-mother, father, step-father, sisters, brothers, and teachers. The situation is so severe that one out of three Indian women has faced violence (sexual or physical) (Saaliq, 2018). Women are considered a threat and usually are given a low position in the power structure in the family, after her marriage (Stephenson, Koenig, Ahmed, 2006).

This chapter deals with the condition of women in India, the role of women's movement in India, laws regarding domestic violence in India, its implementation, and social stigma associated with domestic violence.

II India: Condition of Women

India is a multicultural and multi-lingual society. Rituals and customs followed in one part of the country may not be followed in other parts. The stratification of Indian society, on the basis of caste, creed, culture etc., has made the generalizations difficult to be made.

DOI: 10.4324/9781003264040-12

A Child Marriage and Dowry

Child marriage has been prevalent in India since a long time, though illegal. Child brides are at risk of greater physical and sexual violence in marital relations. It is thought that if the girl's age and education increases, it will be difficult to get a groom. If the groom is available, he may expect a big dowry. Dowry consists of the material possessions that the bride takes with her to the groom's family. At the time of Indian marriage and in other occasions, the paternal family gifts jewellery and assets. This is called *Stridhan*. Though it is called the *stridhan*, which is the property of the bride according to law, but still it actually goes into the hands of the groom and his family. Moreover, the tradition considers that the *stridhan* and the expenditure done during the marriage of the girl is what she can expect from her parents. The father's property should go only to the sons. But, this tradition of leaving aside the women from the father's property has worsened the condition of women, at large. Demands of greater dowry have pushed many Indian women to bear violence within marriage. Dowry deaths are a matter of concern in India.

B Marital Rape

This is not a criminal offense in India. It is assumed that marriage includes consent of the woman to the sexual desires of the husband always. The internalized Indian patriarchal mindset is that even now the wife is the chattel. Section 375 of Indian Penal Code stated that forced sex in marriage is a crime when the wife is under 15 years (Saaliq, 2018). In a study conducted among 1664 married women in Gujarat and West Bengal, two states of India, it was found that 12% and 32% of them faced marital rape frequently and occasionally, respectively. To the study, women who were not familiar with their husband during marriage were more likely to face marital rape. Education can be a protection for unwanted sex (Santhya, Haberland, Ram, Sinha, Mohanty, 2007).

The presumption is that recognition of marital rape would destroy the institution of marriage. To some, marital rape should not be considered a crime because it may create anarchy within the family. The Union government in August 2017 held that the institution of marriage will be destabilized if marital rape is considered a crime. It could be a tool to harass the husband (Former CJI Dipak Misra says Marital Rape should not be a Crime in India, 2019).

The 2013 Criminal Law Amendment does not criminalize marital rape. In India also there have been cases where the woman has faced rape within the sacred institution of marriage. In a case of the Delhi High Court, the Centre has submitted that "what may appear as marital rape to an individual wife, it may not appear so to others". The Supreme Court in *Independent Thought vs Union of India and Anr, 2017* has criminalized sexual intercourse with a minor wife whose age is between 15 and 18 years. But, it has not mentioned regarding marital rape of woman above 18 years of age (Choudhury, 2018).

C "Honour" Killings

Girls or women are killed by members of their family for bringing in shame for the family. It is the version of the family regarding disgrace of the family's honour that pushes them to take the worst step of killing the girl. The girl or the woman may be made responsible for "trivial" reasons. The girl may have been seen with her boyfriend or she may want to marry someone whom her family does not approve or she may have eloped. The woman's "purity" is sacramental. The male in the family has the "responsibility" to protect her "purity". Any "disgrace" for the girl is considered to be disgrace for the family.

D Elder Abuse

Elderly women may face abuse in their homes from their sons, daughters, daughters-in-law, grandchildren or others. India is still a patriarchal society where even now a woman's position in society depends on her husband. Most widows still have a position of second class citizen. She is socialized from young age that she has to depend on father, husband and on her sons. In India, very few women have property in their name. Many are homemakers. So, after their husband's death, they get marginalized and may face torture. They remain silent regarding their pain. They do not report to the police. The Government of India has passed law against elderly abuse. The condition of elderly women is worse than elderly men. Those elderly women who are single, widowed and deserted face several problems (Perappadan, 2016).

III Indian Women's Movement

In the early 1980s, the women's movement brought to glare the serious issue of domestic violence. They supported that every woman has the right to violence-free home. Dowry deaths, bride burning, battering and other abuses were faced by women within the four walls. But, until and unless, women were ready to break the silence and overcome the shame or stigma of accepting publicly that they were facing violence, no one could help them. The support groups helped individual women with legal support and shelter, who suffered from domestic violence. They sensitized the public about the realities of domestic violence. It has been seen that women in India are ready to take action only when the violence has gone beyond the extreme level. Moreover, in most cases, they do not have documentary evidence. The health system is very important in addressing domestic violence. The health providers need to record the history about victimization and recent violent incidents which may merit compensation in divorce and criminal cases. Battered women may go for treatment to the hospital. The pain and trauma due to domestic violence are immense. They may get into self-harming behaviour like refusing to eat and drink water, attempting to suicide, neglecting own health. The Dilaasa centre was established in 2001 as crisis-centre for women based in a public hospital. Women are referred to the Dilaasa crisis-centre from the casualty, inpatient and outpatient departments. Referral process can be tracked now. Doctors and nurses have been already trained to question the patient to identify women under domestic violence. The Management Information System has been modified to include daily record of cases referred to *Dilaasa*. It creates awareness regarding about domestic violence as a public health matter. Feminist counselling helps women facing domestic violence, to locate the problem in the social circumstances and not blaming themselves. The survivors had positive feedback regarding the emotional strength the counselling process had provided. With *Dilaasa's* intervention, success rates of registering complaint with police increase. The success was seen in that another hospital replicated this centre as they were also concerned about the health of the women reporting to the hospital. *Dilaasa* also coordinated with a legal service organization in Mumbai, Majlis; temporary shelters; *MahilaMandals* (Bhate-Deosthali, Sundari Ravindran, Vindhya, 2012).

IV Laws Regarding Domestic Violence

India ratified the Convention on the Elimination of All Forms of Discrimination against Women in the year 1993. Article 15 (2) of the Indian Constitution allows the States to make special provision for women and children.

Domestic violence is considered a crime in India since 1983. A part of the workload of the police relates to cases of domestic violence (Kothari, 2005). Section 498A was added which defined a new cognizable offence, which was "cruelty by husband or relatives of husband". Domestic violence was made a criminal offence. It is specific about cruelty towards married women done by their husband and his family. The police had to take action. In order to support the victim, it allows the woman's family member to complain. The imprisonment could extend to three years and include fine. The definition of cruelty against wife included not only physical harm but also mental harassment.

The Dowry Prohibition Act, 1961 was amended twice in 1980s. Giving and receiving dowry was made a cognizable offence. Section 304B of the Indian Penal Code considered "dowry death" for not less than seven years. It may extend to imprisonment. The burden of proof was on the accused. When a woman dies unnaturally by suicide or murder within seven years of her marriage, it is considered that there must have been some domestic discord.

Protection of Women from Domestic Violence Act, 2005 was passed to uproot domestic violence faced by women. The abuse includes physical, sexual, verbal, emotional and economic forms of violence that women may face within the four walls of the house. It is a civil law which includes those in live-in relationship, joint families and marriages which are legally unrecognized. Traditionally, interference in the domestic privacy was thought to be greater harm than the actual violence committed on women within the four walls of the house. The 2005 Act tried to bridge the gap regarding definition of violence between the public and the private sphere. Objective is protection of victim and not punishment of the perpetrator. It will be done under the area of criminal law. 2005 Act has included the role of the protection officers, service providers, non-government organizations, legal services etc. The registered non-government organization or friend can file a complaint. Both civil and criminal remedies are available. Protection orders, residence order or monetary compensation may be provided. The Act was the result of the success of the long-drawn struggle of the women's movement (Ambast, Sen, 2006). It has provided for emergency relief for those suffering domestic violence. It also provided the right to matrimonial home to the women (Padma, 2012). So, the battered woman could get protection order to end violence at home, continue to stay in the matrimonial home and also not throw the husband behind the bars.

The positive aspect is that the Lawyers Collective monitors the law annually. It brought into notice issues like scarcity of budget, difficulties faced by the protection officers, absence of training regarding the law by the police and the judiciary (Bhate-Deosthali, Sundari Ravindran, Vindhya, 2012). However, the 2005 Act does not include domestic servants, members other than female, or violence against aged male member. Simplification of the procedure of complaint could help.

2005 Act specifically covers right of woman to stay in the matrimonial house. She cannot be evicted from it. If done, she has the right to ask for monetary compensation and safe shelter. She also has the right to seek free legal and medical aid. The Court has the power to pass protection orders. If the protection officer fails to perform the duty, s/he has to face punishment.

2013Justice Verma Committee report on criminal law amendments was submitted to improve condition of women. Many Indian women could not earlier prove their marriage, due to lack of compulsory registration of marriage. It recommended registration of marriage and marital rape to be an offense.

Regarding right to inheritance, the Hindu Succession Act, 1956 was discriminatory to women. The Hindu Succession Act, 2005 gave inheritance rights of daughters in their ancestral assets. Inheritance right was supposed to empower women. But on the contrary, it was seen that female foeticide increased. There was also rise in female infant mortality rates in India. The Economic Survey in 2016–17 substantiated it. Studies by King's College of London and University of Essex also supported this trend. In India, many married women relinquish their hold over their ancestral property (Mehta, 2019). It is thought that in this manner she can keep good relation with her brothers. But, no brother thinks of renouncing the ancestral property for the sake of the married sister to keep good relations. Society has internalized the norm that the son only has the legitimate right on the father's property, not the daughter. When the daughter demands it legitimately, society is still finding it difficult to accept the changing laws. Though slowly, women are becoming aware of their legitimate rights.

V Implementation

Laws can only be effective when the enforcement machinery and the mindset of the people are supportive for proper implementation. Crime against Women Cells has come up in 2010 in the police station of every district, headed by Assistant Commissioner. They have worked sensitively in many cases as mediators.

The neighbours and the community feel that the issue needs to be sorted out within the family. Outside interference will not be appreciated by the family members. But, a campaign called *Bell Bajao*, which stands for ringing the bell, has been started in 2008. Here, intervention of the neighbours is being asked for (Bell Bajao Campaign, 2016). As women usually do not share their saga of pain with others, the incidents grow within four walls of family. So, when outsiders start intervening by just ringing the bell, the perpetrators of violence become aware that people know about their crime. This may prevent domestic violence acts.

Short Stay Homes for women were started in 1969. They cater to women who are facing problem regarding accommodation. They provide medical, counselling and other services.

Even though domestic violence was criminalized through Section 498A and 304B, the patriarchal police prefer conciliation over arrests. In many cases, the judges of the top judiciary have restricted interpretation of cruelty towards women. In the case of *Savitri Devi vs Ramesh Chand and Ors*, it was stated that the definition of cruelty under Section 498A was at a higher degree than civil law (Kothari, 2005).

Misuse of the Section 498A has been done by some women as a bargaining tool for taking vengeance and using it as manipulation against the husband and his family. Misuse of this law has been seen as in most laws. So, misuse of the law is no ground for its abolition. That does not mean that domestic violence law is of no use. It acts as protective armour for many victims of domestic violence.

The police are an important instrument. They should not make arrests indiscriminately. On the other hand, the police, at times, are insensitive to the circumstantial evidence about the wife being killed. They have shown these cases as "suicide". This has been remarked by *Vimochana,* a woman's organization in Bengaluru after survey of cases of domestic violence. In another study by the Tata Institute of Social Sciences and women activists based on police record found that 40% of the women were dead by the time their family lodge complaints against the husbands (Kishwar, 2000).

Social ostracism of the perpetrators of domestic violence is a way out. But, real problem is that the neighbours or the community may be non-intervening or indifferent. Actually, they may enjoy the spectacle. They may also think that beating was justified. Domestic violence can be trivialized not only by the community but also by government actors, like lawyers, police or judges. They may try to maintain unity in family by sacrificing the women.

Legal awareness among women is quite low. It takes a long time for the Courts to adjudicate on cases. Though provision of legal aid is available in India, but women find it difficult to access the Courts. Family counselling centres and family courts have come up. The National Judicial Academy and the State Judicial academies provide capacity building programs, mainly regarding execution of the Protection of Women from Domestic Violence Act, 2005. Trained counsellors regarding domestic violence are less.

National Commission for Women with several non-government organizations has spread awareness of the rights of Indian women throughout the length and breadth of India. *MahilaMandals* or women-community may step in to negotiate and reconciliate. If the woman is perceived to be a good woman performing all her duties, there are more chances that the community will support her. Women may utilize spirituality or religion to cope with domestic violence (Ghosh, 2011).

National Rural Livelihood Mission and other poverty reduction programs do assist in empowering women economically. Women need to be economically independent in order to fight domestic violence.

VI Social Stigma Associated with Domestic Violence

Social stigma is associated with woman fighting domestic violence. They are told to compromise with the situation. Violence by husbands is considered "normal" by the wives in many parts of India. The most common act of violence by husbands is slapping. One in ten women has faced sexual violence committed by their husbands in India. The cycle of domestic violence is repeated in generations. The National Family Health Survey which covered 628,892 households in 2015–16 stated that 54% women and 51% men largely justified domestic violence. In another data, 54.8% of women in the age group of 40–49 supported domestic violence. Overall, 83% and 9% of sexual violence was committed by present and former husband, respectively. For unmarried women, 27%, 18%, 17% and 11% of the perpetrators of sexual violence are relatives, current or earlier boy-friend, friend or acquaintance and family friend, respectively (Saaliq, 2018). A culture of silence and shame are associated with the victims of domestic violence. This crime against women is very much associated with the lower status that women have in the Indian society. Under-reporting of domestic violence is the norm.

The worst part is that women do not seek help when they are abused. They feel that in the eyes of the patriarchal society, it is their responsibility to face the abuses quietly. Women are taught from young age to bear with the injustice of the society. Many women consider that it is their fate that they have to face such violence within the marriage. The real issue is execution of the law.

In India, domestic violence is still considered a private matter, which is supposed to be sorted out among the family members. Outside intervention would make the matters worse. Wife battering is a chronic syndrome. It adds to her powerlessness. Moreover, the police also may ask the victim of domestic violence to compromise or call the offenders to the police station to conciliate. They may exercise discretion to avoid arrest. Many a times, women turn hostile and drop charges. So, the public prosecution rate also gets affected. At the prosecution stage, there are higher rate of dismissal of cases regarding domestic violence (Kothari, 2005).

VII Impact of the Current Pandemic on Domestic Violence

According to the Committee on the Elimination of Discrimination against Women, women are disproportionately affected by gender-based violence. Domestic violence against women in India increases during and after disasters. An example has been given regarding increase in intimate partner violence during tsunami in the Indian Ocean. Intimate partner violence increased from 2005 to 2015 by 48%, according to the study by Rao (Rao, 2020). India declared a "notified disaster" for Covid-19, under the Disaster Management Act, 2005 (Sharma, Talan, Jain, 2020). Quarantine was necessary to prevent the spread of corona virus, but it had disastrous effect on the scenario of domestic violence in India.

With the announcement of lockdown in India due to the pandemic caused by corona virus, the National Commission for Women of India reported that regarding cases of domestic violence, there was 100% rise in complaints. The National Commission of Women launched its national whatsApp number so that registering complaint would be easier. With the relaxation of the lockdown, complaints increased as the victims got an opportunity to come out of the house and contact for help. In May, 2020; there were 552 complaints and in June, 2020, there were 730 complaints (Arora,, 2020). A "shadow pandemic" was being fought within the four walls (Violence against Women and Girls: The Shadow Pandemic, 2020). It was reported that complaints of domestic violence went up tenyear high during the lockdown due to Covid-19. This was just the tip of the iceberg. Overall, 76.6% women who suffered domestic violence remained silent. They did not seek help from anyone. Only 14.3% asked for help. Out of them, only 7% sought assistance from authorities, like police, lawyers. Others asked for help from neighbour, friends and immediate family (Radhakrishnan, Singaravelu, 2020).

There were restrictions on movement due to the lockdown. With some abusive men staying indoors 24x7, it led to violence against women residing in the house. Victims, at times, found it difficult to report the crime as the abuser was always stalking her. They even could not contact their natal families, who could assist in reporting the crime. Pandemic could also lead to unemployment. Increase in male unemployment leads to rise in violence against women, but increase in unemployment for women leads to decrease in violence against women (Bhalotra, Kambhampati, Rawlings, Siddique, 2019). The explanation could be that men may feel greater frustration with their rising unemployment as they fail to serve as a breadwinner. They also think that they are losing ability to control. This feeling transforms in the form of increase in male violence against women (Schneider, Harknett, McLanahan, 2016).

In India, 38% of women have telephones and lesser have internet connection. So, it was difficult for them to reach the National Commission for Women through whatsApp. Another big obstacle for remedial action for redressing grievances for domestic violence was that Protection of Women from Domestic Violence Act was not declared as an essential service during lockdown in India. So, the protection officers and the non-government organizations could not reach the victims in order to help them (Arora, Jain, 2020).

India tried to solve the challenge of domestic violence with One stop centres, Ujjawala homes, Emergency Response Support System etc. Several state governments took up the initiative, like Odisha Police Phone-up programme; campaign by the Uttar Pradesh police of "Suppress corona, not your voice"; Akshara centres of the Maharashtra government, women's tele-counselling facility of the Kerala government (Nikore, 2020).

However, the actions could be improved by publicizing the phone numbers of the protection officers, utilization of Nirbhaya fund, the corpus fund of 10 billion, founded by the Government of India; increase in resources available to the non-government organizations which provides legal aid, counselling etc. Several non-government organizations like Jagori, Swayam, in such trying situations, are trying their best to reach out to the victims of domestic violence. The Aman network has advised to build a shelter home for the victims of domestic violence in Kashmir (Mittal, Singh, 2020). There is need for holistic reform to arrest domestic violence during the pandemic of corona virus.

VIII Impact of Climate Change on Domestic Violence

Globally, climate change can cause gender-based violence. Droughts and bushfires may increase domestic violence in the rural areas (Climate Change Increases the Risk ofViolence against Women, 2019). Violence is a tool to negotiate power (Duncombe, 2020). Due to natural disasters, like floods, famine, parents are forcing their girl child to get forcibly married. Such marriage tends to lead to greater domestic violence, where the girl does not have any support from her parents. With climate change and terrible extreme conditions, women and girls have to walk further to collect food, water or firewood. In this process, they may be vulnerable to sexual violence (Well, 2020). Climate change may increase the household chores which make the married girls become tired and try to remain away from sex. This may lead to domestic violence on them. Extreme climate leads to poor harvest and poverty. Men as provider become frustrated and turn to alcohol. This may lead to increase in domestic violence within the four walls (Gevers, Musuya, Bukuluki, 2020). Women are heavily burdened with responsibilities with extreme hazardous physical conditions (Chan, 2020).

There is need for greater involvement of women in protection of the climate. Existing inequalities of power increase with climate change (Chan, 2020). Two issues of climate change and domestic violence need to be addressed together (Well, 2020). That will lead to better policy making and implementation. The civil society needs to be roped in to deter domestic violence due to climate change. Female networks help in coping up with the increase in domestic violence. They are forming groups to share labour and child care.

IX Conclusion

Domestic violence is indefensible crime. But, toleration of domestic violence has been advised by many conservative quarters in order to protect the Indian family-structure. Even when women are injured, the decision to go to the hospital is taken by the mother-in-law or other elderly members in the family. It has been found that education helps in creating awareness and increase in reporting of domestic violence. Higher levels of education do not automatically translate into lower domestic violence. Patriarchal socialization is entrenched in the Indian social system (Saaliq, 2018). Indian woman has the right to have violence-free home. It has to be provided by the family, State and society. If community is backed by the media in the campaign against domestic violence, India's women's condition may be better off.

References

Ambast, S., & Sen, S. (2006). Into the "Private" — The Domestic Violence Act, 2005. *Student Bar Review*, 18, 112–123.

Arora, K., & Kumar, S. (2020, August 3). *Locked-down: Domestic Violence Reporting in India during COVID-19.* Retrieved September 5, 2021, from Oxfam India: www.oxfamindia.org/blog/locked-down-domestic-violence-reporting-india-during-covid-19

Bell Bajao Campaign. (2016). Retrieved April 21, 2020, from Global database on Violence Against Women: https://evaw-global-database.unwomen.org/pt/countries/asia/india/2008/bell-bajao--ring-the-bell--campaign-on-domestic-violence

Bhalotra, S., Kambhampati, U., Rawlings, S., & Siddique, Z. (2019). Intimate Partner Violence: The Influence of Job Opportunities for Men and Women. *The World Bank Economic Review*, 35, 461–479.

Bhate-Deosthali, P., Sundari Ravindran, T. K., & Vindhya, U. (2012). Addressing Domestic Violence within Healthcare Settings: The Dilaasa Model. *Economic and Political Weekly*, 47, 66–75.

Chan, E. (2020, March 9). *How climate change affects women more—and why they need to be listened to.* Retrieved September 9, 2021, from Vogue: www.vogue.in/culture-and-living/content/why-does-climate-change-affect-women-more

Choudhury, S. (2018, October 29). *Why Criminalisation of Marital Rape is Still a Distant Dream in India.* Retrieved March 16, 2020, from Business Standard: www.business-standard.com/article/current-affairs/why-criminalisation-of-marital-rape-is-still-a-distant-dream-in-india-118102900084_1.html

Climate Change Increases the Risk of Violence Against Women. (2019, November 25). Retrieved September 9, 2021, from United Nations Climate Change: https://unfccc.int/news/climate-change-increases-the-risk-of-violence-against-women

Duncombe, J. (2020, February 6). *Violence Increases with Climate Change.* Retrieved September 9, 2021, from Eos: https://eos.org/articles/violence-increases-with-climate-change

Dutta, D. (2020, February 13). *Sexism in Economy: Women's Unpaid Care Work is still not Acknowledged or Paid.* Retrieved May 10, 2020, from Feminism in India: https://feminisminindia.com/2020/02/13/sexism-economy-womens-unpaid-care-work-not-acknowledged-paid/

Former CJI Dipak Misra says Marital Rape Should Not be a Crime in India. (2019, April 9). Retrieved May 8, 2020, from Scroll. https://scroll.in/latest/919482/former-cji-dipak-misra-says-marital-rape-should-not-be-a-crime-in-india

Gevers, A., Musuya, T., & Bukuluki, P. (2020, January 28). *Why climate change fuels violence against women.* Retrieved September 9, 2021, from UNDP: www.undp.org/blogs/why-climate-change-fuels-violence-against-women

Ghosh, S. (2011). Watching, Blaming, Silencing, Intervening: Exploring the Role of the Community in Preventing Domestic Violence in India. *Practicing Anthropology*, 33, 22–26.

Implement Steps to Curb Domestic Violence during Covid-19 Lockdown: High Court to Centre, Delhi Govt. (2020, April 20). Retrieved April 22, 2020, from The Economic Times: https://economictimes.indiatimes.com/news/politics-and-nation/implement-steps-to-curb-domestic-violence-during-covid-19-lockdown-high-court-to-centre-delhi-govt/articleshow/75249397.cms

Indian Women Spend 16 Billion Hours a Day Doing Unpaid Care Work. (2019, June 8). Retrieved May 10, 2020, from The Times of India: https://timesofindia.indiatimes.com/india/indian-women-spend-16-billion-hours-a-day-doing-unpaid-care-work/articleshow/69699732.cms

Kishwar, M. (2000). *Laws against Domestic Violence: Underused or Abused?* Retrieved March 16, 2020, from India Together: www.indiatogether.org/manushi/issue120/domestic.htm

Kothari, J. (2005). Criminal Law on Domestic Violence: Promises and Limits. *Economic and Political Weekly*, 40, 4843–4849.

Krantz, G., Garcia-Moreno, C. (2005). Violence against Women. *Journal of Epidemiology and Community Health*, 59, 818–821.

Lal, N. (2020, April 17). *India's 'Shadow Pandemic'*. Retrieved May 4, 2020, from The Diplomat: https://thediplomat.com/2020/04/indias-shadow-pandemic/

Mehta, R. (2019, July 29). *Whether you are a wife, daughter or mother, find out what you are entitled to and how you can claim it.* Retrieved May 8, 2020, from The Economic Times: https://economictimes.indiatimes.com/wealth/plan/inheritance-rights-of-women-how-to-protect-them-and-how-succession-laws-vary/articleshow/70407336.cms

Mittal, S., & Singh, T. (2020, September 8). *Gender-Based Violence during COVID-19 Pandemic: A Mini-Review.* Retrieved September 6, 2021, from Front. Glob. Women's Health: www.frontiersin.org/articles/10.3389/fgwh.2020.00004/full

Nikore, M. (2020, November 24). *With Covid-19, comes the "Shadow Pandemic": How the surge of domestic violence gripped India's women in 2020.* Retrieved September 5, 2021, from The Times of India: https://timesofindia.indiatimes.com/blogs/irrational-economics/with-covid-19-comes-the-shadow-pandemic-how-the-surge-of-domestic-violence-gripped-indias-women-in-2020/

Padma. (2012). Addressing Domestic Violence within Healthcare Settings: The Dilaasa Model. *Economic and Political Weekly*, 47, 66–75.

Perappadan, B. S. (2016, August 16). *'Situation worse for old women in India'.* Retrieved May 12, 2020, from The Hindu: www.thehindu.com/news/cities/Delhi/'Situation-worse-for-old-women-in-India'/article14572641.ece

Radhakrishnan, V., & Singaravelu, N. (2020, June 24). *Data | Domestic violence complaints at a 10-year high during COVID-19 lockdown.* Retrieved September 6, 2021, from The Hindu: www.thehindu.com/data/data-domestic-violence-complaints-at-a-10-year-high-during-covid-19-lockdown/article31885001.ece

Rao, S. (2020). A Natural Disaster and Intimate Partner Violence: Evidence over Time. *Social Science and Medicine*, 247.

Ratnam, D. (2020, April 26). *Domestic violence during Covid-19 lockdown emerges as serious concern.* Retrieved May 10, 2020, from The Hindustan Times: www.hindustantimes.com/india-news/domestic-violence-during-covid-19-lockdown-emerges-as-serious-concern/story-mMRq3NnnFvOehgLOOPpe8J.html

Roy, L. D. (2020, April 7). *Domestic Violence Cases across India Swell since Coronavirus Lockdown.* Retrieved April 22, 2020, from Outlook India: www.outlookindia.com/website/story/india-news-rise-in-domestic-violence-across-all-strata-of-society-in-the-coronavirus-lockdown-period/350249

Rukmini, S. (2020, April 18). *Locked down with abusers: India sees surge in domestic violence.* Retrieved May 4, 2020, from Al Jazeera: www.aljazeera.com/news/2020/04/locked-abusers-india-domestic-violence-surge-200415092014621.html

Saaliq, S. (2018, February 8). *Every Third Woman in India suffers Sexual, Physical Violence at Home.* Retrieved April 21, 2020, from News18.com: www.news18.com/news/india/the-elephant-in-the-room-every-third-woman-in-india-faces-domestic-violence-1654193.html

Santhya, K. G., Haberland, N., Ram, F., Sinha, R. K., & Mohanty, S. K. (2007). Consent and Coercion: Examining Unwanted Sex among Married Young Women in India. *International Family Planning Perspectives*, 33, 124–132.

Schneider, D., Harknett, K., & McLanahan, S. (2016). Intimate Partner Violence in the Great Recession. *Demography*, 53, 471–505.

Sharma, G. D., Talan, G., & Jain, M. (2020). Policy response to the economic challenge from COVID-19 in India: A qualitative enquiry. *Journal of Public Affairs*, e2206.

Sharma, P. (2020, April 20). *Delhi HC asks Centre to convene high-level meet to address domestic violence during lockdown.* Retrieved April 22, 2020, from Live Mint: www.livemint.com/

Stephenson, R., Koenig, M. A., & Ahmed, S. (2006). Domestic Violence and Contraceptive Adoption in Uttar Pradesh, India. *Studies in Family Planning*, 27, 75–86.

Violence against Women and Girls: The Shadow Pandemic. (2020, April 6). Retrieved August 16, 2020, from UN Women: www.unwomen.org/en/news/stories/2020/4/statement-ed-phumzile-violence-against-women-during-pandemic

Well, D. (2020, March 4). *Explained: How climate change leads to more violence against women, girls.* Retrieved September 9, 2021, from Indian Express: https://indianexpress.com/article/explained/how-climate-change-leads-to-more-violence-against-women-girls-6299011/

10

COMBATING DOMESTIC VIOLENCE AND SEXUAL AND GENDER-BASED VIOLENCE DURING CONFLICT

The Case of the Rohingyas in Myanmar and Bangladesh

Tonny Kirabira and Fiza Lee-Winter

> "The most significant and common reports of abuse of power include; paying for Bangladeshi nationality papers, diversion of aid, and **sexual exploitation and abuse**."
> ~ *Aung Tun, Rohingya refugee from Cox Bazar, Bangladesh (Milko, 2019).*

Introduction

Even though domestic violence (DV) and gender-based violence (GBV) can affect anyone, according to the United Nations Office of the High Commissioner for Human Rights (OHCHR, 2014), majority of the victims are women and girls. This is further supported by the compilation of worldwide data of the various forms of violence against women (VAW) on UN Women's "Facts and Figures" webpage. The European Institute for Gender Equality (EIGE) further confirms that, regardless of the terminology used, whether DV, GBV, or VAW, it is mostly inflicted on women and girls, by men, describing it as a phenomenon that is "deeply rooted in gender inequality, and continues to be one of the most notable human rights violations within all societies."

According to a UN Human Rights Council (UNHRC) Report titled *Sexual and Gender-Based Violence in Myanmar and the Gendered Impact of its Ethnic Conflicts*, "ethnic [Rohingya] women and girls are doubly victimized" because DV and GBV crimes are perpetrated not only *internally* (within the home), but also *externally* by military forces like the Tatmadaw and ethnic armed organizations (EAOs) (UNHRC, 2019, p. 3). The Rohingyas have been persecuted for generations (Smith & Hassan, 2012, pp. 11–17); but their plight has only recently gained international attention following bouts of sectarian violence stemming from inter-communal conflict since the rape and murder of Thida Htwe, an ethnic Arakanese Buddhist woman in May 2012, allegedly by three Muslim men (ibid., pp. 18–19). Ensuing violence occurred in the following years with two waves of extreme violence and "clearance operations," once in 2016, and the other in 2017, against the Rohingya population in Rakhine state, which was further "accompanied by systematic and widespread sexual and gender-based violence [SGBV] against Rohingya women and girls" (UNHRC, 2019, pp. 19–25). As a result, displacement in the region exacerbated and the region saw "the largest and swiftest refugee exodus" with at least half a million Rohingya refugees fleeing Myanmar into neighboring Bangladesh, joining the "more than 300,000 refugees already in Bangladesh from previous waves of displacement" (United Nations High Commissioner for Refugees [UNHCR], n.d., p. 84). Observers also note that "[t]he widespread threat and use of sexual violence were a driver

DOI: 10.4324/9781003264040-13

and 'push factor' for forced displacement on a massive scale, and a calculated tool of terror aimed at the extermination and removal of the Rohingya as a group" (Quadir, 2017).

Myanmar is a nation made up of hundreds of ethnic minorities; however, the Rohingyas have been excluded and are not considered to be Burmese—the 1982 Citizenship Law has effectively rendered the Rohingyas stateless by depriving them of full citizenship rights, which subjects them to discrimination and other abuses, which include "restrictions on their freedom of movement, discriminatory limitations on access to education, and arbitrary confiscation of property" (Human Rights Watch, 2000, pp. 9–15).

According to Roy (2020), the Rohingya are among the four major Muslim groups residing in the Arakan region. However, there is a historical controversy over the origin of the term "Rohingya" itself, with some scholars linking it to an Arakanese word *Rwa-Haung-ga-kyar*, which means "[t]he Tiger from the Old Village" (p. 9). Due to varying interpretations of early and modern Arakan history, "most citizens of Burma ... do not acknowledge the term Rohingya ... claiming that they [the Rohingyas] are all illegal migrants from what is now Bangladesh," despite the term having been used in published research since the 18th century (Smith & Hassan, 2012, pp. 11–12). In addition, Myanmar's citizenship policies have been a key source of social and political conflict since the 1970s, according to Arraiza and Vonk (2017, p. 2), arguing that the nation is in urgent need for a citizenship law reform which would help guide Myanmar in its democratization process (ibid., pp. 14–15).

Notwithstanding, due to the persistence of military domination within the administration, despite undergoing a democratic transition, promoting legal accountability for GBV and other human rights violations remains a massive challenge; and for the Rohingyas, this is further exacerbated due to their disenfranchisement (International Crisis Group, 2019). To make matters worse, those who have managed to cross the border and sought refuge in Bangladesh are also not afforded a recognized legal status despite Bangladesh's respect for *non-refoulement*, a universally acknowledged legal principle that obligates states to protect refugees fleeing from persecution who are already within their territory from being sent back. Since they "are officially registered as 'Forcibly Displaced Myanmar Nationals [FDMN],' a designation that denies their refugee status and any rights attached to that status" (Frelick, 2018, p. 42), the Rohingyas often find themselves caught in limbo.

Further compounding this is an aspect that cannot be ignored—culture. "Rohingya women suffer systemic gender discrimination as a result of Government policies and practices" (UNHRC, 2019, para. 57) including having limited access to formal education, further confining them to traditional gender roles, "rendering them more prone to gender discrimination" (ibid., para. 56) within their families and out in the society. Ozaki and Otis (2017) explain that aspects of patriarchy are embedded within cultures where traditional gender roles play a dominant role in the family dynamics (pp. 1078–1081; see also Schroeder et.al., 2017, pp. 1–2), confirming the vulnerabilities of the Rohingya women and the unique challenges they face, which further emphasizes the need for us to understand the intersectionality of the factors affecting them.

Most of the Rohingya refugees who have fled to Bangladesh reside in makeshift settlements in Cox's Bazar (United Nations Office for the Coordination of Humanitarian Affairs (UN OCHA), n.d.b.). Not only are they exposed to crowded and generally poor living conditions, there is limited access to food, clean water and sanitation, and basic healthcare, amongst other urgent needs. Further worsening an already dire plight, the Cox's Bazar region is geographically susceptible to torrential rains, landslides, and flooding, particularly during the monsoon seasons. Moreover, the flimsy nature of these temporary shelters—which were built on top of steep hillsides—along with erosion and land slippage further threaten the lives and safety of these refugees (Inter Sector Coordination Group [ISCG], 2020, pp. 14–16). Based on a June 2018 World Bank report, there are fears that "the hilly tracts of Cox's Bazar could foster an environmental crisis brought on by indiscriminate deforestation and vanishing groundwater reservoirs" which would make the region more prone to climate change effects in the long run, especially affecting temperature and precipitation levels, which will then impact living standards adversely (see also Vyawahare, 2018). During the Covid-19 pandemic, Rohingya refugees in Cox's Bazar not only faced reduced access to basic services, but existing hardships were also intensified through the disruption of "self-reliance and income-generating activities and reduced access to basic services" (Rahman et. al., 2020). Ultimately, a link can be made between these humanitarian challenges and the vulnerability of Rohingya women and girls.

This chapter aims to contribute to a better understanding of the approaches needed in addressing SGBV during periods of conflict through a thorough discussion of the factors leading to the intensified vulnerability of women and girls as victims of conflict. It proposes additional humanitarian joint-response approaches that ensure meaningful victim participation and empowerment, highlighting the importance of addressing it through a socio-legal lens while remaining cognizant of exogenous factors such as public health and climate change issues which can put a damper on existing efforts.

Sufficient Normativity?

A strong legal framework is a key pillar in all efforts to provide protection from DV, SGBV, and VAW crimes. This capacity lies primarily within the domestic laws, complemented by the different regional and international treaties and conventions that have been ratified by the situation states, in this case, Myanmar and Bangladesh, as well as the application and enforcement of such laws. Beyond the contemporary state practice of maintaining national law and order, the international human rights regime obligates states to refrain from certain actions, while positively affirming human rights. Both Myanmar and Bangladesh are states party to the Convention on the Elimination of All Forms of Discrimination against Women (CEDAW), the Convention on the Rights of the Child (CRC), and the International Covenant on Economic, Social and Cultural Rights (ICESCR), international treaties that are most relevant to the legal discussion in this section of the chapter (UN Treaty Collection) (UNGA, 1966).

Relevant to the Rohingyas, as laid out in the 2019 UNHRC Report, "[i]international human rights law prohibits SGBV in all its forms" (para. 26). In addition, the CEDAW requires states parties to the convention to prevent SGBV against women and girls as a form of discrimination (CEDAW Committee General Recommendation No. 35), and specifically for Myanmar, this "[does] not cease in periods of armed conflict" (UNHRC, para. 28), something the government has failed to uphold (ibid., para. 98). The CEDAW Committee (2016a,b) expressed particular concern at:

> Continuing sexual violence perpetrated by the military and armed groups against rural women and ethnic minority women, in particular in Kachin, Kayah, Kayin Mon and Rakhine States; widespread impunity enjoyed by perpetrators of such violence as well as threats and revictimization of women who attempt to report such cases; the low rate of prosecution of perpetrators of gender-based violence against women, in particular when such crimes are committed by the military and armed groups; and the conferment of immunity on perpetrators of crimes of sexual violence (see CEDAW Committee, Concluding observations on the combined fourth and fifth periodic reports of Myanmar, 2016, para. 26 (a)).

The report provided further recommendations which suggest a need for Myanmar to provide protection to the Rohingya and other ethnic minorities from DV, SGBV, and VAW crimes, as obligated under international human rights law (Ibid., para. 27). Meanwhile, Bangladesh's reservations to especially Articles 2 and 16 (1) (c) of the CEDAW further contradict the state's commitment to the convention (CEDAW Committee, Concluding observations on the eighth periodic report of Bangladesh 2016, para. 8; also see Khan, 2019). According to Professor Dr. Shahnaz Huda of Dhaka University's law department, in a study she and her colleagues conducted, concerning the legal implications of said reservations: "Hindu women are not allowed to get divorced, and outdated inheritance laws remain in place which deprive women from their right to property" (UNDP Bangladesh, 2019).

Human rights are indeed interdependent and interrelated, in that each right contributes to the realization of a person's human dignity—the fulfillment of a certain right often depends, whether wholly or in part, upon the fulfillment of others. Besides CEDAW, there are two additional international treaties that set standards for state practice, namely the ICESCR and the CRC. The UNHCR Myanmar Fact-Finding Mission team, in its 2019 SGBV report concluded that:

> The Myanmar Government's failure to cease, prevent and take action against sexual and gender-based violence targeting the Rohingya since at least 2012 marks a dismal failure on its part to respect and protect human rights under international law, including its treaty obligations under the [CEDAW], for its use of sexual violence as a prohibited form of discrimination, and under the [CRC], for its use of sexual violence against girls that amounted to sexual abuse, arbitrary deprivation of life, torture or other ill-treatment.
>
> *UNHRC, 2019, para. 98*

The ICESCR complements CEDAW in providing adequate protection ensuring women's equality (Brown & Aggarwal, 2013, pp. 12–14). In particular, Article 12 of the ICESCR places emphasis on "the highest attainable standard of physical and mental health," and Article 19 of the CRC requires states to protect children from sexual abuse; both of which were violated by the government of Myanmar and Bangladesh (UN Committee on Economic, Social and Cultural Rights [CESCR], 2018]; see also UNHRC, 2019, paras. 29–30. Further discussion on right to life and the progressive realization of other rights, see Lee-Winter et al., 2021).

In November 2019, The Gambia filed a suit against Myanmar before the International Court of Justice (ICJ), asserting that it committed acts of genocide against members of the Rohingya community, in violation of the Genocide Convention (*The Gambia v. Myanmar,* Request for the indication of provisional measures, 2020). Among other crimes, The Gambia also contended that Myanmar's military committed acts of rape and other forms of sexual violence against the Rohingya (ibid., para. 29). On 23 January 2020, the ICJ issued provisional orders for Myanmar to comply with its obligations under the Genocide Convention, including the prevention of acts or measures intended to prevent births within the group i.e. Rohingyas (ibid., para. 79). However, Myanmar's Independent Commission of Enquiry (ICOE) rejected the allegations of SGBV crimes (see Global Centre for the Responsibility to Protect and the Global Justice Center, 2020). In general, the ICJ case is part of the international human rights regime, requiring Myanmar to prevent and redress acts of SGBV.

In addition to these international laws, Myanmar derives key guidelines from the regional framework of the Association of Southeast Asian Nations (ASEAN, 2016). However, the 2013 Declaration on the Elimination of VAW and Elimination of Violence against Children in ASEAN (2013 ASEAN Declaration on VAW/VAC), which was built upon the 2004 Declaration on the Elimination of VAW in the ASEAN Region, is legally non-binding. ASEAN is also known for their "soft" approach of non-interference in the domestic affairs of member states (Bui, 2016, pp. 114–118). This is reflected in the 2016 ASEAN Regional Plan of Action on the Elimination of Violence against Women (ASEAN RPA on EVAW)—ASEAN member states (AMS) are presented with a guideline and "calls [the states] for the adoption and full implementation of legal frameworks to hold perpetrators to account and ensure the effective administration of justice" (p. 16). There is unfortunately no regional complaints mechanism for victims to seek justice, with enforcement of laws highly dependent on strength and effectiveness at the national level, further illustrating a regional regime that does not offer concrete protection against DV, SGBV, and VAW (ibid., 2016).

Myanmar has a highly fragmented legal system, due to multi-ethnic social customs and traditional culture for women. This translates into a host of laws which only offer piecemeal protection against DV, SGBV, and VAW crimes (UNHRC, 2019, pp. 6–10); these include the Maternal and Child Welfare Association Law 1990, the Buddhist Women's Special Marriage Law 2015, the Monogamy Law 2015, the Population Control Law 2015, and the Religious Freedom Law 2015 (White, 2015, pp. 10–21). In addition, Myanmar's constitution does provide for fundamental rights including equal rights of women and men (Constitution of the Republic of the Union of Myanmar 2008, Art. 22) and the Penal Code provides for protection against DV/SGBV offences like wrongful restraint, wrongful confinement, rape, procuration of minor girls, and assault (Penal Code of Myanmar, Sec. 369). Recently, the draft bill, Prevention and Protection of Violence against Women (PoVAW), was introduced but its substance remains unclear since it has been in development since 2013 (UNHRC, 2019, para. 34).

It is imperative that the Myanmar's PoVAW meets international human rights standards and best practices, as outlined in the preceding discussions of this section. A legal analysis of the PoVAW reveals significant concerns about its vague terminology and definitions (see Global Justice Center, 2020). According to the Global Justice Center, the law is inconsistent and vague in its definition of crimes and terms like rape and consent (ibid., pp. 2–3). A key recommendation is that the PoVAW is amended in line with international standards like the Rome Statute's broad definition of rape to include any form of

> penetration, however slight, of any part of the body of the victim or of the perpetrator with a sexual organ, or of the anal or genital opening of the victim with any object or any other part of the body.
>
> *Ibid., p. 4; see also International Criminal Court (ICC), Elements of Crimes, 2011, Article 7 (1) (g)–1*

These observations follow earlier recommendations for Myanmar by the CEDAW Committee, to align its laws and definition of rape within the CEDAW Convention and international standards (see CEDAW Committee Report 2016, para. 27 (a))

Besides amending the definitions and terms, another recommendation requires for clarification that the PoVAW law supersedes any contradictory laws (Global Justice Center, 2020, p. 5). A strong and clear legal framework is a key pillar in all efforts to provide protection from DV, SGBV, and VAW crimes for the Rohingyas and other ethnic minorities in Myanmar.

At the domestic level, Bangladesh's Constitution provides for equal protection before the law and an explicit prohibition of gender-based discrimination (Constitution of the People's Republic of Bangladesh, Art. 27–29). DV is defined under the DV Prevention and Protection Act to include physical abuse, psychological abuse, sexual abuse, or economic abuse (2010, Sec. 3). Furthermore, sexual abuse and sexual harassment are prohibited under the Prevention of Women and Child Repression Act 2000 (amended in 2000 and 2003), while dowry-related DV is addressed under Section 5 of the Dowry Prevention Act (2018). Owing to the prevalence of acid throwing as a form of DV/GBV, Bangladesh enacted laws to combat the crimes (The Acid Crime Control Act 2002 and Acid Control Act 2002). The Human Trafficking Deterrence and Suppression Act of

2012 further criminalizes acts of sexual exploitation and labor exploitation (Sec. 3). DV and GBV are also addressed within the law on sexual crimes under Section 375 of the Penal Code 1860 of Bangladesh. It is important to note that Bangladesh is not a member state of ASEAN and therefore not bound to any regional obligations.

Research in radical feminism reveals a prevalence of DV and SGBV in Bangladesh which are deeply rooted in gender norms and social practices under the patriarchal societies (Banerjee, 2020, p. 6). Similarly, early and forced marriages are also considered among the major causes of DV and GBV in Bangladesh (ibid., p. 5). Although marital rape is criminalized under the Penal Code of 1860, it is generally argued that it is impossible to prosecute an offender under this provision, since consent to marriage is also perceived as consent to sexual intercourse, within the traditional Bangladeshi society (ibid., p. 5). Many victims often remain silent because of fear of societal perceptions and compromise in their marriages (Stake et al., 2020, p. 2). Ultimately, a successful implementation of legal frameworks on DV, SGBV requires an understanding of the underlying societal practices and challenges.

Based only on a simple observation of available laws between Myanmar and Bangladesh, it can be said that the more effective DV/SGBV/VAW protection would be derived from Bangladesh's legal framework (see preceding analysis).

However, despite the available normative protection, simply on the basis of the law being there, Rohingya women and children remain unprotected because of their status, or rather, lack thereof as discussed previously; the Rohingyas are not citizens of Myanmar, and Bangladesh does not recognize them as refugees (Swazo, 2020, p. 6). Putting this into context, national laws of both Myanmar and Bangladesh do not offer them adequate protection. Further, even though Myanmar is not a state party to the 1961 Convention on the Reduction of Statelessness, Article 15 of the Universal Declaration of Human Rights (1948) recognizes the right to nationality—this right establishes the most explicit protection for the Rohingyas under international law, based on moral state obligations, as acknowledged by legal scholars (Parashar & Alam, 2018, p. 103). Additionally, also relevant for the Rohingyas, the prohibition against torture is non-derogable (Torture Convention, Art. 2). This normative language assumes causal linkages between state policies and current approaches toward SGBV and VAW. However, the next section highlights a dissonance between the legal norms and local realities.

Responses and Practices toward Achieving Adequate Protection

In order for rights to be meaningful, it first has to be operationalized (Crawley, 2017, pp. 5–6). The Rohingyas really have very limited recourse to justice, whether on-the-run, or in refugee camps (UNHRC, 2019, para. 219). In a 2018 UNHCR review titled *Culture, Context and Mental Health of Rohingya Refugees*, within refugee camps, "Rohingya women and girls are frequently subjected to multiple forms of abuse including harassment, economic deprivations and psychological and physical violence." Along with inadequate medical expertise available, prevailing culturally linked behaviors (such as under-aged marriages for girls who have been raped in order to preserve the family honor and men exhibiting violence and controlling tendencies toward women), and lack of opportunities due to their displacement, Rohingya women are forced to continue to endure physical and mental sufferings (pp. 17–19; see also UNHRC, 2019, pp. 49–51).

Unique to their culture, the Rohingyas rely on the traditional adjudication of disputes by *sordar* or *ukkatas* (in Myanmar) and *majhis* (in refugee settlements in Bangladesh) for cases of DV and intimate partner violence and abuse. Such a system, although informal, has been in place for generations and is traditionally dominated by men with extremely limited participation by women (Tay et al., 2018, pp. 37–38).

Given the limitations and unique needs of Rohingya women and children, current approaches are adapted to the humanitarian context with the goal of "providing culturally relevant Mental Health and Psychosocial Support (MHPSS)" for the Rohingyas. Such a response approach further highlights the need and importance for those involved to understand the "key sociocultural aspects of mental health and wellbeing" in order to provide effective culturally informed services (ibid., pp. 6–8).

A joint-agency GBV sub-sector in Cox's Bazar was established in May 2017 "to prevent and respond to Gender-Based Violence through strengthening community-based GBV programming" (GBV Sub-sector UNFPA, 2017). The group is made up of more than 30 standing member organizations; including participation from UN, non-governmental organizations (NGOs), both international and local, as well as government agencies that are operating in the Rohingya refugee camps and the surrounding affected host community locations. Image 10.1 shows the various activities provided which include psychosocial support, women's empowerment, and the distribution of dignity kits (see image below; on dignity kits) (Dignity Kit Guidance Note: Rohingya Crisis Response, Bangladesh, 2017), see also (United Nations Office for the Coordination of Humanitarian Affairs [OCHA], 2017).

In order to enhance protection and reach as many women and girls as possible, GBV-Service facilities have been set up within the mega-camp, including a *Safe Space for Women and Girls* (SSWG), a safe haven where Rohingya women and girls can find sanctuary from the lawless environment of the camp and support for services including healthcare, psychosocial support, and counseling (Indramalar, 2019; see also Hendessi & Higelin, 2019, p. 9; Marsh, 2019). More than that, the SSWGs are also places where Rohingya women and girls can get empowered through receiving vocational training, as explained by UNICEF Spokesperson, Karen Reidy.

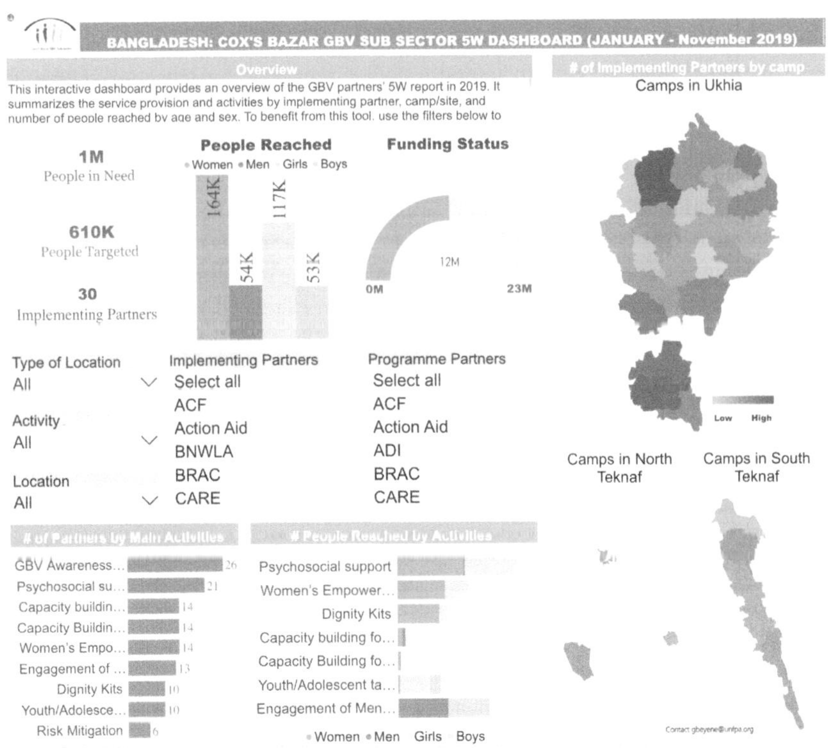

IMAGE 10.1 5W Dashboard by GBV Sub Sector, Cox's Bazar, Bangladesh, OCHA (UNFPA, 2017).

> For adolescent girls, the safe space literally keeps them from being solicited for marriage. 'Child marriage is a big issue in the Rohingya community and also in the Bangladeshi community in the Cox's Bazar area where more than 50% of girls under 18 are married. Poverty is the main driver for child marriages ... families are already struggling to survive and if their daughters are married off, they have one less mouth to feed. Once the girls reach puberty, they start attracting a lot of attention. And so, some stay in the shelters to avoid being harassed. In the Safe Spaces, they can socialize without fear', explains Reidy.
>
> *As cited in Indramalar, 2019; see also UNHRC, paras. 215–216*

However, providing effective services comes with some challenges, which impede the delivery of especially MHPSS services. In an effort to advance the push for accountability toward GBV acts/crimes, a feedback and complaints mechanism has been set up by the GBV sub-sector, according to a 2018 joint-agency research report titled *Rohingya Refugee Response Gender Analysis*. However, the research results revealed that many victims do not know how to submit feedback as they have been poorly informed as to how they can access such services, making it highly likely that many cases are still under-reported. It is important to note that although suggestions to improve the service offering has been made, they are highly focused on information dissemination issues (Toma et al., 2018, pp. 8–9) without considering the relevant factors such as barriers to help-seeking behavior, confidentiality and reprisal concerns, as well as associated stigma (Tay et al., 2018, p. 35; see also Marsh, 2019). It was also found that for cases that do get reported, information was held at the *majhi* level (Toma et al., 2018, p. 9) and *majhis* "have a disproportionate degree of power, and reports have emerged of [such] abuses of power" (Toma et al., 2018, pp. 9 and 37).

Additional Challenges Impeding Service Delivery

During the COVID-19 pandemic, access to SSWGs were particularly challenging due to Bangladesh's nationwide lockdown. In response, SSWGs are not entirely shut; humanitarian staff on the ground ensure that critical GBV and child protection services remain available at all times for those who need them (Jean, 2020a). "While group activities have been discontinued at Safe Spaces for Women and Girls [to minimize the spread of coronavirus], critical services do remain available to address individual needs for new and existing GBV survivors" Gertrude [Mubiru, a Gender-Based Violence Specialist with UNICEF in Cox's Bazar] (as cited in Jean, 2020b).

Because the refugee settlements are located in an area prone to natural disasters such as landslides and floods, the WASH (water, sanitation, and hygiene) sector faces added challenges in maintaining structural WASH facilities in order to adequately address the vulnerabilities of the refugee population. A recent study by WaterAid Bangladesh reveals a host of menstrual health and hygiene (MHH) related challenges, further made worse when Bangladesh entered a nation-wide lockdown (WaterAid Bangladesh, 2020).

While these issues (safety/security, thus protection from DV/SGBV and MHH) may seem separate, they are actually inter-related due to high level of observance and respect for traditional and conservative culture and the practice of *Purdah*, which is the screening of women from men and strangers through the usage of curtains in the home or by way of conservative clothing such as the abaya (Toma et al., 2018). The inevitable link between traditional culture and safety concerns has thus contributed to the unequal access women have to WASH facilities, impacting their ability to manage their MHH, which is a cause for public health concern vis-à-vis gender equality.

Land shortage and crowded spaces means a lack of clean and available facilities—"[l]and shortage in the camp areas hampers effective sludge management. The latrines have shallow pits and are located close to water points, resulting in further contamination of the tube-wells" (Banerjee, 2019;

see also Akhter et al., pp. 3–4). Unsafe and insecure sanitation alone creates several major issues especially in the context of MHH. First, many girls and women have to walk long distances at night to use the facilities. This creates a security risk, as they need someone to move around with in order to avoid becoming victims of SGBV. The second issue relates to their privacy and dignity, which is limited by the inadequacy of the facilities as well as their locations—there were "reports of males holding phones over the top of bathing facilities to take photos when women or girls are using them" (House, 2019, pp. 37–38). Further, Bangladesh's prevention and response plans have largely "overlooked the question of how women and girls would access the facilities and resources needed to manage their periods safely and privately under such restrictive conditions" (WaterAid Bangladesh, 2020).

Currently, NGOs have adopted female-driven participatory approaches in the designing of new sanitation facilities. This new approach was introduced after several women expressed fear about a lack of privacy. Adopting such approaches illustrates that it is vital, especially in contexts of displacements, to design and develop both culturally inclusive and gender-sensitive WASH mechanisms. More significantly, this has led to the construction of a "communal female-friendly WASH unit comprised of separate toilets, a shower stall and a laundering area, all within one structure"—as a Rohingya woman explained, a multi-function design would ensure "nobody would recognize whether I'm going to use the latrine, bathing space or for this [managing my menstruation] reason." Another approach to address these challenges was through the use of community leaders that have personal relationships with many Rohingya girls and women. Additionally, they are able to help sensitize the wider communities about the importance of supporting each other in terms of MHH. These also help to alleviate the gender stereotypes surrounding girls' ages and marriage, as well as other relevant topics (Schmitt et al., 2021).

Other major challenges include a lack of coordination and cooperation amongst stakeholders and involving organizations, a lack of qualified and available MHPSS professionals and specialists, a lack of case detection and referral systems at the community-level, weak inter-sectoral connections (Tay et.al., 2018, p. 40), and most importantly, culturally related challenges which include language barriers and acceptance of concepts and methods of intervention programs (ibid., pp. 44–45). It is imperative that MHPSS stakeholders understand and take into account "culturally sanctioned norms and practices about gender roles and structural gender inequality within a traditionally patriarchal society" (ibid., p. 45) in order for services to be fully accepted by the intended beneficiaries, requiring "efforts from MHPSS workers to work *with* [the] Rohingya refugees and not merely *for* them" (ibid., p. 46).

Conclusion and Recommendations

This chapter has shown us that a better understanding of the various factors is needed in addressing SGBV during periods of conflict. This is crucial especially when we include additional challenges associated with and brought about by the Covid-19 pandemic as well as climate change. It is easy to say that not enough is being done, especially if only viewed from the legal perspective, but changing harmful social and traditional norms, especially that DV is seen as an acceptable social norm, is an important aspect not to be overlooked, especially for the Rohingyas (Toma et al., 2018, pp. 6–8). The idea behind empowerment is that Rohingya women and girls are provided with the first skills they need so that they can change their situation, as exemplified in a recent agreement between the United Nations Population Fund (UNFPA) Bangladesh and the local government, "to implement the Gender-Based Violence (GBV) component of the World Bank Funded Emergency Multi-sector Rohingya Crisis Response Project (EMCRP) project" (UNFPA, 2019).

In exploring unique solutions, there is no one single solution that will fit. Additional efforts which are culturally sensitive and respecting gender-sensitivities should always be considered. However, with that said, a balance must be struck—efforts should also focus on eliminating gender inequalities. For example, stakeholders can reach out to boys in providing them with support (not just SGBV MHPSS services) through various intervention programs with the goal of changing the dominance of patriarchy in their society, and not just to girls as a protection mechanism, as in SSWGs. In improving legal capacities, due to the restricted movement within refugee camps, Bangladesh, as host state, should ramp up additional efforts to strengthen DV/SGBV victims' access to justice; for example, by introducing mobile case mediation for disputes in the camps to even out the imbalance of power possessed by the *majhis*.

These efforts, wholly, are a long-term process that will not yield results overnight; proving even more so the importance to look at the DV/SGBV/VAW through a socio-legal lens, with the aim of providing a suite of culturally suitable responses. Moreover, the regional regime is also lackluster in providing adequate protection. In the end, the law only protects so much, especially if one is stateless, and changing perceptions is a challenge in and of itself. For the Rohingyas, it is an ongoing struggle—but it is a fight that must continue to be fought.

References

Acid Control Act 2002 (Bangladesh).

Acid Crime Control Act 2002 (Bangladesh).

Akhter, M., Uddin, S. M. N, Rafa, N., Hridi, S. M., Staddon, C., and Powell, W. (2020). Drinking Water Security Challenges in Rohingya Refugee Camps of Cox's Bazar, Bangladesh. *Sustainability, 12* (18). https://doi.org/10.3390/su12187325

Arraiza, J. M. & Vonk, O. (2017). *Report on Citizenship Law: Myanmar [Country Report 2017/14]*. European University Institute (EUI). https://cadmus.eui.eu/bitstream/handle/1814/48284/RSCAS_GLOBALCIT_CR_2017_14.pdf?sequence=1

Association of Southeast Asian Nations (ASEAN). (2016). *ASEAN Regional Plan of Action on the Elimination of Violence against Women (ASEAN RPA on EVAW)*. www.asean.org/wp-content/uploads/2012/05/Final-ASEAN-RPA-on-EVAW-IJP-11.02.2016-as-input-ASEC.pdf

Banerjee, S. (2019, July 15). The Rohingya Crisis: A Health Situation Analysis of Refugee Camps in Bangladesh. *Observer Research Foundation—Issue Briefs and Special Reports*. www.orfonline.org/research/the-rohingya-crisis-a-health-situation-analysis-of-refugee-camps-in-bangladesh-53011/

Banerjee, S. (2020). Identifying Factors of Sexual Violence against Women and Protection of their Rights in Bangladesh. *Aggression and Violent Behavior*, 52. 1–7. www.sciencedirect.com/science/article/pii/S1359178919301843#bb0740

Brown, R. and Aggarwal, A. (2013, April). Claiming Women's Economic, Social, and Cultural Rights. *International Network for Economic, Social and Cultural Rights (ESCR-Net) and International Women's Rights Action Watch–Asia Pacific (IWRAW)*. www.escr-net.org/sites/default/files/guide_on_womens_escr_-_final_3.pdf

Bui, H. (2016). The ASEAN Human Rights System: A Critical Analysis. *Asian Journal of Comparative Law, 11* (1). 111–140 https://doi.org/10.1017/asjcl.2016.9

Constitution of the People's Republic of Bangladesh, 4 November 1972, Articles 27–29.

Constitution of the Republic of the Union of Myanmar 2008.

Crawley, H. (2017). Ensuring Respect for Rights in the Provision of Refugee Protection and Assistance: Summary of an Expert Meeting held at UNHCR, Geneva 13 November 2017. *Chair in International Migration Centre for Trust, Peace and Social Relations, Coventry University*. www.refworld.org/pdfid/5a5dbf534.pdf

Declaration on the Elimination of Violence against Women in the ASEAN Region adopted at the 37th ASEAN Ministerial Meeting (AMM) on 30 June 2004.

Domestic Violence (Prevention and Protection) Act, 2010 (Act 58 of 2010). Bangladesh.

Dowry Prohibition Act, 2018 (Act No. XXXV of 1980). Bangladesh.

European Institute for Gender Equality (EIGE). (n.d.). *What is Gender-Based Violence?* Retrieved 11 May 2020, from https://eige.europa.eu/gender-based-violence/what-is-gender-based-violence

Frelick, B. (2018). *"Bangladesh Is Not My Country" The Plight of Rohingya Refugees from Myanmar.* Human Rights Watch. Retrieved 14 May 2020, from www.hrw.org/report/2018/08/05/bangladesh-not-my-country/plight-rohingya-refugees-myanmar

Global Centre for the Responsibility to Protect and the Global Justice Center. (2020). *Q&A: The Gambia v. Myanmar, Rohingya Genocide at The International Court of Justice,* Global Centre for the Responsibility to Protect and the Global Justice Center. Retrieved 01 October 2021 from www.globalr2p.org/publications/myanmarqav2/

Global Justice Center. (2020). Myanmar's Proposed Prevention of Violence against Women Law: A Failure to Meet International Human Rights Standards. Global Justice Center. Retrieved 01 October 2021, from https://globaljusticecenter.net/files/20200710_MyanmarPOVAWlawAnalysis.pdf

Hendessi, M. & Higelin, M. (2019). *A Feminist Approach to Safe Spaces for Women and Girls in Humanitarian Response.* ActionAid. Retrieved 14 May 2020, from https://actionaid.org.au/wp-content/uploads/2019/10/a-feminist-approach-to-safe-spaces-for-women-and-girls-in-humanitarian-response-actionaid-uk-publication_0.pdf

House, S. (2019). Strengthening the Humanity in Humanitarian Action in the work of the WASH Sector in the Rohingya Response: Gender, GBV and Inclusion Audit of the Work of the WASH Sector and Capacity Development Assessment. *WASH Sector Cox's Bazar and UNICEF.* www.humanitarianlibrary.org/sites/default/files/2020/01/House_Humanity%20in%20WASH_Main%20Report.pdf

Human Rights Watch. (2000). Burma/Bangladesh Burmese Refugees in Bangladesh: Still No Durable Solution. Human Rights Watch. www.hrw.org/reports/2000/burma/burm005-02.htm

Indramalar, S. (2019, April 26). Rohingya Girls, Women Vulnerable to Abuse, Rape, Violence in Refugee Camps. *The Star.* www.thestar.com.my/lifestyle/living/2019/04/26/rohingya-women-finding-voice#0xBWq5vK7LKGD6px.99

Inter Sector Coordination Group (ISCG). (2020, January–December). *2020 Joint Response Plan: Rohingya Humanitarian Crisis.* Retrieved 16 January 2021 from https://reporting.unhcr.org/sites/default/files/2020%20JRP%20-%20March%202020_0.pdf

International Court of Justice (ICJ) (2020). *Application of the Convention on the Prevention and Punishment of the Crime of Genocide (The Gambia v. Myanmar) – Request for the indication of provisional measures,* Order of 23 January 2020.

International Criminal Court (ICC), Elements of Crimes. (2011). www.refworld.org/docid/4ff5dd7d2.html

International Crisis Group. (2019). *Peace and Electoral Democracy in Myanmar (Crisis Group Asia Briefing N°157).* https://d2071andvip0wj.cloudfront.net/b157-peace-and-electoral-democracy.pdf

Jean, K. (2020a, April). Essential Protection Services in Rohingya Camps during COVID-19 Lockdown. *United Nations Children's Fund Website.* https://reliefweb.int/report/bangladesh/essential-protection-services-rohingya-camps-during-covid-19-lockdown

Jean, K. (2020b, April 29). Preventing a Silent Crisis for Rohingya Women and Girls during COVID-19 Pandemic. *United Nations Children's Fund Website.* www.unicef.org/coronavirus/preventing-silent-crisis-rohingya-women-and-girls-during-covid-19-pandemic

Khan, M. (2019, March 8). CEDAW at a Dead End in Bangladesh? *The Daily Star.* www.thedailystar.net/star-weekend/news/cedaw-dead-end-bangladesh-1711840

Lee-Winter, F., Kirabira, T., and Collins, L. (2021, April 8). The Right to Live under Threat: On the Armed Forces (The Tatmadaw) Taking Power in Myanmar. *Völkerrechtsblog.* doi: 10.17176/20210408-100939-0

Marsh, S. (2019, December 3). 'My Dignity Is Destroyed': The Scourge of Sexual Violence in Cox's Bazar. *The Guardian.* www.theguardian.com/global-development/2019/dec/03/my-dignity-is-destroyed-the-scourge of sexual violence in coxs bazar

Milko, V. (2019, August 22). 'Conditions Here are Inhumane': Rohingya in Bangladeshi Camps. *Al Jazeera.* www.aljazeera.com/news/2019/08/rohingya-refugees-bangladesh-face-hope-repatriation-190821062348499.html

OHCHR. (2014). Women's human rights and gender-related concerns in situations of conflict and instability. OHCHR and women's human rights and gender equality. Retrieved from: https://www.ohchr.org/en/women/womens-human-rights-and-gender-related-concerns-situations-conflict-and-instability

Ozaki, R. & Otis, M. D. (2017). Gender Equality, Patriarchal Cultural Norms, and Perpetration of Intimate Partner Violence: Comparison of Male University Students in Asian and European Cultural Contexts. *Violence against Women, 23* (9), 1076–1099. https://doi.org/10.1177/1077801216654575

Parashar, A., & Alam, J. (2018). The National Laws of Myanmar: Making of Statelessness for the Rohingya. *International Migration, 57* (1), 94–108. https://doi.org/10.1111/imig.12532

Penal Code 1860 of Bangladesh, Act No. XLV of 1860, 6 October 1860.

Penal Code of the Union of Myanmar of 1861.

Prevention and Suppression of Human Trafficking Act, 2012 [Bangladesh], Act 3 of 2012, 20 February 2012.

Prevention of Women and Child Repression Act 2000.

Quadir, S. (2017, November 12). U.N. Official Says Will Raise Sexual Violence against Rohingya with ICC. *Reuters.* www.reuters.com/article/us-bangladesh-myanmar/u-n-official-says-will-raise-sexual-violence-against-rohingya-with-icc-idUSKBN1DC0N7

Rahman, M. M., Baird, S., and Seager, J. (2020, December 21). COVID-19's Impact on Rohingya and Bangladeshi Adolescents in Cox's Bazar. *UNHCR Blogs.* www.unhcr.org/blogs/covid-19s-impact-on-rohingya-and-bangladeshi-adolescents-in-coxs-bazar/

Roy, S. (2020). The Archaeological and Historical Validation of Rohingya Citizenship in Burma. *International Journal on World Peace, 37* (1), 7–22.

Schmitt M. L., Wood, O. R., Clatworthy, D., Rashid, S. F., Sommer, M. (2021, February 26). Innovative Strategies for Providing Menstruation Supportive Water, Sanitation and Hygiene (WASH) Facilities: Learning from Refugee Camps in Cox's Bazar. *Conflict & Health 15.* https://conflictandhealth.biomedcentral.com/articles/10.1186/s13031-021-00346-9

Schroeder, J.A., Scharff Peterson, D., Osby, O., & Omari, S. (2017). Introduction: International Response to Domestic Violence. In Scharff Peterson, D. & Schroeder, J.A. (Eds.). *Domestic Violence in International Context* (1st ed.). Routledge. https://doi.org/10.4324/9781315618098

Smith, M. & Hassan, T. (2012). *"The Government Could Have Stopped This" Sectarian Violence and Ensuing Abuses in Burma's Arakan State.* Human Rights Watch. Retrieved 14 May 2020, from www.hrw.org/report/2012/07/31/government-could-have-stopped/sectarian-violence-and-ensuing-abuses-burmas-arakan

Stake, S., Ahmed, S., Tol, W., Ahmed, S., Begum, N., Khanam, R., Harrison, M., and Abdullah H., & Baqui, A.H. (2020). Prevalence, Associated Factors, and Disclosure of Intimate Partner Violence among Mothers in Rural Bangladesh. *Journal of Health, Population and Nutrition, 39* (14), 1–11 https://jhpn.biomedcentral.com/articles/10.1186/s41043-020-00223-w

Swazo, N. K. (2020). Special Issue on the Rohingya Crisis. *International Journal on World Peace, 37* (1), 3–6 https://ijwp.org/special-issue-on-the-rohingya-crisis/

Tay, A.K., Islam, R., Riley, A., Welton-Mitchell, C., Duchesne, B., Waters, V., Varner, A., Silove, D., & Ventevogel, P. (2018). *Culture, Context and Mental Health of Rohingya Refugees: A Review for Staff in Mental Health and Psychosocial Support Programs for Rohingya Refugees.* United Nations High Commissioner for Refugees (UNHCR). www.refworld.org/docid/5bbca9377.html

Toma, I., Chowdhury, M., Laiju, M., Gora, N., Padamada, N., Novales, C., Opolot, S., Haider, D., & Debebe, S. (2018). *Rohingya Refugee Response Gender Analysis: Recognizing and Responding to Gender Inequalities* [Research Report]. Oxfam International Policy & Practice. Retrieved 10 May 2020, from https://reliefweb.int/sites/reliefweb.int/files/resources/rr-rohingya-refugee-response-gender-analysis-010818-en.pdf

UN Committee on the Elimination of Discrimination against Women (CEDAW Committee). (2016a). *Concluding observations on the eighth periodic report of Bangladesh.* 65th Session. UN Doc CEDAW/C/BGD/CO/8. 18th Nov 2016. www.refworld.org/docid/583864444.html

UN Committee on the Elimination of Discrimination against Women (CEDAW Committee). (2016b). *Concluding observations on the combined fourth and fifth periodic reports of Myanmar.* 1407th and 1408th meetings. UN Doc CEDAW/C/MMR/CO/4-5. 7th July 2016. https://undocs.org/CEDAW/C/MMR/CO/4-5

UN Committee on the Elimination of Discrimination against Women (CEDAW Committee).. (2017). *General Recommendation No. 35 on gender-based violence against women, updating General Recommendation No. 19.* UN Doc CEDAW/C/GC/35. https://tbinternet.ohchr.org/_layouts/15/treatybodyexternal/Download.aspx?symbolno=CEDAW/C/GC/35&Lang=en

UN Development Program (UNDP) Bangladesh. *Withdrawal of CEDAW reservations is necessary to ensure gender equality.* Retrieved 4 October 2021 from www.bd.undp.org/content/bangladesh/en/home/presscenter/pressreleases/2019/06/24/withdrawal-of-cedaw-reservations-is-necessary-to-ensure-gender-e.html

UN Committee on Economic, Social and Cultural Rights (CESCR). (2018). *Concluding observations on initial report of Bangladesh*. 18th April 2018. UN Doc E/C.12/BGD/CO/1. https://tbinternet.ohchr.org/_layouts/treatybodyexternal/Download.aspx?symbolno=E/C.12/BGD/CO/1&Lang=En

United Nations General Assembly (UNGA) (1984). *Convention against Torture and Other Cruel, Inhuman or Degrading Treatment or Punishment*, 10 December 1984, United Nations, Treaty Series, vol. 1465, p. 85, www.refworld.org/docid/3ae6b3a94.html

UNGA. (1989). *Convention on the Rights of the Child*, 20 November 1989, United Nations, Treaty Series, vol. 1577, p. 3.

UNGA. (1966). *International Covenant on Economic, Social and Cultural Rights*, 16 December 1966, United Nations, Treaty Series, vol. 993, p. 3.

United Nations High Commissioner for Refugees (UNHCR). (2014, October). *Sexual and gender-based violence in the context of transitional justice*. https://www.ohchr.org/en/women/womens-human-rights-and-gender-related-concerns-situations-conflict-and-instability

UNHCR. (n.d.). Global Appeal 2018–2019 | Global Focus (UNHCR Global Appeals). United Nations High Commissioner for Refugees. Retrieved February 29, 2020, from http://reporting.unhcr.org/sites/default/files/ga2018/pdf/Global_Appeal_2018_full_lowres.pdf

United Nations Human Rights Council (UNHRC). (2019). *Sexual and gender-based violence in Myanmar and the gendered impact of its ethnic conflicts*. 42nd Session. 22 August 2019. UN Doc A/HRC/42/CRP.4. www.ohchr.org/Documents/HRBodies/HRCouncil/FFM-Myanmar/sexualviolence/A_HRC_CRP_4.pdf

United Nations Office for the Coordination of Humanitarian Affairs (OCHA): Gender-Based Violence Sub-sector. (2017). *Dignity Kit Guidance Note: Rohingya Crisis Response, Bangladesh*. www.humanitarianresponse.info/sites/www.humanitarianresponse.info/files/documents/files/dignity_kit_guidance_note_23_dec_2017_3.pdf

United Nations Office for the Coordination of Humanitarian Affairs (UN OCHA). (n.d.a). *Gender Based Violence (GBV)*. United Nations Office for the Coordination of Humanitarian Affairs (OCHA). Retrieved 21 May 2020, from www.humanitarianresponse.info/en/operations/bangladesh/gender-based-violence-gbv

United Nations Office for the Coordination of Humanitarian Affairs (UN OCHA). (n.d.b). *Rohingya Refugee Crisis*. Retrieved 2 December 2020 from www.unocha.org/rohingya-refugee-crisis

United Nations Population Fund (UNFPA). (2017). Gender-Based Violence (GBV) Sub Sector Coordination Structure in Cox's Bazaar 2017. United Nations Population Fund. www.humanitarianresponse.info/en/operations/bangladesh/gender-based-violence-gbv

UNFPA. (2019). UNFPA Collaborates with the Government to Prevent Gender-Based Violence in Rohingya Camps. United Nations Population Fund. https://bangladesh.unfpa.org/en/news/unfpa-collaborates-government-prevent-gender-based-violence-rohingya-camps

UN Women. (n.d.). Facts and figures: Ending violence against women various forms of violence. UN Women Website. Retrieved 12 May 2020, from www.unwomen.org/en/what-we-do/ending-violence-against-women/facts-and-figures

Universal Declaration of Human Rights, 10 December 1948, 217 A (III).

Vyawahare, M. (2018, December 19). Cox's Bazar: Rohingya Camp to Be Hardest Hit by Climate Change. *Aljazeera*. Retrieved 3 October 2021, from www.aljazeera.com/features/2018/12/19/coxs-bazar-rohingya-camp-to-be-hardest-hit-by-climate-change

WaterAid Bangladesh (2020), Menstrual Health and Hygiene: Challenges Associated with the COVID-19 Pandemic in Bangladesh, https://reliefweb.int/sites/reliefweb.int/files/resources/Report-%20MHH%20-%20Challenges%20Associated%20to%20COVID-19%20Pandemic%20in%20Bangladesh-.pdf

White, C. (2015). Protection for Whom? Violations of International Law in Myanmar's New 'Race and Religion Protection' Laws. *Georgetown Institute for Women, Peace & Security*. https://giwps.georgetown.edu/wp-content/uploads/2017/10/Violations-of-International-Law-in-Myanmar-2.pdf

11

MALAYSIA RESPONDING TO DOMESTIC VIOLENCE

A Corpus-Assisted Discourse Analysis

Mohd Muzhafar Idrus, Habibah Ismail, Bahiyah Dato Haji Abd Hamid and Ruzy Suliza Hashim

Introduction

Reactions to domestic violence in Malaysia have, to this end, been discussed in three socio-political ways. First, the number of assistance from (non)politically affiliated institutions. Second, (online) grassroots responses to domestic violence. Three, real-life cases captured both on official and nonofficial accounts. When politically affiliated institutions, hegemony-centered or not, disperse directives or tangible links to "understanding" and "addressing" policy and its related interventions (Parliament of Malaysia, 2019), the public, public offenders, crime manipulators, and victims, just to name a few, get a first-hand view of the impact domestic violence has on personal and public levels. This chapter highlights the way in which domestic violence is dealt by taking into account a corpus-assisted discourse analysis across select Malaysian official and non-governmental organizations (NGOs) reports as examples. A corpus analysis, an analysis based on word collocation and frequencies, can describe thematic responses to domestic violence. By looking through the ways of how these reports provide reactions to domestic abuse, we will be able to produce descriptions and representations of recommendations related to domestic violence, exposing the fact that both (non)government documents are essential for successful legal, social, and political relations among the abusers and abused. They are considered integral to putting an end to domestic-oriented politics, so their initiatives with the public are remembered as a union of important consequences. On broader levels, our contribution focusing on corpus-assisted discourse analysis could highlight words and themes surrounding recommendations of dealing with domestic violence, asserting official and NGOs' agency.

The chapter will be outlined as follows; we will firstly begin by presenting official and nonofficial accounts highlighting Malaysian family and community social order. Of particular interest are the ways in which these accounts warrant an investigation into Malaysian responses to domestic violence. Secondly, we will provide backgrounds on corpus employed and the methodology in which corpus-assisted discourse analysis is carried out. After that, we will present our analysis. Implications for future studies, particularly on how these reports articulate reactions to domestic violence, are highlighted. By focusing on corpus-assisted discourse analysis across these reports, we are able to highlight convergence and divergence of points, highlighting implications of Peterson and Schroeder's (2016) work on *Domestic Violence in International Context*. The existing COVID-19 pandemic and the American Psychological Association (APA) guidelines, *Mental Health and Our Changing Climate: Impacts, Implications, and Guidance,* will also be linked to interrogate the spaces

DOI: 10.4324/9781003264040-14

with which the findings of our investigation concerning domestic violence overlap. Through the various multi-faceted elements of the guidelines, we will be able to draw the connections between climate change and the profound and often deadly chaos of domestic violence, as the ensuing discussions will show.

"Strategizing" NGO Report: the Malaysian State of Family and Community Social Order

One of the many noteworthy trends in domestic violence is its interdisciplinary approach. In this chapter, we combine corpus-assisted analysis with discourse analysis to dissect the layers as provided in the reports. In this section, we will present a necessarily brief look at the Malaysian state of community social order and conflict; of the complex relation between particular streams of official, centralized approach and the unofficial, decentralized accounts of reactions to domestic violence.

Firstly, official accounts of responses to domestic violence within the Malaysian landscape suggest growing sensitivities to implicit and explicit effects of domestic violence. Precisely because homes are not the ideal environments for "erupting" violence; in other words, to gain perspectives on domestic violence is not something that can be executed at homes, for its ramifications reach far beyond spouses, children, and community's traumatic experiences. Government bureaucrats debating conflicts and traumatic experiences of domestic violence perpetrators and victims, at times raising concerns, and at other times recommending solutions, are forms of educating public masses on how disputes on domestic violence are treated. *Dewan Rakyat* Hansard, the official records of Parliament proceedings, are among notable examples of how Malaysia deals with and implements some measures of domestic violence issues that both transcend and bridge what it means growing up within volatile landscapes of the world both inside and outside homes. Malaysia structures its governmental offices and puts in place several necessary measures to execute plans to mediate domestic violence. According to the Malaysian Ministry of Women, Family and Community Development (hereafter MWFCD) whose advocacy centers on privileging "caring and developed society" (Ministry of Women, Family and Community Development, 2019), the MWFCD is further aided by its primary department, Department of Social Welfare (DSW, 2019), all of whom came with the holistic and integrative mission to empower "community in need towards social well-being" (DSW, 2019). It is holistic in the sense that they believe domestic violence requires district and regional-based enforcement, citing "every parliamentary constituency" is involved in "intervention programs" (Zainudin, 2019). The enforcement, among other things, is designed to allow victims to file for "safe place," "emergency protection orders," " (interim) protection orders," and "counselling" (My Government, 2019). On various occasions, DSW often holds meetings in which all views could be heard before decisions are made to "complaints," "applications," and "incidents" irrespective of "districts" or "straits" (My Government, 2019). More recently, the global use of hashtags MeToo (#MeToo) and TimesUp (#TimesUp) was also linked to the holistic and integrative approach in navigating the Malaysian landscape of domestic violence (Ministry of Women, Family and Community Development, 2019). These, apart from organizing "legal clinics," "De'Stress Clinics," "Women Anti-Crime Programs," and "Violence Against Women Campaign" properly rank the position of MWFCD and DSW, as they help to amend various laws to mediate domestic violence, including but not limited to Domestic Violence Act (DVA) 1994 and Code of Practice on the Prevention and Eradication of Sexual Harassment in the Workplace (Ministry of Women, Family and Community Development, 2019).

The challenge, as many of these reports have summarized, mirrors major difficulty for carrying out domestic violence duties, as officials and NGOs negotiate sociocultural traditions and worldviews. In other words, many of these responses to domestic violence are essentially understood as an interconnectedness of things, and that household arguments, for instance, are not just about how plain conversations take place. Parents, spouses, (un)married couples, guardians, next-of-kins, just to name a few, often contend that the lack of emotional and psychological channels sends a powerful message to decision-makers, policy-drafters, and government bureaucrats that domestic violence is not just the "tip of the iceberg," but is "out there." This, of course, presents nothing new or an easy feat to execute, given the sociocultural complexities to which one needs to comply. Norms, traditions, moral values, cultural beliefs, and religious precepts governing reactions to domestic violence are complex, yet, official elaborations have documented that actions concerning domestic violence have, more often than not, fraught with difficulties (Ministry of Women, Family and Community Development, 2019). By focusing on elite constructions about their reactions to domestic violence, we will be able to highlight the centrality of the social, emotional, and physical well-being of households by taking Malaysia as an example.

Secondly, discussions surrounding the realities of domestic violence must be accompanied by what is left unsaid. That is, unofficial accounts regarding the prevalence of domestic violence must be situated within profound, intense experiences of the "natural" world, making it relatable to individuals across diverse communities; domestic violence is also contingent upon readings that are freed from the influence of government or officials in power. One does not need to look further for recent examples in Malaysia. A search entry of "domestic violence" across Google platforms can point to multiple, often deadly domestic violence-related experiences. Stories related to domestic violence (Alhabshi, 2019; Indramalar 2018) that range from (1) safety of physical and social environments, (2) physical and social supports, (3) threats to daily, domestic roles and duties, (4) freedom to choose values, beliefs, and skills, and (5) freedom to enhance thinking and emotional values are some but many aspects responsible for the rise in domestic violence and the degradation of victims.

Unofficial interactions involving domestic violence associations can be found everywhere. In 2019, for instance, the Malaysian Women's Aid Organization (WAO) and Women's Institute of Management, for example, have continued to (re)energize responses to adequately align the interests of victims and perpetrators, and their interactions not only call for putting aside race, gender, and religious differences but also illustrate the necessity to address hazardous physical and mental abuse. In her statement, the chief executive officer of the Women's Institute of Management argues, "There should also be programs for men. A lot of them take domestic violence as taboo and don't want to talk about it. You have to face it and win over those who indulges in domestic violence" (Ng, 2019, online Free Malaysia Today). Accounts of domestic violence as seen in the Asia Pacific contexts centralize patriarchy and/or gender politics (Fulu et al., 2013). The following accounts are specifically reproduced to depict how domestic violence is contextualized:

"In many sites, male dominance over women, especially in the family sphere, and normalization of violence" is

> a form of disciplining women and children. Still, there was wide variation by the site in gender attitudes, which appears to reflect genuine differences in how violence against women is viewed across diverse socio-cultural contexts. This may be related to differing social norms, different levels of male domination, gender inequality, and patriarchy across these diverse settings.
>
> *Fulu et al., 2013, p. 66*

Stories as documented by Sahdan, Pain, and McEwan (2021) bear a resemblance to the issue of gender politics. Culled from stories comprising individuals of multi-ethnic backgrounds, Sahdan, Pain, and McEwan (2021) highlighted three important tenets: (1) intimate captivity, (2) abuse, and

(3) symptoms of trauma. For instance, the investigation focusing on the victims' stories highlighted the multivocality of roles played by Malay-Muslim perpetrators who somewhat used religion to "control their wives" (p. 12) and that the ideals of "obedient" women are prevalent at the beginning of marriages to make permanent the subjugation, manipulation, and control over wives (p. 13). The links between spouses' families who meddle in marriages illustrate the peripheralization of the victims as can be seen from the verbatim below:

> He (the husband) always listened to his father and sister. Both of them dislike me. They liked to contact my husband. He (father-in-law) called him (the husband), asked my husband to go to his home. My husband went there, my father-in-law complained, 'You can't allow Chumy to dress up, she can't work, ask her to quit, forbid her from going out, ask her to take care of the kids' ... Even if I'm dead, I will remain as his son's slave (Chumy).
>
> *Sahdan, Pain, & McEwan, 2021, pp. 14 and 15*

The sporadic interactions among activists on their integral contribution to preventing domestic violence bolster the need to acknowledge victims' precarious situations, female or not, and the agencies of these interactions across official and unofficial accounts signify a change in the midst of derangement. And although typically domestic violence victims and survivors are typically female, their classification into distinct groups of people also indicates that domestic violence is also shaped by cultural beliefs and patterns of socialization. In the remainder of this chapter, we hope to contribute to this dialogue on domestic violence and recontextualize the discussions to accentuate the actions as exemplified in reports, official or not. Our analysis introduces readers to a preliminary study on how some of the many interventions placed on understanding and regulating measures on domestic violence are perceived and given due attention. Corpus-assisted discourse analysis, as we shall see, explores some of the many thematic examples of how (non) (official) discourses alert the public about domestic violence, particularly pertaining to the ways of how individuals, couples, spouses, next-of-kin, and children deal with shame, guilt, and vulnerability. In other words, corpus-assisted discourse analysis may explain the preponderance of word choices, including their related phrases and expressions that form reactions to domestic violence.

The Corpus

Reports which contain the keyword, domestic violence, were collected to build the Reports on Domestic Violence corpus (RDV corpus, hereafter). By combining official and non-government reports, two sub-corpora, NGO reports sub-corpus and government report sub-corpus, are created. The NGO reports contain 301, 911 running words, while the government reports contain 307, 683 running words. A corpus can be as small as 77, 000 words (e.g. Alrabia, Alhelewh, & Al-Salman, et al., 2014) or as large as 1.5 billion words if not more (Baker et al., 2012). In this chapter, the RDV corpus is made up of 609, 594 words, which is quite small but acceptable since it is a specialized corpus.

With the availability of the corpus, analysis and examination of data were undertaken using corpus-assisted discourse analysis. This approach is simply an integration of corpus linguistics with the discourse analysis approach. The latter is a qualitative method, while the former is more quantitative in nature, and by integrating these two, the best qualities of these approaches were utilized. They foil each other in a way that they complement each other's strengths and weaknesses. For example, discourse analysts were criticized for "cherry-picking" their sample and data, whilst corpus linguists were criticized for ignoring contexts and discourse (Baker & Levon, 2015). When used together, corpus-assisted discourse analysis approach helps researchers to point out obvious patterns and tease out hidden elements in discourses, in a systematic, time-efficient way without ignoring the context, simultaneously avoiding the researchers' bias in sampling data.

Responses to Domestic Violence in Malaysia: An Overview of RDV

Using word lists, we examined the most frequent words occurring in the reports written both by officials and NGOs. Table 11.1 shows an overview of the two sub-corpora focusing on lexical words (nouns, adjectives, verbs, and adverbs). The rank of the word as it appears in the word list is written in parentheses followed by the frequency of occurrences in the respective sub-corpus.

As an overview, these reports do not only address domestic violence but also some of the many substantive issues related to women's rights. By women's rights, the inclusion and exclusion of women and the gaps between the official discourse and their representation in practice exhibit the many ways in which abusive relationships and women's social justice overlap. For example, apart from domestic violence, NGOs also discuss gender-based violence and violence against women (VAW) in a broader context which includes cases of human trafficking and sex workers. Words that are semantically related to the narratives of domestic violence are highlighted in bold in Table 11.1. As expected, the most frequently occurring words, *domestic* and *violence*, appear highest in the ranks since these are the keywords we used to build the corpus. On the one hand, the reports written by NGOs highlight the dominance of the following words: *law, court, legal,* and *husband*. The first three words indicate the emphasis on law and regulations. On the other hand, in government and government-affiliated reports, words such as *men, physical, protection, abuse,* and *victims* are abundant. It can be surmised that the focus of government reports lies more on the actions and reactions to increasing domestic violence cases, including but not limited to *abuse* and *protection*. Our preliminary analysis also shows that the words commonly used in official reports are more generic, for example, the word, *men*, is frequently chosen than *husband*. The dominance of *men* in the analysis suggests an emphasis on gender as opposed to spousal roles, exposing the cautions and opposition against private, household duties when abusive relationships generally take place at homes. This brings us to the next point; an examination concerning the contexts in which these words appear

TABLE 11.1 Top 100 words in NGOs and government reports based on the word list

Most frequent words in NGO reports	*Most frequent words in government reports*
women (8/3920); Malaysia (12/2162); government (27/1086); gender (28/1028); available (29/1007); **violence (32/952)**; **domestic (33/929)**; rights (37/853); Malaysian (38/846); report (41/758); **CEDAW (48/636); law (49/625)**; development (53/571); family (55/560); state (59/536); national (60/528); children (62/517); human (63/493); marriage (64/493); workers (66/474); sexual (67/469); **court (68/467);** case (71/454); online (73/451); article (74/439); work (75/437); health (77/432); public (79/422); **husband (81/411);** police (85/399); discrimination (86/397); trafficking (87/393); access (89/383); social (91/378); education (94/368); committee (95/367); employment (98/359); **legal (99/359)**; federal (100/358).	women (7/6091); **violence (10/2754)**; health (21/1186); development (28/994); rights (32/894); children (33/853); sexual (34/810); gender (37/770); national (39/756); family (42/740); other (46/696); Malaysia (47/667); international (49/649); united (51/641); human (53/609); social (54/603); action (55/595); partner (56/583); education (59/551); services (60/528); study (61/528); **men (62/504);** city (63/495); child (64/487); government (66/462); world (69/451); conferences (71/439); programs (71/439); community (74/432); nations (80/408); economic (81/403); public (82/400); support (84/398); province (85/391); **physical (86/384);** countries (89/377); **protection (90/377);** committee (91/374); **abuse (93/373);** work (95/363); ensure (96/362); female (97/355); **victims (100/348)**

TABLE 11.2 Collocates of *domestic violence* in the reports written by NGOs and the government

Significant collocates in NGO reports	*Significant collocates in government reports*
DVA, situations, each, standards, reported, include, shelters, **survivors**, since, cases, shelter, **act**, through, **Tina**, rape, but, **survivor**, may, community, response, case, including, there, also, had, must, when, **laws**, are, can, it, us, by, who, she, as, not	**amendment**, mental, **act**, cases, multi, trafficking, **victims**

to ascertain if they are precisely related to domestic violence. Thus, a collocate analysis was undertaken for the phrase *domestic violence* in the sub-corpora. Its results are shown in Table 11.2.

Based on Table 11.2, more collocates were found in NGO-related documents as opposed to government (-affiliated) reports. These may be due to the frequency of occurrences of the phrase, *domestic violence*, which appears 530 times in the NGO reports as opposed to 263 times in official publications.

If we can recontextualize our discussions previously about NGO reports' emphasis on law and regulations using collocate analysis, we could deduce a number of similarities and differences about the words chosen and contexts employed to demonstrate reactions to domestic violence. Firstly, since both NGO and government records put emphasis on the law, our analysis shows that collocates such as *act* and *laws* commingled in NGO publications, while another collocation surrounding law and legal nexus such as *amendment* and *act* were dominant in government-affiliated reports. In other words, the dominance of words, *act* and *laws*, might suggest the glorification of legal issues subsequent to domestic violence, involving individuals, men or not. Secondly, the acronym, DVA, appears 80 times, while the noun phrase, DVA, written in full appears 42 times. This act was mentioned and discussed in all seven (7) reports as highlighted by NGO. While it is also common for government reports to mention the acronym, DVA, and its full form, Domestic Violence Act, they were only used 21 times in six (6) publications, specifically five (5) times as acronyms and sixteen (16) times spelled out in full. Thus, we can surmise that NGOs were far more active in discussing and evaluating DVA, as opposed to the government.

Thirdly, we found that the collocate, *Tina*, refers to a fictional character who was used as a means to portray a fictionalized narrative to depict (actual) experiences of various survivors of domestic violence. The character was used quite extensively in one particular report; one hundred six (106) instances of the word, *Tina*, were found in that report alone. The emphasis on the fictionalized character, *Tina*, might suggest two things. First, it may glorify the superiority of men over women as it is women who need to make adjustments to various household (or not) circumstances. Second, the dominance of the word, *Tina*, might suggest that women typically do not have the agency, authority, position, or power to protect against husbands' violence; therefore, it is women who need to craft and employ strategies to keep the abuse at bay. Specifically, in terms of style, reports written by NGOs are more directed toward discussing the abused from the lens of women/survivors. This is evinced from the collocate such as *Tina* and *she*. Six hundred two (602) instances of the pronoun, *she*, were found in NGO reports, while only one hundred seventy (170) occurrences of the pronoun were found in government reports. To compare, we also searched for the pronoun, *he*, and found two hundred eight (208) instances of *he* appearing in NGO reports and only seventy-two (72) in government publications. Fourthly, further examination of the pronoun, *he*, found that the word, *threatened*, is one of its most prominent collocates, which may indicate that *he* (i.e. male/man) is usually framed as the "abuser" in domestic violence cases. Other examples of abusive acts were additionally found in NGO reports including *he would beat her*; *he would divorce her*; *he would scald her with hot water*. Finally, what is really interesting in Table 11.2 is the presence of the collocates, *survivor/survivors*, in the NGO reports, and *victims* in government records. These refer to the same person, i.e. the abused, but varying terminologies were nevertheless used to exemplify much that is significant about some of the many Malaysians who respond to domestic abuse.

Conclusions and Some Implications Involving the Consequences of Climate Change and the Global COVID-19 Pandemic on Domestic Violence

Issues involving domestic violence drawn from a combination of official and NGO reports highlight the words and contexts in which they are presented. Particularly, apart from the following two words, *domestic* and *violence,* NGO reports are preoccupied with *law, court, legal,* and *husband*, highlighting their concentrations on law and its regulations. In government-affiliated reports, words such as *men, physical, protection, abuse*, and *victims* are abundant, elaborating the centrality of heightened awareness of domestic violence issues that have since prompted actions across the district, municipal, and national levels. While it is commonly understood that there is no definite, comprehensive, one-size-fits-all abatement to domestic violence, corpus-assisted discourse analysis above has illuminated the seriousness with which inequality, prejudices, and abuse are dealt despite chaotic circumstances given increasing statistics on severe injuries.

Corpus-assisted discourse analysis above is also aligned with Peterson and Schroeder's (2016) work on *Domestic Violence in International Context.* As our colleagues, Peterson and Schroeder argue,

> the 'system' needs to be sensitized to our female experiences. No woman can be 'owned,' and thus forced to comply with male demands or be abused. She has a human right to be her own person, free, unharmed, even autonomous.
>
> *Peterson & Schroeder, 2016, p. xvii*

Their spirit allows us to move beyond what is presented in the texts (reports) to associate the words employed to (sociocultural, sociopolitical) circumstances at public, collective levels. That is, through words and phrases as elaborated in this chapter, Malaysian coping mechanism against domestic violence is a force to be reckoned with, as Malaysia attempts to make visible these abuses and measures against the odds.

So, what do these corpus-analysis findings on domestic violence say about their links to climate change? Climate change exacerbates what is already messy and uncomfortable for victims who are often placed in disadvantaged positions. For example, the dramatic increase in reports involving polluted water, heat-related illnesses, and allergies demonstrates that the victims of domestic violence may have to treat these illnesses before they are able to file reports to higher ranking officials. As such, with the dramatic transition of climate change to individuals and communities, the depictions of uncertainty, fear, and conflicts concerning the individuals involved in domestic violence are at all-time alarming. Women and men who confront their lives in the middle of "chaotic" climate change indicate the movements of the self that somewhat cannot be conceived and practiced. We are witness to the emergence and development of weakened infrastructure and spaces. We are privy to the stress from climate impacts that could cause "changes in behavior, development, memory, executive function, and decision-making," in which the complex personality traits of the selves are shaped and conflicted (Clayton et al., 2017, p. 6). Uncertainty, helplessness, and denial influence the way people interact within domestic spaces, for example, in contesting, complying, and disagreeing with the spouse, including the family pressures that they experience in various households in one sense, a consequence of climate change.

At this juncture, the consequences of climate change on domestic violence could involve mitigations at personal and public levels. First, human-oriented organizations and community health experts continue to serve and mediate the ways in which climate change affects domestic violence. Among the recommendations include but are not limited to (1) evaluating and rebuilding helpline and health resources, (2) reducing socio-economic gaps and emphasizing domestic help across underdeveloped communities, and (3) encouraging community members to be trained to face and assist community members who are at risk of domestic violence. Second, individuals may respond to the extreme climate conditions in order to control and provide security to impacted individuals, particularly, single, and divorced individuals. As such, individuals get together to understand what it means to live in changing and challenging chaos in the following ways: (1) engage and train family, colleagues, and friends to keep in touch consistently, (2) normalize mindfulness and healthy behavior, and (3) identify and practice emergency tactics, either verbally/non-verbally or online/offline. By emphasizing these recommendations, individuals and community members play significant agency to "reconcile" the adverse effects of climate change across abusive relationships.

Spouses and children who are vulnerable to abuse and violence may continue to seek help, especially so with the recent COVID-19 pandemic. The greater risks associated with the pandemic such as obesity, loss of jobs, increased mortality rates, increased rental/housing fees, and increased gas prices may pose greater risks to victims of domestic violence. The insurmountable risks experienced by the abused victims are generally not apparent since a lot of these incidents take place inside their homes or secluded areas. Some recommendations might better be considered to prepare for and recover from pandemic-related effects across vulnerable groups such as spouses and children: (1) consider reporting to schools, and in exchange, schools could offer free therapy or provide various check-ins at regular times, (2) consider legislating flexible stay-at-home restrictions following reports of domestic violence within their homes, and (3) consider creating home rental and legal service collaborations to temporarily help house individuals in abused relationships. By looking through the ramifications of COVID-19 and what it means growing up in tumultuous places, vulnerable communities and individuals could disassociate themselves from physically and emotionally abusive environments.

The *Time* Magazine, as recently as March 18, 2020, puts on its website an image of a helpless mask-wearing woman staring out of a window, placed below a bold headline, "As cities around the world go on lockdown, victims of domestic violence look for a way out" (Godin, 2020, online *Time* magazine). The picture and words chosen for the headline carry a loud and clear message about the need for continued interventions across domestic violence perpetrators and victims. In the midst of an unprecedented pandemic, domestic violence reports surge exponentially, indicating the centrality of mental health issues, depression, and a sense of loss (Ustun, 2021). "Her partner strangled her tonight. While talking to her, it sounded like she has some really serious injuries" (Godin, 2020, online *Time* magazine) is just the tip of the iceberg. This chapter goes on to show that physical and mental assaults are not race-based, religion-based, or class-based; they are relatable to everyone. One can only hope that the global circumstances in the near future are less shaped by fear, hatred, and uncertainties.

References

Alhabshi, S. A. (2019, June 20). Help to end child and domestic abuse. *Facebook*. www.facebook.com/photo.php?fbid=10156558556861478&set=a.10151566130451478&type=3&theater

Alrabia, M., Alhelewh, N., Al-Salman, A., & Atwell, E. (2014). An empirical study on the Holy Quran based on a large classical Arabic corpus. *International Journal of Computational Linguistics*, *5* (1), 1–13.

Baker, P., Gabrielatos, C., & McEnery, T. (2012). Sketching Muslims: A corpus driven analysis of representations around the word "Muslim" in the British Press 1998–2009. *Applied Linguistics*, 1–25. https://doi.org/10.1093/applin/ams048

Baker, P., & Levon, E. (2015). Picking the right cherries? A comparison of corpus-based and qualitative analyses of news articles about masculinity. *Discourse and Communication, 9* (2), 221–236. https://doi.org/10.1177%2F1750481314568542

Clayton, S., Manning, C. M., Krygsman, K., & Speiser, M. (2017). *Mental health and our changing climate: Impacts, implications, and guidance*. Washington, DC: American Psychological Association and ecoAmerica.

DSW. (2019, May 30). *Department of social welfare*. Malaysia. www.jkm.gov.my/

Fulu, E., Warner, X., Miedema, S., Jewkes, R., Roselli, T. & Lang, J. (2013). *Why do some men use violence against women and how can we prevent it? Quantitative findings from the United Nations multi-country study on men and violence in Asia and the Pacific*. Phra Nakhon, Bangkok: UNDP, UNFPA, UN Women, and UNV.

Godin, M. (2020, March 18). As cities around the world go on lockdown, victims of domestic violence look for a way out. *Time*. https://time.com/5803887/coronavirus-domestic-violence-victims/

Indramalar, S. (2018, November 30). *Malaysian fights her way out of 20-year abusive marriage, lives to tell her story*. The Star. www.thestar.com.my/lifestyle/family/2018/11/30/from-victim-to-warrior

Ministry of Women, Family and Community Development. (2019, May 29). International day for the elimination of violence against women, unite campaign to end violence against women. *Minister's Speeches*. www.kpwkm.gov.my/kpwkm/uploads/files/TextUcapan/Ucapan%20YB%20Menteri/ERA%20BARU%202018/SPEECH%20YB%20HANNAH%20YEOH%20-%20EVAW%20UNFPA.pdf

My Government. (2019, May 29). *Domestic violence*. Managing family institution. www.malaysia.gov.my/portal/category/1575

Ng, N. (2019, October 6). Spend more to prevent domestic violence, say women's groups. *Free Malaysia Today*. www.freemalaysiatoday.com/category/nation/2019/10/06/spend-more-to-prevent-domestic-violence-say-womens-groups/

Parliament of Malaysia. (2019, May 29). The official portal of parliament Malaysia. *Government of Malaysia*. www.parlimen.gov.my/hansard-dewan-rakyat.html?uweb=dr&lang=en

Peterson, D. S., & Schroeder, J. A. (2016). *Domestic violence in international context*. Oxford and New York: Routledge.

Sahdan, Z., Pain, R., & McEwan, C. (2021). Demonic possession: Narratives of domestic abuse and trauma in Malaysia. *Transactions of the Institute of British Geographers*, 1–32. https://doi.org/10.1111/tran.12485

Ustun, G. (2021). Determining depression and related factors in a society affected by COVID-19 pandemic. *The International Journal of Social Psychiatry, 67* (1), 54–63.

Zainudin, F. (2019, November 21). Thousands of domestic violence cases not reported to welfare department. *Free Malaysia Today*. www.freemalaysiatoday.com/category/nation/2019/11/21/thousands-of-domestic-violence-cases-not-reported-to-welfare-dept/

12

FROM PRIVATE MATTER TO PUBLIC PROBLEM

Relocating Gender-Based Violence in China

Dongling Zhang

Domestic Violence and an Anti-Domestic Violence Law

Domestic violence is one of the most serious and pervasive public health problems on a global scale, with approximately one-third of women being subject to some form of physical and/or sexual violence at the hands of their intimate partners and roughly 40 percent of all murders of women committed by intimate partners (WHO, 2021). Victims of domestic violence in China constitute a vast yet mostly silent group. Often, domestic violence is defined as "the actual or threatened physical, sexual, psychological, or economic abuse of an individual by someone with whom they have or had an intimate partnership" (Coker, 2005, p. 1). Nevertheless, the focus of this chapter is a specific type of domestic violence—gender-based violence within a current or former romantic relationship that is directed against a person solely based upon his/her sex and gender identity and includes "acts that inflict emotional, physical, mental or sexual harm or suffering, threats of such acts, coercion and other deprivations of liberty" (Dlamini, 2021, p. 583; UN Women, 1992).

According to a journalist for the state-sponsored *China Daily* who used findings from the most recent national survey (disclosed by the All-China Women's Federation [ACWF] in late 2013), nearly one quarter of Chinese families have experienced some type of domestic violence ("Twenty-Five Percent of Married Women Suffer Domestic Violence in China", 2017). Given that official statistics exclude non-spousal violence and most if not all accounts of emotional abuse when counting domestic violence, however, the real incidence of domestic violence in China is, no doubt, far greater than those findings suggest.

China's Anti-Domestic Violence Law (henceforth, the DV Law) came into effect in March 2016, following a decade-and-a-half-long fight waged largely by Chinese feminist scholars, women's rights activists, and survivors of domestic violence. This law, the first of its kind in China, represents a solid step, taken by the central and local governments, both to protect victims of gender-based violence and to galvanize the general public's support of the fight against the violence. A matter that had long been relegated to the private sphere, difficult to see beneath layers of Confucianism and patriarchal understandings of gender roles (which included a husband's right to discipline his wife), it seemed, was gradually being relocated to the public sphere—first via daytime television, later via social networking platforms, and then in 2016, when it seemed as if domestic violence might at last achieve its due legitimacy: via the halls of Chinese lawmakers.

About half a decade later, however, it is of loopholes and weak enforcement that women's rights activists, academics, victims, lawyers, and most onlookers speak when discussing the DV Law. Wang

DOI: 10.4324/9781003264040-15

et al. (2020) compiled a number of media reports on incidents of domestic violence from March 2016 onward, illustrating the grim current reality that making the DV Law actually work for victims of domestic violence is an uphill battle: up until the end of November 2016 in Dezhou, a city in northwestern Shandong Province, local police departments across the city received 238 reports of domestic violence in total but ended up issuing only two formal written warning letters; during the same period of time in Shanghai, police processed over 2,700 domestic violence-related cases but issued only 44 written warnings. The written warning letter mechanism, which is considered the most important innovation made by the DV Law, supposedly allows state inventions in minor conflicts in intimate relationship before they escalate into real criminal behaviors. The numbers, however, clearly indicate that the mechanism has been underutilized. To put it differently, the problem that seemingly motivated the law's enactment (that of domestic violence) remains widespread.

State-affiliated organizations, including the ACWF, the Beijing Institute of Marriage and Family, and the Population Research Institute at the Chinese Academy of Social Sciences, conducting large-scale empirical studies that date back to the late 1980s (see, for example, Sun, 1997; Tong, 1999), have reported that anywhere from 1.6 percent to more than a quarter of women in China have experienced some form of gender-based violence during their lifetimes (with most contemporary, foreign journalists citing the higher number). Consequently, "Is it working?" is the question most often asked of China's DV Law today. And this is an especially complicated question, given that there is a lack of aggregated national data that can be drawn upon to map the landscape of China's fight against domestic violence in the wake of the DV Law's implementation. As I mentioned above, the most recent comprehensive survey on the scope and nature of gender-based violence in China dates back only to 2013. Also, existing survey reports to date are one-off measurements that lack mechanisms for ongoing data collection.

In the absence of statistical data, in-depth examination of individual court cases has become the most reliable strategy for interpreting the whos, whats, wheres, whens, and hows of gender-based violence in China following the DV Law. Thus, taking as a point of departure the case study of a single Chinese divorcee, one whose gender-based, violence-related court cases were particularly high-profile just after the DV Law was passed, what follows is an examination of what went wrong with the DV Law and ultimately of what must change if the fight against domestic violence (and specifically gender-based violence) in China is to be won.

The Case of Dai Xiaolei

Dai Xiaolei is a Chinese-born, Canadian citizen who was living in Beijing and married to famous, Chinese movie stuntman Liu Jie. That marriage started to founder in 2014. Later, from July 2016 to November 2017, evidence from the former couple's divorce case repeatedly made headlines in China's and eventually global mainstream media outlets. Carefully documented for the public was a soap-opera rivaling, morality tale of love turned sour. Dai's soon to be ex-in-laws had forcefully snatched her son from her in early 2014, journalists wrote; Dai had not seen her son since that time. Equally shocking, a selfie of Dai's badly bruised face and swollen eyes went viral via social networking platforms, along with Dai's claim, corroborated by airport footage and a prior case settlement, that soon to be ex-husband Liu had punched her at an airport in Hangzhou, the capital city of Zhejiang Province, in mid-2014.

Three months after the implementation of the DV Law, evidence led a court in Beijing to grant Dai a divorce. The judge, however, granted Dai's abusive, former husband full custody of the only child. Once this verdict went public, it indeed threw a wet blanket over the celebratory intentions of those who wished to hail the DV Law as a landmark piece of legislation. Seven months later, in November 2017, Dai's appeal of the custody ruling was rejected. A judge at that point in the process found that any change to the child's relatively stable living environment would not be beneficial to the child's physical and mental health.

The DV Law, if Dai Xiaolei's case is to be taken as exemplary, did not offer tangible protections for victims of gender-based violence. Ironically, perhaps, the law served instead as a justification for the victimized parent's loss of child custody, ultimately re-victimizing Dai and exacerbating her traumatic experiences. Looking more closely at the DV Law, however, it turns out that the law did precisely what it was designed to do.

Article 1 of the DV Law declares as its primary goal the following: to "prevent domestic violence and protect the legal rights and interests of all family members *as a way of maintaining not only an equal, harmonious, and civilized family relationship, but also social stability*" (emphasis author's own). A gender-neutral approach to tackling gender-based violence is salient in this assertion. Deemphasizing the vulnerability of female victims, the DV Law describes male-on-female gender-based violence as a family matter. More importantly, it is a family matter that is able to influence broader social stability. The rationale for criminalizing gender-based violence, it becomes apparent, may have had less to do with the protection of individuals and the prevention of violence against women and more to do with the threat that rampant gender-based violence posed and continues to pose to Chinese family stability and, by extension, to Chinese social stability.

Seeing Domestic Violence in China

Stemming from patriarchal beliefs and social ordering deeply rooted in Confucianism, men historically were allowed to beat their wives, an act that was understood to be appropriate for disciplining women and asserting men's dominance within the household (Gallin, 1992). These cultural notions of male authority and privilege within the family are evident in many traditional Chinese aphorisms, such as "After three days without beating your wife, your house would fall apart", "Beating is love, and scolding is intimacy", and "The wife I have taken, the horse I have bought: I can ride and whip both". In light of China's traditional patriarchal family culture, a good Chinese woman must demonstrate obedience at every stage of her life: as a child, she should follow and obey her father; after getting married, she must follow and obey her husband; and even after the death of her husband, she is required to follow and obey her grown son (Arsella et al., 1985; Tu, 1998). As the home became the man's domain, to be ruled as male heads of households saw fit, beating one's wife was deemed to be not a form of violence but rather a family's private matter.

One result of the above is that even while women made great strides toward women's empowerment and gender equality during the first decade of the Communist rule (1949–1959), aspiring at that time, as the central government had instructed, to "hold up half the sky", prior to the 1980s, gender-based violence in China was largely invisible in mainstream political and academic discourse (Hershatter, 2004; Xu et al., 2001). China's market-oriented economic reforms since 1978 have spread unprecedented wealth and inequality simultaneously across the nation. In particular, the reforms have provided new choices and opportunities for women, at the same time posing new challenges to their pursuit of full equality with men in all aspects of social life. While making inroads into many traditionally masculine fields (e.g., women's entry, en masse, into entrepreneurship), tensions in intimate relationships (especially the husband-wife relationship) could arise because of men who are dissatisfied with their partners' participation in the labor force as well as increasing work hours and earnings; these tensions very likely escalate into violent threats and/or acts as victims decide to prioritize work over family (Zhang, 2021). Though the problem of gender-based violence in China is as pervasive as it is hidden, there has almost no serious thought given to raising public awareness and eliminating such violence by social and legal means until the mid-1980s.

Saying Domestic Violence in China

Compared to Western nations, China's history of research into gender-based violence is brief. In 1987, Li Xiaojiang, an eminent women's studies scholar, established China's first women's studies research center at Zhengzhou University. In spite of Tiananmen Square Incident of 1989 causing considerable setbacks to many humanities and social science disciplines, the fast growth of the field of women's studies kept its momentum. By 1993, the so-classed "One Institute and Four Centers"—the ACWF's Institute of Women's Studies and the four women's studies research centers based, respectively, at Beijing University, Tianjin Normal University, Zhengzhou University, and Hangzhou University (taken over by and merged with Zhejiang University in 1998)—constituted the leading force creating and shaping efforts to address issues of gender inequality, in general, and violence against women, in particular (Chow et al., 2004).

As a large number of non-governmental organizations (NGOs) joined forces to support and further advance the development of the academic field in the 1990s (Du, 2001), activists, academics, and others participating in the fight against gender-based violence have worked to shift the discourse in which gender-based violence is discussed. The phenomenon of violence against women was, until only recently, predominantly described as either "wife-beating" (*da laopo*) or "maltreatment" (*nuedai*), a violent act in which a man inflicts upon his wife or female partner unnecessary pain or suffering. The popularity and widespread use of these terms perpetuated understandings of gender-based violence as biologically inevitable or individualistic rather than gender-based and socially constructed (Hester, 2005). In other words, the previous terms themselves worked to entrench understandings of gender-based violence as a private, family affair rather than a socio-legal, and thus public, problem.

Foreign experience, especially that from the Western world, provided a useful reference point in China's search for a terminology that can accurately capture the phenomenon of gender-based violence. Adopting literal translations of the terminology used in the global north, domestic violence became *jiating baoli*. Activists emphasized gender awareness by specifically using the term "domestic violence against women" (*zhendui funv de jiating baoli*). Due to their persistence, the term "domestic violence" appeared in China's nation-wide legislative efforts for the first time in 2001, the year in which the Supreme People's Court issued the amended Marriage Law explicitly defining and outlawing behaviors of family violence (Zhao & Zhang, 2017). An important breakthrough was made in 2015 when the State Council, the chief administrative authority of the country, enacted the Law on the Protection of Women's Rights and Interests. Notably, this law put forward a broad definition of domestic violence and thereby shed light on many different forms of abuse and violence in intimate relationship, such as physical and psychological abuse, verbal abuse, and infringement of freedom. The law also provided guidelines for punishment and prevention that explicitly establish the Chinese government's responsibilities for the control and prevention of gender-based violence (Leggett, 2017). Nevertheless, although the recognition and emphasis of gender-based violence in both the amended Marriage Law and the Law on the Protection of Women's Rights and Interests is a milestone in China's history of anti-domestic violence legislation, the two laws offered neither basic measures to protect women's basic human rights to live free of violence from their domestic partners, nor pragmatic guidelines to transform the definition into actual legal and judicial actions (Keith & Lin, 2006).

Legislating Domestic Violence in China

In contrast, enacting the DV Law of 2016 should be recognized as evidence of China's increasingly deep commitment to combating domestic violence as a serious social problem. Unlike pre-existing local ordinances and national statutory laws that utilized literal translations of global north terminology without context-specific judicial interpretation and law enforcement guidelines, the DV Law establishes a fairly explicit clarification on the definition of domestic violence—"infliction of physical, psychological, or other harm between family members through the use of such methods as beating, restraint, maiming, restrictions on physical liberty, as well as recurrent verbal abuse or intimidation" (Article 2). This definition is indeed flawed, to some extent a field guide to remaining yet resilient societal stereotypes and blind spots. It does not include sexual violence, for one thing (the concept of physical violence could be extracted to encompass sexual violence but the absence of explicit language and emphasis is worrying). For another, the long-awaited statutory definition does not go far enough to provide institutionalized safeguards for same-sex partners, former spouses, and intimate partners who do not live together even if academics, women's rights activists, and victims spoke loudly about the limitation during the public comment period prior to the enactment of the DV Law in 2016. Albeit imperfect, the definition makes it possible to not only outlaw concrete, recognizable gender-based violence behaviors, but also raise public awareness of the domestic violence problem.

Most importantly, perhaps, the DV Law seeks to create and provide new legal protections for victims through comprehensive legal procedures, mainly including temporary personal safety protection orders (similar to restraining orders) (Articles 23–32), and as mentioned above, the written warning mechanism that mandates early public intervention by employers, social workers, law enforcers, and other government officials (Articles 13–22). It is also noteworthy to mention that the DV Law establishes special protections for victims who are underage, elderly, disabled, pregnant or lactating, and seriously ill (Article 5). In response to critics (see, for example, Jiang, 2019; Rauhala, 2017) charging that the DV Law fails at almost every step, from gathering evidence to winning a court case to finally enforcing a judgment, the Supreme People's Court—China's highest court—issued the most recent guideline in July 2022 in order to provide easier access to those legal protections. Major measures include easing the burden of proof on a victim petitioning for protection order and adding ten more scenarios to further concretize the definition of domestic violence (e.g., denying food to family members, constant insults, stalking, and harassment) (Cao, 2022). Despite facing many other problems and challenges, the DV Law does make legal protections available to vulnerable victims, especially those women who have endured severe and sustained forms of gender-based violence.

Implications of China's DV Law

Once again, the DV Law is imperfect. Especially when the interests of female victims are inconsistent with those of the state, the DV Law is most likely to protect the state's socio-political interests at the cost of victims' legal rights and emotional well-being (Jiang, 2019). As was illustrated by Dai Xiaolei's lawyer, who said in a statement following his and his client's second failed attempt in the child custody battle:

> Almost any court around the globe, except those in China, would deny custody to a parent who has been accused of domestic violence because the abuser is normally seen as a threat to the child and the child's other parent, the domestic violence victim. The judge did not seriously consider the accusation of domestic violence in today's child custody determination and disappointingly favored the parent who already had the physical custody of the child. In the judge's words, the rationale behind this ruling is to avoid further disruption to the former couple and thereby clear obstacles to the enforcement of the civil judgment.
>
> *Xinmeiti nvxing, 2016*

If the work of governance is sustaining macro-level, social stability, then the work of adjudicating becomes the same, as was evinced in this case. At the trial's end, the judge spoke of avoiding "further disruption" while ignoring: first, Dai's legal claims to her child; second, contemporary notions that domestic violence and gender-based violence are criminal; and also, third, the possibility that it might not be in the child's best interest to live with a convicted perpetrator of domestic violence.

Dai Xiaolei's case is one of several high-profile cases which suggest that China's criminal justice approach to gender-based violence, including its legislative efforts, cannot on its own resolve the problem of gender-based violence. The court rulings, time and again in these cases, dovetail neatly with China's increasingly vintage, patriarchal ideas about social order, and a man's freedom to do what he wishes within his home. And such rulings ultimately thwart the progress suggested, for example, by rapidly shifting public perceptions of gender-based violence on Chinese social networking platforms.

The DV Law defines domestic violence, but it does not challenge socio-cultural norms of the past. In so failing, it fails, too, to facilitate the recovery of gender-based violence survivors and/or enforce real repercussions for perpetrators. Progress reports published by one of China's most influential gender-based, violence-related NGOs today—an NGO bearing the name Beijing Equality—suggest that the next battle to reduce gender-based violence must be a socio-cultural battle rather than a criminal justice one.

Suggestions for a More Just Future

Beijing Equality, a grantee of the United Nations (UN) Trust Fund to End Violence against Women, was established in October 2014 and has since become one of China's most influential NGOs dedicated to eradicating gender-based violence and promoting gender equality (Beijing Equality, 2022). Immediately after the DV Law came into effect, Beijing Equality recognized the importance of periodically scrutinizing each component in and step of the lawmaking and implementation processes. In doing so, Beijing Equality has been serving as a platform through which Chinese government officials and agencies, academia, grassroots human rights activists and groups, and the UN can work jointly to not only update the general public on the progress of the law implementation as well as its consequences (both intended and unintended), but also advocate to improve anti-domestic violence legislation and public policymaking. These efforts so far have resulted in seven separate progress assessment reports being published in February 2017, December 2017, March 2018, March 2019, November 2019, April 2020, and December 2021, respectively.

"Can the implementation of the DV Law across the country make any difference to the extent and severity of the gender-based violence problem?" the first three reports asked. In order to answer this question, these reports presented comprehensive assessments of how the law implementation worked to prevent gender-based violence, and to treat both perpetrators and victims when the violence does occur (Beijing Equality, 2017a, 2017b, 2018). The report, which Beijing Equality (2019a) released in March 2019, was about a special investigation into the performance of the personal safety protection order mechanism from March 2016 through December 2018. Released in the same year, the third annual assessment report resumed the yearly overall assessment of the efficiency and effectiveness of the DV Law during the third-year implementation period (Beijing Equality, 2019b). Meanwhile, it shifted attention to the opportunities and challenges facing NGOs' participation in joint endeavor to tackle the problem of gender-based violence through the law implementation. In the fourth and fifth annual assessment reports, the organization shifted the focus again to compare the actual performances of different societal institutions and organizations with the new duties and responsibilities of those institutions and organizations as outlined by the DV Law (Beijing Equality, 2020, 2021).

The seven reports are of great importance in disclosing limitations with both the DV Law itself and the law implementation, along with advice for next steps of legal and public policy reform. For instance, the aforementioned flawed statutory definition of domestic violence, as specified by Article 2, needs to be expanded so that: first, legal protections from the DV Law are accessible to not only victims who are legally married, but also same-sex couples, former spouses, and separated partners; second, in addition to physical abuse, the DV Law can recognize and take seriously the use or attempted use of sexual abuse and economic control. On the condition that the definition becomes much broader, education on and increasing public awareness of gender-based violence—another two pieces of advice that the reports have repeatedly stressed—would work to cultivate a social environment favorable to the law implementation.

Furthermore, the reports have garnered considerable attention from the authorities and reminded them of how much more there is to be done (Beijing Equality, 2022). This achievement illustrates the significance of ongoing systematic monitoring and assessment of the entire law cycle; it can achieve transparency in the law implementation process, increase stakeholder engagement and accountability, emphasize achievements toward law objectives, and keep the general public informed of the consequences and impacts of the DV Law. Whereas Beijing Equality initially planned to study achievements and challenges of the law implementation only, the actual impacts of the organization's assessments have gone far beyond the purview of lawmaking and implementation processes as well as that of the criminal justice system. More important, as implicitly suggested by the law and policy recommendations from the reports, the Chinese state's sole reliance on the criminal justice approach renders questionable its capability (as well as the capability of the DV Law) to change socio-cultural norms that constantly restrict the social problem of gender-based violence within the private, family sphere, let alone put an end to historical cycles of violence. Without transforming the socio-cultural context, no anti-domestic violence legislation and public policy can effectively address gender-based violence and enhance the well-being of victims.

More Challenges Down the Road: Fostering a Public Stance on Gender-Based Violence

The COVID-19 pandemic and climate change are delivering an extra double blow to the interests and safety of women as well as gender and sexual minorities across the globe, many of whom were already disproportionately victimized by gender-based domestic violence. China is not an exception. Ever since the outbreak of the virus, emerging data and news reports from those on the front lines have indicated a sharp rise in domestic violence against women. As cited by Zhang (2022), the number of domestic violence-related police reports in Jianli, a small city in Hubei Province, nearly tripled when the first wave of the pandemic peaked in February 2020. More than two years into the pandemic, the spread of the virus in China has not yet stopped as the progress of vaccinations is racing against new variants of the virus and the Chinese government's extremely stubborn stance on the zero-COVID approach. In such extraordinary circumstances, we keep seeing and hearing the same story over and over again that a victim of domestic violence is in urgent need of legal protections and assistance, but strict lockdown and quarantine regulations deprive her of what the DV Law and associated policies literally make available to all victims and survivors (see, for example, Wu & O'Donnell, 2022).

In contrast, the impacts of climate change on China's problem of gender-based violence are largely unknown and therefore could be more concerning. It is primarily because there has been no academic research or media coverage on how climate crisis has impacted gender-based violence and inequalities in China. According to UN Women (United Nations Entity for Gender Equality and the Empowerment of Women, 2022), approximately 80 percent of the population being displaced by climate change are women, and forced migration and displacement are two major negative consequences of the climate crisis that are currently influencing millions of people in the world. Worsening socio-economic and natural conditions exacerbated by the overlapping influences of climate change and the pandemic have led to the fact that women are among the hardest hit—those who are more likely to experience increased caring responsibilities, job loss and insecurity, and violence at home (UNHCR, 2022). In order to leverage the DV Law and other relevant government policies to address these new challenges, we must explore best practices through which members of the general public can be educated on the root causes of gender-based violence as well as the remaining and newer roadblocks on the path to solve the problem.

"Fostering a public stance", here, is intended to suggest the project of cultivating shifting, democratic, culturally appropriate, and also socially just understandings—about gender relations, about violence, and about the family—at a community-wide level. Education of course is of the utmost importance to such a project. Though the seven reports briefly touched upon this recommendation, they did not take into account current challenges to educational reform in China which, like the challenges to reducing gender-based violence, are linked to the persistence of patriarchal norms and social ordering.

Calls for education on gender-based violence are likely to collide head-on with dated yet resilient moral tenets that underlie and sustain broader structured power relations in contemporary China. Central to gender-based violence education, for example, are teachings on gender sensitivity and justice—both topics which remain peripheral and even taboos in daily conversation for many Chinese. Despite this obstacle, recent progress on anti-domestic violence education has been commendable. The Standing Committee of the National People's Congress, the highest legislative body of China, passed an amendment to the Law on the Protection of Minors in 2020 that mandates "age-appropriate sex education" in all schools (Zhou, 2020). Albeit not clearly stated, education on the public's ability to recognize and protect themselves against all kinds of sexual violence can serve as an ideal platform where specific domestic violence-related education can be undertaken. The Ministry of Education and its branches across the country, I suggest, should take the next step to not only bring gender-based violence-related course contents to the forefront, but also integrate those in classroom spaces and at various stages in the elementary, junior, and senior high school curricula. In this way, formerly sensitive subjects will become normative, and perhaps even someday, they will become daily topics in public conversation.

Finally, in addition to new education endeavors, the fight against gender-based violence in China will require full use of the mass media. It is the mass media that, since 2001, has been able to transform gender-based violence into spectacle: following high-profile court cases, analyzing fictional television (especially soap opera) content in which gender-based violence is used to drive plot lines, and beyond. It is well known that the mass media has, since its origins, been capable of drawing and then maintaining the attention of the masses, but this power has left us mostly dubious—rightfully not only critical of media moral panics, but also hesitant to harness the powers of the fourth estate when it can be used for good.

Learning to see, say, and legislate domestic and gender-based violence, just like other relatively recent plights to expand human rights, has been key to establishing China's credibility, as the nation assumes a renewed position of global leadership. Central to each of these lessons, and a struggle which continues today, is the transformation of gender-based violence from private matter, one that is unseen and unaddressed, to public problem. Only as public problem can gender violence command the attention it requires. Once public, it can be taught, it can be reported on, it can be shared, and, ideally, it can be defeated.

References

Arsella, A. J., DeVos, G., & Hsu, F.L.K. (Eds.). (1985). *Culture and self Asian and Western perspective.* Tavistock.

Beijing Equality (2017a, March 17). *The first annual evaluation report of the implementation of the DV Law.* www.equality-beijing.org/newinfo.aspx?id=31

Beijing Equality (2017b, December 15). *The 20 months evaluation report of the implementation of the DV Law.* www.equality-beijing.org/newinfo.aspx?id=69

Beijing Equality (2018, March 7). *The second annual evaluation report of the implementation of the DV Law.* www.equality-beijing.org/newinfo.aspx?id=71

Beijing Equality (2019a, March 13). *The third annual evaluation brief report of the implementation of the DV Law.* www.equality-beijing.org/newinfo.aspx?id=73

Beijing Equality (2019b, November 29). *The 45 months evaluation report of the implementation of the DV Law.* www.equality-beijing.org/newinfo.aspx?id=77

Beijing Equality (2020, April 29). *The fourth annual evaluation report of the implementation of the DV Law.* www.equality-beijing.org/newinfo.aspx?id=80

Beijing Equality (2021, December 8). *The fifth annual evaluation report of the implementation of the DV Law.* www.equality-beijing.org/newinfo.aspx?id=86

Beijing Equality (2022). About us & our works. www.equality-beijing.org/about.aspx?id=2

Cao, Y. (2022, July 16). *Domestic violence guideline provides enhanced safeguards.* www.chinadaily.com.cn/a/202207/16/WS62d206bca310fd2b29e6ca9d.html

Chow, E. N., Zhang, N., & Wang, J. (2004). Promising and contested fields: Women's studies and sociology of women/gender in contemporary China. *Gender & Society, 18* (2), 161–188. https://doi.org/10.1177/0891243203261128

Coker, A. L. (2005). Opportunities for prevention: Addressing intimate partner violence in the healthcare setting. *Family Violence Prevention and Health Practice, 1* (1), 1–9.

Dlamini, N. (2021). Gender-based violence, twin pandemic to COVID-19. *Critical Sociology, 47* (4–5), 583–590. https://doi.org/10.1177/0896920520975465

Du, F. (2001). Maneuvering fate and following the call: Development and prospects of women's studies. In P. Hsiung, M. Jaschok, & C. Milwertz (with R. Chan) (Eds.), *Chinese women organizing: Cadres, feminists, Muslims, queers* (pp. 237–249). Berg.

Gallin, R. S. (1992). Wife abuse in the context of development and change: A Chinese (Taiwanese) case. In D. A. Counts, J. K. Brown, & J. C. Campbell (Eds.), *Sanctions and sanctuary: Cultural perspective on the beating of wives* (pp. 219–227). Westview.

Hershatter, G. (2004). State of the field: Women in China's long twentieth century. *The Journal of Asian Studies, 63* (4), 991–1065.

Hester, M. (2005). Transnational influences on domestic violence policy and action: Exploring developments in China and England. *Social Policy & Society, 4* (4), 447–456. https://doi.org/10.1017/S1474746405002630

Jiang, J. (2019). The family as a stronghold of state stability: Two contradictions in China's anti-domestic violence efforts. *International Journal of Law, Policy and the Family, 33* (2), 228–251. https://doi.org/10.1093/lawfam/ebz004

Keith, R., & Lin, Z. (2006). *New crime in China: Public order and human rights.* Routledge.

Leggett, A. (2017). Online civic engagement and the anti-domestic violence movement in China: Shifting norms and influencing law. *Voluntas: International Journal of Voluntary and Nonprofit Organizations, 28* (5), 2251–2277. https://doi.org/10.1007/s11266-016-9680-9

Rauhala, E. (2017, February 7). *Despite a new law, China is failing survivors of domestic violence.* www.washingtonpost.com/world/asia_pacific/despite-a-new-law-china-is-failing-survivors-of-domestic-violence/2017/02/02/ae7948a4-e31f-11e6-a419-eefe8eff0835_story.html?noredirect=on&utm_term=.0b55ad3a7080

Sun, X. (1997). The cause of violence in Chinese families and its prevention. In *Expert workshop on fighting domestic violence against women: Social, ethical, and legal issues* (pp. 29–31). China Women Publishing House.

Tu, W. (1998). Probing the three bonds and the five relationships in Confucian humanism. In G. De Vos & W. Slote (Eds.), *Confucianism and the family* (pp. 121–136). State University of New York Press.

Tong, X. (1999). The production and reproduction of unequal gender relations: An analysis of domestic violence in China. In L. Stearns (Ed.), *Chinese women's rights* (Working paper no. 10, pp. 42–56). Institutt for Mennskerettigheter.

Twenty-five percent of married women suffer domestic violence in China. (2017, March 2). CCTV. COM. http://english.cctv.com/2017/03/02/VIDEsd8TYsYQVyXgo86BjANx170302.shtml

United Nations Entity for Gender Equality and the Empowerment ofWomen. (1992). General recommendation No. 19 made by the Committee on the Elimination of Discrimination against Women. www.un.org/womenwatch/daw/cedaw/recommendations/recomm.htm

United Nations Entity for Gender Equality and the Empowerment of Women. (2022, July 12). Climate change exacerbates violence against women and girls. www.ohchr.org/en/stories/2022/07/climate-change-exacerbates-violence-against-women-and-girls

United Nations High Commissioner for Refugees. (2022, March 8). Covid-19 and climate crisis worsen inequalities for displaced women and girls. www.unhcr.org/news/press/2022/3/622755294/covid-19-climate-crisis-worsen-inequalities-displaced-women-girls.html

Wang, J., Zhang, L., & Wu, T. (2020). Fanjiabaofa shishi sinian duoxiang cushi shijianzhong yulen [To put the Anti-Domestic Violence Law into practice is has been challenging during the past four years]. *Xinhua Net*, www.xinhuanet.com/legal/2020-11/25/c_1126782389.htm

World Health Organization. (2021, March 9). Violence against women. www.who.int/news-room/fact-sheets/detail/violence-against-women

Wu, H., & O'Donnell, K. (2022, June 9). In locked down Shanghai, a "shadow pandemic" of domestic violence. www.sixthtone.com/news/1010484/in-locked-down-shanghai%2C-a-shadow-pandemic-of-domestic-violence

Xinmeiti nvxing [New media women] (2016, May 31). Changqi jiabao zhixu peiyang wuqian: Sicang haizi haineng de fuyangquan? [Paying five thousand yuan for a long-term domestic violence: Being granted with the child custody by snatching the child away?]. *Sina Blog*, http://blog.sina.com.cn/s/blog_5b09f6cd0102won6.html

Xu, X., Campbell, J. C., & Zhu, F. (2001). Intimate partner violence against Chinese women: The past, present, and future. *Trauma, Violence, & Abuse*, *2* (4), 296–315.

Zhang, D. (2021). The "she power" that was not: A contextual-interfaces analysis of Chinese women micro-entrepreneurs' experiences of gender-based violence. *American Review of China Studies*, *22* (2), 1–29.

Zhang, H. (2022). The influence of the ongoing COVID-19 pandemic on family violence in China. *Journal of Family Violence*, *37*, 733–743. https://doi.org/10.1007/s10896-020-00196-8

Zhao, R., & Zhang, H. (2017). Family violence and the legal and social responses in China. In E.V. Buzawa & C. G. Buzawa (Eds.), *Global responses to domestic violence* (pp. 189–206). Springer. https://doi.org/10.1007/978-3-319-56721-1_10

Zhou, V. (2020, November 11). "China has a national sexual illiteracy": The challenges in the way of developing sex education in the country. www.scmp.com/lifestyle/family-relationships/article/3109184/china-has-national-sexual-illiteracy-challenges-way

13

SOCIAL TABOOS AND LEGAL CONSTRAINTS

The Status of Domestic Violence in Kuwait

Alanoud AlSharekh and Nour AlMukhled

Introduction

Domestic violence is a complex issue in Kuwait culture complicated by norms and beliefs that pertain to family hierarchy and the concept of "honor". As with other forms of abuse that can occur within the family, domestic violence is considered a private matter that should not be addressed publicly, even when it comes to seeking legal protection or medical treatment. Reflections of such attitudes can be seen in Kuwait's penal code, which defends these practices in the name of honor and guardianship by treating some of these abuses as a misdemeanor rather than a crime. As a legal and social framework to assist abuse survivors has yet to be implemented, many have no option other than to file a complaint with the police, which will file a report and in many cases request documentation from a hospital on injuries sustained. In most cases, the police will ask the perpetrator to sign a statement "of intended future good conduct" which is a non-legally binding pledge stating that such actions will not happen again. This statement does not even serve as a restraining order, and since most survivors would have no option but to return home to their abusers, many do not file an official complaint with the police.

Although there is a lack of up-to-date figures, domestic violence seems to be prevalent in Kuwait, affecting 53.1% of women according to a 2018 study (AlSalem, 2018). The latest official statistics come from Kuwait's last submission to CEDAW on the issue, which quoted statistics from the Ministry of Justice that showed that 447 domestic violence cases had been through the court system (with only 76 resulting in a conviction) in 2016 (Kuwait State Party Report, 2016). Given the difficulties of reporting and getting a case to court, it is not a far stretch to assume that the actual figures of abused women are much higher than 447 a year.

Although Kuwait claims to have several official bodies dealing with the issue of ending violence against women, it has been left up to the civil society sector to both highlight and effectively deal with the plight of abuse survivors. In November 2014, an NGO called Tabeebat (female doctors) launched a marathon with a number of other NGOs to draw attention to the issue of ending violence against women (WCSS, 2020). It was the first time that the issue of ending violence against women had taken shape in an organized public forum in Kuwait. Unfortunately, that would be the first and last such event that Tabeebat would hold. However, that very year Abolish 153 was established and had been leading the fight to end violence against women in Kuwait since then. Working alongside Abolish 153 is its registered sister organization Eithar, Soroptimist Kuwait and the Women's Cultural and Social Society.

DOI: 10.4324/9781003264040-16

The campaign to abolish article 153 of Kuwait's penal code is led by five Kuwaiti female activists concerned with ending all forms of violence against women in the Arabian Gulf and the neighboring region. The campaign aims to raise awareness about the existence of legal and social practices that justify the killing of mothers, daughters, sisters and wives in the name of protecting "family honor". In light of the absence of laws that criminalize violence against women, as well as the lack of administrative and executive measures to protect women subjected to violence within the family, the campaign has trained over 400 people on how to advocate for abuse survivors through holding seminars and workshops with volunteers and specialists. Spreading the culture of anti-violence, the campaign organized poetry evenings and free film and documentary evenings in public facilities and public and private universities (Abolish 153, 2015).

Currently in Kuwait, there are no working shelters, hotlines or any other resources to assist women facing domestic abuse and gender-based violence.[1] Therefore, Abolish 153 and Eithar are trying to fill that gap. While Abolish 153 aims at filling the legal vacuum, Eithar works to provide victims of domestic violence with the necessary resources and support. The advocacy campaign launched by Abolish 153 is focused on making sure that a domestic violence legislation gets passed on the governmental and parliamentary levels to activate a working shelter for abused women and provide them with legal cover from abusive guardians. Meanwhile, Eithar is working in parallel to provide abused women and their families with immediate financial and emotional support. As of today, Eithar has assisted more than 120 abuse survivors and their families in Kuwait by helping them find housing and providing them with legal, medical and financial assistance.

Official Resources Available to Survivors

In their closing statement to the OHCHR in January 2015, Kuwaiti delegate's official response to the issue of resources available for survivors of domestic violence was delineated in comments 7 and 8: setting up a dedicated police force called the "social police" by the Ministry of Interior to oversee and help resolve domestic violence cases, and to offer psychological and social aid to abuse survivors (OHCHR, 2015). This report also stated that when reporting abuse at the police stations most resorted to finding a resolution between the parties (as opposed to filing a report of the case) to "preserve peace within the family and maintain Kuwaiti mores and traditions". It also stated that the country was providing sufficient training to those in the field to deal with survivors of abuse, which according to several members of the committee to oversee the opening of the Fanar center for domestic abuse and advisory services under the Higher Council of Family Affairs, the main body overseeing the implementation and operation of Kuwait's domestic abuse shelter is simply not true.[2] There is also a reference to the Committee for Women's Affairs under the Council of Ministers in comment 10, which is headed by the former Crown Prince's wife Latofa al Sabah, whose remit is to follow up and oversee a range of female empowerment initiatives, yet has not been active in pushing anti-violence legislations since its inception in 2012.

The Kuwaiti Diwan for Human Rights is another governmental body supposedly working toward ending violence against women. The organization was mentioned by the Kuwait Delegation in their response to the experts at the Convention on the Elimination of All Forms of Discrimination Against Women (CEDAW) in 2017 (OHCHR, 2017), as one of the organizations that would be responsible for dealing with the issue of violence against women. The Diwan was established in September 2018 as part of an agreement between Kuwait and the UN that took place in 2015 (Abdullah, 2018), but it has not yet taken official action to push for a domestic violence law or the operation of the domestic abuse shelter.

History of the Domestic Violence Law

In 2015, Kuwait stated in a report submitted to the Office of the United Nations High Commissioner for Human Rights (OHCHR) that according to articles 160–164 of its penal code, the country forbids domestic violence (OHCHR, 2015). As of today, Kuwait still has no laws on domestic violence and does not explicitly criminalize marital rape. A law passed in 2015 led to the creation of a family court in each of Kuwait's five governorates to "combat domestic violence", but the law requires that the center prioritized reconciliation between family members over protection of domestic violence survivors (Human Rights Watch, 2020).

In 2016, a member of parliament (MP) Saleh Ashoor requested a formal inquiry into article 153 and its unconstitutional status during a parliamentary session (Aamer, 2016). Later in 2017, he submitted a domestic violence bill while heading the Women and Family Affairs Committee (WFAC). The bill was signed by four other MPs – Safa AlHashem, Ahmad AlFadhel, Khalil AlSaleh and Faisal AlKanderi. However, there have been different reiterations from that day to today. (Domestic Violence Bill 2017).

Supporting the efforts of putting an end to domestic violence, in 2017, MP Omar AlTabtabaee requested that shelters be created for victims of domestic violence. In May of that same year, AlTabtabaee, along with four other MPs, signed an official parliamentary request to abolish article 153, thereby giving it urgent status (Abolish Article 153, 2017).

In January 2018, MPs Khalid AlShatti, Ahmad AlFadhel, Yousef AlFadhala, Rakan AlNusif and Ouda AlRuwaie submitted a bill made up of 17 articles that address the issue of combating domestic violence (Kuwait National Assembly [KNA], 2018).

> In their explanatory note, the lawmakers said that despite the global developments in the are of human rights in general, and the rights of women and children in particular, domestic violence remains prevalent in most communities due to the inability of concerned institutions to curb this phenomenon and identify the real causes.
>
> *Abubakar, 2018*

A few months later, *AlQabas* newspaper published a statement made by MP Saleh Ashoor justifying the reason for the delay of the bill. Ashoor explained that the domestic violence law would be delayed because the WFAC was examining a legislation suggested by another MP and that after comparisons are completed a new combined legislation would be presented to the national assembly (AlQabas, 2018). On March 7, 2018, a few days after his statement in AlQabas, Ashoor submitted a proposal for a domestic violence legislation with MP Safa AlHashem containing 15 articles (Kuwait National Assembly [KNA], 2018).

In October 2019, MP Mohammed Al Dalal issued a press statement that the WFAC was awaiting comments from the government to move ahead with the domestic violence law and the activation of the shelter (AlWatan, 2019). A week later, MP Safa AlHashem stated that the domestic violence legislation, made up of 32 articles, would be ready to present to the national assembly shortly (AlTurki, 2019). The law would include a six-month jail sentence for domestic violence offenders and even stricter sentences for repeat offenders and community service like cleaning streets (Alanba, 2019).

However, it wasn't until January 27, 2020, that the head of the committee MP Safa AlHashem issued a press statement which stated that the domestic violence law had been voted on and approved in the WFAC and would include a suggestion for the inclusion of a family mediation center within the general framework of the law (AlShammari, 2020). In her statement, MP AlHashem clarified that in this final form the law included 26 articles inclusive of 9 suggestions by multiple stakeholders. This legislation guarantees the psychological, political, legal and financial protection of abuse survivors through building dedicated centers or through activating the shelters that already exist in each governorate (a problematic statement since there is only one shelter in existence and it is yet to be activated), and setting up a fund to assist affected families. She added that the law includes a provision to protect informants and will empower the social police force to intervene and issue arrests in domestic violence cases (Abdulhafith & AlFaam, 2020).

On August 19, 2020, the "family protection" law, as it is formally called, was passed in Kuwait's national assembly with 38 votes, one MP abstaining, and another voting against it (The National, 2020). A total of 17 MPs were conspicuously absent from the room including the WFAC rapporteur himself, known for his human rights activism, signaling the complex social and political issues associated with domestic violence in Kuwait. The official version of the family protection law contains 26 articles, some of which were discussed in detail the day after in an article published in AlQabas newspaper (AlQabas, 2020). These include the formation of a "National Family Protection Committee" which will draw up plans to counter the spread of violence in Kuwait, and the review and amendment of national laws that run counter to ending violence. Other provisions cover mandatory training programs for all government sectors involved in family protection; awareness programs on detection, reporting and survivor advocacy; and issuing an annual report about domestic violence statistics.

Article 5 of the law concerns the activation of the domestic violence shelter and offering rehabilitation and advisory services, while article 13 concerns penalizing those who try and coerce survivors not to report abuse. Within the suggested articles of the family protection law, there is also an important provision for cooperation with civil society organizations that work in this field.

The Aborted Fanar Center

As early as 2012, there was a reference made to an email service offered by Kuwait's social police to facilitate "early intervention" in cases of domestic violence or abuse within family members (KUNA, 2012). A hotline service meant to deal with domestic abuse and with other "family-related" issues was activated through the social police in 2015 (Aboush, 2015), but this service was only available from 9 am to 9 pm on weekdays and only in Arabic. The social police themselves were limited in what help they could offer due to the lack of legislation prohibiting domestic violence and a shelter.

A few years later there was a mention of "soon to be activated" domestic abuse shelters in the budget assigned to family affairs by the Ministry of Justice according to an article published by KUNA, quoting the deputy minister Dr. Adel AlZamanan (AlDaqbasi, 2015).

Kuwait's official delegation to CEDAW in 2017 claimed that the country had already taken administrative steps with regard to violence against women: it had enabled the police to receive complaints and set up shelters and had not waited for this law to take concrete steps to support victims of violence. The delegation stressed that all forms of violence against women and children were prohibited in Kuwait, and the laws provided women with an opportunity to access justice and take their attackers to court (OHCHR, 2017).

In November 2017, the shelter for abused survivors and center for advisory service called "Fanar" was first announced before CEDAW. An inauguration of the building took place, with members of several NGOs (including Abolish 153) invited to the event, but it has never been functional due to the delay of the legislation needed to make it operational (AlKhaldy, 2019). Hanan al Zayed's report in *AlQabas* newspaper in the summer of 2019 called it "A stillborn dream" and showed images of the empty building surrounded by sewage water (AlZayed, 2019). The report also included interviews with the former deputy minister of Social and Labor Affairs and a former member of the Higher Council of Family Affairs who was heading the committee overseeing the Fanar advisory center and abuse shelter Dr. Malak AlRushaid. Both conveyed the message that the government was not serious enough about pushing forth with the activation of the shelter.

AlQabas newspaper reported on October 1, 2019, that MP Safa AlHashem had stated that part of the delay with the legislation and activation of the shelter was due to the fact that there were too many official bodies involved such as the Ministry of Interior to the Ministry of Social and Labor Affairs, all of which have different agendas. She also stated that the committee was trying to provide all legal responsibility with regard to dealing with abuse survivors to the Higher Council for Family Affairs.

Post COVID-19

Domestic violence in Kuwait during the COVID-19 pandemic has been rising according to the activists and experts interviewed in an article in *AlAnba* newspaper during the coronavirus lockdown (AlAnba, 2020). According to those interviewed, this has been aggravated by the lack of legal resources and a shelter for survivors. This unfortunate situation, and worldwide interest in the issue of domestic violence within the current epidemic, led to renewed media interest in the issue of resolving violence against women in Kuwait and brought the lack of resources available to abuse survivors once more to the public eye. This may have facilitated governmental and parliamentary mobilization on the family protection law (which was published in the official gazette and became an enforceable law in September 2020), especially as Kuwait enters into an election cycle in late November 2020, which, alongside the press and publication law passed that same day in parliament, is considered a win for liberal civil society activists lobbying to change dangerous and restrictive legislations in Kuwait.

In January 2021, there has been much more interest in issues of protecting women against violence because of a sexual harassment campaign, #Lan_Asket (I will not be silent), that has been launched by young activists in Kuwait as a reaction to the influx of sexual harassment incidents that have occurred (Makhoul, 2021).

Several members of parliament proposed new laws to combat sexual harassment after the launch of the online sexual harassment campaign. MP Yousef AlFadhala proposed a government-sponsored mobile application designed to document and report instances of harassment and allow for immediate registration of a crime, MP Dr. Abdulaziz AlSaqabi proposed an amendment to the penal code, adding punishments that include up to a year in prison and a fine of $10,000 and lastly MP Abdullah AlMudhaf suggested adding punitive measures to the penal code (AlKhaleej, 2021). However, none of the aforementioned proposals have been implemented as of October 2021.

However, on September 27, 2021, the Minister of Commerce and Industry and the Chairman of the Public Authority for Manpower, Abdullah AlSalman, issued directives to end discrimination in the private sector and criminalize harassment in the workplace (Ministry of Commerce and Trade of Kuwait, 2021).

In an article published by *AlRai* newspaper, prominent lawyer and member of the International Bar Association Alaa AlSaeedi stated that the only way women can be protected from sexual harassment and domestic violence is through enforcing a sexual harassment legislation and operating the domestic violence shelters immediately. According to her, even women who have obtained protective orders from the court cannot be guaranteed protection without the shelter (Dashti, 2021). This brings us to the high-profile murders that occurred since the beginning of the pandemic, which amount to six women.

Now that there are no women in parliament, the Women, Children and Family parliamentary committee, which consists of only men at this point, released a statement on September 9, 2021, which suggests that femicide is not a legislative issue but a societal one, stating that preventing violence against women is a governmental responsibility (AlJarida, 2021).

Climate Change and Domestic Violence

According to research conducted by the UNDP, climate change can be a direct cause of violence against women (Gevers, Musuya, & Bukuluki, 2020). And while there are no studies directly linked to Kuwait, it has been predicted that summer temperatures in the Middle East and Africa will rise over twice as fast as the global average (The Economist, 2018). This rise in temperature is accompanied by frequent dust storms and hotter heat waves, and according to Dr. Craig Anderson, these factors may cause an increase in aggression. In one of his laboratory tests, Dr. Anderson concluded that people in warmer conditions tend to choose harsher punishments than those who are in cooler environments (Anderson, 1987).

Another study conducted by the Carnegie Middle East Center suggests that while it may not be a direct causation, climate change may exacerbate problems that are already present in the Middle East which include domestic violence (Young, & Lazard, 2020).

The authors, as active members of the Abolish 153 campaign and Eithar, witnessed an increase in cases asking for help with domestic violence during the peak summer months in Kuwait.

Conclusion

Due to the lack of the availability of comprehensive statistics of domestic violence cases in Kuwait, several independent entities have conducted surveys and studies regarding the matter. Two lawyers representing the Women's Cultural and Social Society have visited Arab shelters and rehabilitation centers in a regional study tour and in their findings highlighted the importance of having a functioning shelter with its different services running throughout the country. The most common problem in all the countries they have visited was the lack of societal awareness on the issue of gender-based violence and its outcomes on society as a whole. Another common problem that was underlined in the study is the lack of budget and funding given to organizations that are handling the shelters. Based on the results of the study, the main struggle Arab women encounter is the fear of breaking their silence and bringing shame upon their families (WCSS, 2017).

Due to the cultural similarities between the various Arab countries, similar obstacles exist in Kuwait and have been pointed out in the findings of a survey done by Dr. Fatema AlSalem, Assistant Professor of Mass Communication in Kuwait University, in collaboration with Abolish 153. The survey was given to 767 adults in Kuwait proportionately between men and women and revealed that over 51% of Kuwaitis have been subjected to violence, yet only half of that number think ending violence against women should be a social priority. Furthermore, the perception of violence against women among men seemed to be of less importance than violence against children and the elderly, which were perceived as very important. (AlSalem, 2018).

Another academic study conducted by the College of Social Sciences in Kuwait University revealed that 54% of the survey takers believe that there is an exponential number of marital abuses at the hands of the husband. Unfortunately, there is no other scientific data available because victims and their relatives – in particular in outer districts in Kuwait – fear to report abuses, and seek legal protection or medical treatment. People choose silence over social humiliation and prefer to deal with their problems privately (AlKhashaab, 2019).

Findings of Justin Gengler et al's study on "*Who Supports Honor-Based Violence in the Middle East?*" indicate that the majority of Kuwaitis do not know about the existence of violent legislations and this attitude also makes itself apparent in their refusal to acknowledge the occurrence of domestic violence in Kuwait (Gengler, AlKazemi, & AlSharekh, 2018).

Another issue is that the awareness of the prevalence of domestic violence cases among primary care nurses is poor, and shortage of knowledge is a barrier to an effective clinical response by medical professionals. Between 60 and 90% of patients are inadequately managed (AlSafy, AlHendal, AlHawaj, Shazly, & Kamel, 2011).

One of the main issues in addressing the problem of domestic violence in regard to activating the shelter and approving the legislation is mistrust of victims, which is part of a universal phenomenon first documented by William Ryan in his book "Blaming the Victim" (Patry, 1978). In an article published in *AlSeyassa* newspaper in October 2019, it was revealed that one of the fears that was brought up by stakeholders during the WFAC meeting discussing the legislation is that women and especially young girls would use this law to falsely accuse their guardians and family members for "revenge" or to gain more freedom of movement. This may also explain the aversion to reporting cases and holding "family peace" as more important than stopping abuse as reported by Kuwaiti officials themselves to the OHCHR in 2015 (OHCHR, 2015).

Mona al Sager, a member of the Higher Council for Family Affairs, has stated that she believes that a culture of patriarchy and of misaligned social practices contributes to violence against women in Kuwait (KUNA, 2019). Many of those who argue that physical admonishment of women is permitted within certain parameters in the Quran use a particular verse from Surah An-Nisa (also referenced as Quran 4:34). This verse discusses the husband's role as protector and provider, and how he should progressively deal with disobedience, first by verbal admonishing, then withhold sex and finally physical discipline.

This brings us to an understanding of why disciplinary violence against women is tolerated so widely and why any act seen as disrespecting male kin or elder females may be punished under the pretext of moral guardianship (AlSharekh, 2017). In legal terms, many disciplinary actions give more rights to guardians over those they "guard", such as placing difficult young men and women in governmental social care homes until a guardian consents to releasing them, and reporting young women, even those above the legal age of 21, for "absconding" at local police stations. Articles 29, 182 and 153 of Kuwait's penal code are especially problematic with the intersection of rights of a male guardian and women's safety from sexual and physical harm.

Notes

1 There are some shelters specific to abused domestic staff, whether operated by the government or by embassies and church groups.

2 Discussions conducted with members of the committee and members of Abolish 153 on provision of training services for government employees specifically on domestic abuse during 2018 and 2019.

References

Aamer, M. (2016, January 9) Women and Family Affairs Committee Discusses Abolishing Adultery Article in Penal Code. AlJarida. www.aljarida.com/articles/1468122715704254000/

Abdulhafith, S., & AlFaam, R. (2020, January 27). Plain Clothes Police force to counteract Domestic Violence. AlAnba.https://menafn.com/arabic/1099610717/الكويت-بالفيديو-فرق-أمنية-بلباس-مدني-لمواجهة-العنف-الأسري

Abdullah, A. (2018, September 19). The board of "Human Rights Diwan" sees the light. *AlRai* www.alraimedia.com/Home/Details?id=653c131d-3264-4aeb-a70f-ff4635fd8530

Abolish Article 153. (2015). Winner of the 2016 Chaillot Prize for Human Rights in the GCC. www.abolish153.org

Abolish Article 153. [@abolish153]. (2017, May 10). When you lobby a politician and he actually listens. [Instagram photograph] www.instagram.com/p/BT6J0lXBuau/

Aboush, Q. (2015, August 12). "Will a hotline end the problems of Kuwaiti families". Erem News. www.eremnews.com/entertainment/329768

Abubakar, I (2018, January 24). Legislators Submit Bill on Domestic Violence. Arab Times. www.arabtimesonline.com/news/legislators-submit-bill-domestic-violence/

Alanba. (2019, October 10). "Women and Family Affairs Committee: Immediate 6 month Imprisonment for violators of the new domestic violence law".. *Alanba*. www.alanba.com.kw/ar/kuwait-news/parliament/928468/10-10-2019-المرأة-والأسرة-السجن-الفوري-أشهر -عقوبة-مخالفة-قانون-العنف-الأسري/

Alanba. (2020, April 14). "The First Murder Committed Between Spouses Sheds Light on the Psychological Suffering of Some Families Amidst the Lockdown". Alanba. www.alanba.com.kw/ar/kuwait-news/961984/14-04-2020-

AlDaqbasi, N. (2015, May 5). AlZamanan: Ministry of Justice to Launch Projects that Will Benefit Citizens. Kuwait National News Agency. www.kuna.net.kw/ArticleDetails.aspx?id=2439809&language=ar

AlJarida. (2021, September 9). "The Family Committee: The increase in gender-based violence is a societal problem and not a legislative one". *AlJarida*. https://www.aljarida.com/articles/1631193268541418800/

AlKhaldy, K. (2019, January 18). "Campaigns to end violence against women in Kuwait". *Alaraby*. www.alaraby.co.uk/society/2019/1/17/1-حملات-ضد-العنف-المنزلي-في-الكويت

AlKhaleej (2021, December 2). Kuwait: 7 MPs Present Proposals to Combat the Phenomenon of Sexual Harassment. http://khaleej.online/ZWZWY4

AlKhashaab, Y (2019, May 22). Violence Is Increasing in Kuwait. *AlQabas*. https://alqabas.com/article/671678

AlQabas. (2018, March 5). "Women and Family Affairs (Committee): Domestic Violence Law Postponed". *AlQabas*. https://alqabas.com/article/508739-المرأة-والأسرة-تأجيل-قانون-العنف-ال

AlQabas. (2019, October 1). "Parliamentary Women and Family Affairs Committee; Domestic Violence Law will be ready before sessions commence". *AlQabas*. https://alqabas.com/article/5712890-المرأة-والأسرة-البرلمانية-قانون-العنف-الأسري-سيكون-جاهزا-قبل-الانعقاد

Alsafy, Nagham & Alhendal, Entisar & Alhawaj, Shurooq & Shazly, Medhat & Kamel, Mohamed. (2011). Knowledge of primary care nurses regarding domestic violence. *Alexandria Journal of Medicine*, 47, 173–180. 10.1016/j.ajme.2011.02.002

AlSalem, F (2018, November 24). 53% of Kuwaiti Women are Abused by Men. AlQabas. https://alqabas.com/article/607181

AlShammari, F (2020, January 27). AlHashem to AlRai (newspaper): The Women's committee has approved the Family Violence Law and listed it for discussion at a national assembly session. AlRai. www.kuwaitpress.net/show34742.html

AlSharekh, A. (2017, December 19). "Disciplinary Violence in Kuwait". LSE. https://blogs.lse.ac.uk/mec/2017/12/19/disciplinary-violence-in-kuwait/

AlTurki, F (2019, October 8). MP Al Hasehm to AlJarida (newspaper): The Domestic Violence Legislation is Made up of 32 articles and it will be completed tomorrow. AlJarida. www.aljarida.com/articles/1570464692475871500/

AlWatan. (2019, October 1). "The Women and Family Affairs parliamentary committee awaiting the government's comments with regards to the family violence law". *AlWatan*. http://alwatan.kuwait.tt/articledetails.aspx?id=600256&yearquarter=20194

AlZayed, H. (2019, August 18). "The Domestic Abuse Shelter ... a stillborn dream". *Alqabas*. https://alqabas.com/article/5699558-مركز-إيواء-المعنفات-حلم-ولد-ميتا

Anderson, C. (1987). (PDF) temperature and aggression: Effects on Quarterly, Yearly, and City Rates of Violent and Nonviolent Crime www.researchgate.net/publication/19562791_Temperature_and_Aggression_Effects_on_Quarterly_Yearly_and_City_Rates_of_Violent_and_Nonviolent_Crime

Dashti, M. (2021, May 05). "The Family Protection Law Saw the Light ... With One Eye!". *AlRai*. https://bit.ly/3v9srj5

Domestic Violence Bill (2017). https://raqib50.s3.amazonaws.com/uploads/suggestion/file/1633/62.pdf

The Economist. (2018, May 31). Climate change is making the Arab World More Miserable. www.economist.com/middle-east-and-africa/2018/05/31/climate-change-is-making-the-arab-world-more-miserable

Gengler, J. J., Alkazemi, M. F., & Alsharekh, A. (2018). Who Supports Honor – Based Violence in the Middle East? Findings from a National Survey of Kuwait. *Journal of Interpersonal Violence*. https://doi.org/10.1177/0886260518812067

Gevers, A., Musuya, T., & Bukuluki, P. (2020, January 28). Why climate change fuels violence against women. www.undp.org/blog/why-climate-change-fuels-violence-against-women

Human Rights Watch. (2020). Kuwait: Events of 2019. https://www.hrw.org/world-report/2020/country-chapters/kuwait

KUNA. (2012, May 21). "Ministry of Interior activates email service for social police". *KUNA*. www.kuna.net.kw/ArticleDetails.aspx?id=2241921&language=ar

KUNA. (2019, November 25). "Kuwaiti Development Office:Violence Against Women is a Global Issue that requires Preventative Programs and Legislations". *KUNA*. www.kuna.net.kw/ Art icle Deta ils.aspx?id=2838046

Kuwait National Assembly. (2018, January 25). MPs submit a law to protect against Domestic Violence. http://www.kna.kw/clt-html5/news-details.asp?id=29210

Kuwait's State Party Report (2016, January 11). *CEDAW* http://tbinternet.ohchr.org/_layouts/treatybodyexternal/Download.aspx?symbolno=CEDAW%2fC%2fKWT%2f5&Lang=en

Makhoul, Mark. (2021, January 21). "Harassment in Kuwait". TWOFORTYEIGHTAM. https://248am.com/mark/complaining/harassment-in-kuwait/

Ministry of Commerce and Trade of Kuwait. (2021, September 27). The Minister's decision to criminalize discrimination in the private sector aims to improve Kuwait's rank in the work environment indicators. https://www.kuna.net.kw/ArticleDetails.aspx?id=2999985&language=ar

The National. (2020, August 20). Kuwait's National Assembly Passes Domestic Violence bill. https://www.thenationalnews.com/world/gcc/kuwait-s-national-assembly-passes-domestic-violence-bill-1.1066150

OHCHR. (2015), Kuwait's Report 2015. http://docstore.ohchr.org/SelfServices/FilesHandler.ashx?enc

OHCHR. (2017, November 1). Committee on the Elimination of Discrimination against Women reviews the situation of women in Kuwait.. Retrieved from www.ohchr.org/en/NewsEvents/Pages/DisplayNews.aspx?NewsID=22341&LangID=E

Patry, W. (1978). Book Reviews: William Ryan, Blaming The Victim (New York: Pantheon Books, 1971. *Review of Radical Political Economics, 10* (4), 66–67. https://doi.org/10.1177/048661347801000406

Report of the Office of the United Nations High Commissioner for Human Rights (Rep.No.A/HRC/WG.6/35/KWT/3). (2019, November 6). Retrieved from www.ecoi.net/en/file/local/2021634/A_HRC_WG.6_35_KWT_3_E.pdf

"Understanding a Difficult Verse, Qur'an 4:34: Additional Translations. The Feminist Sexual Ethic Project|Brandeis University. www.brandeis.edu.

WCSS. (2017, July 12). *The Philosophy of Shelters and Rehabilitation Centers: A Mechanism to Protect Women From Domestic Violence* (Rep. No. P115-51OS-01). https://www.wracati.com/uploads/book_new_final_resize.pdf

WCSS. (2020, May 11). "AlQatan: Kuwaiti Legislations have preserved women's dignity against any violence". *WCSS*. https://wcss-kw.org/?p=93

Young, M., & Lazard, O. (2020, November 19). Will the Middle East remain habitable? www.carnegie-mec.org/diwan/83256

14

"MOBILIZING FOR PUNISHMENT"

Legal Activism, Women's NGOs and the Grassroots in Lebanon

Sirin Knecht

1 Introduction

This paper assesses the significance of advocacy work and rights-based activism of grassroots women's NGOs in Lebanon and their impact on legal reforms in penal and judicial code tackling intimate relationships, family matters, and violence against women. The paper argues that activist work intends to guarantee protection and security. The activists' claims further strive towards increasing preventive measurement awareness while providing justice to suffering but surviving subjects affected by criminal actions harming women. Women's activists refer to international law such as the (women's) human rights Convention on the Elimination of All Forms of Discrimination against Women (CEDAW) with the UN Charter (UNRIC 2020)[1]. This way, they use the international law and human rights framework as a tool to hold a state's institutions accountable for eliminating and attempting to criminalize gender violence.[2]

The case study of the KAFA law serves as an excellent example to illustrate efforts to criminalize domestic violence. KAFA – a women's NGO based in Beirut – launched a campaign in the early 2000s to pass a law that punishes domestic violence, mainly when it takes place within marital relationships. The campaign and activists' work demonstrates tactics to manoeuvre around the legal status quo and patriarchal legal structures that give legal power and authority to religious laws and authorities in governing family and personal status matters. The campaign demands the implementation of gender justice by promoting legislation on domestic violence that protects women in the penal code.

The patriarchal structures display a male-dominated system that involves the constitution and the sectarian power-sharing political system intertwined with the political economy of clientelism and familialism.

This paper explores how activism tackles legality and the judicial system by mobilizing and lobbying, as well as non-state actors' involvement on the ground and in legislation reforms. This paper analyses the relationship between local non-state actors and their involvement in political affairs, intimate relationships and decision-making processes. The paper scrutinizes women's NGOs' demands to amend discriminatory legislation against the backdrop of Lebanon's legal and political sectarian census system and pluralism. The Lebanese constitution prescribes that family matters and personal and intimate relationship matters are considered religious affairs and separates them from civil affairs that are rooted in French mandate imperialism as well as in the Ottoman occupation and the introduction of the *"millet system"*. This paper critically examines developments

DOI: 10.4324/9781003264040-17

and challenges to internationalize and institutionalize the process of "judicialization" (Couso et al., 2010; see Hirschl, 2006; Hirschl, 2008; Moustafa, 2003; Shapiro & Sweet, 2002; Zenker, 2015) by developing a global legal culture (see Randeria, 2007).[3]

This paper contains three parts. The first part deals with violence, intimacy and visibility as generally accepted concepts by institutionalized women's rights and international activism. The women's activists' endeavour is to problematize and make claims for women's rights rejection and violation by exercising violence. It further establishes the importance of the topic by also referring to the first concept of penal populism that will be discussed throughout the paper. The second part centres on a case study to offer an illustration of activism and lobbyism that is backed by international legal culture. The third and last part discusses the case study's findings related to the conceptual/theoretical ramifications of transnational activism.

2 Violence, Intimacy and Visibility

In recent years, violence and oppression against women have increasingly been mentioned in public discourses and on media platforms thanks to the diligent efforts of activists around the world. Reasons for its increased recognition in public can be tied to the process of the issue, and the media paid greater attention to documented or reported cases. Developments of broader abilities to spread and disseminate information and reports on social media allow for reaching a broad spectrum of a mainstream global society. The specific form of violence presented and made the centre of attention regarding societal topics has impacted or affected (feminist) mainstreaming. Such mainstreaming constructed gender inequality or discrimination against women more visible in mainstream media and the public. These developments use both mainstream and the media to tackle the status quo of patriarchal grounding norms in society, based on law and decided on through politics. Nevertheless, critical players in documenting gender violence are activists who advocate the end of women's discrimination and legitimized violent acts against them in their institutional work. Women's rights activists are vital players who mobilize themselves as well as each other, to form coalitions and organize to make visible the issue that is finally tackled and disseminated by the media. The concept of visibility is, in general, a common concept used in a wide field of institutionalized activism (related not only to grassroots, non-governmental activities but also, beyond that, in academic circles and scholarship). The term's rhetorical but symbolic meaning comprises illustrating alternative representations that favour diversity. Throughout this paper, the concept of visibility will refer to the action of shedding light on gender injustice and therefore transforming this injustice into equality. Such transformation occurs concretely in jurisdiction, and women's NGOs seek to gain more representation in public and societal norms through their women's rights campaigns.

The importance and global societal implications of the arrival in the mainstream of injustice across media and among the public can be illustrated by one example of black women's activism in the United States of America. The debate aimed to make sexual harassment visible, including assault and violence against black women. Black human rights activist Tarana Burke coined the term "Me Too" and the social movement with the same name (Me Too Movement, 2020, URL).[4] The *Me Too* movement went viral as a hashtag, enabling women to testify to their experience as survivors of sexual harassment. The testimonies sparked outrage on a global scale, and one major victory of the movement was that it prompted a judicial trial, in which eventually the American movie mogul and producer Harvey Weinstein was punished for innumerable cases of sexual violence against women. He was sentenced and jailed for rape (The Guardian, 2020, URL).

As this case very clearly demonstrates, it is essential to recognize transnational connectedness and dissemination as a powerful tool to reach out and mobilize the public. Criminologist John

Pratt (2007) formulates such action as "penal populism", where (scandalizing) pressure on existing legal bodies is exerted in public. The increasing demand for structural penal law reforms to criminalize actions harming women in everyday life is fast becoming a key instrument in combatting gender violence globally. In light of recent events that report scandals of crimes and assaults, it is becoming challenging to ignore the existence of gender injustice exercised structurally but also in everyday life. However, actions need to be situated and contextualized related to their transnational connections and local circumstances. Regarding the penal populism concept after Pratt (2007), this paper extends the theoretical framework of the idea by its contribution of an analysis of the concept against the backdrop of domestic violence and violence against women. Accordingly, criminalizing violence against women calls for legal reform and changes in societal norms and moralities.

3 Going Public and the Power of the Public

It has previously been observed that studies over the past two decades have provided important information on legal activism, grassroots and non-governmental organizations working on contemporary issues tackling violence in the private realm that begin to impact more effectively in public. One concept that has theoretical ramifications on the influence on public (opinion) regarding punishment is the concept mentioned above of penal populism (Pratt, 2007). Pratt suggests that penal populism tries to influence public opinion using images, sentiments, and collective affects (see also Bens & Zenker, 2017, 2019; Slaby, 2017). These can evoke positive reactions and feelings such as empathy, sympathy or compassion towards a case or situation presented through reports, documentation or images. Negative emotions, such as rejection, disgust or deterrence, may also be responsible for feelings of reservation. Such images can also cause scandal, which means the information or contexts regarding an opinion to be shaped might also be presented in a way that anticipates a specific reaction towards it. It is thus presented in a manipulative manner, where information, images or narratives are deliberately exaggerated and presented in this way, whether this might reflect reality or not. The exaggeration of descriptions is relevant as media tends to be driven by a particular imperative to scandalize stories while retaining interpretational sovereignty over its decision as well as the motivation behind them. In sum, feelings and affects related to justice and a moral understanding of them are intentionally evoked.

In the Lebanese context presented in this paper (and more detailed in the case study in the following section), this kind of penal populism aims at creating sympathies and compassion of unjust situation and treatment. However, a sort of rational feeling of assessing the problem is somehow wanted to be depicted as I would interpret and consider it.

In addition to his later work, John Pratt, together with Marie Clarke published on penal populism in New Zealand (2005), forwarding a concept similar to the one Pratt published by himself. In a subsequent article (2008), he also confirmed the limitations of his concept. In 2002, the authors Julia Roberts, Loretta Stalans, David Indermaur and Mike Hough published an edited volume on penal populism as a comparative study of five countries. Michael Tonry has made a stance in opposition to the general observation of penal populism. In his article (2007), he argues that the established concept of penal populism is not applicable in Western countries, stating that statistics do not show an increase in incarcerations. In light of this discussion, I would argue that penal populism is not necessarily about imprisonment but rather about the act of being sentenced and, therefore, the recognition of a criminal, violent act such as assault. In general terms, there are even fewer cases reported, filed and brought to court based on domestic violence globally, and even fewer are legally punished as criminal actions.

Nevertheless, my aim in this paper is not to comparatively demonstrate and approve the hypothesis by judging whether this is the case in non-Western contexts or not. Instead, I intend to illustrate the influence of law, norms and society through the concept of penal populism as advanced by the rights-based campaigns of women's NGOs in Lebanon. The relevant impact is, therefore, the act of visibility and recognition by society and subsequent changes or reforms in the law. Imprisonment, thus, is secondary in my analysis.

4 KAFA and the KAFA Law – A Case Study

Before discussing in the following section, the women's NGO KAFA and its work, a summary about the constitutional and political composition of Lebanon is necessary. Without this, it would be impossible to talk about law and implementation as well as its constraints and reservations. The short overview of the legal system in Lebanon also helps us understand the relevance of non-governmental actors such as women's NGOs tackling the status quo of the legal system employing public opinion and mobilization.[5] Family and private matters are usually considered intimate in the sense of inner family-oriented and do not become the topic of public discussion. If state's institutions make decisions on family affairs, they do it in traditionalized ways that reflect and maintain men-dominated structures. Alternatively, the state's institutions transmit this sovereignty by acting through religious institutions.

In Lebanon, the constitution prescribes in article 3[6] that religious authorities govern family affairs. The political system of Lebanon is a proportional system that was reinforced by French colonial power during the mandate period, which has since been slightly tailored several times. The religious majority determine political positions, and the classification of Muslims and Christians served as two general denominational categories. Significant changes in the political system due to the (in-)balances and other privileges for specific religious and confessional subgroups – designated in the political framework as sects – occurred in the aftermath of Lebanon's civil war in 1990 as part of a peace agreement. Sects and confessional belonging are therefore tied to political parties and vice versa. Officially recognized religious groups number 18 in Lebanon with 15 religious courts and the recognition of family laws. The judicial legitimacy of religious authority dates back to the Ottoman Empire and the legal tradition of the *"millet system"* (see Abu Jaber, 1967). The process of sectarianism or confessionalism shapes and interferes into a public, private, and everyday life. Sectarianism demonstrates the essential formation of sects as both identificatory and distinctive features when their strength and power in the context of political decisions and position become relevant.[7] Sects display to be fixed and undynamic, which is the case from a political and legal perspective, where sects as structural entities are legally defined. Given this framework and without a surprise, alleged sectarian differences were instrumentalized politically and have prompted the long-lasting conflict (see Assi, 2016, 2018; Zamir, 1997, 1999).

The religious judiciary is relevant insofar as women's rights activism strives to universalize family law by transforming it into civil law. Personal status laws are confessional-bond, as well. Contemporary women's NGOs in Lebanon work on gender violence through advocacy and rights-based lens.

4.1 Institutional Background of KAFA

KAFA means "enough" in Arabic and is the name of women's NGOs based in Beirut. The organization's real name is *Enough Violence and Exploitation* and founded in 2005 (KAFA, 2020, URL). The organization considers itself to be a " (…) feminist, secular, Lebanese, non-profit, non-governmental civil society organization" (URL). Yara[8] has been working at KAFA since its foundation (in fact, she was a member of the founding KAFA team). During our interview held in Beirut in 2017, she told me that she has specialized in the field of violence against women since 1985 after the UN-organized third International World Conference on Women in Nairobi.[9] Leyla, another employee of KAFA, confirms the longevity and whole experience of KAFA's staff on the topic of violence against women that Yara pointed out. Leyla adds that the people who founded KAFA have been working on women's issues for longer and have even launched a women's umbrella organization *The Lebanese Council To Resist Violence Against Woman* (LECORVAW), the "first organization of its own kind in Lebanon".[10] Rita, a project manager at KAFA and a member of its executive board, explains the goal of the organization in tackling violence against women broadly. Their primary focus within the domain of violence against women is on family violence as well as violence/abuse against children. However, they aim at reaching out into several sectors of violence against women, such as women trafficking, domestic worker abuse/violence and sexual harassment in public or at workplaces, as Rita confirmed. Rita also said that throughout the years of women's rights activism, there had been a shift to transform violence from a private to a public issue. Leyla mentioned that there has also been a recognizable structural shift of grassroots organizations towards institutionalized activism throughout the last 25 years. Leyla said that in the late 1970s, and beginning of the 1980s, all NGO sector work was voluntary ("during the civil war, people were enthusiastic about helping").

4.2 The KAFA Law and Domestic Violence Campaign

The KAFA law was passed in 2013, after seven years of constant strenuous campaigning. In 2013, the parliament approved the legal draft. A joint political committee of members in the parliament of different political parties had lobbied to gain the majority of votes for approval of the draft. However, the legal draft received some revisions from the original demands. The approved draft did not meet the needs of prosecuting domestic violence in marital relationships with particular regard to violence against women were not met. Personal status law still gives leeway to the exercise of violence within the family, particularly between spouses, where exercising violence for disciplinary purposes can be deemed allowable depending on the judges' religious beliefs.

According to Yara, KAFA's strategy was not to have any further overlap with personal status law amendments in their campaign and draft because they wanted "just to pass the law". Personal status laws are connected to religious legal codes. They would, therefore, cause further complications to enforce any significant changes in the legislation as the religious authority would further be weakened. Personal status laws are relevant as they are connected to family laws and the representation of legal subjects. Yara's statements hint at the complicated relationship of personal status laws within politics and society, the separation of which is aimed for through women's rights activism. From this perspective, the campaign team navigated around personal status laws and intimate relationships and directed it towards criminal law and punishment. Yara further states that "[religious authorities] thought that it is the first time an actor from the civil sector is interfering in family issues. But I think it was a big step forward". KAFA, as an NGO, entered into the realm of religious governance, which they regard as a significant success of the campaign (KAFA, 2013, URL).

The new draft of the penal law refers to a less fixed umbrella term of domestic violence against all types of a family member. KAFA initially wanted to call it "domestic violence against spouses", as Rita told me. Rita further explained that the name of the legal draft would have been a political statement, referring to feminist interference into a religious and patriarchal terrain. Moreover, assault as part of domestic violence and as a criminalized act is not considered. The penal law also does not apply to minors, which is regressive for women as they are not able to protect their children (KAFA, 2013, URL).

The family law campaigned for by KAFA had more enormous implications on several levels. The campaign gained international attention within the field of global developments and politics and attracted external, foreign funding and support. The organization received recognition, popularity and prestige within the context of international aid (but also, they were confronted with accusations of being too radical and unwilling to compromise and collaborate with religious authorities). The legal draft became personally associated with the organizations, and they are known as "the dinosaurs" of women's NGOs within international aid circles.

The campaign served as a role model for advocacy work tackling gender violence and family law among the MENA region and beyond. But unfortunately, the reference to the precedent was not made, as Leyla pointed out: "The campaign work was replicated all over the world - without referring to us!"

4.3 COVID-19 and Environmental Issues Implications on Gender and Violence

Domestic violence expanded worldwide during the pandemic and is also problematized as a shadow pandemic (UN Women, 2021, URL). As isolation, quarantine and confinement generally characterized daily pandemic life, the domestic setting became the only place to stay to protect oneself from the virus. However, this also told that many women could not defend themselves from violence because they had no other options for places of refuge. This retreat to the home again gave the intimate setting of family and privacy more space. Traditional gender roles were hardened again, and with them, the domestic context and social relationships.

Lebanese gender expert Abir Chebaro (2021), in a report published at the Issam Fares Institute for Public Policy and International Affairs at American University (AUB), suggested that cross-cutting links between gender and the impact of COVID-19 in Lebanon are evident. Classically "female" occupations such as nursing work are the most vulnerable during the pandemic, exposing staff to multiple risks. Most vulnerable here are migrant domestic workers, most of whom are stuck unpaid due to the lockdown that has shut down public life, without travelling documents and any entitlement to health care. Other precarious sectors of the economy where women work part-time, such as tourism, body-care professions or, in some cases, the catering industry, have been cut off due to the pandemic. Sexual and reproductive health centres remain closed (Chebaro, 2021, URL). Especially sexual minorities from LGBTQI$^+$ groups, such as transgender or non-binary people, lose essential places of retreat and contact points to find shelter due to the temporary closure.

For the work of women's NGOs, the pandemic meant that their work focused more on supply and support work, as they did during the civil war, for instance. Due to contact restrictions, local organizations could not carry out organized activities and initiatives such as campaign work, demonstrations, and even educational work. Their work and activism in the public sphere were temporarily suspended, and they had difficulties reaching their target groups. KAFA used testimonies to document the daily lives of women affected by violence who could barely leave the house or find public transportation, such as a *Service,* a shared cab (KAFA, 2020, URL). Local NGOs with support hotlines noted a dramatic overall increase in the use of the telephone service (Rose, 2020, URL).

An accumulation of different historical causes and compositions led to Lebanon's current highly precarious economic situation, which I cannot discuss further in the context of this paper.

The pandemic has exacerbated the already ongoing inflation. Prices for medicines, gas and food continue to rise sharply. As if that were not enough, on August 3, 2020, Beirut experienced one of the worst explosions in the port of Beirut. Highly explosive ammonium nitrate fertilizer stored for six years at the port was exploded and levelled entire neighbourhoods to the ground. Several hundred people were killed, and over several thousand people were injured and left homeless (Chehayeb, 2021, URL).

In addition to the extent of suffering, loss and grief, this meant another economic and political relapse for Lebanese society. With the devastation of offices, bars, clubs, health centres, recreational centres and shelters, the already precarious situation for domestic and sexual violence victims was further worsened by the pandemic. The same applies to the work of local organizations active in this field.

5 Legal Activism as International Response

5.1 Transnationalism in Action

Let me come back to women's rights advocacy and gender violence work. These findings support the conceptual premise that women's NGOs mobilize activists, lobby in political domains to gain influence in decision-making processes, interfere in law-making processes and shape public discourse. Moreover, they found a strategy to impact existing legislation by referring to international law as well as pressuring the Lebanese state as a signatory of the CEDAW convention – even though they passed the convention with some reservations.[11] It further connects social movements and developments of what Cecilia MacDowell Santos (2007) understands as transnational legal activism. Women's activists are not only consultants but also active representatives who are practically involved. They form coalitions and launch campaigns. An explanation might be that they activate transnational materiality, networks and relations (and money, which is donor-driven). There are internationalization and institutionalization that are recognizable. Through established conferences, preferably by United Nations agencies, women can gather, exchange, debate and communicate their issues. Such a transnational connectedness is materialized in the visibility of partnerships and cooperation that extends to a regional, local, international and global scale. In particular, the transnational exchanges are of great significance among activists in the MENA region as they are confronted with similar challenges. There are commonalities in the legal systems among the MENA region due to legal traditions derived from colonialism and occupation. Legal, colonial legacies are transmitted and not adjusted in many modern states' constitutions after they have gained independence from former colonial mandates or colonial powers (with particular regard to French legal influence). Therefore, they are tackling the same legal issues, such as the visibility of domestic violence in marital relationships, while addressing them as citizens and not religious matters. It can be said that, in general, women's rights activists in the MENA region deal with the same issues. Similarities and commonalities are essential to share the experiences of each organization in dealing with violence and in terms of legal activism and lobbying. Women's NGOs and women's rights activists exchanged documents and legal drafts. Strategies on how to involve the media, how to raise awareness in the public realm and how to attract foreign funding partners are shared among them.

5.2 State, Law and Mobilization

The majority of women's rights movements in the MENA region date back mainly to the independence of modern states from former colonial empires or mandates in the second half of the 20th century. Such historical events and contextualization are of great significance as many former women's rights activism endeavours were engaged in supporting resistance forces led by Lebanese men that aimed to advance independence from the French colonial mandate (1943). Therefore, women demanded independence from their husbands, cousins, fathers or sons. Lebanon symbolizes a patchwork in the sense that there is already a considerable amount of religious diversity that is recognized. In these very first moves towards independence, women's activism joined forces institutionally because, previously, women had organized themselves by religious or sectarian affiliation.[12]

This historical contextualization is relevant to the fact that there is a correlation between women's rights and activism in Lebanon and their demand to stand together to unite beyond sectarian, religious, generational and political and regional boundaries both in the past and now in the country's contemporary struggles. In the past, the colonial and occupational powers would have oppressed their visibility, while now they face a lack of visibility within the family and personal matters and intimate relationships. In both cases, it is a patriarchal legal culture that has rendered them invisible, embedded in a state structure. While referring to domestic violence and its punishment, the state's responsibility, and the question of whether the state structure is still an adequate reflection of the present, has been made. Here comes Donald Black's ageing yet valuable concept forwarded by Donald Black regarding legal mobilization. Black (1972, p. 126) states that "without the mobilization of the law, a central legal system lies out of touch with the human problems is designed to oversee. Mobilization is the link between the law and the people served or controlled by the law". I would not entirely share Black's dimensional and vertical-scalar view from a conceptual point of view. However, I second that between law and people is the powerful force of social mobilization that can negotiate, evoke and create change. In other words, legal mobilization embodies the power of living, dynamic law being able to be shaped and changed. On a political level, legal mobilization requires allies such as political parties and partners to be able to enter the political sphere.

Gender justice has advanced in its practical development and humanitarian work (international aid) through supporting projects on the topic run by UN institutions. As previously stated in this paper, there is a trend towards gender mainstreaming in the media and public, which positively impacts gender justice and its recognition. Therefore, I argue that the visibility of domestic violence issues is shifting from a personal, private concern to a public one, allowing it to be openly tackled and penalized. Such a perspective reflects a gender mainstream shift that has taken place within international aid in previous years.

5.3 Transition on the Ground

Stricter criminal penalties for sexual crimes, violence or abuse have been demanded, and laws and legal subjects have to be created that define the criminal act against them. Concretely, this means recognizing women as legal subjects (not affiliated as wives, mothers, or daughters, unmarried) and recognizing illegal actions against them. However, they also seek to amend former French colonial civil laws that forbid the transmission of citizenship and exempt rapists from penal punishment if they marry their victims.[13]

In his article, Turkish anthropologist Hikmet Kocamaner (2019) explores the undertakings of the Turkish state to involve religion in matters of the family and intimate relationship by employing religious authorities by the state so they can govern over family matters. Unlike this Turkish case, the Lebanese constitution already legitimates religious personal status and family laws, including family matters and intimate relationships, particularly between spouses and therefore in a marital relationship. This disguise or increasing control of the religious authority in legitimized state power is what women's NGOs are trying to avoid and mainly to get it to be abandoned. By criminalizing domestic violence, women's activism enters the contentious domain of religious power, family and personal status laws.

Sally Engle Merry's comprehensive study on "vernacularized" (legal) activism (2006a, 2006b) contributes to contemporary issues tackling violence in the private realm that had begun to matter more effectively in public through international law. In her book entitled "Human Rights and Gender Violence: Translating International Law into Local Justice" (2006a), she shows how international law (about human and women's rights) is translated from the international scale, as she calls it, to local courts that address domestic violence. Empirical data exemplifies her conceptual framework, and she highlights the transnational activism and legal mobilization that travels from the international sphere and arrives and ends in a local court and a local judicial verdict. This translation, transmission and transitional moment within a legal culture and its adaption and implementation were ground-breaking within legal anthropology scholarship. It paved the way for further research and study on the topic. However, what is important to note here is that Merry's concept focused less on looking at the mediating procedures of institutional organizations on the ground and their agency while shifting importance to international scales. Grassroots NGOs and, therefore, women's NGOs are brokers in the sense that they need to find strategies to navigate their activism using the tool of international legal culture to adjust and frame it in ways that their demands are made visible. It is their agency that shapes their needs. In the case of this case study, the KAFA law aimed to establish another alternative way of tackling patriarchal legal culture. The KAFA law demands secularizing the judicial process and making it universal for all women in Lebanon, no matter their religious background and sectarian affiliation.

6 Conclusion

The case study of the KAFA law confirms the importance of criminalizing intimate relationship violence by going public. Institutionalized NGO activism brings issues to the public stage to help it influence and shape public discourse and the media landscape. Transnational activism demonstrates how legal mobilization, NGO work, lobbyism, and networking are practised in structural and legalistic ways. It is hence an international response to domestic violence. This paper described the design and implementation of criminalization and punishment of domestic violence to raise awareness and change societal structures and norms in public. Women's rights activists pursue legal activism by lobbying and mobilizing political parties, committees and external partners. They use international human rights language regarding gender justice and use CEDAW to mediate and deliver their claims. The cases study further supports the idea of a transformation among grassroots NGOs. As Pratt (2007) has shown us with his framework of "penal populism", NGOs and their involvement in penal populism have transformed themselves into political entities in the sense of shaping and influencing public discourse and procedures. In the case of the established women's NGOs in Lebanon that women's NGO KAFA is part of, a considerable shift of institutional organization is noticeable. The first allegedly solely business-oriented, bureaucratic, outcome-delivering and reproducing organization transitioned into a political entity that participates in decision-making and law-making procedures and actions. Research has also indicated the extent of existing gender inequality in legislation recognized by Lebanon's legal system. Legality and (religious) authority are thereby questioned, and punishment and criminalization of violent social behaviour and norms against women are sought. Public opinion is targeted to be re-oriented in terms of perceptions of women and their role within society. Influencing the public can lead in a seminal direction towards gender and social justice in order to abandon and penalize the legitimation of violence against women. Challenges that now exist include legal implementations after laws have been passed and lobbying and mobilizing for them. The practical implementation of legal reforms on political, judicial levels, and governmental institutions, including the security agency, needs to be controlled and monitored. A reasonable approach to tackle this issue could be to establish impartial organizations, which evaluate institutions such as state agencies and courts in Lebanon.

The case study has identified how grassroots NGOs advance the politics of gender equality on the ground in Lebanon while the NGO work increases its professionalization and institutional structure. Nevertheless, grassroots Lebanese NGOs' perseverance and hard work in their everyday advocacy and rights-based institutional work should not be ignored. Their activism and institutionalization in problematizing social issues expose them to risks, rejection and crises. Funding limits, withdrawal of support and unstable political backing manifest such a state of uncertainty and precarity.

Finally, this paper examined the growing transnational impacts of international legal culture on judicialization globally.

Notes

1 For detailed information, see https://unric.org/en/un-charter-app/.

2 I do not refer to the debate on whether "women rights are human rights" as well as to the discussion whether women's rights should be framed as women's human rights due to its historical origins.

I am aware that women's rights originate from the human rights framework and, therefore, women's rights as a particular rights discourse embed itself around human rights universalist claim. However, I prefer to use women's rights to centre the centrality and universality of rights claims for women but with less emphasis on the universalist human rights framework as such because most of the women's activists working on advocacy and in NGOs in Lebanon do so. In this way, it opens up for divers perspectives on the translation of women's rights and its comparative analysis.

For further information to this debate, see Bunch (1990); Cook (1994); Grewal (1999); Hesford & Kozol, (2005) and van Leeuwen (2009).

3 Human rights gained primary focus and impact in global and international politics after World War II, from where views on morality, ethics of goods, as well as questions on humanity and humanitarian action, had evolved.

Furthermore, it is a widely held view that significant and increased cultures of legislation, in general, are historically tied to the contextualization of legal activism starting in the 1990s (Hesford et al., 2005). Through the end of the Cold War, inter-state affairs have been eased in the sense that there are more peaceful negotiations than in the past. It also means that intra-state matters have become more central in politics, and that is why human rights as a practice and not only as a discourse gained more attention. Additional reasons for this establishment are the "Millennium Development Goals" (MDGs), and the augmentation of non-governmental organizations in post-conflict and peacebuilding programs and initiatives.

4 For further information regarding the *Me Too* movement, see https://metoomvmt.org.

5 I am aware of the fact that the concept of penal populism is broadly and more likely to be used to illustrate how populist and conservative ideologies might sway public opinion, which has more tremendous implications on normative order and morality in society. I do not want to compare the case study of KAFA and the organization's agenda with the endeavours, as mentioned earlier. On the contrary, I intend to show the increasing impact on feminist policies and politics in existing politics as well as on public order and structures.

6 For further information, see the Lebanese constitution online https://mjp.univ-perp.fr/constit/lb1926.htm.

7 For further analysis and background information regarding the political system in Lebanon and sectarianism, see Mikdashi (2011) and Majed (2016, 2019).

8 All names of employees are anonymized. I gained informants' knowledge during interviews and fieldwork between 2016 and 2017 in Beirut. The collected data serves as ethnographic material for my currently unpublished doctoral thesis. The interviews with Yara, Leyla and Rita were made in June 2017 in Beirut.

9 For further information, see UN Women's website www.unwomen.org/en/how-we-work/intergovernmental-support/world-conferences-on-women.

10 For further information on LECORVAW NGO, see its website www.lecorvaw.com/index.php/en/.

11 In Yara's view

> (…) [a]ll the reservations Arab countries [had about] CEDAW articles are related to cultural specificities. Nevertheless, we know that it is a patriarchal mentality; it is nothing else. That is behind these reservations. It is as if they put all the sacred status laws in a sacred place which nobody should talk about, but we are breaking this taboo.

The Lebanese state has ratified the CEDAW convention apart from three articles (9, 16, 29) in 1997. See URL: www.ohchr.org/en/professionalinterest/pages/cedaw.aspx.

12 The scope of this paper does not allow me to discuss the history of women's rights and activism in Lebanon in a more detailed way.

13 A campaign was launched on this issue in 2016 by the grassroots NGO, ABAAD. In 2017, one major victory of the campaign was the approval of the political committee within the parliament to amend this article through legislation. For further information, see ABAAD's website www.abaadmena.org/.

Bibliography

Literature

Abu Jaber, K. S. (1967). The millet system in the nineteenth-century Ottoman Empire. *The Muslim World*, 57 (3), 212–223.

Assi, A. (2016). *Democracy in Lebanon: Political parties and the struggle for power since Syrian withdrawal.* I.B.Tauris.

——. (2018). Lebanon's consociational model, Christian parties and the struggle for political power in the post-2005 period. In *Sectarianism in the Contemporary Middle East*, (pp. 100–122) Routledge.

Bens, J., & Zenker, O. (Eds.) (2017). *Gerechtigkeitsgefühle: Zur affektiven und emotionalen Legitimität von Normen.* Transcript Verlag.

——. (2019). Sentiment. In Slaby S. (Ed.), *Affective Societies,* (pp. 96–106) Routledge.

Black, D.J. (1973). The mobilization of law. *The Journal of Legal Studies*, 1 (2), 125–129.

Bunch, C. (1990). Women's rights as human rights: Toward a re-vision of human rights. *Human Rights Quarterly*, (12), 486–498.

Chebaro, A. (2021). *The gendered dimension of COVID-19 in Lebanon.* American University of Beirut Press.

Cook, R. J. (1994). State responsibility for violations of women's human rights. *Harvard Human Rights Journal*, 7, 125–176.

Couso, J., Huneeus, A., & Siedler, R. (2010). *Cultures of legality: Judicialization and political activism in Latin America.* Cambridge University Press.

Grewal, I. (1999). 'Women's rights as human rights': Feminist practices, global feminism, and human rights regimes in transnationality. *Citizenship Studies,* 3 (3), 337–354.

Hesford, W. S. et al. (2005). *Just advocacy?: Women's human rights, transnational feminisms, and the politics of representation.* Rutgers University Press.

Hesford, W. S., & Kozol, W. (Eds.) (2005). Introduction. In: Just advocacy?: Women's human rights, transnational feminisms, and the politics of representation (pp. 1–29). Rutgers University Press

Hirschl, R. (2006). The new constitutionalism and the judicialization of pure politics worldwide. *Fordham Law Review*, 75, 721–754.

——. (2008). The judicialization of mega-politics and the rise of political courts. *Annual Review of Political Science,* 11, 93–118.

Kocamaner, H. (2019). Regulating the family through religion: Secularism, Islam, and the politics of the family in contemporary Turkey. *American Ethnologist,* 46 (4), 495–508.

Majed, R. (2019). Sectarianization: Mapping the new politics of the Middle East. *Global Change, Peace & Security*, 31 (1), 121–124.

Merry, S. E. (2006a). Human rights and transnational culture: Regulating gender violence through global law. *Osgoode Hall Law Journal 4 (1)*, 53–77.

——. (2006b). Transnational human rights and local activism: Mapping the middle. *American Anthropologist*, 108 (1), 38–51.

Mikdashi, M. (2011, March 25). What is political sectarianism. *Jadaliyya—*جدلية.. www.jadali yya.com/Deta ils/23833

Moustafa, T. (2003). Law versus the state: The judicialization of politics in Egypt. *Law & Social Inquiry*, 28 (4), 883–930.

Pratt, J. (2007). *Penal populism.* Routledge.

— —. (2008). When penal populism stops: Legitimacy, scandal and the power to punish in New Zealand. *Australian & New Zealand Journal of Criminology*, 41 (3), 364–383. https://journals-sagepub-com.ezproxy.eth.mpg.de/doi/pdf/10.1375/acri.41.3.364

Pratt, J., & Clarke, M. (2005). Penal populism in New Zealand. *Punishment & Society*, 7 (3), 303–322.

Randeria, S. (2007). The state of globalization: Legal plurality, overlapping sovereignties and ambiguous alliances between civil society and the cunning state in India. *Theory, Culture & Society*, 24 (1), 1–33.

Santos MacDowell, C. (2007). Transnational legal activism and the state: Reflections on cases against Brazil in the Inter-American Commission on Human Rights. *SUR-Int' l Journal on Human Rights*, 7–29. www.scielo.br/j/sur/a/53tc4SDrrHtL85tJhzpvkDB/?lang=en

Shapiro, M., & Sweet, A. S. (2002). *On law, politics, and judicialization*. Oxford University Press.

Slaby, J. (2017). More than a feeling: Affect as radical situatedness. *Midwest Studies in Philosophy*, 41, 7–26. https://philarchive.org/archive/SLAMTA-3

Tonry, M. (2007). Determinants of penal policies. *Crime and Justice*, 36 (1), 1–48.

van Leeuwen, C . F. (2009). *Women's rights are human rights: The practice of the United Nations human rights committee and the Committee on economic, social and cultural rights*. Intersentia Cambridge University Press.

Zamir, M. (1997). *Lebanon's quest: The road to statehood 1926–1939*. IB Tauris.

——. (1999). From hegemony to marginalism: The Maronites of Lebanon. In Bengio, O., & Ben-Dor, G. (Eds.), *Minorities and the State in the Arab World*, (pp. 111–128) Kumarian Press.

Zenker, O. (2015). De-judicialization, outsourced review and all-too-flexible bureaucracies in South African Land Restitution. *The Cambridge Journal of Anthropology*, 33 (1), 81–97. https://doc.rero.ch/record/288884/files/2015_Zenker_Dejudicialization.pdf

Internet Sources

ABAAD. (2020). URL: www.abaadmena.org/, [accessed date 18.07.20].

Chehayeb, K. (2021). A year on, politicians accused of hindering Beirut blast justice. URL: www.aljazeera.com/news/2021/8/3/a-year-on-lebanon-politicians-accused-hindering-beirut-blast-justice, [accessed date 12.12.2021].

Digithèque de matériaux juridiques et politiques (MJP). (2011). Liban. Constitution du 23 mai 1926. URL: https://mjp.univ-perp.fr/constit/lb1926.htm, [accessed date 18.07.20].

——. (2020). About KAFA. www.kafa.org.lb/en/about, [accessed date 15.07.20].

KAFA. (2013). Campaign for Legislating the Protection of Women from Domestic Violence. Domestic Violence. URL: Campaign for Legislating the Protection of Women from Domestic Violence, https://kafa.org.lb/en/node/10 [accessed date 15.07.20].

——. (2020). Between the Corona epidemic, and that of domestic violence: Kafa's March report. URL: https://kafa.org.lb/en/node/407, [accessed date 12.12.2021].

Majed, R. (2016). In the Arab World, Sectarianism Is Real, Sects Are Not. Al Jazeera [Online] 16. URL: www.aljazeera.com/news/2016/10/16/in-the-arab-world-sectarianism-is-real-sects-are-not, accessed Date [16.10.2020].

Me Too Movement. (2020). URL: https://metoomvmt.org, [accessed date 18.07.20].

Rose, S. (2020). Lebanon's spike in lockdown domestic violence cases reveals a legal system left wanting. URL: www.thenationalnews.com/world/mena/lebanon-s-spike-in-lockdown-domestic-violence-cases-reveals-a-legal-system-left-wanting-1.1005916, [accessed date 12.12.2021].

The Guardian. (2020). Harvey Weinstein begins 23-year sentence at New York state prison URL: www.theguardian.com/world/2020/mar/19/harvey-weinstein-new-york-state-prison-maximum-security, [accessed date 01.07.20].

The Lebanese Council to Resist Violence Against woman (LECORVAW). (2020). URL. www.lecorvaw.com/index.php/en/, [accessed date 20.07.20].

United Nation (UN). (2020). Charter of the United Nations. URL: www.un.org/en/charter-united-nations/, [accessed date 03.07.20].

United Nations of Human Rights Office of the High Commissioner (OHCHR) (2020). Convention on the Elimination of All Forms of Discrimination against Women New York, December 18, 1979. URL. www.ohchr.org/en/professionalinterest/pages/cedaw.aspx, [accessed date 01.07.20].

UN Women. (2020). Definition of domestic violence. URL: www.endvawnow.org/en/articles/398-definition-of-domestic-violence.html, [accessed date 18.07.20].

——. (2021). The Shadow Pandemic: Violence against women during COVID-19. URL: www.unwomen.org/en/news/in-focus/in-focus-gender-equality-in-covid-19-response/violence-against-women-during-covid-19, [accessed date 12.12.2021].

15

DOMESTIC VIOLENCE IN THAILAND

An In-Depth Examination of How Culture and Resource-Seeking Barriers Impact Victim Safety

Tanya Grant

Introduction

Domestic violence is an intention to use force or power to threaten or hurt family members. It often develops from conflicts and quarrels and results in physical and mental injuries and loss of rights. Domestic violence can be committed physically, verbally, and sexually – usually characterized by some combination of forcing, threatening, beating, kicking, and limiting and/or obstructing another person's rights and freedom (Laeheem, 2019). It focuses on physical, sexual, and mental abuses toward family members, especially between husbands and wives. Furthermore, domestic violence reeks of anger, fright, and apprehension clearly inflicted on the victim with the intent of severe harm, sometimes even resulting in death. Most of the incidents are committed by husbands who want to display power and control their wives by injuring them physically, mentally, and sexually and to force and threaten their wives to do something for them. Beyond the individual family members affected, domestic violence has made an unmistakably negative impact on society as a whole. For example, children whose parents use violence against each other might learn and absorb these violent tendencies (Kongsakon & Pojam, 2008).

It is estimated that of the 87,000 women who were intentionally killed in 2017 globally, more than half (50,000 or 58%) were killed by intimate partners or family members, meaning that 137 women across the world are killed by a member of their own family every day. More than a third (30,000) of the women intentionally killed in 2017 were killed by their current or former intimate partner (United Nations, 2019).

Despite the amount of data regarding domestic violence throughout the world, scant official Thai data exist on violence against women. The magnitude of the domestic violence problem in Thailand is underestimated and has rarely been documented. However, a survey of 2,500 Thai women in four provinces was conducted by Cheumchit, Chernkwanma, Rugkua, Daengthern, Abdullakasim, and Wieringa in 2018. The survey revealed that one in six Thai women faced intimate partner violence (IPV). In Thai society, IPV is considered a private issue and a family matter because the family is an important social institution and portrayed as a space of love and care, even when the reality of family violence exists. Most Thais learn they should not tell outsiders about internal family matters. As a result, IPV remains an invisible and unrecognized issue in Thai society, and women victims must deal with their intimate violence in solitude.

Over the past 50 years, Thailand has undergone significant social and economic changes. It has experienced the forces of industrialization and urbanization and, thus, the position of women in

DOI: 10.4324/9781003264040-18

Thai society has begun to change. Polygamous marriage was outlawed in 1935, arranged marriages are less common, families have migrated to urban centers, and Thai women are now more likely to be educated and to participate in the paid labor force (Knodel, 1997; Quicker, 2002). Unfortunately, however, this increase in resources and status among Thai women has coincided with an increase in domestic violence (www.nationthailand.com/national/30352831).

So, the question remains, how do we protect the women who are exposed to the horrors of IPV? How do we provide resources and ensure safety for these women? First, Thailand must acknowledge the issue that exists and then institute laws to protect victims of IPV.

Thailand

Brief Political History

Thailand is located in the center of mainland Southeast Asia. Thailand, which has about the same land area as Spain or France, consists of two broad geographic areas: a larger main section in the north and a smaller peninsular extension in the south. The main body of the country is surrounded by Myanmar (Burma) to the west, Laos to the north and east, Cambodia to the southeast, and the Gulf of Thailand to the south (Keyes, Keyes, & Hafner, 2018). In order to understand how laws are passed in Thailand, one must have a general idea of the political climate that encompasses the country.

Siam, as Thailand was officially called until 1939, was never brought under European colonial domination. Independent Siam was ruled by an absolute monarchy until a revolution there in 1932. Since the far-reaching changes of 1932, progress toward a stable, democratic political system has been erratic. Politics has been dominated by rival military cliques headed by powerful generals. These cliques have caused frequent coups d'état and have imposed prolonged periods of martial law on the country.

Today the country has a fledgling democracy watched over by the military and the new king who recently took over the reins from H.M. King Bhumibol Adulyadej, the ninth king of the Chakri Dynasty, who was the country's longest reigning monarch until his death in 2016. Currently, King Vajiralongkorn is the tenth king of the Chakri dynasty to sit at the throne. In April 2017, King Vajiralongkorn (known as King Rama X) signed into law a new constitution which has aided in a significant movement toward true democracy for the Thai people.

Today, Thailand categorizes itself as a constitutional monarchy, where the king has little direct power under the constitution and exercises power through the National Assembly, the Council of Ministers, and the Courts in accordance with the 2017 constitution. The king, as the head of state, is the symbol of national identity and unity (Merieau, 2019).

Religion and Culture

Overall, 93% of the Thai population is Buddhist. While Buddhism is not Thailand's official religion, Thailand's new 2017 constitution mandates that the Thai government assist the Theravada school of Buddhism and guard Buddhism against all forms of desecration (Tongsakulrungruang, 2018). Within Thai Buddhism, women are inherently inferior to men. Women's major role in Thai Buddhism is to provide support for monks (who are always men) and temple activities; this, along with providing offerings, is one of the only ways for a woman to earn religious merit. The belief is that women's "lower karma" subjects them to a life of suffering which they should endure with bravery so that they can eventually be reborn as a man in their next lifetime. Women in Thailand who've experienced domestic violence are often advised by Buddhist monks to be patient and compassionate with their perpetrators since their suffering is a product of bad karma from a past life.

Moreover, in traditional Thai families, husbands are assigned the role of head and master of the household. Wives are expected to be gentle, pure, obedient, and subordinate in relation to their husbands. These roles can be traced back to eighteenth- and nineteenth-century legislation in Thailand that recognized wives as property of husbands that could be subjected to corporal punishment and/or be sold (Kerley, Xu, Sirsunyaluck, & Alley, 2010). Additional traditional Thai family values emphasize the dichotomy of public and private lives in this country. According to their customs, families are encouraged to keep their conflicts and problems private in order to maintain family honor. Family members are also taught by tradition to hide their expression of feelings and thoughts from others (Xu, Kerley, & Sirsunyaluck, 2011).

The Evolution of Women's Rights in Thailand

Attempts to use public spaces to raise questions about power relationships relating to gender and sexual oppression started before the 1932 Revolution in Thailand that changed the country from an absolute monarchy to a democratic regime. Most attempts took place outside the formal political system, in social platforms used by women and men who sought to raise public awareness and demand social change. The platforms – specifically, bringing together print media and literature, women's organizations, and coalitions – have included social movements aimed at leveraging the political agenda to push for new laws or amendments and to scrutinize government mechanisms, with the goal of advancing the status and rights of women (Buranajaroenkij, 2017).

In 1974, Kanitha Wichiencharoen became a founder of the Association for the Promotion of the Status of Women (APSW), an association made up of both women and men campaigning to revise and amend laws to provide better protections for women and children (Falk, 2007). In the 1977 Constitution of Thailand, women were required to receive equal rights and protections. However, some inequalities remain in the law. The greatest barrier to gender equality is in relation to domestic violence and trafficking. Sexual harassment became illegal in 1998, but there have been few reported cases and even less that reach prosecution because of the difficulties involved in proving a case.

The most immense barriers to gender equality and the empowerment of women in Thailand remain in the areas of lack of sex-disaggregated data, traditional attitudes and stereotypes which underpin domestic violence and violence against women, low participation of women in politics and decision-making positions, discrimination and vulnerabilities of ethnic and rural women as well as women in the informal sector, HIV prevalence, trafficking, and exploitation. Thailand ranks 69th in the Gender Inequality Index as of 2011 (Buranajaroenkij, 2017).

Domestic Violence in Thailand

Thailand is a country with strong family dynamics and a political history that continues to marginalize women. The exact rates of domestic violence are impossible to determine, but there are a few numbers worth considering. According to a report by the United Nations, up to 44% of women in Thailand have been hurt (either sexually or physically, or both) by their romantic partner, and 63% of the Thai population thinks it's acceptable for a husband to beat his wife. It is perhaps that very attitude that elevates Thailand to number 2 among 49 countries for domestic violence (United Nations, 2019).

In 2007, the country passed its first-ever domestic violence law to protect victims abused by their partners. The act was praised for enforcing harsher punishments, more prosecutions, and better protection for women (as well as gay men and transgendered victims). Prior to the 2007 act, the majority of perpetrators served no time, received no fines, and rarely went to court. Marital rape wasn't even considered a crime in Thailand then, even though sexual abuse is known to be a common form of domestic violence. And on the rare occasion when a case was brought before the court, the legal system pushed for family reconciliation rather than prosecution (Sroigsong, Triamchaisri, Kongsakon, Bennett, & Ross, 2018).

In 2007, The National Legislative Assembly of Thailand passed a law criminalizing IPV. The Domestic Violence Victim Protection Act of 2007 vowed harsher punishments for abusers and better protections for victims; unfortunately, this has not proven a major deterrent, as few cases are reported (Nuygen, 2013). Fortunately, this abundant lack of reporting of domestic violence should change under the new law, which now puts the onus on law enforcement. Police are now allowed to enter a home upon notification that abuse is taking place. They are obligated to help arrange for the victim to receive treatment and for the perpetrator to get rehabilitation, even punishment. The new law even requires police to pass the case to a prosecutor who, at the request of the victim, can then proceed to court. If abusers are convicted, they now face serious consequences of a fine, a jail term, or both.

When Thailand launched the "Domestic Violence Victim Protection Act, B.E. 2550" and amended the criminal law B.E. 2550 section 276 (Penal Code Amendment Act (No.19) B.E. 2550 (2007)), it comprised 18 sections; many of these sections are crucial to victims, perpetrators, and government officers. For example, section 4 states that "Whoever conducts any act of domestic violence or is said to commit domestic violence shall be liable to imprison for a term of not exceeding six months or to a fine of not exceeding six thousand Baht or both"; section 5 states that "A domestic violence victim or a person who has found or known of domestic violence shall have the duty to notify a competent official for the execution of this Act." Prior to 2007, the criminal law B.E. 2550 section 276 did not include marital rape as a crime, so a spouse was not legally protected against sexual abuse by their partner (Penal Code Amendment Act (No.16) B.E. 2546, (2003)). However, changes to the law in 2007 added legal protection for a spouse who has been a victim of sexual violence by their partner (www.Thailaws.com).

Moreover, an update to the 2007 law was passed in 2019. This law, the Family Institute Protection Act, hopes to reduce the increasing number of IPV cases. In addition to criminal action, domestic abusers will also be required to undergo behavioral adjustment, such as substance abuse treatment in cases of alcoholism. However, a major area of concern facing victims of IPV continues to be help-seeking. Sroisong, Triamchaisri, Kongsakon, Bennett, and Ross (2018 conducted a study on experiences of survivors of domestic violence. In this study, again, help-seeking behavior of victims is addressed.

UN Women in Thailand works with the National Human Rights Commission, National Law Reform Commission, and other partners to build capable judges and legal personnel on CEDAW and women's human rights and improving gender-sensitivity in the handling of cases. This has resulted in significant advancements toward a more female-friendly judicial process in the Thonburi Criminal Court, which is now regarded as a model court (UN Women, 2020).

Help Seeking: Family, Organizations/Supportive Networks

Family/Friend Support

Victims of IPV who are able to turn to family and friends for support have been found to be more likely to leave the abusive relationship (Flasch, Murray, & Crowe, 2015). For some abused women, there is a great deal of support when they seek help from family and friends, not only to cope emotionally with the abuse, but also to protect themselves and their children. When women can turn to their family and friends not only for advice, inspiration, and encouragement but also for tangible support (e.g. financial assistance, help with children, a place to stay), this leads to greater psychological well-being and higher self-esteem. On the other hand, for those victims who do not have such assistance, the need for more formal avenues of support is vital. As noted previously, family preservation is a large piece of the Thai culture; many family members are reluctant to aid a victim if they believe that support will possibly assist in ending a marriage (Goodkind, Gillum, Bybee, & Sullivan, 2003).

Organizations/Network Supports

In Thailand, there are emergency hotlines, counseling services, and temporary shelters that are backed by non-governmental organizations (NGOs) in the country (US 11 Mar. 2010, Sec. 6). A *Bangkok Post* news article, reporting on the high number of domestic violence cases in Thailand's Upper North provinces, also indicated that there are ten branches of the Friends of Women Foundation set up across the country that help women and children victims of domestic violence (21 Aug. 2010). To address the increasing violence in the North, a hotline was established to receive complaints about violence against women and children and a network of residents and local government agencies was created to protect children (Glahan, 2010). Various support services are available for women seeking help in cases of domestic violence, such as Shelters for Children and Families or One Stop Crisis Centres, which were established in all provinces. Some of the social workers employed there were already trained and registered as competent officers assigned by the law to assist victims (regardless of gender and age) in reporting a case to police; however, the number of competent officers is still low and not all of the trained competent officers of gender-based violence can enforce the law effectively.

Another channel that female victims of domestic violence can go to for help is women's NGOs. Some local NGOs, at least in Bangkok, have worked to promote women's rights for decades. They have also provided legal, as well as social welfare, assistance to women who have experienced domestic violence (www.humanrights.asia/countries/thailand/). The Asian Human Rights Commission also states that the barriers to accessing domestic violence support services include not knowing that services are available, the gender bias in Thailand's health-care system, and the limited funding/loans available to women to "establish a new residence or source of livelihood."

The Network of Women and Constitution is a cooperative organization comprising women from women's organizations, the political, public, and civil society sectors, and universities. The network received backing from international organizations to arrange activities aimed at educating and raising public awareness about issues pertaining to women and the Constitution. They also undertook research and produced publications justifying and supporting women's issues, making them more persuasive when presented to the Constitution Drafting Assembly of Thailand (CDA), and they sponsored members running for election to the CDA as a way to participate in the drafting process and motivate political activeness and involvement (Doneys, 2002). The most significant achievement of this network was the push for the inclusion of Article 53 in the B.E. 2540 Constitution, calling upon the state to protect family members from violence and unfair treatment (A.D. 1997). This article changed the conception of domestic violence from a personal problem into a political issue that requires legal protection. Currently, this network remains a platform to build pressure for relevant political agendas and to solicit cooperation from women's organizations and others (such as those in the academic, private, and public sectors) when working toward seeking social justice.

Under the leadership of Her Royal Highness Princess Bajrakitiyabha as UN Women's Goodwill Ambassador, Thailand has contributed to the UN Secretary General's UNiTE Campaign to End Violence against Women, in partnership with UN Women. A total of 3,123,679 signatures, out of the globally collected 5 million signatures, were amassed from Thailand in support of the Say No to Violence Campaign in 2008, and 622,189 actions were collected in 2010 in support of UNiTE.

UN Women in Thailand has worked with national partners to promote relevant legislation and its implementation, notably the Domestic Violence Legislation. Ongoing activities include supporting implementation of the Domestic Violence Act, development of the National Action Plan on Ending Violence against Women and Domestic Violence, and working with young people (notably high school students and police cadets) as change agents to end violence against women. UN Women in Thailand promotes the implementation of activities toward the five UNiTE outcomes: legislation, National Action Plan, data, social mobilization working with youth and media, and ending sexual violence in conflict (UN Women, 2020).

Moreover, long-term experience working together has enabled both public and private organizations to continue to collaborate to drive greater change. Examples are as follows: (1) pushing for the appointment of female police investigators, (2) development of an aid-provision system for women, and (3) creation of the system and the form of feminist counseling. Training programs were conducted for both male and female police investigators and for the counselors from both public and private sectors. The efforts in the area of ending violence against women have therefore concentrated on creating measures to cope with violence simultaneously in three dimensions: direct violence (providing protection and rehabilitation from the impacts of physical violence), structural violence (the system for aid provision and amendment of laws), and cultural violence (campaigns and education to reduce biases of officers, workers, and the public).

Climate Change and Domestic Violence in Thailand

What Is Climate Change?

Climate change describes the increasingly extreme variation of long-term average weather conditions worldwide. Climate change specifically refers to the effects of the greenhouse gas emissions caused by more than a century and a half of burning fossil fuels like coal, oil, and gas resulting from industrialization, as well as increased deforestation, fertilizer use, and livestock production to feed and house our growing societies.

While climate change affects all aspects of our world, because of the Earth's varied environmental zones, different regions will be impacted differently by slow-onset and sudden-onset hazards. In Asia, the Intergovernmental Panel on Climate Change (IPCC) forecasts that freshwater availability will decrease by 2050 and coasts will experience greater flooding. The geographical location and topography of Small Island Developing States in Asia, the Pacific, and Africa also make them particularly vulnerable to the adverse impacts of climate change such as rising temperatures and rising sea levels. These lead to changes in precipitation patterns, increased likelihood of flash floods, intensified cyclones and storm surges, and coastal degradation and salinization (www.usgs.gov/faqs/what-are-long-term-effects-climate-change-1?qt-news_science_products=0#qt-news_science_products).

Environmental degradation and natural resource scarcity pose significant threats to ecosystems and livelihoods, resulting in or exacerbating biodiversity loss, food insecurity, poverty, displacement, violence, and loss of traditional and cultural knowledge. Ensuing tension and competition over scarce resources in and between communities, households, and industries amplifies normative, discriminatory, and exploitative gender inequalities, giving way to a rise in gender-based violence as a means of control and reinforcement of power imbalances.

Link between Climate Change and Gender-Based Violence

The fight against climate change is not only a struggle to keep our planet livable – for many women, it can be a strong determining factor of violence. Global research demonstrates the link between adversity and violence, in particular the exacerbating effects disasters have on pre-existing rates of gender-based violence. The Pacific region, where gender-based violence rates are already high by global standards, is no exception to this trend; the Asia and Pacific regions are recognized as two of the most vulnerable to climate change and disaster impacts globally. While Asian economies are growing, so are the levels of temperature, pollution, and greenhouse gas emissions. The retreat of glaciers, rising temperatures, and permafrost in Asia are occurring at an unprecedented rate. Climate change is no longer a concern just for the distant future. As a consequence, every country in Asia is facing the various impacts of this phenomenon (Dankelman, 2016).

Gender-based violence response is also impeded by cultural factors that discourage reporting, including shame, stigma, and a culture of silence (Gevers, Musuya, & Bukuluki, 2020). Disasters create conditions that intensify pre-existing gender-based violence risk factors such as stress and trauma (both of which are drastically heightened following disasters and significantly reduce normal coping capacities and heighten the risk of violent response to pressure or strain).

Help-Seeking Barriers due to COVID-19 Pandemic

Although government services for women who experience domestic violence in Thailand have considerably expanded over the past two decades, women's advocates were seeing setbacks even before COVID-19 began disrupting the typical channels for help. The country's hotline service had been reduced from one call center per province to only one centrally located in the capital of Bangkok. And five years ago, the government shifted the hotline's focus from violence against women and children (as well as human trafficking, child labor, and teenage pregnancy) to any social problem, thus diluting the strength of this resource for women and children experiencing domestic violence.

Media reports have highlighted increases of reported domestic violence in countries around the world due to the lockdown stresses, and the situation in Thailand is consistent with this data. Incidences of aggravated domestic violence have risen as a result of falling household incomes and increased alcohol consumption during the Covid-19 pandemic, the Thai Health Promotion Foundation says.

According to a nationwide survey carried out by the foundation, cases of domestic violence surged by 66% since virus control measures were introduced in March 2020, said Thai Health's Director of Wellbeing Promotion for Vulnerable Individuals, Poranee Phuprasert. The South showed the highest increase in the number of domestic violence cases, where cases surged by 48%, while Bangkok saw the smallest increase at 26%.

The increases in domestic violence cases were mainly driven by frustration over dwindling household incomes as jobs disappeared due to the pandemic and an increase in alcohol intake during lockdown, the report said. The director said Thailand has one of the highest rates of violence against women in the world, as per the United Nations Office on Drugs and Crime's figures.

Data indicate that the number of clients appearing at One Stop Crisis Centre units in hospitals in April 2020 more than doubled from a year earlier, from 85 to 183. These walk-ins included violence both inside and outside the family. But the Ministry of Social Development and Human Security's 1300 hotline, which was dedicated to violence against women in 2013 and was considered a major step forward in the government's response, registered a significant drop in family violence reports for March and April 2020, compared with a year ago. "Those who experience domestic violence may have difficulty accessing the hotline during COVID-19, because the lines have been flooded with calls about social assistance and grants," notes a hotline official who asked not to be named (https://th.boell.org/en/2020/07/01/covid-19-domestic-violence).

As the pandemic interrupted people's livelihoods and earnings with unpaid bills and sometimes nothing to eat, other grievances grew. The 24-hour helpline was flooded with more than 28,000 calls in March and April 2020 – more than double for that period a year earlier. But most of the calls were complaints or inquiries about government relief.

In Thailand, domestic violence cases are often reported by outsiders, such as teachers and friends who notice signs of abuse, according to Boonwara Sumano, a researcher with the Thailand Development Research Institute. In lockdown at home, this first line of support was largely cut off and abusers were able to keep their spouses or partners from reaching out for help.

Additionally, Boonwara speculated, the threat of virus infection likely scared many people from seeking hospital care. Government and private shelters for women and children had to take preventive COVID-19 measures and limit the number of people staying in their facilities or shut down their services altogether. Furthermore, when abuse happens at night, many non-government organization directors explain, the curfews imposed by the authorities became another possible barrier to seeking help. In some provinces, roads were even blocked to prevent people from traveling during the pandemic (www.nationthailand.com/news/30386542?utm_source=category&utm_medium=internal_referral). With or without a pandemic, a major barrier to women reporting violence in Thailand has long been and remains societal attitudes, among public servants like the police.

Conclusion

It is quite apparent that while Thailand has made much progress to address the issue of IPV, more work must be done. Tackling an established masculine-driven culture, while simultaneously trying to educate and empower the women who have been raised within that environment, is no easy task. Additional services must be made available for Thai women to feel safe, encouraged, and educated, while Thai police officers need to understand their moral obligations to victims of IPV. Creating a diverse police department, allowing women to be in elected positions, and balancing the inequality that Thai women face is the first step in creating this much-needed, permanent, widespread change in Thailand; it is possible if everyone joins together and realizes this is a public health issue that cannot be ignored.

Works Cited

Asian Human Rights Commission. (2020). Retrieved on July 8, 2020 from www.humanrights.asia/countries/thailand/.

Buranajaroenkij, D. (2017). *Political Feminism and the Women's Movement in Thailand: Actors, Debates, and Strategies*. Bangkok: Friedrich-Ebert-Stiftung Foundation.

Chuemchit, M., Chernkwanma, S., Rugkua, R., Daengthern, L., Abdullakasim, P., & Wieringa, S. E. (2018). Prevalence of Intimate Partner Violence in Thailand. *Journal of Family Violence, 33* (5), 315–323. https://doi.org/10.1007/s10896-018-9960-9

Dankelman, I. (2016). *Action Not Words. Confronting Gender Inequality through Climate Change Action and Disaster Risk Reduction in Asia*. Thailand: UN Women. Retrieved on October 25, 2021. www2.unwomen.org/ /media/field%20office%20eseasia/docs/publications/2017/04/ccdrr_130317 s.pdf?la=en&vs=5239

Doneys, P. (2002). 'Political Reform through the Public Sphere. Women's Groups and the Fabric of Governance'. In D. McCargo (Ed.), *Reforming Thai Politics* (pp.163–182). London: Routledge.

Falk, M. L. (2007). *Making Fields of Merit: Buddhist Female Ascetics and Gendered Orders in Thailand*. Copenhagen, Denmark: NIAS Press. pp. 207–208.

Flasch, P., Murray, C. E., & Crowe, A. (2015, August). Overcoming abuse: A phenomenological investigation of the journey to recovery from past intimate partner violence. *Journal Interpersonal Violence, 32* (22), 3373–3401. doi: 10.1177/0886260 515599161

Foundation urges people to step in as domestic violence cases rise. (2018). Retrieved June 11, 2020, from www.nationthailand.com/national/30352831.
Gevers, A., Musuya, T., & Bukuluki, P. (2020). Why climate change fuels violence against women. *United Nations Development Programme*. Retrieved October 25, 2021, from www.undp.org/blogs/why-climate-change-fuels-violence-against-women.
Glahan, S. (2010). "Despite laws Asian women still suffer." *Bangkok Post*. 25 November 2010.
Goodkind, J. R., Gillum, T. L., Bybee, D. I., & Sullivan, C. M. (2003). The impact of family and friends' reactions on the well-being of women with abusive partners. *Violence against Women, 9* (3), 347–373. doi: 10.1177/1077 801202250083
Kerley, K. R., Xu, X., Sirisunyaluck, B., & Alley, J. M. (2010). Exposure to family violence in childhood and intimate partner perpetration or victimization in adulthood: Exploring intergenerational transmission in urban Thailand. *Journal of Family Violence, 25* (3), 337–347.
Keyes, E. J., Keyes, C. F., & Hafner, J. A. (2018). Thailand | Geography, Economy, History, & Facts | Britannica. Retrieved June 11, 2020, from www.britannica.com/place/Thailand.
Knodel, J. (1997). The closing of the gender gap in schooling: The case of Thailand. *Comparative Education, 33*, 61–86.
Kongsakon, R., & Pojam, N. (2008). *Family Violence*. Bangkok, Thailand. Srinakharinwirot University (in Thai).
Laeheem, K. (2019). Casual relationships between religious factors influencing ethical behavior among youth in the three southern border provinces of Thailand. *Children and Youth Services Review, 108*.
Langerak, A., & Korolczuk, E. (2020, July 1). Thailand's silent pandemic: Domestic violence during Covid-19: Heinrich Böll Foundation: Southeast Asia regional office. *Heinrich-Böll-Stiftung*. Retrieved September 27, 2021, from https://th.boell.org/en/2020/07/01/covid-19-domestic-violence.
Mérieau, E. (2019, March 20). How Thailand Became the World's Last Military Dictatorship. Retrieved June 12, 2020, from www.theatlantic.com/international/archive/2019/03/thailand military-junta election-king/585274/.
Nation Thailand. (2021, April 21). *Covid-19 crisis triggering "increased domestic violence'*. Retrieved September 27, 2021, from www.nationthailand.com/news/30386542?utm_source=category&utm_medium=internal_referral.
Nguyen, M. (2013). *Kiss with a Fist: A Look at Thailand's Domestic Violence Act*. Citylife: Chiang Mai.
Quicker, J. C. (2002). Thailand. In R. W. Summers & A. M. Hoffman (Eds.), *Domestic Violence: A Global View* (pp. 155–167). Westport, CT: Greenwood Press.
Sroisong, S., Triamchaisri, S.K., Kongsakon, R., Bennett, T., & Ross, R. (2018). The experiences of survivors of intimate partner violence in Thai women. *Journal of Health Research, 32* (2), 132–141.
Thailand Domestic Violence Laws. (n.d.). Retrieved June 15, 2020, from http://ilo.org/dyn/natlex/natlex4.detail?p_lang=en
The United Nations Office on Drugs and Crime (2019). *Global Study on Homicide 2019 edition*, p. 10. UNODC. https://www.unodc.org/unodc/en/data-and-analysis/global-study-on-homicide.html
The United Nations Statistics Divisions (2019). The World's Women 2015: Trends and Statistics. Retrieved https://unstats.un.org/unsd/gender/worldswomen.html on February 24, 2020.
Tongsakulrungruang, K. (2018, January 30). The Dangerous Buddhist Card in Thailand's New Constitution. Retrieved June 09, 2020, from https://thediplomat.com/2018/01/the dangerous-buddhist-card-in-thailands-new-constitution/.
UN Women (2020). Retrieved July 07, 2020, from https://asiapacific.unwomen.org/en/countries/thailand/ending-violence-against-women.
What are the long-term effects of climate change? (n.d.). Retrieved November 9, 2021, from www.usgs.gov/faqs/what-are-long-term-effects-climate-change-1?qt-news_science_products=0#qt-news_science_products.
WHO. (2016). *Fact Sheet on Violence against Women*. Geneva: World Health Organization. Retrieved from www.who.int/mediacentre/factsheets/fs239/en/.
Xu, X., Kerley, K. R., & Sirisunyaluck, B. (2011). Understanding gender and domestic violence from a sample of married women in Urban Thailand. *Journal of Family Issues, 32* (6), 791–819. https://doi.org/10.1177/0192513X10386306

16

DOMESTIC VIOLENCE IN THE MICRONESIAN CONTEXT

Past and Future Challenges

Hiroaki Matsuura

Introduction

The Pacific Island countries are among the least advanced in terms of gender equality. Women are significantly underrepresented in parliamentary politics in the region. Micronesian countries, which are located north of Polynesia and Melanesia, particularly lag behind. In 2000, the United Nations Millennium Development Goals (MDGs) used the proportion of seats held by women in national parliaments as a key indicator of the progress for gender equality. However, in the final year of the MDGs, the Federated States of Micronesia and Palau still had no women in their lower or only house of parliament. At the same time, only 3 percent and 6.7 percent of seats were held by women in the Marshall Islands and Kiribati, respectively (UN, 2015). The Federated States of Micronesia and Palau were two of four countries with no women in parliament, alongside Qatar and Yemen in the Middle East (UN, 2015).

One of the most significant consequences of women's underrepresentation in politics is the high level of domestic violence and insufficient access to protection in the Pacific Islands region. Women face many different forms of violence perpetrated by family members or intimate partners, including physical, sexual, and psychological abuse, as well as economic abuse and exploitation. Other forms of violence, such as forced marriage, sex trafficking, and commercial sexual exploitation, are also prevalent in the region.

Over the past twenty years, significant data collection and legislative efforts have been undertaken to help eliminate domestic violence in the region. According to the United Nations Population Fund (UNFPA), on average, 48.9 percent of women in Pacific Island countries experience physical and/or sexual violence by a partner in their lifetime (UNFPA, 2019). This is a much higher rate than the global average of 35 percent, yet some Micronesian countries, such as Kiribati and the Marshall Islands, have recorded even higher rates (WHO, 2013). Between 2009 and 2015, nine Pacific Island countries, including Kiribati, the Marshall Islands, and Palau, enacted legislation to better protect women from domestic violence (UN Women, 2016).

The UN Sustainable Development Goals (SDGs) adopted in 2015 explicitly target the elimination of all forms of violence against women (Target 5.2) and other harmful practices, such as forced marriage and female genital mutilation (Target 5.3) (UNGA, 2015). These targets reflect the global concern that violence against women has continued to hinder women's empowerment and provide an opportunity to tackle domestic violence and promote gender equity in the region. However, the 2020 COVID-19 pandemic has brought additional challenges to the battle against

DOI: 10.4324/9781003264040-19

domestic violence in the region. During the pandemic, the existing gender power imbalance within households was magnified due to economic problems and mobility restrictions, leading to an increase in cases of domestic violence. At the same time, the pandemic has limited the activities of public and private organizations that deliver services in the field of domestic violence, making victims harder to reach.

The SDGs and COVID-19 pandemic pose both positive and negative challenges to women in Micronesian countries. The rest of this paper reviews the achievements and challenges of the policy response to domestic violence in Micronesian countries (Federated States of Micronesia, Kiribati, the Marshall Islands, and Palau) in the context of the SDGs and the COVID-19 pandemic. Micronesia is unique from the rest of the Pacific Island countries in terms of its history, legal system, and matrilineal social system. It has also been the least studied sub-region of the Pacific Islands in terms of domestic violence. The next section discusses the results of the Family Health and Safety Study (FHSS) conducted by UNFPA and the Pacific Community. The study provides the first comprehensive set of data covering domestic violence for Micronesian countries. The section on international human rights instruments discusses the ratification status of the major UN human rights treaties, such as the Convention on the Elimination of All Forms of Discrimination against Women (CEDAW), and how they apply to the domestic laws in each country. The section on national legislative responses discusses the progress of national anti-domestic violence legislation and identifies the common features of these laws in the region. The section on domestic violence during the pandemic discusses the new challenges of implementing this legislation during the COVID-19 pandemic. The section also discusses the effect of climate change, which is one of the primary focuses of the SDGs. Finally, the last section provides discussion and concluding remarks.

Family Health and Safety Study

Much work has been carried out to understand the nature and consequences of violence against women in the region, as evidenced by the FHSS conducted by UNFPA and the Pacific Community. The FHSS provides the first comprehensive and comparable set of data covering the high prevalence and severity of violence against women in Pacific Island countries. The study also reveals that the prevalence varies from country to country across the region. While Kiribati (68 percent) recorded the highest rates of physical and/or sexual violence against women by a partner, Palau had the lowest rate at 25 percent (UN Women, 2016).

In all Micronesian countries, as in the case of other Pacific Island countries, cultural acceptability of domestic violence and persisting gender inequality are the two main reasons for the continuation of violence against women (Secretariat of the Pacific Community, 2006, 2007, 2010, 2013). There is widespread support among women for the use of violence by husbands to control and punish their wives, but the degree of support varies by country. In Kiribati and the Marshall Islands, respectively, where a higher rate of physical and/or sexual violence was recorded, 56 percent and 66 percent of women believe a husband should be able to physically assault his wife if she has not completed her housework, 60 percent and 71 percent if she disobeys him, 35 percent and 38 percent if she refuses to have sex with him, and 60 percent and 75 percent if he discovers that she has been unfaithful (Secretariat of the Pacific Community, 2006, 2010). However, in Palau, only 1.2 percent believe husbands should be allowed to physically assault their wives if she has not completed her housework, 3 percent if she disobeys him, 1.6 percent if she refuses to have sex with him, and 12.8 percent if he discovers that she has been unfaithful (Secretariat of the Pacific Community, 2007). The Federated States of Micronesia is somewhere between Palau and Kiribati/the Marshall Islands. In the Federated States of Micronesia, 22.6 percent of women believe a husband is justified in physically assaulting his wife if she has not completed her housework, 40.7 percent if she disobeys him, 22.6 percent if she refuses to have sex with him, and 32.4 percent if he discovers that she has been unfaithful (Secretariat of the Pacific Community, 2013). Most abused women in these countries had not told anyone about their partners' violence and rarely approached any formal service for support.

Except for Kiribati, Micronesian countries are commonly matrilineal societies. The results of the FHSS suggest that cultural acceptability of domestic violence is high not only in a traditional patriarchal society such as Kiribati's but also in a traditionally matrilineal society such as that of the Marshall Islands.

Gender inequality is reinforced by cultural gender norms and customary practices in the region. Although specific customs vary between countries and communities, the practice of "bride price" is performed widely across the region, which increases the perception of male ownership of women (Biersack & Macintyre, 2017). Gender norms of masculinity also encourage men to control their wives, often through domestic violence, while women feel that bride price has prevented them from escaping their husbands (Biersack & Macintyre, 2017).

International Human Rights Instruments

Many Pacific Island countries have yet to ratify all of the major international human rights instruments (UN, 2021). However, all countries in Micronesia have ratified the Convention on the Rights of the Child (CRC) and, except for Palau (albeit signed in 2011), all have ratified the CEDAW (UN, 2021), illustrating their commitment to the human rights of women and children. In Palau, a resolution to ratify CEDAW in 2008 was approved by the Senate but not by the House of Delegates. Unlike CRC, which explicitly protects children from all forms of child abuse (Article 19), there is no provision for violence against women in CEDAW. However, General Recommendation 19, which defines discrimination to include all forms of violence against women in Article 1 of CEDAW, has been adopted (CEDAW Committee, 1992).

Although a significant number of countries in the region have ratified CEDAW, the application of international human rights instruments in domestic courts largely depends on the origin of a country's legal system. The Micronesian group occupies the territory of three independent states—the Federated States of Micronesia, the Marshall Islands, and Palau—which are historically unique from the rest of the region. After the defeat of the Japanese Empire in 1945, these countries were given to the United States for administration by the United Nations. Therefore, these countries followed the American common law system, while the rest of the Pacific Island countries inherited the British system. In American common law countries, such as the Federated States of Micronesia and Palau, once a convention is ratified, the convention's provisions have immediate applicability in the courts and for domestic law in general (Pacific Islands Legal Information Institute, 2020). However, British common law countries, including Kiribati, must enact domestic legislation before a convention comes into effect in domestic law, including CEDAW (the dualist approach). The Marshall Islands seem to be the exception to this rule, with their Supreme Court recently recognizing that they are a dualist state in the decision of Chubb Ins. v Eleni et al. 2017 (Pacific Islands Legal Information Institute, 2020).

National Legislative Responses

Over the past twenty years, Micronesian and other Pacific Island countries have made significant efforts to align their family protection and domestic violence legislation with international human rights standards. Between 2009 and 2015, nine countries passed such legislation to better protect women from violence (UN Women, 2016). Much of this work has been supported by the Regional Rights Resource Team of the Pacific Community, established in 1995.

In 2008, Vanuatu passed the Family Protection Act and became the first Pacific Island nation to enact comprehensive laws on violence against women and was followed by other Pacific Island countries. Three out of four Micronesian countries followed this trend, passing the Domestic Prevention and Protection Act in 2011 (revised in 2018) (Marshall Islands), the Family Protection Act in 2012 (Palau), and the Family Peace Act in 2014 (Kiribati). In the Federated States of Micronesia, state-level legislation has been enacted instead of at a national level. All four states—Chuuk, Kosrae, Pohnpei, and Yap—have introduced domestic violence provisions into state law. For Kosrae and Pohnpei, the maximum imprisonment duration is ten years: more than anywhere else in the region (Singh et al., 2018).

There are several distinctive common features in the national legislation of Micronesia and other Pacific Island countries. First, many of these acts define domestic violence broadly, including physical, sexual, and psychological abuse. Later legislation enacted in the 2010s, including in Kiribati, the Marshall Islands, and Palau, added "economic abuse", which includes the act of restricting a partner's access to financial resources, denial of food and other basic needs, and controlling access to health care and employment (Dipty, 2010). In many Pacific Island countries, domestic violence was historically not regarded as a crime. Incidents of domestic violence had typically been reported as assaults or batteries to the police. The result was that the many forms of domestic violence beyond physical abuse were rarely reported. While this new legislation may change people's perceptions in the future, in Kiribati, only 3 of the 1,100 abuse cases reported in 2017 concerned economic abuse, compared to 608 for physical abuse, 380 for psychological abuse, and 39 for sexual abuse (Republic of Kiribati, 2019).

Furthermore, in Micronesia and other Pacific Island countries, extended families are common and some household members are often non-family members. The acts in almost all Pacific Island countries have extended protection to various family relationships, including de facto ones. However, there is no distinction between family violence and violence perpetrated by an intimate partner (Singh et al., 2018).

These pieces of legislation provide both criminal punishment for the perpetrators and civil protection orders for the victims (Forster, 2010). However, the severity of the penalty varies from country to country. Under Vanuatu's Family Protection Act, the perpetrators of domestic violence can be sentenced to up to five years in prison (or fined up to VUV100,000 or both) regardless of the number of previous penalties. However, the legislation in Micronesian countries imposes more lenient penalties. In Kiribati and the Marshall Islands, first-time perpetrators can be sentenced to up to six months (or fined up to $250 or $1,000, respectively), and up to one year (and no fine for the first offense) in Palau. Kiribati, the Marshall Islands, and Palau impose longer sentences and higher maximum fines for second and third offenses (Singh et al., 2018). In addition to the criminal charges against perpetrators, victims can access immediate and long-term protection orders. The courts may also issue family protection orders enabling the victim and her family to remain at home to exclude the perpetrator. Anyone who violates a protection order will be imprisoned or required to pay a fine separate from their charge of domestic violence (Singh et al., 2018).

Such legislation has been significantly adjusted to each Pacific Island nation's individual situation. Customary laws are still influential in these countries. In Palau, statute and customary law are equally authoritative under Article V of the Constitution (Singh et al., 2018). The Family Protection Act of 2012 can supersede customary law only if the act does not conflict with the underlying principles of customary law. In other Micronesian countries, such as Kiribati and the Federated States of Micronesia, the courts may consider customary laws as long as they do not conflict with anti-domestic violence legislation (Singh et al., 2018). The customary laws have a stronger influence in rural areas where there is limited access to a formal court system.

Finally, a "no-drop" policy has been adopted in many Pacific Island countries to ensure that cases of domestic violence cannot be withdrawn (Forster, 2010). The no-drop policy requires both legal and non-legal support for victims to proceed with their cases in the judiciary (Pacific Community, 2017). At the same time, police are also trained to not wrongfully drop cases of domestic violence. If the victim wishes for an official complaint to be withdrawn, they must make a formal request to the court (Pacific Community, 2017).

While these legislations are well designed and meet the standards of international best practice, their implementation remains a challenge. Kiribati has made significant efforts in this area. Before the 2014 Family Peace Act, in 2011, the government adopted the ten-year Elimination of Sexual and Gender-Based Violence Policy and National Action Plan and developed mechanisms for collaboration and coordination between government, donors, NGOs, and civil society actors. This led to a wide range of programs supporting the implementation of the act. A recent report noted the positive outcome of training police officers to better understand their role in issuing protection safety orders (Republic of Kiribati, 2019). Police also ran a 24-hour hotline for victims of domestic violence, significantly improving their access to protection services. Providing education and public awareness programs can also help to protect women from domestic violence.

However, a lack of funding and delays in the administrative process still hinder the implementation of the Family Peace Act (Pacific Community, 2017). In particular, this is because Kiribati is a country of scattered islands, and communities in the outer islands may find it difficult to reach a police officer or a court to lodge a complaint of domestic violence. Local community settings also make it difficult to guarantee confidentiality and privacy for victims. More recently, telecommunications have been used for victims to access judicial and police services from the outer islands, but this creates new challenges for both victims and service providers.

The aforementioned efforts led to a significant increase in the number of reported domestic violence cases in Kiribati following the enactment of the Family Peace Act. In 2017, there were 1,110 reported cases, including 53 reported to the Crisis Center, 278 to the Ministry of Health and Medical Services, 750 to the police, and 29 to the Social Welfare Division (Republic of Kiribati, 2019). This demonstrates increasing awareness among the general public that domestic violence is a criminal offense. Unfortunately, we know little about how the judiciary has responded to these cases because data on the number of cases filed at court and any protection orders are not publicly available in Kiribati.

In Palau, however, these data are available. The number of restraining order cases related to domestic abuse brought to the court under the 2012 Family Protection Act increased from 0 to 60 between 2013 and 2016 (Supreme Court, 2017). The court granted 94 percent of all applications for a restraining order. Meanwhile, the number of criminal domestic violence cases filed was almost constant before and after the Family Protection Act's implementation, reflecting the fact that criminal charges for domestic violence are relatively small in this country.

Although it is unclear how many criminal cases are brought to the judiciary, the number of victims seeking civil protection orders is likely to have increased due to domestic violence legislation in Micronesian countries. However, compared to the number of potential victims speculated from the FHSS, this will account for only a tiny fraction of victims.

Domestic Violence during the Pandemic

Almost all Pacific Island countries locked down or declared national emergencies in the early stages of the COVID-19 pandemic, even before any confirmed cases were recorded (Tukuitonga,

2020). While the rest of the world struggled with the pandemic, the Pacific Island countries had the lowest number of confirmed cases of COVID-19 globally (Dong, Du, & Gardner, 2020).[1] This was especially true for Micronesian countries, where only a few cases of COVID-19 infection have been reported until now. However, their economies have been severely affected by the disruptions to global trade and travel restrictions. Many of these countries are geographically isolated and have limited resources, making them vulnerable to the disruption on global trade. All four depend on agriculture, fishery, and tourism: the sectors most affected by the pandemic. In Palau, tourism accounts for more than 60 percent of economic activity and 90 percent of employment (South Pacific Tourism Organisation, 2018). According to the World Economic Outlook, Palau's economy shrank by 8.7 percent last year, while the Marshall Islands', the Federated States of Micronesia's, and Kiribati's economies contracted by 2.4 percent, 1.8 percent, and 0.5 percent, respectively (IMF, 2021). The decline of tourism, one of the few sectors that make a significant contribution to women's employment outside of agriculture and fishery, has affected the living standards of many women in Palau and other Pacific Island countries that are dependent on tourism.

The COVID-19 pandemic has disproportionally affected women in these countries. Women and girls have faced even higher rates of domestic violence or the rationing of food and other resources during lockdown. The pandemic has also affected service providers. Except for the police, domestic violence service providers, including crisis centers, were not considered essential services; therefore, they could not continue operating as usual during lockdown.

Soon after the World Health Organization declared the pandemic on March 11, 2020, crisis centers across the Pacific Islands began to intensively promote their helpline numbers on radio, television, and social media (UN Women, 2020). The situation was particularly serious in the Melanesian countries affected by the combined effect of Tropical Cyclone Harold and the pandemic in April 2020. Fiji's national domestic violence helpline recorded a significant increase in calls (from 187 in March to 527 in April), while the women's crisis centers in Tonga recorded a 54 percent increase in the number of cases during that period (UN Women, 2020).

In Micronesia, the ability for women to access telephone counseling was more disrupted due to limited awareness about availability. Marshall Island's Women United Together Marshall Islands (WUTMI) and Federated States of Micronesia's Chuuk Women's Council (CWC), which both operate crisis support centers in these countries, encouraged victims to make contact via social media in order to meet their needs while face-to-face counseling was suspended (Pacific Women, 2020).[2]

In Kiribati, more women experiencing domestic violence came to access a shelter during the pandemic, despite the closure of the country's only shelter due to the fear of infection in April 2020 (OCHA, 2021). As a result, it was difficult to find out where to place women who needed protective custody. In response to the situation, the Kiribati Women and Children Support Centre (KWCSC) established a temporary shelter called "Orange Door" with the support of the Australian government.

The pandemic is certainly a time of trouble for victims of domestic violence, but it is also an opportunity to expand existing crisis center activities in Kiribati and other Micronesian countries. Before the pandemic, it was difficult for KWCS to reach victims in Kiritimati and other islands outside of Tarawa, the capital of Kiribati. The center had provided telephone counseling support for women who experienced domestic violence in these outer islands. However, women may find telephone counseling challenging given the situation of confinement and close monitoring by the perpetrator at home. With the support of the Australian government, the KWCSC opened its second branch on Kiritimati Island in July 2021 (UN Women, 2021). In the Marshall Islands, with the support of the EU-UN Spotlight Initiative complemented by the government of Australia, the WUTMI also opened its second branch on Ebeye Island in February 2021 (Pacific Women,

2021). These new branches provide women living in these outer islands a safe space to share their experiences in a way that is confidential and where empathy is practiced by the counselors.

The Marshall Islands recently reported a surge in mental health cases and domestic violence complaints to the High Court in the first half of 2021 (Johnson, 2021). It is not clear why the numbers are surging this year and not last year. However, an increase is an increase. The question is whether the expansion of the crisis centers in these countries can sufficiently meet the increasing demand for shelter and services for such domestic violence survivors.

So far, Palau has more than 99 percent of its eligible population fully vaccinated, making it the world leader for COVID-19 vaccination rates (Ministry of Health & Human Services, 2021). However, less than 10 percent of Kiribati is vaccinated (Kaye, 2021). A country like Palau can soon go back to normal life, but the other three countries will take some time.

Climate change may also pose an even greater threat to women in the region. The overall impact of climate change on domestic violence is still unknown, but it exacerbates the underlying risk factors for gender-based violence. The region's economy and environment have already been affected by a rising sea level and the threat of stronger storms. Cyclone Harold and its destruction in Vanuatu, Fiji, and Tonga serve as a grim reminder of how tropical storms have become more severe with climate change. The urgency of increasing vaccination rates in the region was pressured by the upcoming Pacific cyclone season, which could cause additional damage to livelihoods already impacted by the pandemic. Cyclone Harold did not affect Micronesian countries, but there is no guarantee that the next cyclone will not hit one or more of these countries.

All four Micronesian countries are vulnerable to climate change and are likely to suffer serious adverse environmental and economic losses. Increases in temperature and intensified extreme weather can lower agriculture and fisheries output, degrade natural tourist attractions, increase the vulnerability of critical infrastructure, and worsen human health. They may affect a country's economy, which depends on agriculture, fishery, and tourism, and lead to a higher level of violence against women. For example, approximately one-third of Palau's corals died, with coral mortality as high as 90 percent in some areas (NOAA & CRTF, 2008). This had severe, adverse impacts on the nation's important marine tourism industry. The exact mechanism of climate change affecting domestic violence is still unclear, and various pathways exist between climate change and domestic violence. However, economic losses due to climate change will be one of the main mechanisms where climate change can increase domestic violence.

Discussion

While many governments in Micronesian countries have passed national legislation to address domestic violence through their family and criminal law frameworks, this has had limited impact on the prevalence and severity of domestic violence. It is evident that legal reform is the first step toward the elimination of violence against women in this region. Such laws must be supported by significant budgetary allocations for effective implementation, public-private partnerships, and through education and other awareness-raising activities.

The COVID-19 pandemic has led to policy measures that address how women are disproportionately affected in these countries and how they face even higher rates of domestic violence and the rationing of food and other resources under lockdown. Despite police and crisis centers' efforts to address violence against women, new challenges have emerged for the effective implementation of domestic violence legislation in the context of the emergency situation, related to disease pandemics, natural disasters, and climate change. Given the high vulnerability of Micronesian countries to these risks, there is an imminent need to construct a social system that provides seamless prevention of domestic violence as well as protection to victims in both non-emergency and emergency situations in this region to achieve Target 5.2 and other targets of Goal 5 of the SDGs.

Notes

1 As of October 14, 2021, there have been five confirmed cases of COVID-19 in Palau, four in Marshall Islands, two in Kiribati, and one in the Federated States of Micronesia.

2 Crisis centers across the Pacific continue to assist each other to support survivors of domestic violence in the region. In 2019, Kiribati set up the Kiribati Women and Children Support Centre (KWCSC), which has offered domestic violence counseling, management of the victim support fund, case management, support, and an advocacy service for the women and children. In the Republic of the Marshall Islands, Women United Together Marshall Islands has been operating the country's first counseling service, Weto in Mour, since 2016. In Chuuk State in the Federated States of Micronesia, the Chuuk Women's Council launched the Tongen Inepwineu Counseling Center, which is the first crisis support center for women in 2020. As of today, Palau does not have such a crisis center. As a result, there is no safe shelter for survivors other than a 48-hour emergency shelter located in the courthouse for survivors whose petitions for protective orders are not immediately executed for some reasons.

References

Biersack, A., & Macintyre, M. (2017). *Emergent Masculinities in the Pacific*. London: Routledge.

CEDAW Committee. (1992). *General Recommendation 19*. New York: UN Committee on the Elimination of Discrimination against Women, Retrieved from www.un.org/womenwatch/daw/cedaw/recommendations/recomm.htm.

Dipty, M. D. (2010). *The Three Dimensions of Domestic Violence*. London: Tate Publishing.

Dong, E., Du, H., & Gardner, L. (2020). An Interactive Web-based Dashboard to Track COVID-19 in Real Time. *Lancet Infectious Diseases, 20* (5), 533–534.

Forster, C. (2010). Ending Domestic Violence in Pacific Island Countries: The Critical Role of Law. *Asian Pacific Law and Policy Journal, 12*, 123–144.

IMF. (2021). *World Economic Outlook: Recovery during a Pandemic—Health Concerns, Supply Disruptions, Price Pressures*. Washington, DC: International Monetary Fund Retrieved from www.imf.org/-/media/Files/Publications/WEO/2021/October/English/text.ashx.

Johnson, G. (2021). *Marshalls Sees Spike in Domestic Violence, Depression, Drug Misuse*. Wellington: Radio New Zealand, Retrieved from www.rnz.co.nz/international/pacific-news/445221/marshalls-sees-spike-in-domestic-violence-depression-drug-misuse#:~:text=Marshalls%20sees%20spike%20in%20domestic%20violence%2C%20depression%2C%20drug%20misuse,-5%3A19%20pm&text=But%20it%20is%20following%20the,with%20extended%20lockdowns%20and%20quarantines.

Kaye, B. (2021). *Tiny Pacific nation beats the world with 99% COVID vaccination, says Red Cross*. Retrieved from www.reuters.com/world/asia-pacific/tiny-pacific-nation-beats-world-with-99-covid-vaccination-says-red-cross-2021-10-14/.

Ministry of Health & Human Services. (2021). *Palau COVID-19 Situation Report*. Koror: Ministry of Health and Human Services, Retrieved from www.palauhealth.org/2019nCoV_SitRep/MOH-COVID-19%20Situation%20Report.pdf.

NOAA, & CRTF. (2008). *The State of Coral Reef Ecosystems of the United States and Pacific Freely Associated States: 2008*. Silver Spring: National Oceanic and Atmospheric Administration.

OCHA. (2021). *Pacific Humanitarian Team: COVID-19 Response Plan: Final Report*. New York/Geneva: United Nations Office for the Coordination of Humanitarian Affairs, Retrieved from https://reliefweb.int/sites/reliefweb.int/files/resources/PHT%20HRP%20COVID-19%20Final%20Report%202021_05_12.pdf.

Pacific Community. (2017). *Implementation Plan for the Te Rau N Te Mwenga (Family Peace) Act 2014*. Suva: Pacific Community Retrieved from www.spc.int/DigitalLibrary/Doc/HDP/Gender/Implementation_Plan_for_the_Te_Rau_N_Te_Mwenga.pdf.

Pacific Islands Legal Information Institute. (2020). *Pacific Islands Legal Information Institute Database*. Port Vila: University of the South Pacific School of Law, Retrieved from www.paclii.org/.

Pacific Women. (2020). Pacific Women: Supporting Gender-Inclusive COVID-19 Responses Suva: Pacific Women, Retrieved from https://pacificwomen.org/news/pw-supporting-gender-inclusive-covid-19-responses/.

Pacific Women. (2021). Women United Together in Marshall Island's (WUTMI) Expands Its Support Service for Women to Ebeye. Suva: Pacific Women, Retrieved from https://pacificwomen.org/news/women-united-together-in-marshall-islands-wutmi-expands-its-support-service-for-women-to-ebeye/.

Republic of Kiribati. (2019). Responses to CEDAW/C/KIR/Q/1-3. Convention on the Elimination of All Forms of Discrimination against Women, Retrieved from https://undocs.org/en/CEDAW/C/KIR/Q/1-3.

Secretariat of the Pacific Community. (2006). *Kiribati Family Health and Support Study*. Noumea: Secretariat of the Pacific Community, Retrieved from https://asiapacific.unfpa.org/sites/default/files/pub-pdf/Kiribati-Family-Health-and-Support-Study.pdf.

Secretariat of the Pacific Community. (2007). *Balau Family Health and Safety Study*. (9822039778). Secretariat of the Pacific Community Retrieved from https://asiapacific.unfpa.org/sites/default/files/pub-pdf/Palau_family_health_safety_survey_report_2014.pdf.

Secretariat of the Pacific Community. (2010). *RMI Family Health and Safety Study*. Noumea: Secretariat of the Pacific Community, Retrieved from https://pacific.unfpa.org/sites/default/files/pub-pdf/RMIFHSSReportweb.pdf

Secretariat of the Pacific Community. (2013). *Federated States of Micronesia Family Health and Safety Study*. Palikir: Secretariat of the Pacific Community, Retrieved from https://pacific.unfpa.org/sites/default/files/pub-pdf/FSMFHSSReportweb.pdf

Singh, H., Singh, J., Leese, R., Huts, S., Goddard, E., & Harris, S. (2018). *Sexual and Gender-Based Violence in the Pacific Islands: Handbook on Judicial Sentencing Practices*. London: ICAAD/Clifford Chance Retrieved from www.cliffordchance.com/content/dam/cliffordchance/briefings/2018/10/icaad-sgbv-sentencing-handbook.pdf.

South Pacific Tourism Organisation. (2018). *Annual Visitor Arrivals Report*. Retrieved from https://pic.or.jp/ja/wp-content/uploads/2019/07/2018-Annual-Visitor-Arrivals-ReportF.pdf.

Supreme Court, P. (2017). *Press Release: Palau Judiciary Reviews Family Protection Act Cases 2014–2016*. Koror: Supreme Court Retrieved from www.palausupremecourt.net/upload/P1406/17831090603382.pdf.

Tukuitonga, C. (2020). Pacific Defences: Ocean, Isolation and Lockdown. Retrieved from www.newsroom.co.nz/ideasroom/2020/04/10/1122230/colin-tukuitonga-pacific-defences-ocean-isolation-and-lockdown.

UN. (2015). *Millennium Development Goals Indicators*. New York: United Nations Retrieved from https://milleniumindicators.un.org/unsd/mdg/Data.aspx.

UN. (2021). *United Nations Treaty Collection*. New York: United Nations Retrieved from https://treaties.un.org/.

UNFPA. (2019). *Violence against Women – Regional Snapshot*. New York: United Nations Population Fund, Retrieved from https://asiapacific.unfpa.org/sites/default/files/resource-pdf/kNOwVAWdata%20regional%20VAW%20map%20April%2013%202019.pdf.

UNGA. (2015). *Transforming Our World: The 2030 Agenda for Sustainable Development*. New York: United Nations Retrieved from https://sustainabledevelopment.un.org/content/documents/21252030%20Agenda%20for%20Sustainable%20Development%20web.pdf.

UN Women. (2016). *Global Database on Violence against Women*. New York: United Nations Entity for Gender Equality and the Empowerment of Women Retrieved from https://evaw-global-database.unwomen.org/en.

UN Women. (2020). *Across the Pacific, Crisis Centres Respond to COVID-19 amid Natural Disasters* New York: United Nations Entity for Gender Equality and the Empowerment of Women, Retrieved from www.unwomen.org/en/news/stories/2020/6/feature-pacific-crisis-centres-respond-to-covid-19-amid-natural-disasters.

UN Women. (2021). *From Where I Stand: "I Really Want to Support Women"*. New York: United Nations Entity for Gender Equality and the Empowerment of Women Retrieved from https://asiapacific.unwomen.org/en/news-and-events/stories/2021/09/fwis-i-really-want-to-support-women.

WHO. (2013). *Global and Regional Estimates of Violence against Women: Prevalence and Health Effects of Intimate Partner Violence and Non-Partner Sexual Violence*. Geneva: World Health Organization.

SECTION THREE
Africa

17

DOMESTIC VIOLENCE IN ETHIOPIA

An Overview

Fikresus Amahazion

Introduction

Domestic violence, which involves a pattern of assaultive and coercive behaviors perpetrated by intimate partners and other family members, is a pressing global problem. It is present in every country and occurs in all settings, cutting across all boundaries of culture, religion, class, education, wealth or income, ethnicity, and age. Around the world, domestic violence represents a significant social, economic, health, and development issue, while it is also widely recognized as a grave violation of fundamental and basic human rights (UNICEF, 2000, 2006). In the Federal Democratic Republic of Ethiopia (hereafter Ethiopia), a populous, low-income, developing country located in the Horn of Africa, domestic violence is a major and persistent challenge.

General Country Background

A large, landlocked country, Ethiopia shares borders with Eritrea to the north, Djibouti and Somalia to the east, Sudan and South Sudan to the West, and Kenya to the south. It has a population of approximately 110 million people, making it the second most populous nation in Africa (after only Nigeria). A longtime key Western security ally in the Horn of Africa, Ethiopia is extremely diverse. It has more than 80 ethnolinguistic groups, the largest of which are Oromo, Amhara, Somali, Tigrean, and Sidama. The major religions in Ethiopia are Christianity and Islam, while the major languages include Oromo, Amharic, Somali, Tigrinya, and Sidamo. Addis Ababa (meaning "New Flower" in Amharic, one of Ethiopia's main languages), the country's capital, is home to the headquarters of a number of regional and international organizations, including the African Union (which was formerly the Organisation of African Unity), the Intergovernmental Authority on Development, and the United Nations Economic Commission for Africa. Ethiopia is a predominantly agricultural country, with more than 80% of the population living in rural areas. Although it has experienced recent economic growth and made considerable progress toward eliminating extreme poverty, Ethiopia remains one of the poorest, least developed countries in the world, with a per capita income of about $US790 (CIA, 2020; World Bank, 2018). Image 17.1 shows the geographic setting of Ethiopia.

DOI: 10.4324/9781003264040-21

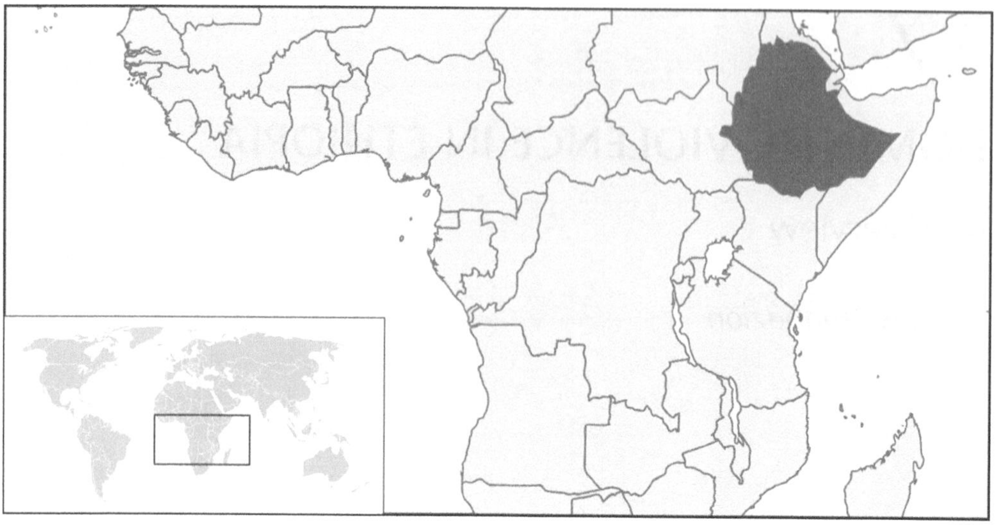

IMAGE 17.1 Ethiopia geographic setting.

Domestic Violence in Ethiopia

Although complete and comprehensive data are unavailable, domestic violence is a pervasive problem in Ethiopia. It is widespread and remains prevalent within both urban and rural areas. Most commonly, the victims of domestic violence are girls and women (although it is also possible for males and boys to be victims of violence). According to the 2005 *Multi-country Study on Women's Health and Domestic Violence against Women*, sponsored by the World Health Organization (WHO), about 71% of ever-partnered women experienced either physical or sexual violence, or both, over their lifetime – one of the highest prevalence rates in the world (WHO, 2005). More recently, the 2016 Ethiopia Demographic and Health Survey (EDHS) found that approximately one-third (34%) of ever-married women aged 15–49 in the country had experienced intimate partner violence (EDHS, 2016). Notably, a number of other reports and studies conducted in the country have also shown that significantly high percentages of Ethiopian women and girls have experienced domestic violence (Abeya, Afework, & Yalew, 2011; Andarge & Shiferaw, 2018; Semahegn & Mengistie, 2015). Importantly, actual prevalence rates of domestic violence in the country are quite likely higher since domestic violence may be under-recorded by legal or health officials and because it is often under-reported by victims.

As within many other settings around the world, domestic violence in Ethiopia takes several different forms, many of which often coexist and are intricately related. For example, many Ethiopian girls and women may experience murder or attempted murder, or suffer battering, which is characterized by the use of physical force, or the threat of such force. Such violence often includes kicking, punching, biting, slapping, burning, throwing sulfuric acid, beating with fists or objects, and strangling. Sexual abuse and violence are also prevalent in Ethiopia. Many girls and women may experience rape or attempted rape, marital rape, intimidation, pressure, threats, or harassment, and unwelcomed sexual advances or unwanted touching (Adinew & Hagos, 2017; Nimani & Hamdela, 2015; Tora, 2013). Additionally, women and girls in Ethiopia are exposed to psychological and emotional violence, including repeated verbal abuse, belittling, calumny and defamation, monitoring and stalking, threats and harassment, isolation and confinement, and deprivation of physical, financial, and personal resources.

In addition to these forms of violence, female genital cutting/mutilation (FGC/M) and child marriage, two harmful traditional practices that have existed for centuries, are quite common in Ethiopia and they have a profoundly negative impact on the lives of millions of girls and women. FGC/M, which comprises all procedures that involve partial or total removal of the external female genitalia, or other injury to the female genital organs for non-medical reasons (WHO, 2008: 8), is common among Ethiopian girls and women. The practice crosses ethnolinguistic and religious boundaries, and it is practiced in all regions. According to the 2016 EDHS, about 65% of women between the ages of 15 and 49 had undergone the practice (EDHS, 2016). Child marriage, which refers to any formal marriage or informal union between a child under the age of 18 and an adult or another child (UNICEF, 2014), is also relatively common in the country. The 2016 EDHS revealed that the median age at first marriage in the country was 17.1, and 58% of women aged 25–49 were child brides (EDHS, 2016).

While prevalence rates for FGC/M, child marriage, and other traditional harmful practices (e.g., forced marriage and abduction of girls for marriage) have reportedly declined in recent years, the practices remain widespread and they still persist, particularly within rural areas and among the poorest households.

Legal Framework and Response

Ethiopia is a party to a number of important regional and international human and gender-related rights instruments, including the *United Nations Convention on the Elimination of All Forms of Discrimination against Women*, the *United Nations Convention on the Rights of the Child*, the *African Charter of Human and People's Rights*, the *Protocol to the African Charter on the Rights of Women in Africa*, the *African Charter on the Rights and Welfare of the Child*, and the *United Nations Protocol to Prevent, Suppress and Punish Trafficking in Persons, especially Women and Children*. Generally, these instruments affirm the principles of fundamental rights and freedoms of every human being and they commit governments to protect women and change discriminatory practices and laws, including those that permit early marriage, bar women from inheriting property, or relegate them to a secondary status.

Additionally, women's rights and gender equality are incorporated into Ethiopia's constitution (Ethiopia Constitution, 1994), while the country has enacted a number of laws which aim to eliminate domestic violence and violence against girls and women. For example, the revised *Ethiopia Criminal Code*, officially proclaimed in 2004 and which repealed the *Penal Code of the Empire of Ethiopia* (1957), and the *Revised Special Penal Code of the Provisional Military Administration Council* (1982) outlaw "violence against a marriage partner or a person cohabiting, even in an irregular union" (Ethiopia Criminal Code, 2004: Article 564). Additionally, rape is a criminal offence, as is the trafficking of women or children (Ethiopia Criminal Code, 2004: Articles 597, 620, 621). Furthermore, FGC/M is prohibited, with stiff criminal penalties for medical practitioners, parents, and other practitioners, while child marriage, forced marriage, and abduction for marriage are illegal (marriage is based on the free and full consent of both spouses, and the minimum legal age for marriage is 18) (Ethiopia Criminal Code, 2004: Articles 565, 587, 648).

In addition to legislative measures, the Government has established child and women protection units in police stations responsible for handling cases of violence, and violence investigation and prosecution teams in some regions. In 2013, the Government launched the *UNiTE* program to end violence against women and girls and assist survivors, while also adopting the *National Strategy and Action Plan on Harmful Traditional Practices against Women and Children in Ethiopia*. The former seeks to eliminate gender-related violence and support victims, while the latter initiative aims to address the issue of harmful traditional practices. Several other educational and awareness-raising programs on domestic violence and gender equality have been conducted in the country, involving cooperation between the government, civil society organizations, nongovernmental organizations (NGOs). As well, the country's Growth and Transformational Plan (commonly known as GTP II and from 2015) includes ending violence against women as a priority.

Notwithstanding the fact that domestic violence is a significant issue in Ethiopia, relatively few resources are available to support victims in the country. There are a limited number of shelters and safe houses, which provide victims with inadequate rehabilitation, medical, psychosocial, legal, or judicial support services. These resources are mostly run or supported by NGOs and generally found within urban regions, thus limiting access to victims in remote, rural areas.

Notably, in December 2019, the Ethiopian Federal Office of the Attorney General, in collaboration with the United Nations Office on Drugs and Crime, a UN agency focusing on the trafficking in and abuse of illicit drugs, crime prevention and criminal justice, international terrorism, and political corruption, held the first in a series of widely publicized National Consultative Workshops focusing on strengthening the criminal justice response to violence against women and girls in the country and a commitment toward ensuring accountability (UNODC, 2020).

Causes and Associated Factors

While Ethiopia has undertaken important steps to address domestic violence, the issue remains a major challenge in the country. A large body of empirical work has shown that there is no one single factor to account for domestic violence (Abramsky et al., 2011; Koenig et al., 2006; Naved & Persson, 2005; Stith et al., 2004). In Ethiopia, domestic violence is associated with a number of different factors, many of which are interrelated.

Traditional Norms and Sociocultural Perspectives

Ethiopia remains a highly conservative, tradition bound country (Molvaer, 1995). A broad array of longstanding traditional norms and entrenched sociocultural attitudes condone, support, or tolerate violence against women. For example, notions of manhood or masculinity are linked to authority, dominance, control, sexual activity or virility, and aggression, while deeply ingrained patriarchal norms privilege or ascribe higher status to men and lower status to women. Furthermore, there are widespread beliefs, held by both men and women, that a man has a right to physically discipline a woman for "incorrect" or "disrespectful" behavior, among other reasons, that once a woman enters into a contract of marriage, the husband has the right to unlimited sexual access to his wife, and that physical violence is an acceptable way to resolve conflicts within a relationship (Abeya, Afework, & Yalew, 2012).

Both FGC/M and child marriage are also motivated by strong patriarchal norms and generally associated with cultural ideals of femininity, modesty, and appropriate sexual behavior. For example, FGC/M is often considered as a fundamental, necessary part of raising a girl, and the proper way to prepare her for adulthood and marriage. The procedure is seen as a way to ensure premarital virginity and marital fidelity. In terms of child marriage, marriage is often regarded as the only way to ensure sexual purity and uphold family honor.

Tradition and norms can often also play a significant role in forcing many victims to stay silent and remain within abusive relationships. For example, many victims do not report cases of violence by their spouse or intimate partner due to strong pressures and social taboos against speaking out and the fact that they may be blamed or stigmatized by relatives, neighbors, and the surrounding community. Additionally, there are commonly held beliefs that a woman should tolerate domestic violence in order to keep the family together and that domestic violence is solely a family matter, thus making it a "private" issue (Jones et al., 2014).

Poverty, Inequality, and the Low Socioeconomic Status of Women

Domestic violence in Ethiopia is also related with the poverty, illiteracy, high levels of socio-economic inequality, and the largely nonexistent social safety net in the country. Although illiteracy and poverty affect both genders in Ethiopia, they tend to affect women much more. For example, about 63.1% of women remain outside of the economically active population. As a result, victims of violence are frequently forced to remain in abusive relationships because their partners serve as vital opportunities for financial and social security, or for satisfying material aspirations. Notably, an empirical study conducted in South Ethiopia zone found that the prevalence of domestic violence was significantly higher among women from food insecure households as compared to women from food secure household (Andarge & Shiferaw, 2018), while another study conducted in Sidama zone found a strong positive association between food insecurity and domestic violence (Regassa & Stoecker 2012).

Similarly, poverty and inequality can serve to drive child marriage in Ethiopia, where it is particularly common in rural areas and among the poorest households. Some Ethiopian families may choose to marry off their daughters in order to reduce the number of children they need to feed, clothe, and educate, while others may do so because they believe it will secure their daughters' futures.

Furthermore, poverty, inequality, and unemployment can contribute to increased levels of stress, hardship, and the abuse of alcohol or drugs among men, which are often associated with reduced self-control, increased aggression, and the perpetration of violence against partners.

Underreporting

Another important factor associated with domestic violence is that most victims never report the abuse that they suffer. This is due to a variety of reasons. For one, in Ethiopia, domestic violence is often downplayed, condoned, or tolerated, seen as a family issue, and thus a "private" affair, and victims are often either blamed or stigmatized for abuse. Furthermore, victims are strongly encouraged to reconcile with and return to their abusive partners, rather than reporting violence, while divorces are considered as dishonorable or shameful (Tafere et al., 2020). Additionally, victims may refrain from reporting violence due to fear of reprisals from their abuser or the community, or because they lack access to information or knowledge about viable alternatives or legal rights. As well, many victims in remote, rural areas may face significant barriers to seeking assistance or accessing justice. Generally, these various factors can lead to a sense of helplessness and despair among victims, causing them to suffer in silence, while also contributing to a sense of impunity among abusers.

Inadequate Legal Framework and Lack of Enforcement

The poor legal framework and lack of implementation or enforcement of laws is also associated with domestic violence in the country. For instance, in Ethiopia there is no comprehensive law on domestic violence or violence against women. Common forms of violence, such as marital rape or gang rape, acid attacks, economic and psychological violence, as well as sexual or gender harassment and stalking, are not legally proscribed. There is also an absence of civil remedies for victims of violence, while there are no procedures for victims to obtain protection or restraining orders against abusers. Furthermore, existing laws are neither enforced nor fully implemented, with law enforcement often failing to investigate or prosecute domestic violence accusations. Often, officials (e.g., police and health) lack the general awareness or necessary training to properly identify violence or respond appropriately (Freedom House, 2019; USDS, 2017; Woldeyesus, Domingo, & Bekele, 2018).

When there is an inadequate legal framework, poor implementation or enforcement of laws, and frequent dismissal or downplaying of complaints, abusers can act with impunity and they are seemingly encouraged to continue with their abuse. Victims are left helpless in seeking protection from and justice against perpetrators of violence.

Impact of COVID-19

Coronavirus disease (COVID-19), an infectious disease caused by a recently discovered coronavirus, was declared a pandemic by the WHO in early March 2020. Since the onset of the global pandemic, tens of millions around the world have been infected, several million have died due to the virus, and the livelihoods of hundreds of millions have been severely disrupted. Past crises and outbreaks have demonstrated that men and women are differently affected, while preexisting inequalities and challenges for women and girls are often exacerbated (Chattu & Yaya, 2020; Davies & Bennett, 2016).

Ethiopia, with a relatively weak health system, limited infrastructure and resources, and a chronic shortage of health workers, has had one of the largest COVID-19 caseloads in Africa. The pandemic also contributed to an increase in domestic violence and exacerbated existing barriers to justice. A community-based cross-sectional study conducted in Northern Ethiopia during the pandemic found "a relatively higher prevalence of violence against women" (Gebrewahd, Gebremeskel, & Tadesse, 2020: 7), while there were also reports of a resurgence of harmful traditional practices and child marriages. Importantly, with the news of the violence, several measures were taken, including the opening of a temporary emergency shelter in Addis Ababa, as well as an announcement by the Federal Supreme Courte to prioritize domestic violence (Zeleke, 2020).

Increased stress and tensions, related to health concerns or economic insecurity, likely contributed to the violence and abuse, while the pandemic also led to various challenges for victims. Economic issues made accessing care or services more difficult, many supportive services for victims were cutback or reallocated to the pandemic response, and many victims have been hesitant to travel to hospitals or clinics due to lockdowns and fear of the virus or being harassed by police. Across the country, shelters also experienced great strain, housing more people than can be safely accommodated under physical distancing rules and lacking adequate resources (e.g., food, water, electricity, and personal protective equipment). Additionally, with national resources directed to the pandemic response, efforts to stop sexual exploitation of young girls and children were interrupted, placing many at risk.

The pandemic also contributed to a rise in unemployment and economic insecurity in Ethiopia (Weiser, Ambel, Bundervoet, & Haile, 2020). As a result, some families have been forced to push their young daughters into arranged or early marriages, or sent them to cities for work, where they are at greater risk of labor or sexual exploitation. Many Ethiopian women and girls were laid off after COVID-19 struck the country and some were forced into the commercial sex trade, exposing them to abuse, violence, and exploitation.

Climate Change

Climate change, which refers to long-term shifts in temperatures and weather patterns, has been increasingly regarded as a global emergency that goes beyond borders and is one of the greatest threats facing humanity (UN, 2021). Despite the country's extremely low contribution to global greenhouse gas emissions, Ethiopia is one of the most vulnerable countries to climate change in the world (World Bank, 2021). According to the WHO, climate change, particularly in terms of increased temperatures, intense heat waves, and more extreme rainfall, floods, and landslides, is exacerbating health problems in Ethiopia (WHO, 2015). Climate change also threatens to fuel and increase the risk of violence against women and girls in the country. For instance, as a result of more periods of prolonged drought, Ethiopian women and girls may be forced to make more frequent and longer journeys to obtain food or water, thus exposing them to sexual assault. Additionally, greater food scarcity or economic insecurities associated with climate change may push vulnerable families to push young daughters into marriage as a mechanism to cope.

Moving Forward

Domestic violence is a truly global problem. In Ethiopia, despite some progress it remains a massive and multi-faceted challenge. Although important steps have been made to address domestic violence in the country, moving forward, continued attention is critically required in order to increase general awareness, reduce its occurrence, and better protect the rights and interests of girls and women.

There are a number of possible steps that can be taken in this direction. For example, more and methodologically rigorous population-based studies and data collection are necessary to better estimate the prevalence, burden, and impact of domestic violence and provide critically relevant information for government, policymakers, and health-care professionals.

Ethiopia can also enact comprehensive, progressive legislation on domestic violence that is in-line with international legal and human rights norms, principles, and standards, and which includes all forms of violence against women (including marital rape, gang rape, and acid attacks). It is vital that access to protection or restraining orders for victims is legally ensured. Additionally, Ethiopia can improve the application and enforcement of laws. Stronger, more comprehensive laws and policies, as well as better enforcement mechanisms are important and can convey a strong message that domestic violence is not tolerated and reduce impunity for abusers.

Notably, in 2018, against a backdrop of growing turmoil, mounting discontent, and widespread unrest in Ethiopia, Hailemariam Desalegn resigned as prime minister, with Dr. Abiy Ahmed being appointed as his replacement. The bold new PM quickly pursued an aggressive, reformist agenda, promising a more inclusive form of politics, calling for tolerance and preaching reconciliation. One of his major moves was initiating an unprecedented and dramatic increase in the participation of women in public and private life; Abiy reshuffled the cabinet, appointing half the seats in parliament to women – one of the highest rates of female representation in parliament in the world. Importantly, this may prove to be a far-reaching move with tangible outcomes; a considerable body of research has examined how an increase in females elected to legislative branches of government may correspondingly increase the policies addressing issues concerning women (Dodson & Carroll, 1991; Lovenduski, 2005; Swers, 2002; Trimble, 2008).

As well, the government will need to allocate more human or financial resources to support victims of violence and allow them to find ways of exiting from abusive relationships. This can include the establishment of more shelters and safe houses, income assistance, and improved access to health care and social services, including counseling, legal aid, and psychosocial services. Geographic coverage of shelters and supportive services must also be expanded in order to ensure that victims in remote, rural areas have improved access to resources.

Additionally, there should be more done to sensitize police, judges, and social workers about domestic violence and train them in responding to the needs of survivors holistically and empathetically. Front-line health-care workers can be trained to recognize the signs of violence during interactions with women seeking routine services (e.g., pre-natal care and family planning). This type of training for health-care workers can help ensure early identification of women who are experiencing violence and provide them with appropriate referral and support. As well, gender desks or similar departments can be established within police stations to allow women to safely report domestic violence.

A genuine paradigm shift within Ethiopian culture is also imperative in order to confront this deep-rooted social problem. Cultural and social norms supportive of domestic violence must be firmly challenged, while more should be done to raise general awareness about the harmful impact of domestic violence. Awareness campaigns can involve public workshops and seminars or utilize local media outlets and general communication opportunities. Various communities, elders, and other respected figures should be involved in design and dissemination of awareness-raising materials and messages. Egalitarian norms can be promoted as part of life skills and comprehensive sexuality education curricula taught to young people. The messages to all must be based on gender equality, that domestic violence is damaging to everyone, and that it can be stopped.

Finally, girls and women should be supported and empowered. For example, they should be provided equal access to quality primary and secondary education, as well as social, economic, and civic opportunities. Women should receive vocational training, as well as general support to increase their opportunities to find a job and compete with their skills in the labor market. Economic independence can increase women's power and agency and provides them the freedom to escape abusive domestic relationships, particularly economic violence. A considerable body of research has shown, for example, that an improvement in women's economic and employment opportunities may lead to a decline in violence (Aizer, 2010; Bowlus & Seitz, 2006; Farmer & Tiefenthaler, 1997; Heise & Kotsadam, 2015).

References

Abeya, Sileshi Garoma, Mesganaw Fantahun Afework, and Alemayeh Worku Yalew. 2011. "Intimate Partner Violence against Women in Western Ethiopia: Prevalence, Patterns, and Associated Factors." *BioMed Central Public Health*. 11 (913): 1–18.

Abeya, Sileshi Garoma, Mesganaw Fantahun Afework, and Alemayeh Worku Yalew. 2012. "Intimate Partner Violence against Women in West Ethiopia: A Qualitative Study on Attitudes, Woman's Response, and Suggested Measures as Perceived by Community Members." *Reproductive Health*. 9 (14): 1–11.

Abramsky, Tanya, Charlotte H. Watts, Claudia Garcia-Moreno, Karen Devries, Ligia Kiss, Mary Ellsberg, Henrica A.F.M. Jansen, and Lori Heise. 2011. "What Factors are Associated with Recent Intimate Partner Violence? Findings from the WHO Multi-country Study on Women's Health and Domestic Violence." *BioMed Central Public Health*. 11 (109): 1–17.

Adinew, Yohannes Mehretie and Mihiret Abreham Hagos. 2017. "Sexual Violence against Female University Students in Ethiopia." *BioMed Central International Health and Human Rights*. 17 (19): 1–7.

Aizer, Anna. 2010. "The Gender Wage Gap and Domestic Violence." *American Economic Review*. 100 (4): 1847–1859.

Andarge, Eshetu and Yohannes Shiferaw. 2018. "Disparities in Intimate Partner Violence among Currently Married Women from Food Secure and Insecure Urban Households in South Ethiopia: A Community Based Comparative Cross-Sectional Study." *BioMed Research International*. 2018: 1–12.

Bowlus, Audra J. and Shannon Seitz. 2006. "Domestic Violence, Employment, and Divorce." *International Economic Review*. 47 (4): 1113–1149.

Chattu, Vijay Kumar and Sanni Yaya. 2020. "Emerging Infectious Diseases and Outbreaks: Implications for Women's Reproductive Health and Rights in Resource-Poor Settings." *Reproductive Health*. 17 (43): 1–5.

CIA. 2020. *The World Factbook: Ethiopia*. The Central Intelligence Agency. Available at www.cia.gov/library/publications/the-world-factbook/geos/et.html.

Davies, Sara E. and Belinda Bennett. 2016. "A Gendered Human Rights Analysis of Ebola and Zika: Locating Gender in Global Health Emergencies." *International Affairs*. 92: 1041–1060.

Dodson, Debra and Susan J. Carroll. 1991. *Reshaping the Agenda: Women in State Legislatures*. New Brunswick, NJ: Eagleton Institute of Politics.
EDHS. 2016. *Ethiopia Demographic and Health Survey*. Addis Ababa, Ethiopia: Central Statistical Agency.
Ethiopia Constitution. 1994. *The Constitution of the Federal Democratic Republic of Ethiopia*. Addis Ababa, Ethiopia. Available at www.wipo.int/edocs/lexdocs/laws/en/et/et007en.pdf.
Ethiopia Criminal Code. 2004. *The Criminal Code of the Federal Democratic Republic of Ethiopia*. Proclamation No. 414/2004; in force May 9, 2005. Addis Ababa, Ethiopia.
Farmer, Amy and Jill Tiefenthaler. 1997. "An Economic Analysis of Domestic Violence." *Review of Social Economy*. 55 (3): 337–358.
Freedom House. 2019. *Freedom in the World 2018: Ethiopia Profile*. Washington, DC: Freedom House. Available at https://freedomhouse.org/report/freedom-world/2019/ethiopia.
Gebrewahd, Gebremeskel Tukue, Gebreamlak Gebremedhn Gebremeskel, and Degena Bahrey Tadesse. 2020. "Intimate Partner Violence Against Reproductive Age Women During COVID-19 Pandemic in Northern Ethiopia, 2020: A Community-based Cross-sectional Study." *Reproductive Health*. 17 (152): 1–8.
Heise, Lori L. and Andreas Kotsadam. 2015. "Cross-national and Multilevel Correlates of Partner Violence: An Analysis of Data from Population-based Surveys." *The Lancet Global Health*. 3 (6): 332–340.
Jones, Nicola Anne, Bekele Tefera, Janey Stephenson, Taveeshi Gupta, Paola Pereznieto, Guday Emirie, Betlehem Gebre, and Kiya Gezhegne. 2014. *Early Marriage and Education: The Complex Role of Social Norms in shaping Ethiopian Adolescent Girls' Lives*. London: Overseas Development Institute.
Koenig, Michael A., Rob Stephenson, Saifuddin Ahmed, Shireen J. Jejeebhoy, and Jacquelyn Campbell. 2006. "Individual and Contextual Determinants of Domestic Violence in North India." *American Journal of Public Health*. 96 (1): 1–7.
Lovenduski, Joni. 2005. *Feminizing Politics*. Cambridge: Polity.
Molvaer, Reidulf Knut. 1995. *Socialization and Social Control in Ethiopia*. Wiesbaden: Harrassowitz Verlag.
Naved, Ruchira Tabassum and Lars Ake Persson. 2005. "Factors Associated with Spousal Physical Violence Against Women in Bangladesh." *Studies in Family Planning*. 36 (4): 289–300.
Nimani, Wegu and Belayneh Hamdela. 2015. "Sexual Violence and Associated Factors among High School Students in Butajira Town, South Ethiopia." *General Medicine*. 3 (4): 1–8.
Regassa, Nigatu and Barbara J. Stoecker. 2012. "Household Food Insecurity and Hunger Among Households in Sidama District, Southern Ethiopia." *Public Health Nutrition*. 15 (7): 1276–1283.
Semahegn, Agumasi and Bezatu Mengistie. 2015. "Domestic Violence against Women and Associated Factors in Ethiopia; Systematic Review." *Reproductive Health*. 12 (78): 1–12.
Stith, Sandra M., Douglas B. Smith, Carrie E. Penn, David B. Ward, and Dari Tritt. 2004. "Intimate Partner Physical Abuse Perpetration and Victimization Risk Factors: A Meta-analytic Review." *Aggression and Violent Behavior*. 10 (1): 65–98.
Swers, Michele L. 2002. *The Difference Women Make: the Policy Impact of Women in Congress*. Chicago, IL: University of Chicago Press.
Tafere, Yisak, Nardos Chuta, Alula Pankhurst, and Gina Crivello. 2020. *Young Marriage, Parenthood and Divorce in Ethiopia*. Oxford: Young Lives.
Tora, Abebayehu. 2013. "Assessment of Sexual Violence against Female Students in Wolaita Sodo University, Southern Ethiopia." *Journal of Interpersonal Violence*. 28 (11): 2351–2367.
Trimble, Linda. 2006. "When Do Women Count? Substantive Representation of Women in the Canadian Legislature." pp. 120–133 in Marian Sawer, Manon Tremblay, and Linda Trimble (eds.), *Representing Women in Parliament: A Comparative Study*. London: Routledge.
UN. 2021. "Climate Action." United Nations. Available at www.un.org/en/climatechange.
UNICEF. 2000. *Domestic Violence against Women and Girls*. Florence: United Nations Children's Fund (UNICEF) Innocenti Research Centre.
UNICEF. 2006. *Behind Closed Doors. The Impact of Domestic Violence on Children*. New York: United Nations Children's Fund (UNICEF).
UNICEF. 2014. *Ending Child Marriage: Progress and Prospects*. New York: United Nations Children's Fund (UNICEF).
UNODC. 2020. *Addressing Violence against Women and Girls in Ethiopia*. 12 January 2020. Vienna, Austria: United Nations Office on Drugs and Crime. Available at www.unodc.org/easternafrica/en/addressing-violence-against-women-and-girls-in-ethiopia.html.

USDS. 2017. *United States Department of State Bureau of Democracy, Human Rights and Labor, Country Reports on Human Rights Practices for 2017: Ethiopia.* Washington, DC: United States Department of State Bureau of Democracy, Human Rights, and Labor.

Weiser, Christina, Alamayehu A. Ambel, Tom Bundervoet, and Asmelash Haile 2020. *Monitoring COVID-19 Impacts on Households in Ethiopia.* Washington, DC: The World Bank Group.

WHO. 2005. *World Health Organization (WHO) Multi-country Study on Women's Health and Domestic Violence against Women.* Geneva: World Health Organization.

WHO. 2008. *Eliminating Female Genital Mutilation: An Interagency Statement (WHO, UNFPA, UNICEF, UNIFEM, OHCHR, UNHCR, UNECA, UNESCO, UNDP, UNAIDS).* Geneva: World Health Organization.

WHO. 2015. *Climate Change to Impact on Human Health in Ethiopia.* 4 December 2015. Geneva: World Health Organization. Available at www.afro.who.int/news/climate-change-impact-human-health-ethiopia.

Woldeyesus, Elshaday K., Pilar Domingo, and Bezawit Bekele. 2018. *Policy and Legal Analysis Notes – Ethiopia: A Review of the Strategic Plan for a Multisectoral Response to Violence against Women and Children.* London: Overseas Development Institute and GAGE Programme Office.

World Bank. 2018. *Ethiopia: Overview.* Washington, DC: The World Bank Group. Available at www.worldbank.org/en/country/ethiopia/overview.

World Bank. 2021. *Climate Risk Country Profile: Ethiopia.* Washington, DC: The World Bank Group. Available at https://climateknowledgeportal.worldbank.org/sites/default/files/2021-05/15463A-WB_Ethiopia%20Country%20Profile-WEB.pdf.

Zeleke, Meron. 2020. *We Need a National Conversation in Ethiopia as Covid-19 Hits Women Hard.* 11 August 2020. Danish Institute for International Studies. Available at www.diis.dk/en/node/24151.

18

BETWEEN REALITY AND EXPECTATIONS

Tackling Domestic Violence in Egypt

Hiam Elgousi

Introduction

Gender-based violence remains a significant subject that attracts global attention to women's rights. Violence is perceived as a vital obstacle that hinders women's development and progress due to it negatively affecting their mental and physical health. In 1979, the Convention on the Elimination of All Forms of Discrimination Against Women (CEDAW), adopted by the UN General Assembly, was a turning point in women's rights in modern history as it represented a significant vision of equitable human rights for both women and men. Based on the CEDAW definition,

> gender-based violence constitutes any form of violence that is directed at a person on the basis of gender and sex. It includes acts that inflict physical, mental or sexual harm or suffering, the threat of such acts, coercion and other deprivations of liberty.

This definition constitutes a broad understanding of acts which result in jeopardizing female lives and well-being, such as domestic violence, domestic abuse, Female Genital Mutilation (FGM), amongst other examples.

According to the key-fact sheet published by the World Health Organization (WHO) "1 in 3 (35%) of women worldwide have experienced either physical and/or sexual intimate partner violence or non-partner sexual violence in their lifetime" and in addition "almost one third (30%) of women who have been in a relationship report that they have experienced some form of physical and/or sexual violence by their intimate partner in their lifetime" (WHO, 2017, p. 1). Such violence occurs in both upper and lower middle-income countries irrespective of economic, educational, and social status. It is a global phenomenon which all too often has the most serious consequences for women who experience it, for example, globally 38% of all murders of women are committed by intimate partners (WHO, 2017, p. 2). And yet only 7.2% of the total victim's report experiencing sexual violence by other perpetrators (WHO, 2014, p. 14).

This chapter will focus on one form of gender-based violence, which is domestic violence in Egypt. It will also touch upon the impact of the COVID-19 pandemic and climate change and examine to which degree these two factors have affected the well-being of Egyptian women and girls. Thus, the chapter is arranged into several sections: the first section following the introduction covers a brief background to the term and its definition; domestic violence in the Egyptian context; the impact of the COVID-19 pandemic and climate change on Egyptian women and girls;

DOI: 10.4324/9781003264040-22

current measurements to defy gender-based violence in general and domestic violence, particularly in normal contexts/ circumstances; and, finally, ways forward (a set of recommendations).

Defining the Term Domestic Violence

The term "domestic violence" refers to abuse and violence that occur in the domestic sphere. It has also been known as family violence, a term that is

> often preferred in communities where there are prominent extended family connections, such as indigenous communities or families from culturally and linguistically diverse back grounds. This is in recognition that family violence is more broad than intimate partner violence and that it impacts on a wide range of kin and community members.
>
> *Nursing and Health Sciences, 2015, p. 2*

There is also another term which has been adopted by the WHO to describe such an act which is "Intimate partner violence" or IPV. WHO define IPV as "behavior by an intimate partner that causes physical, sexual or psychological harm, including acts of physical aggression, sexual coercion, psychological abuse and controlling behaviors" (2013a, p. vii). These definitions fall under the umbrella of violence against women stated in Article 1 of the Declaration on the Elimination of Violence Against Women by the United Nations General Assembly in 1993.

In this chapter, I have used the term "domestic violence" as it involves the mixture of physical and sexual violence by employing several techniques to maintain male domination over females. These techniques are varying from a misinterpretation of religious text, economic dependency, cultural, and approval of customary norms.

Setting the Context: Domestic Violence in Egypt

In 2009, the Egyptian Cinema House produced a film entitled "*Scheherazade, Tell Me a Story*".[1] The film is about Heba, a young and popular TV presenter, who is interested in broadcasting stories that touch on the everyday secret lives of women and the social injustices they face. Her honest style in broadcasting puts her husband's job and his ambitions to be appointed as editor-in-chief of the leading governmental newspaper in jeopardy. Even though her program focuses on women's issues and considerations are non-political, it becomes distasteful to the authorities. This eventually results in her husband losing his promotion. Due to that, he pours all his anger on her violently. The film received many criticisms for its boldness in shedding the light on different forms of gender-based violence which Egyptian women face regardless of their education and socio-economic status, and how the society deals with such violence.

There is no doubt that the film can be regarded as a case study to understand how violence against women functions in Egyptian society. It exposes the patriarchy nature of both the society and the political system. Suad Joseph defines the term patriarchy in the Arab context as: "patriarchy is the prioritizing of the rights of males and elders (including elder women) and the justification of those rights within kinship values which are usually supported by religion". She continues by stating that her definition "differs from some western feminists, who do not consider age or kinship" (1996, p. 14). According to her, there are many forms of patriarchy: social, economic, political, religious, as well as patriarchy as a condition in its own right.

With the understanding of this term and by looking to the mechanism of decision-making processes in Egyptian society, it is possible to explain why almost the majority of decisions are taken by men, even those relating to women's issues often mean solutions that result in a ratcheting up of domination of men over women. Eventually, the repulsive process of controlling women's lives results in a loss of any sense of individuality, dignity, or ability to be independent. It is also peculiar how, in the process, women oppress other women. For example, older women, who become saturated with male-dominated visions, and who have been indoctrinated for long enough by men within a societal environment that seeks to subdue women, take active part in making the younger women in their kin become submissive to male authority in the family (Elgousi, 2016).

A recent finding from a World Bank report of 2018 echoed observations I made previously in 2016 (see Elgousi, 2016, p. XVI), as according to this study[2] conducted on the economic cost of gender-based violence it was estimated that:

> 7.9 million Egyptian women suffered from all forms of violence yearly, perpetrated by spouses, close relatives and strangers in public spaces. Domestic Violence within marriage is considered socially acceptable, especially in rural areas and among the less educated. Moreover, many women do not recognize domestic violence as an unacceptable act, but rather as part of married life.
>
> *The World Bank, 2018, p. 34*

Women's justifications for being beaten or hit by their husband vary from: going out without permission; neglecting taking care of the children; refusal to have sexual intercourse; arguing on matters; and burning the food. These justifications provided by women who are likely to agree with wife-beating are from rural Upper Egypt did not attend a school, or have basic education, and belong to the lowest wealth quintile (The World Bank, 2018). In addition, in a 2017 survey conducted by UN Women on gender attitudes, it was asked: "should a wife tolerate violence to sustain and keep the family together". The result of the study demonstrated that 90% of Egyptian men and 71% of women agreed with the statement. It is worth noting that "domestic violence is prevalent and commonly accepted across religious communities and socio-economic levels" (Australian Government, Department of Foreign Affairs and Trade, 2019, p. 31). While marital rape is considered as violence against women, it is not criminalized or recognized as rape by the society.

> Moreover, most of the violated women by their family members[3] or anyone within their surrounding environment did not seek the help of the authorities for protection, or any services, with the exception of only 5% who received health services.
>
> *(National Strategy for the Empowerment of Egyptian Women 2030 Vision and Pillars, 2017, pp. 51–52*

The Impact of the COVID-19 Pandemic on Egyptian Women and Girls

The available literature has suggested that violence against women and girls tends to escalate during any type of emergency. Such emergencies can vary from displacement, refugee camps, living in conflict-affected zones, etc. It also includes an outbreak of an epidemic. The outbreak of the COVID-19 pandemic in late 2019, "has exacerbated violence against women and girls in public and private spaces" (UN Women, 2020a,b, p. 1).

Globally, a large number of the population has been under distancing measures, the businesses have been shut down, schools have been closed, movement has been restricted. At the beginning of 2020, the situation was getting worse. Lockdown policy was carried out in almost all countries. People have been encouraged to stay at home, yet in some countries they were forced to do so. Lockdown policy poses another challenge in terms of economy, as it increased the severe financial strain on communities especially those how are already vulnerable, such as lower-paid, informal employment, where there is a lack of income and social security protection umbrella.

Women in abusive relationships are trapped inside their homes with their violent partners, leaving women exposed to severe violence day and night. In addition to the shortage in financial capacity, women are left with increased care work as children are at home, having fewer contacts with their friends and families, living under stress, and potential job losses. These concerns resulted in the increasing level of vulnerability of women, adding more burdens to their livelihood.

A brief published by the UN Women in 2020 stated that

> the existing crisis of violence against women and girls (VAWG) is likely to worsen in the context of COVID-19. Emerging data shows that since the outbreak of COVID-19, reports of violence against women, and particularly domestic violence, have increased in several countries as security, health, and money worries create tensions and strains accentuated by the cramped and confined living conditions of lockdown.
>
> *2020a, p. 3*

The emerging evidence of the impact of COVID-19 on violence against women and girls urged governments to form and put in place a set of measures in cooperation with international organizations and civil society organizations aiming at preventing and responding to the violence against women (VAW). At the same time, international organizations such as UN Women, and WHO continue to release recommendations and guidelines for governments to respond to the current pandemic.

The situation in Egypt was not different from the rest of the world, as the Egyptian government took several measures to respond to COVID-19. These measures have been compiled and published by the National Council for Women (NCW) in five series with the title "Women Policy Tracker on Responsive Policies and Programs During the New COVID-19 Pandemic". The fifth and final edition of the series (which comes in 33 pages) published in January 2021 covering the period from March 14, 2020 to January 20, 2021. By establishing the "Women policy Tracker", The National Council for Women was aimed to serve the following purpose as stated in the tracker document (2021, p. 2):

1. Monitor all issued policies and procedures responsive to the needs of Egyptian women directly and/or indirectly in light of the efforts made to reduce the spread of COVID-19;
2. Design an easier tool that can be used as reference to all women related issued policies that can be used by decision makers for a more collaborative and comprehensive vision on means of moving forward;
3. Document the efforts and highlight the outcome of the coordinated efforts of the government on women related policies to protect them and their families from the COVID-19; and
4. Reflect on all those policies with necessary supporting programs and initiatives.

The measures covered several issues, such as economic concerns, raising awareness about COVID-19, mental health during the lockdown, and violence against women. For example:

1. The Ministry of Manpower launched as part of its website a registration form of irregular workers to receive an exceptional allowance of EGP 500, as part of the government plan to protect them due to the pandemic. The financial provision included both genders.
2. In cooperation with Baseera Center and partnership with UN Women, a phone survey was launched during the period of the 4th–14th of April, 2020 aiming at examining the effect of

the COVID-19 pandemic on women and girl's life. "The survey included 1518 women with a minimum age of 18 years old". The results showed that "7% of the wives reported that they had already been subjected to violence by the husband (verbal abuse or insult); that this did not happen before the pandemic occurred" (2021, p. 10). It also showed that "33% was the rate of increased problems with in the family; and 19% increase in violence among family members" (Ibid).

3. In June 2020 the Anti-Harassment Unit in Cairo University delivered a campaign raising awareness on all forms of cybercrimes and violence against women through the internet targeting the university population (Ibid).
4. In December 2020, in cooperation with the Ministry of Higher Education and Scientific Research and development partners, "a three Women Safety Units" was launched in the hospitals of Al-Qasr Al-Aini, Mansoura, and Ain Shams universities to deal with women victims of violence. Launching the Units included training program targeting "190 doctors and nurses" (Ibid, p. 26).

Finally, in January 2021, the draft law submitted by the National Committee for the eradication of FGM had been approved by the Egyptian Cabinet after the study and review of Ministry of Justice – "amending some provisions of the Penal Code to increase the punishment of FGM crimes, the amendments were stipulated in Article (242 bis & 242 (a) bis)" (Ibid, p. 31).

Having highlighted on the above procedures and measures, still the gravity resulting from the increase of violence against women under COVID-19 took another turn. In a shocking news covered by a local newspaper "Youm 7"[4]dated on June 24, 2020:

> A husband throws his wife from the balcony as she has been affected by COVID-19. The husband denies this charge. He explains that the quarrel was on economic shortages resulted from COVID-19, and he didn't know about his wife.

Setting the Context: Climate Change and Its Linkage to Gender-Based Violence

There is growing evidence that climate change has an undoubted linkage to violence in general and gender-based violence in particular. Environmental Studies indicate links between "environmental pressures and gender-based violence, and that the degradation of nature, competition over increasingly scarce resources and environmental crime can all exacerbate violence" (International Union for Conservation of Nature Issues Brief, 2020).

It is crucial to underline how the term "environmental crime" is understood. Hence this paper draws on the definition stated by Nellemann et al. (2016, p. 17):

> Although the definition of "environmental crime" is not universally agreed, it is most commonly understood as a collective term to describe illegal activities harming the environment and aimed at benefitting individuals or groups or companies from the exploitation of, damage to, trade or theft of natural resources, including, but not limited to serious crimes and transnational organized crime.

Environmental crime is composed of a wide range of activities and practices that cause damage to natural resources. It affects public health and well-being of communities that depend directly and indirectly on natural resources for their lives and livelihoods. Examples of such activities include: illegal wildlife and logging trades, illegal fishing, illegal mining, illicit resource extraction (IUCN, 2020), illegal dumping, and trade in hazardous and toxic waste (Nellemann et al., 2016).

According to Nellemann et al. (2016), the cost of environmental crime has an estimated annual value of US$ 90–258 billion. It also comes in fourth place of transnational organized crime globally, just after drug trafficking, counterfeiting, and human trafficking. Studies indicate that women and girls are the most vulnerable segments affected by environmental crime in their communities in terms of safety and health. Indeed, resource scarcity, conflicts, and displacement caused by environmental degradation play an enormous role in deepening existing inequalities.

> In such cases, gender-based violence is often used as a means of reinforcing privileges and control over resources. Climate change worsens these effects. During prolonged drought, for example, child marriage is used by families as a strategy to cope with scarcity of food and income.
>
> *IUCN Issues Brief, 2020*

The following are examples of different forms in which women and girls have been subject to gender-based violence as a result of environmental crimes and climate change:

- In some parts of Africa, for example, the Democratic Republic of Congo, the illegal charcoal trade involves a range of crimes and human rights violations, including extortion, forced labor, murder, and sexual slavery (Dranginis, 2016).
- In Zimbabwe after cyclone Idai in 2019 "Women and girls faced challenges of unsafe shelter, exposure to gender-based violence (GBV) and negative coping mechanisms, including transactional sex. Their burdens of unpaid care work intensified" (Chatiza, 2019, p. 13).
- In Darfur, during the war waged by Al-Bashir's[5] regime, Sudanese women have reported being subjected to rape, abduction, and sexual abuse by the militants who supported the government. According to Médecins Sans Frontières "Between October 2004 and mid-February 2005, MSF doctors in numerous locations in South and West Darfur treated almost 500 women and girls who were raped. MSF believes that these numbers reflect only a fraction of the total number of victims because many women are reluctant to report the crime or seek treatment". Violence occurred when women and girls carried out activities indispensable to the survival of their families, such as searching for firewood or water.

The Impact of the Climate Change on Egyptian Women and Girls[6]

The term "Land is like honour" makes explicit the importance and the significant value of the agricultural land in the Egyptian rural context. "The notion of honour (*sharaf*) is a central concept that guides behaviour and significantly influences interactions in Egyptian culture. It is deeply intertwined with people's ideas about their dignity (*karama*). Traditionally, a man's honour was determined by his ability to protect the women in his care" (Cultural Atlas, 2021), in addition to the female's behavior inside the family. Some traditional communities acted violently to preserve and restore honor – traditional practices such as FGM; honor crimes, done under the pretext of saving family honor.

It is crucial to understand the historical roots of valuing the land, especially the fertile tracts in Egyptian rural communities. According to a report published by Statista Research Department in December 2020: "Agriculture was the main driving factor for the establishment of the Egyptian civilization. Archaeologists dated the beginning of agriculture in Egypt back to the prehistoric period of 6,000-3,150 BCE, although some evidence suggests its beginning back to 8,000 BCE". About 20–30% of Egypt's GDP is generated by the agricultural sector and 30% of the labor force in the country is employed in the agricultural sector (Food and Agricultural Organization of United Nations, 2021). This illustrates the significant role played by the agriculture sector in the Egyptian economy.

Following January 2011, the rate of illegal construction and violations of the agriculture land was sped up due to the security vacuum as a result of the 2011 revolution. Yet, it is worth mentioning that the violations of the agricultural land are not just recent and have been occurring for many decades. Egyptian Prime Minister Dr Mustafa Madbouli in his meeting with a number of Egyptian editors-in-chief, announced that Egypt has lost more than 400,000 feddans (one feddan equals about 1.038 acres) over 40 years, including 90,000 feddans since 2011 due to encroachment activities on the agriculture lands. According to him "Construction [on farmlands] causes a food crisis for 100 million citizens. We will deal decisively with any attempt of encroachment" (Egypt Today, 2019).

Having stated that, the violation of women's inheritance rights in some traditional communities in Egypt could be understandable within this prerequisite condition. Women in some traditional communities, such as in the rural areas and in Upper Egypt, still face discrimination by their own kin or family. The discrimination takes different forms – examples include:

- Semi-exclusion: women are compensated with cash and gold in exchange for their share in inheritance, particularly in the case of physical assets, and especially agricultural land. However, the value of the cash and gold cannot sustain women in the long term, in contrast with productive assets such as land or business;
- Limited control: women inherit their share according to Islamic law.[7] However, control over the land remains in the hands of male family members. Thus, women only receive a share of the revenue, while decisions to rent or sell are subject to the discretion of the male family members;
- Exclusion: women are excluded from inheritance in the case of agricultural land.

There is a kind of unwritten agreement within such communities to conceal this issue in order to prevent any changes that might drive women to claim their rights according to Islamic law. In other words, the issue of inheritance is considered a private family matter, in which other members of the community have no right to intervene. This results in the continuation of unfair and discriminatory distribution of wealth, with serious implications for the financial autonomy of women. It leads to women having low economic capacity and being subject to gender subordination. There are examples of women who accepted such discriminatory acts and rejected the ideas of seeking justice from the judiciary system for the sake of provision of security, economic, and kin/family support. Adding to that is a lack or limited knowledge of their rights, regarding access to management bodies, and this has limited their opportunity to secure their interests and livelihoods. Having said that, due to men having more control over and access to housing, land, and property, women are often reliant on their relationships with men to access these rights. Economic violence is common and is the primary form of overlap between housing, land and property rights, and gender-based violence (NRC, 2014, p. 7).

Current Measurements to Defy Gender-Based Violence in General and Domestic Violence in Particular in a Normal Context/Circumstance

There are a set of measurements which the state and women's rights civil society organizations have put in place aimed at combating gender-based violence. The following are examples of these measurements.

International Legal Framework

The Arab Republic of Egypt ratified the CEDAW on September 18, 1981 and had reservations on the Articles 2, 16, and 29.[8]

> Egypt has acceded most of the key UN conventions[9] related to human rights, women's rights, and elimination of violence. Those conventions, thus, became part of the Egyptian law[10] after being duly ratified by the Parliament and published in the State's official journal.[11]

National Legal Framework and Civil Society

In 2000, Egyptian government established the National Council for Women (NCW) to govern women's rights issues in the country. NCW works closely with international and national organizations advocating for women's rights. The council submitted several draft bills aiming at amending the existing law to guarantee a full protection for Egyptian women and girls against physical and sexual violence, whether the same takes place in the public or private domain. The latest attempt by the NCW was a draft bill that criminalizes domestic violence, "puts punitive sanctions, reaching one-year imprisonment, for fathers, brothers and husbands who are proven guilty of physically or verbally assaulting women in their family" (Egypt Independent, 2017). Following that, in 2018 a coalition of seven civil society organizations submitted a draft bill on "a unified law to combat violence against women" to be discussed in the Egyptian parliament.

Furthermore, in 2015 the NCW drafted its National Strategy for Combating Violence against Women 2015–2020, laying down its strategic vision[12] including identifying the current existing challenges in law or society, existing gaps, its counterparts from different ministries (e.g., the Ministry of Education, Ministry of Justice, Ministry of Health and Population, and Ministry of Endowment), and their role.

There are only eight government-run shelters that operate nationwide (in Cairo, Giza, Qalyubia, Alexandria, Beni Suef, Fayoum, and Minya). These shelters[13] provide social, family, and psychological counseling, along with referrals to other service providers (DFAT, 2019).

With a general aim to offer quality services to survivors and reduce levels of gender-based violence, the Ministry of the Interior played a significant role in dealing with the matter, through establishing the Department of Combating Violence against Women aiming at raising women's awareness, encouraging women to report crimes of violence to the police, informing women of their rights, and referring women to support, including the NCW and the Office of the Public Prosecutor. In addition, the Ministry has increased the number of women police officers throughout Egypt and "Women's units have been established within the offices of the Forensic Medicine Department in Cairo and Giza, operating 24 hours per day 7 days per week, to preserve evidence in cases of GBV" (Egypt Gender Justice & The Law, 2018, p. 14). Moreover, Al-Azhar Al-Sharif University issued a document on women's rights in the Islamic faith to challenge the misinterpretation of Islamic teaching regarding women's rights.

Legislation

The Constitution

According to George Sadek, the 2014 Constitution did not only preserve the rights granted to women by previous Egyptian Constitutions but also introduces more rights aimed at protecting women from other forms of violence and discrimination. As an example, Article 11 focuses on promoting gender equality, stating that "[t]he State shall ensure the achievement of equality between women and men in all civil, political, economic, social, and cultural rights in accordance with the provisions of this Constitution" (Sadek, 2016, p. 5).

As a result of this Article, women currently represent about 16% of parliamentarians for the first time (87 members) and have a quota in municipality elections of 25%. In addition, this Article also obligates the State to protect women against all forms of violence.

The Criminal Code

The Egyptian Criminal Code has divided crimes of sexual violence against women into two categories: misdemeanors and felonies. Misdemeanors include sexual harassment, while felonies consist of FGM, rape, the kidnapping of a female, and sexual assault. According to Article 306 of the Criminal Code, the offense of sexual harassment involves the harasser (the offender), the victim (female), and an inappropriate act against the victim's will. There are two types of sexual harassment: physical and verbal. Physical sexual harassment is an obscene act that is perpetrated by the offender on the body of the victim or on his own body. Verbal sexual harassment encompasses obscene gestures and words made in public. Article 306 proscribing sexual harassment aims at protecting the dignity of the victim from any obscene gestures in public that are deemed offensive (Sadek, 2016, pp. 6–7).

As for domestic violence there is no law, some domestic violence offences may be punishable under the Penal Code and Law No. 6 of 1998, but only if the battery exceeds the accepted limits of discipline decided by the judge and if the injuries are apparent when filing the complaint at the police station. Having said that, many women fail to report it because the Egyptian personal status law puts up serious challenges for women to prove that their spouses have harmed them.

Gaps that Obstruct the Application of Laws Regarding Gender-Based Violence in Public and Private Spaces

According to the National Strategy for Combating Violence against Women (2015–2020)

> the Egyptian legal system and the enforcement of laws could play a pivotal role in combating violence against women. Therefore, it is not sufficient that the laws directly guarantee the physical and sexual protection of women, but they should also prevent physical and psychological violence against women, whether in private or public life, before it occurs.

However, a number of gaps could obstruct the application of laws such as:

1. The most crucial gap requiring rapid attention being the absence of comprehensive legislation that covers all forms of violence against women and girls in one article.
2. Absence of legal support on the part of the State to women victims of violence by providing those who cannot afford a legal counsel with a lawyer
3. Shortage and small number of specialized policewomen who are properly and technically trained to receive reports on acts of violence and to handle accordingly cases of violence at the police station.
4. The negative role of the media and drama giving a negative image of women.
5. Women victims of violence remain silent due to many reasons such as lack of family support, isolation, fear from being harmed, lack of knowledge on how to seek help in addition to their fragile economic status, and for fear of losing home or shelter.

6. Lack of active engagement by religious institutions in providing the required guidance and counseling.
7. The complete lack or the extremely low degree of awareness among women and girls of their rights guaranteed to them by the Constitution, religious teaching, and civic laws – particularly women with very fragile economic conditions and those who are living in conservative communities where cultural norms dominate.

Ways Forward

To conclude, the following are recommendations for reaching a better understating of gender-based violence with its broader meaning and of domestic violence in Egypt:

1. The Egyptian Government has a tremendous responsibility for undertaking actions to address violence against women, with greater attention on domestic violence at different levels of society. In particular, the government should address the needs of the most marginalized communities, to protect women's human rights and to work toward reducing all forms of violence against women. Violence against women not only affects victims, but it also has a negative impact on the children that results in an increasing number of street children in the major cities. Moreover, it has negative consequences for society's socio-economic and political progression, thus there is an urgent need to conceptualize VAW as part of the development priorities of governmental policies.
2. There is a need to conduct more research on violence against women to understand the problem in Egyptian society to develop more effective and strategic actions at different levels (macro, community, family/relationship, and individual). Operational research and program evaluations to increase knowledge about how to design effective programs and policies to prevent and respond to VAW are also priorities.
3. An increase in quantitative and qualitative research on the nature and prevalence of sexual violence, especially where information is not available, ideally using well-designed, large-scale surveys on gender-based violence in general with a special focus on domestic violence.
4. Access to accurate and updated data on VAW in general and domestic violence in particular should be facilitated by NCW with a collaboration with civil society. This could be achieved by strengthening the official data collection systems, including mechanisms for collecting official information, particularly in rural and marginalized areas.
5. Identifying mechanisms to monitor the enforcement of laws and norms throughout the country, particularly in marginalized settings.
6. Lobbying media outlets to play a significant role in covering and highlighting the issue of gender-based violence within its broader picture, including domestic violence.
7. Extensive work needs to be done in the educational sector in terms of designing a gender-based violence subject and included in the education national curriculum aiming at raising awareness about the subject targeting students at different educational levels.

Notes

1 Original title in Arabic "Ehky ya Scherazade" written by Wahid Hamid and played by Mona Zaki, a popular film star in Egypt.

2 The 2015 study conducted by Central Agency for Public Mobilization and Statistics (CAPMAS), United Nation Population Fund (UNFPA), and National Council for Women (NCW) – Egypt.

3 According to the demographic and health survey, which was conducted in Egypt in 2005, it covered data on violence against women and girls. The result shows that 47.4% of married women indicated that they had been victims of domestic violence ever since they were 15 years' old, and that their partners (that is the present or past husband) was the perpetrator of such violence; almost half of the women surveyed (45%) indicated that they had been victims of violence at the hands of males other than their husbands; 26% stated that they were victims of violence perpetrated against them by women; the rate of violence committed by fathers against girls was 53% and is double the rate of violence committed by brothers (at 23%). Females committing acts of violence against girls were mostly by their mothers (at 10%). (*The National Strategy for Combating Violence against Women 2015–2020* – First Edition 2015.)

4 Youm 7 Newspaper (2020) Youm7.com

5 Omar al-Bashir: came to power in a military coup in 1989 and ruled Sudan for three decades before being deposed in 2019.

6 There are no available studies that comprehensively examined the relationship between climate change and gender-based violence especially domestic violence in the Egyptian context. However, there are studies that examined the impact of climate change on agricultural and water sector.

7 Islamic teachings provide clear rules regarding women's shares in the inheritance system.

8 Article (2) "States Parties condemn discrimination against women in all its forms, agree to pursue by all appropriate means and without delay a policy of eliminating discrimination against women".

Article (16) "States Parties shall take all appropriate measures to eliminate discrimination against women in all matters relating to marriage and family relations and in particular shall ensure, on a basis of equality of men and women".

Article (29)

> Any dispute between two or more States Parties concerning the interpretation or application of the present Convention, which is not settled by negotiation shall, at the request of one of them, be submitted to arbitration. If within six months from the date of the request for arbitration the parties are unable to agree on the organization of the arbitration, any one of those parties may refer the dispute to the International Court of Justice by request in conformity with the Statute of the Court.

For full text of the Convention: www.un.org/womenwatch/daw/cedaw/text/econvention.htm

9 The international conventions and declarations to which Egypt is committed, taking into consideration Egypt's reservations over certain provisions: The Universal Declaration of Human Rights (1948), which Egypt participated in the drafting of as a founding member of the United Nations; The International Covenant on Civil and Political Rights and the International Covenant on Economic, Social and Cultural Rights (1966); The Convention on the Rights of the Child (CRC) (1990); The Declaration on the Elimination of Violence Against Women (1993); The International Conference on Population and Development (ICPD) Programme of Action (1994); The Beijing Declaration and Platform for Action (BPFA) (1995).

10 Egyptian Constitution 2014, article (93) "The State shall observe international conventions, treaties, covenants, and instruments on human rights endorsed by Egypt and shall have the power of law after publication as per the stipulated conditions". This eventually ensures abidance by Egypt by CEDAW and other women-related conventions ratified by Egypt except for the articles to which Egypt has reservation.

11 *The National Strategy for Combating Violence against Women 2015-2020* – First Edition 2015

12

> The Vision of the National Strategy is to ensure a secure community free of all forms of violence that guarantees the protection of women and the availability of all services to them, as well as the commitment to respect women's rights and encourage their effective and active participation in the development of their community.
>
> *(NCW, 2015, p. 21)*

The National Strategy to Combat Violence against Women is a five-year plan that relies on 24 protocols signed with a number of ministries, the Orthodox Church, and many specialized national councils and civil society organizations.

13 Human rights observers reported that "the shelters focus primarily on reconciling women with their abusive husbands and tend to shelter women on a limited basis" (DFAT 2019,p. 31).

Bibliography

Arab Republic of Egypt. (2019). *Constitution of The Arab Republic of Egypt 2014*. https://constitutions.unwomen.org/en/countries/africa/egypt

Australian Government, Department of Foreign Affairs and Trade. (2019). *DFAT country information report Egypt*. www.dfat.gov.au/sites/default/files/country-information-report-egypt.pdf

Castañeda Camey, I., Sabater, L., Owren, C. and Boyer, A.E. (2020). *Gender-based violence and environment linkages: The violence of inequality*. Wen, J. (ed.). International Union for Conservation of Nature. https://genderandenvironment.org/agent-gbv-env/

Chatiza, K. (2019). *Cyclone Idai in Zimbabwe: An analysis of policy implications for post-disaster institutional development to strengthen disaster risk management*. https://oxfamilibrary.openrepository.com/bitstream/handle/10546/620892/bp-impact-response-cyclone-idai-zimbabwe-071119-en.pdf?sequence=1&isAllowed=y

Cultural Atlas. (2021). *Egyptian culture core concepts*. https://culturalatlas.sbs.com.au/egyptian-culture/egyptian-culture-core-concepts

Dranginis, H. (2016). *The Mafia in the park: A charcoal syndicate is threatening Virunga, Africa's oldest national park*. https://enoughproject.org/files/report_MafiaInThePark_Dranginis_Enough_June2016.pdf

Egypt Today. (2019). 15 Egyptian laws, rulings that protect, support, empower women. www.egypttoday.com/Article/1/66500/15-Egyptian-laws-rulings-that-protect-support-empower-women

Elgousi, H. (2016). *Women's rights in authoritarian Egypt: Negotiating between Islam and politics*. London: I.B.Tauris.

Food and Agricultural Organization of United Nations. (2021). *Family farming knowledge platform*. www.fao.org/family-farming/countries/egy/en/

Holland office of Médecins Sans Frontiers. (2005). *The crushing burden of rape sexual violence in Darfur*. www.msf.org/crushing-burden-rape-sexual-violence-darfur

International Union for Conservation of Nature. (2020). *Gender-based violence and the environment*. [Issue brief]. https://www.iucn.org/resources/issues-brief/gender-based-violence-and-environment

Joseph, S (1996). Patriarchy and development in the Arab world. *Gender and Development*, 4, (2), 14–19. www.jstor.org/stable/4030482

National Council for Women, Egypt. (2015). *National strategy for combating violence against women 2015–2020, First edition*. https://evaw-global-database.unwomen.org/en/countries/africa/egypt/2015/national-strategy-for-combating-violence-against-women-2015-2020

National Council for Women, Egypt. (2017). *National strategy for the empowerment of Egyptian women 2030 vision and pillars, First edition*. http://ncw.gov.eg/wp-content/uploads/2018/02/final-version-national-strategy-for-the-empowerment-of-egyptian-women-2030.pdf

Nellemann, C., Henriksen, R., Kreilhuber, A., Stewart, D., Kotsovou, M., Raxter, P., Mrema, E. & Barrat, S. (eds.). (2016). *The rise of environmental crime – A growing threat to natural resources peace, development and security. A UNEP-INTERPOL Rapid Response Assessment*. United Nations Environment Programme and RHIPTO Rapid Response–Norwegian Center for Global Analyses. https://wedocs.unep.org/bitstream/handle/20.500.11822/7662/-The_rise_of_environmental_crime_A_growing_threat_to_natural_resources_peace%2C_development_and_security-2016environmental_crimes.pdf.pdf?sequence=3&isAllowed=y

Noureldin, O. (2017, Sept 6). Egypt's parliament to discuss bill that criminalizes domestic violence. *Egypt Independent*. www.egyptindependent.com/egypts-parliament-discuss-bill-criminalizes-domestic-violence/

Richardson, A. & Hannay, L. (2014). *Violence against women and housing, land and property in Monrovia – Published by NRC (Norwegian Refugee Council)*. http://womenshlp.nrc.no/wp-content/uploads/2014/02/Violence-against-women-and-HLP-Liberia.pdf

Sadek, G. (2016) *Egypt: Sexual violence against women* (LL File No. 2016-013851 LRA-D-PUB-002377). The Law Library of Congress, Global Legal Research Center. https://tile.loc.gov/storage-services/service/ll/llglrd/2016590020/2016590020.pdfp

Samir, S. (2020, Sep 12). Cancerous building on agricultural lands should be curbed in Egypt. *Egypt Today*. www.egypttoday.com/Article/1/91878/Cancerous-building-on-agricultural-lands-should-be-curbed-in-Egypt

Sobhy, K. (2020, June 24). *Youm 7 Newspaper*. www.youm7.com/story/2020/6/24/4842918

Statista Research Department. (2020). *Agriculture in Egypt - statistics & facts*. www.statista.com/topics/5674/agriculture-in-egypt/#topicHeader__wrapper

The National Council for Women, Egypt. (2021). *Women policy tracker on responsive policies and programs during the new COVID19 pandemic.* http://ncw.gov.eg/Pdf/476/Fifth-Edition-Women-policy-Tracker-on-Responsive-Policies-and-Programs

UN Women. (2020a). *COVID-19; Ending violence against women and girls.* www.unwomen.org/sites/default/files/Headquarters/Attachments/Sections/Library/Publications/2020/Issue-brief-COVID-19-and-ending-violence-against-women-and-girls-en.pdf

UN Women. (2020b). *Recommendations into action brief COVID-19: Safe cities and safe public spaces for women and girls.* www.unwomen.org/sites/default/files/Headquarters/Attachments/Sections/Library/Publications/2020/Brief-Recommendations-COVID-19-Safe-Cities-and-Safe-Public-Spaces-en.pdf

United Nation Human Rights – Office of the High Commissioner – Committee on the elimination of discrimination against women. *General recommendations.* www.ohchr.org/EN/HRBodies/CEDAW/Pages/Recommendations.aspx accessed 2021.

United Nations Development Programme. (2018). *Egypt gender justice and law: Assessment of laws affecting gender equality and protection against gender-based violence.* https://arabstates.unwomen.org/sites/default/files/Field%20Office%20Arab%20States/Attachments/Publications/2018/Gender%20Justices%20and%20The%20Law%20in%20the%20Arab%20Region/Country%20Assessments/Egypt%20Country%20Assessment%20-%20English.pdf

Walsh, J., Spangaro, J. & Soldatic, K. (2015). Editorial: Global understandings of domestic violence. *Nursing and Health Sciences*, 17, (1), 1–4. https://onlinelibrary.wiley.com/doi/full/10.1111/nhs.12197

World Bank. (2018). *Women Economic Empowerment Study.* Egypt, p. 34. https://documents.worldbank.org/en/publication/documents-reports/documentdetail/861491551113547855/women-economic-empowerment-study

World Health Organization. (2002). *World report on violence and health.* https://apps.who.int/iris/bitstream/handle/10665/42495/9241545615_eng.pdf?sequence=1

World Health Organization. (2013a). *Global and regional estimates of violence against women: Prevalence and health effects of intimate partner violence and non-partner sexual violence.* https://apps.who.int/iris/bitstream/handle/10665/85239/9789241564625_eng.pdf?sequence=1

World Health Organization. (2013c). *Responding to intimate partner violence and sexual violence against women: WHO clinical and policy guidelines.* http:// apps.who.int/rhl/guidelines/9789241548595/en/

World Health Organization. (2014). *Global status report on violence prevention.* www.who.int/violence_injury_prevention/violence/status_report/2014/report/report/en/

World Health Organization. (2017). *Violence against women.* [key facts]. www.who.int/en/news-room/fact-sheets/detail/violence-against-women

19

DOMESTIC AND SEXUAL VIOLENCE AMONG UNIVERSITY STUDENTS IN GHANA

Michelle L. Munro-Kramer, Lindsay M. Cannon, Eugene K. M. Darteh, Ruth Owusu-Antwi and Sarah D. Compton

Gender-based violence (GBV) is a global public health crisis that is occurring across geographic and cultural contexts. It is part of a broader societal problem in which gender inequality and social mores "normalize" violence and prime youth for later relationship violence. GBV can encompass domestic violence, sexual violence, and stalking. Worldwide, one in three women are victims of intimate partner violence and/or non-partner sexual violence and estimates suggest that the prevalence of domestic violence in sub-Saharan Africa is among the highest in the world at 33% (World Health Organization, 2021). A multi-national study of university students, with data from 30 sites around the world, showed a generally high prevalence of both dating violence and sexual violence (Hines, 2007; Straus, 2004). These results are consistent with findings from studies conducted in individual low and middle-income countries, including Ghana (Britwum & Anokye, 2006; Contreras, Bott, Guedes, & Dartnall, 2010; Jejeebhoy, Shah, & Thapa, 2005; Jewkes & Abrahams, 2002; Norman, Aikins, & Binka, 2013; Philpart et al., 2009). The purpose of this chapter is to describe the scope of the problem in Ghana, as well as recent efforts to address the knowledge, attitudes, and behaviors that precipitate domestic violence by providing case studies of research, programing, and policy on university campuses in Ghana.

Ghanaian Social and Cultural Context

According to a cross-country measure of discrimination against women in social institutions (i.e., formal and informal laws, social norms, and practices), Ghana scores as highly discriminatory (African Development Fund, 2008; Social Institutions and Gender Index, 2015). National surveys and qualitative research support a culture of gender inequality where domestic violence is justified and excused (Dickson, Ameyaw, & Darteh, 2020). Results from the 2014 Demographic and Health Survey provide evidence for the social acceptability of physical violence in Ghana, with nearly a third of women agreeing that wife beating is justified under certain conditions, such as neglecting one's children (Darteh, Dickson, Rominski, & Moyer, 2021; Ghana Statistical Service [GSS], Ghana Health Service [GHS], & ICF Macro, 2015). The role of patriarchy and gender inequitable attitudes have been highlighted as contributing to a culture where men are seen as the decision-makers, heads of household, "owners" of their female partners, and entitled to use physical or sexual force as legitimate means of disciplining their partners (Sikweyiya et al., 2020). Although violence experienced across the life course can have stark social, physical, and mental

DOI: 10.4324/9781003264040-23

health consequences, early life exposure to violence can shape an individual's susceptibility to and experiences of violence later in life (McMahon et al., 2015; Voith, Anderson, & Cahill, 2017). This makes it particularly important to concentrate education and prevention efforts on youth and young adults.

In Ghana, responding to and preventing GBV, particularly domestic violence and sexual violence, on university campuses has become a priority area; however, information about effective interventions to prevent violence is lacking. Our focus on university students is purposeful, as many of these students will go on to be leaders in the country. Addressing their views about domestic violence and healthy relationships can have far-reaching effects for the country by informing future program and policy development that will ultimately change the social norms that perpetuate these forms of violence. Efforts over the last two decades to address domestic violence with policies, police response, and survivor resources have had limited impact due to lack of resources and the inability to change the social norms that perpetuate domestic violence (Agbitor, 2012; GSS, GHS, & ICF Macro, 2015).

The Scope of the Problem

Domestic Violence

Domestic violence is a pervasive problem in Ghana. Findings from the 2016 Ghana Family Life and Health Survey suggest that 71% of both men and women surveyed reported having experienced at least one form of violence (domestic and/or non-domestic) in their lifetime, which could include physical, sexual, emotional, or economic abuse (Institute of Development Studies & Ghana Statistical Services and Associates, 2016). A more recent population-based survey conducted in the Central Region of Ghana in 2018 found that 34% of women had experienced domestic violence in the past year (Alangea et al., 2018). According to the 2008 Ghana Demographic and Health Survey, youth are also severely impacted by violence, with 41% of 15–19-year-old females reporting sexual or physical violence (GSS, GHS, & ICF Macro, 2008).

Prior work on university campuses has described a culture of violence, which is undoubtedly linked to the high levels of domestic violence outside of universities (Britwum & Anokye, 2006; Norman et al., 2013). In one study of university students, 27.8% of males and 37.1% of females reported that they had been insulted by a partner (Munro-Kramer et al., 2020). When these same questions were asked to a second sample of participants, we found even higher rates of psychological abuse (40.6% of males and 40.0% of females have been insulted by a partner) (Munro-Kramer et al., 2020). These results demonstrate that one form of domestic violence, psychological abuse, is common among Ghanaian university students. Further work is needed to understand university students' experiences with physical violence and economic abuse.

Stalking

Research suggests that stalking is often perpetrated by intimate partners (Pengpid & Peltzer, 2014). In Ghana, there has been very limited research on stalking. One study of 371 male and female university students found that more than half of participants had experienced stalking, with significantly more female participants experiencing stalking than male participants (Chan, Sheridan, & Adjorlolo, 2020). Another exploratory mixed-methods study examined the prevalence of stalking among 117 Ghanaian midwifery students using a survey modeled after the *Stalking Behavior Checklist* (Coleman, 1997) and focus group discussions. Survey results indicate 79.7% of the participants had experienced at least one stalking behavior. Specifically, they experienced unwanted calls (64.1%), unwanted texts (53.0%), received unwanted images (47.0%), and had their activities monitored through social media (52.1%) (Zagurny et al., 2021). Although there is limited research on stalking, these data indicate that stalking, particularly using digital mediums, is a form of power and control that is being used within the context of domestic violence in Ghana.

Sexual Violence

Global research demonstrates that sexual violence is pervasive on university campuses (Britwum & Anokye, 2006; Contreras et al., 2010; Hines, 2007; Jejeebhoy et al., 2005; Jewkes & Abrahams, 2002; Norman et al., 2013; Philpart et al., 2009; Straus, 2004). From January to March 2015, residential university students at a university in Ghana (n=1,036) completed a survey in their residence using a tablet computer to ascertain information about their sexual debut and most recent episode of sexual intercourse (Rominski, Moyer, Darteh, & Munro-Kramer, 2017). Similar to Bingheimer and Reed (2014), later in the survey, all participants, regardless of if they reported having sexual intercourse, were asked, "Has anyone ever physically forced, hurt or threatened you into having sexual intercourse?" More than 20% of females and 10% of males reported having been forced to have sexual intercourse at some time in their lives. Further exploration revealed the following factors were associated with forced or coerced sexual intercourse: being female, reporting a pregnancy that resulted in an abortion, and receiving gifts or money in exchange for sex.

An additional study demonstrated that experiences of violence within a relationship were not uncommon for university students (n=70), with 25.0% of males and 28.6% of females reporting they have been physically forced to have sex when they did not want to (Munro-Kramer et al., 2020). A follow-up study with a second sample of students (n=57) found similar rates of sexual violence (21.9% of males and 20.0% of females have been physically forced to have sex when they did not want to) (Munro-Kramer et al., 2020). These results indicate that university students are experiencing sexual violence at relatively high rates and highlight the need to recognize the myriad ways that power and control may be displayed within relationships.

Knowledge and Attitudes Related to Domestic and Sexual Violence

Research has shown that acceptance of negative and inequitable attitudes toward women and girls and belief in rape myths, which are prejudicial, stereotyped, and false beliefs about sexual assaults, rapists, and rape victims, serving to excuse sexual aggression (Burt & Albin, 1981), are associated with violence perpetration (Tharp et al., 2012). Further, belief in gender stereotypes and rape myths may increase the risk of victimization (Cense, Bay-Cheng, & Van Dijk, 2018). In Ghana, country-wide measures to address knowledge and attitudes related to domestic violence have demonstrated pervasive gender inequitable attitudes and acceptance of rape myths (Sikweyiya et al., 2020). However, there has been little exploration of these attitudes specifically focused on young adults enrolled at university.

Our research team explored knowledge and attitudes related to gender equity and rape myth acceptance among Ghanaian university students prior to participating in a healthy relationship education and sexual violence prevention workshop using the Gender Equitable Men (GEM) scale (Pulerwitz & Barker, 2008) and adapting the Illinois Rape Myth Acceptance Scale (IRMA-SF; McMahon & Farmer, 2011) through cognitive interviews. Both male and female participants (n=70) demonstrated high gender equity at baseline (57.6+6.8) (Munro-Kramer et al., 2020). Although there is no standardized threshold for high versus low rape myth acceptance, similar to findings in other settings, including Kenya and the United States (Tavrow et al., 2013), we found high levels of rape myth acceptance among these university students (mean baseline score of 65.6±14.8; range 22–100) (Rominski, Darteh, & Munro-Kramer, 2017). As in other settings, women had lower rape myth acceptance (71.1±14.4) compared with men (60.1±13.1) ($p<.001$) (Rominski, Darteh, & Munro-Kramer, 2017).

Ongoing Challenges

There are a number of global challenges that are exacerbating women's experiences of violence. One acute challenge is the COVID-19 pandemic. In the past, crises ranging from earthquakes to tsunamis to disease have been associated with an increase in domestic violence (Enarson & Fordman, 2001; Palermo & Peterman, 2011). The Ebola outbreak in West Africa exposed many women and girls to domestic violence, as they were unable to escape their abusers due to quarantines (Onyango, Resnick, Davis, & Shah, 2019).

Global pandemics, such as COVID-19, do not create new risks for women and girls. Rather, they compound pre-existing gender inequalities and vulnerabilities leading to increased risk for abuse (United Nations, 2020). While many instances of domestic violence occur while living on campus, our pilot campus climate survey showed a large number of university students are exposed to violence in their homes. The risk to these students is further escalated by measures intended to protect individuals from infection, such as the closure of university campuses. While necessary to reduce the spread of a contagious disease, these measures remove protective factors like social support, education, economic activities, and resources when violence occurs, while increasing stress and strain within the home. As students transition to conducting more of their lives physically distanced from their schools and their peers, the potential for online and electronic forms of sexual harassment increase (Lim & Teo, 2009). As we have found in our investigations in Ghana, many students were already experiencing digital forms of harassment and violence (Zagurny et al., 2021), and it is likely that this has increased during the COVID-19 pandemic.

Although there are limited studies on the link between extreme whether events precipitated by climate change and domestic and sexual violence, there is growing recognition of the gendered effects of natural disasters (World Health Organization, 2014a). For example, the *World Disaster Report* notes that, particularly among women who have experienced domestic violence in the past, there is the potential for increased violence post-disaster (International Federation of Red Cross and Red Crescent Societies, 2018). Similar to global pandemics, such as COVID-19, this is thought to be related to displacement, psychological stress, and decreased income-generating opportunities. As we consider how to provide primary, secondary, and tertiary prevention for domestic violence in Ghana, it is essential that we also consider emerging factors such as global pandemics and climate change. These two factors will continue to change the landscape related to experiences and responses to GBV.

Help-Seeking Resources

Domestic violence can result in the need for acute and chronic health care, social services, legal assistance, housing, child care, and safety recommendations (Tenkorang, 2019). When victims of domestic violence engage in help-seeking, they often do so with the intent to find resources to best meet their unique needs. Unfortunately, in low and middle-income countries, these services may be very limited or not present at all. Furthermore, many women may not know about or trust existing resources and there are concerns about seeking out services due to fear of re-victimization, retribution, and stigma (Anyemedu, Tenkorang, & Dold, 2020; Tenkorang, Owusu, & Kundhi, 2018). For this reason, many survivors of domestic violence in Ghana are more likely to seek help from informal resources (e.g., family, friends) than formal domestic violence services.

Legal Response

The government of Ghana has taken steps to attempt to protect citizens from domestic violence. The Ghana Police Service established a Women and Juvenile Unit in 1998, which was later renamed the Domestic Violence and Victims Support Unit (DOVVSU) between 2004 and 2005. The establishment of this unit resulted in increased reports of violence against both women and children (Amoakohene, 2004). However, it was not until 2007 with the passage of Domestic Violence Act 732 that domestic violence was specifically defined, prohibited, and attempts were made to provide protection to survivors (Pool et al., 2014; World Health Organization, 2014b). Despite these legal provisions, there is an atmosphere of mistrust around the DOVVSU, which is the only agency providing domestic violence services in all ten regions of Ghana (Tenkorang et al., 2018). University students also remain unfamiliar with formal sources of legal support for domestic violence.

Social Services

Formal domestic violence social services are also lacking nationwide and universities are taxed with creating systems and policies to provide support for their students. Specifically, there are no open shelter services in Ghana for survivors to seek respite from abuse, despite specific language in the Domestic Violence Act of 2007 instructing that each district in the country should have a shelter (Parliament of the Republic of Ghana, 2007). A shelter was in the process of being constructed in the capital city of Accra by the DOVVSU but was abandoned because of a lack of funding (GhanaWeb, 2018). Non-governmental organizations, like The Ark Foundation, have attempted to step in to help provide shelter for survivors of domestic violence but have also been limited due to difficulty raising money. The Ark Foundation does provide counseling, social support, and training but this work is limited to the greater Accra region in which it is located. With ten public universities and a growing number of private universities throughout the country, this leaves many university students experiencing domestic violence without social services.

Health-Care Provider Response

Health-care systems and providers serve a key role in responding to domestic and sexual violence, as survivors may sustain physical injuries or require mental health support as a result of violence. Our team conducted a situational analysis at two hospitals to better understand the health-care provider response to sexual violence at one university in Ghana (Cannon et al., 2020). The study included an observational facility assessment about health-care services for survivors of sexual violence as well as an in-depth exploration of health-care providers' knowledge, attitudes, and practices related to sexual violence ascertained via a 113-item questionnaire and in-depth semi-structured interviews. Results indicated that both sites lacked critical supplies, such as pre-packed rape kits, post-exposure HIV prophylaxis, and informational handouts on medications and support services for survivors. Health-care providers cited a lack of training on GBV, including best practices for caring for survivors during medical-forensic exams and evidence collection. Providers also verbalized that many survivors seek health care as a requirement of the "police form," as a health-care provider must complete a portion of this form in order for a sexual assault report to be filed. Health-care providers noted a lack of mental health services in Ghana, as these services are limited by a shortage of providers, stigma, and the geographic location of service provision (Ofori-Atta, Read, & Lund, 2010). Health-care providers also noted a number of barriers to accessing post-assault health care, which included stigma related to disclosing sexual violence and structural barriers, such as cost of medical supplies and lack of privacy within the health-care facilities. Due to the substantial health consequences associated with domestic violence (Campbell, 2002), it is concerning that survivors face significant personal and systemic barriers in accessing necessary health-care services.

Promising Interventions

Rural Response System

The Rural Response System intervention used community-based action teams to raise awareness about domestic violence and support survivors in Central Ghana. Between 2002 and 2008, the intervention was piloted in four regions of Central Ghana, followed by a community randomized controlled trial to evaluate outcomes (Alangea et al., 2020). Results indicated a reduction in women's past year experience of sexual violence by a partner, past year physical violence by a partner, and severe domestic violence (Alangea et al., 2020). Secondary analyses indicated a reduction in depression scores and decreased reports of controlling behavior by a male partner (Alangea et al., 2020). Although studied in a community-based setting, this intervention warrants further research and consideration, particularly among university students.

Bystander Intervention

Our research team explored whether or not bystander intervention techniques are socially and culturally acceptable in Ghana by conducting six gender-separated focus groups with a total of 57 participants. University students felt that preconceived notions about violence, such as assuming domestic violence is only physical; the sociocultural construction of gender inequality; concerns about intervening in someone's private relationship; and a lack of knowledge about external resources, could complicate their ability to intervene (Munro-Kramer et al., under review). Despite these potential barriers, overall university students were supportive of the concept of bystander intervention and the potential it holds to disrupt domestic and sexual violence.

Relationship Tidbits

Primary prevention programs seek to avert violent behaviors before they occur. By adapting a pre-existing evidence-based program focused on values-based decisions and healthy relationships, our research team was able to engage faculty, staff, and university students in a rapid adaptation and dissemination of a primary prevention program. *Relationship Tidbits* is a peer-delivered program with ten building blocks that include information and interactive activities to reinforce the concepts of healthy relationships, consent, and communication (Choi et al., 2020; Munro-Kramer et al., 2020). Pilot testing of the program demonstrated increased gender equitable attitudes and reduced rape myth acceptance among participants. The *Relationship Tidbits* program has now been implemented at both the University of Cape Coast and the Kwame Nkrumah University of Science and Technology. Although the results are preliminary, and we do not yet have data on impacts on behaviors, the attitudinal changes are promising (Munro-Kramer et al., 2020).

Abuse Clinic

Members of our team have also been involved with developing the novel *Abuse Clinic* located at the Komfo Anokye Teaching Hospital (KATH) in the central belt of Ghana. The *Abuse Clinic* is a multidisciplinary one-stop clinic, comprising 16 different professionals (including pediatricians, psychiatrists, clinical psychologists, emergency physicians, family physicians, obstetricians, nurses, police, art therapists, lawyers, social workers, pharmacists, and an ethicist). The *Abuse Clinic* provides services for survivors of all forms of abuse. The clinic runs once a month and has been running since late 2019. The aim of the clinic is to give both clinical and psychological support in a respectful and less complicated manner to survivors of abuse and to anonymously report on abuse trends in the catchment area. Patients have been referred to the clinic with complications of abuse, including depressive illness, unwanted pregnancies, declining academic performance, and physical injuries. Services are provided at no cost to patients due to the observation that lack of economic power is a significant barrier to seeking help.

Implications for Research, Practice, and Policy

Although the above interventions demonstrate promise in preventing and disrupting violence and its precipitating causes, it is imperative that we continue to address GBV earlier in the life course, ideally in early adolescence. Primary prevention programs are needed when youth and young adults are first forming relationships and when they are amenable to change. University students represent a population that experiences high levels of domestic and sexual violence and can be targeted for prevention programming within their university environments (Gonzales, Schofield, & Schmitt, 2005). Implementing primary prevention programs among this age group also has the ability to disrupt the acute and chronic health consequences and interruption to a survivor's education that can result from violent intimate and non-intimate partner relationships. In order to meet the diverse needs of university survivors experiencing domestic violence, universities must establish pathways that providers can use to facilitate timely referral of survivors to health-care systems, social services, and legal assistance. This coordinated, multi-sectoral response must be supported through university, local, and national-level policies.

References

African Development Fund. (2008). *Ghana country gender profile*. www.afdb.org/fileadmin/uploads/afdb/Documents/Project-and-Operations/ADF-BD-IF-2008-237-EN-GHANA-COUNTRY-GENDER-PROFILE.PDF

Agbitor, K. A. (2012). *Addressing domestic violence cases in Ghana: A study of the practice methodologies of Accra regional DOVVSU* [dissertation]. Accra: University of Ghana.

Alangea, D. O., Addo-Lartey, A. A., Chirwa, E. D., Sikweyiya, Y., Coker-Appiah, D., Jewkes, R., & Adanu, R. M. K. (2020). Evaluation of the rural response system intervention to prevent violence against women: Findings from a community-randomised controlled trial in the Central Region of Ghana. *Global Health Action, 13* (1), 171136. doi:10.1080/16549716.2019.1711336

Alangea, D. O., Addo-Lartey, A. A., Sikweyiya, Y., Chirwa, E. D., Coker-Appiah, D., Jewkes, R., & Adanu, R. M. K. (2018). Prevalence and risk factors of intimate partner violence among women in four districts of the central region of Ghana: Baseline findings from a cluster randomized controlled trial. *PLoS One, 13* (7), e0200874. doi:10.1371/journal.pone.0200874

Amoakohene, M. I. (2004). Violence against women in Ghana: A look at women's perceptions and review of policy and social responses. *Social Science & Medicine, 59* (11), 2373–2385. doi:10.1016/j.socscimed.2004.04.001.

Anyemedu, A., Tenkorang, E. Y., & Dold, P. (2020). Ghanaian women's knowledge and perceptions of services available to victims of intimate partner violence. *Journal of Interpersonal Violence, 35* (3–4), 682–706. doi:10.1177/0886260517689886

Bingheimer, J. B. & Reed, E. (2014). Risk for coerced sex among female youth in Ghana: Roles of family context, school enrollment and relationship experience. *International Perspectives on Sexual and Reproductive Health, 40* (4), 184–195. doi:10.1363/4018414

Britwum, A. O. & Anokye, N. A. (2006). *Confronting sexual harassment in Ghanaian universities*. Accra: University of Cape Coast and Ghana University Press.

Burt, M. R. & Albin, R. S. (1981). Rape myths, rape definitions, and probability of conviction. *Journal of Applied Social Psychology, 11* (3), 212–230. doi:10.1111/j.1559-1816.1981.tb00739.x

Campbell, J. C. (2002). Health consequences of intimate partner violence. *The Lancet, 359* (9314), 1331–1336. doi:10.1016/S0140-6737 (02)08336-8

Cannon, L. M., Sheridan-Fulton, E. C., Dankyi, R., Seidu, A. A., Rominski, S. D., Darteh, E., Odoi, A., & Munro-Kramer, M. L. (2020). Understanding healthcare provider response to sexual violence in Ghana: A situational analysis. *PLoS One, 15* (4), e0231644. doi:10.1371/journal.pone.0231644

Cense, M., Bay-Cheng, L., & Van Dijk, L. (2018). 'Do I score points when I say "no"?': Negotiating sexual boundaries in a changing normative landscape. *Journal of Gender-Based Violence, 2* (2), 277–291. doi:10.1332/239868018X15266373560443

Chan, H. C., Sheridan, L., & Adjorlolo, S. (2020). Stalking and intrusive behaviors in Ghana: Perceptions and victimization experiences. *International Journal of Environmental Research and Public Health, 17* (7), 2298. doi:10.3390/ijerph17072298

Choi, C. M., Munro-Kramer, M. L., Cannon, L. M., Owusu-Antwi, R., Akorsu, A. D., & Compton S. D. (2020). Building master trainers to facilitate sexual violence prevention: A pilot study in Ghana. *Annals of Global Health, 86* (1), 134. http://doi.org/10.5334/aogh.2747

Coleman, F. L. (1997). Stalking behavior and the cycle of domestic violence. *Journal of Interpersonal Violence, 12* (3), 420–432.

Contreras, J. M., Bott, S., Guedes, A., & Dartnall, E. (2010). *Sexual violence in Latin America and the Caribbean: A desk review.* Pretoria: Sexual Violence Research Initiative. http://new.paho.org/hq/dmdocuments/2010/sexual_violence_LA_Caribbean_e.pdf

Darteh, E. K. M., Dickson, K. S., Rominski, S. D., & Moyer, C. A. (2021). Justification of physical intimate partner violence among men in sub-Saharan Africa: A multinational analysis of demographic and health survey data. *Journal of Public Health, 29*, 1433–1441. doi:10.1007/s10389-020-01260-9

Dickson, K. S., Ameyaw, E. K., & Darteh, E. K. M. (2020). Understanding the endorsement of wife beating in Ghana: Evidence of the 2014 Ghana demographic and health survey. *BMC Women's Health, 20*, 25. doi:10.1186/s12905-020-00897-8

Enarson, E. & Fordman, M. (2001). From women's needs to women's rights in disasters. *Global Environmental Change Part B Environmental Hazards, 3*, 133–136. doi:10.3763/ehaz.2001.0314

Ghana Statistical Service (GSS), Ghana Health Service (GHS), & ICF Macro. (2008). *Ghana Demographic and Health Survey 2008.* Accra, Ghana: GSS, GHS, ICF.

Ghana Statistical Service (GSS), Ghana Health Service (GHS), ICF Macro. (2015). *Ghana Demographic and Health Survey 2014.* Accra, Ghana: GSS, GHS, ICF.

GhanaWeb. (2018). *Pearl Safe Haven project to provide shelter for abused young women.* www.ghanaweb.com/GhanaHomePage/NewsArchive/Pearl-Safe-Haven-project-to-provide-shelter-for-abused-young-women-705803

Gonzales, A. R., Schofield, R. B., & Schmitt, G. R. (2005). *Sexual assault on campus: What colleges and universities are doing about it.* Washington, DC: United States Department of Justice. https://catalog.data.gov/dataset/sexual-assault-on-campus-what-colleges-and-universities-are-doing-about-it-617d2

Hines, D. A. (2007). Predictors of sexual coercion against women and men: A multilevel, multinational study of university students. *Archives of Sexual Behavior, 36* (3), 403–422. doi:10.1007/s10508-006-9141-4

Institute of Development Studies (IDS) & Ghana Statistical Services and Associates (GSS). (2016). *Domestic violence in Ghana: Incidence, attitudes, determinants, and consequences.* Brighton: IDS.

International Federation of Red Cross and Red Crescent Societies. (2018). *World disaster report.* Geneva: International Federation of Red Cross and Red Crescent Societies. www.ifrc.org/en/publications-and-reports/world-disasters-report/

Jejeebhoy, S. J., Shah, I., & Thapa, S. (2005). *Sex without consent: Young people in developing countries.* London: Zed Books.

Jewkes, R. & Abrahams, N. (2002). The epidemiology of rape and sexual coercion in South Africa: An overview. *Social Science & Medicine, 55* (7), 1231–1244. doi:10.1016/S0277-9536 (01)00242-8

Lim, V. K. G. & Teo, T. S. H. (2009). Mind your e-manners: Impact of cyber incivility on employees' work attitudes and behavior. *Information Management, 46* (8), 419–425. doi:10.1016/j.m.2009.06.006

McMahon, S. & Farmer, G. L. (2011). An updated measure for assessing subtle rape myths. *Social Work Research, 35* (2), 71–81.

McMahon, K., Hoertel, N., Wall, M. M., Okuda, M., Limosin, F., & Blanco, C. (2015). Childhood maltreatment and risk of intimate partner violence: A national study. *Journal of Psychiatric Research, 69*, 42–49. doi:10.1016/jpsychires.2015.07.026

Munro-Kramer, M. L., Dankyi, R., Seidu, A. A., Sheridan-Fulton, E. C., Britwum, A. O., Darteh E. K. M., & Compton, S. D. (under review). Exploring bystander intervention in Ghana. *Journal of Interpersonal Violence.*

Munro-Kramer, M. L., Rominski, S. D., Seidu, A. A., Darteh, E., Britwum, A. O., & Stephenson, R. (2020). Adapting a sexual violence primary prevention program to Ghana utilizing the ADAPT-ITT framework. *Violence Against Women, 26* (1), 66–88. doi:10.1177/1077801219828533

Norman, I. D., Aikins, M., & Binka, A. (2013). Sexual harassment in public medical schools in Ghana. *Ghana Medical Journal, 47* (3), 128–136.

Ofori-Atta, A., Read, U. M., & Lund, C. (2010). A situation analysis of mental health services and legislation in Ghana: Challenges for transformation. *African Journal of Psychiatry, 13*, 99–108.

Onyango, M. A., Resnick, K., Davis, A., & Shah, R. R. (2019). Gender-based violence among adolescent girls and young women: A neglected consequence of the West African Ebola outbreak. In: Schwartz D, Anoko J, Abramowitz S, (eds). *Pregnant in the time of Ebola. Global maternal and child health (medical, anthropological, and public health perspectives)*. Springer. doi:10.1007/978-3-319-97637-2_8

Palermo, T. & Peterman, A. (2011). Undercounting, overcounting, and the longevity of flawed estimates: Statistics on sexual violence in conflict. *Bulletin of the World Health Organization, 89*, 924–926. doi:10.2471/BLT.11.089888

Parliament of the Republic of Ghana. (2007). *Ghana Domestic Violence Act, ACT 732*. www.africalegalaid.com/download/domestic_violence_legislations/Ghana_Domestic_Violence_Act_2007.pdf

Pengpid, S. & Peltzer, K. (2014). Sexual assault and other types of intimate partner violence in women with protection orders in Vhembe District, South Africa. *Violence & Victims, 29* (5), 857–871. doi:10.1891/0886-6708.VV-D-13-00008

Philpart, M., Goshu, M., Gelaye, B., Williams, M. A., & Berhane, Y. (2009). Prevalence and risk factors of gender-based violence committed by male college students in Awassa, Ethiopia. *Violence & Victims, 29* (1), 122–136.

Pool, M. S., Otupiri, E., Owusu-Dabo, E., de Jonge, A., & Agyeman, C. (2014). Physical violence during pregnancy and pregnancy outcomes in Ghana. *BMC Pregnancy & Childbirth, 14*, 71–78. doi:10.1186/1471-2393-14-71.

Pulerwitz, J. & Barker, J. (2008). Measuring attitudes toward gender norms among young men in Brazil: Development and psychometric evaluation of the GEM scale. *Men & Masculinities, 10* (3), 322–338. doi:10.1177/1097184X06298778

Rominski, S. D., Darteh, E., & Munro-Kramer, M. L. (2017). Rape-myth acceptance among students at the University of Cape Coast, Ghana. *International Journal of Gynecology & Obstetrics, 136* (2), 240–241. doi:10.1002/ijgo.12054

Rominski, S. D., Moyer, C. A., Darteh, E. K., & Munro-Kramer, M. L. (2017). Sexual coercion among students at the University of Cape Coast, Ghana. *Sexuality & Culture, 21* (2), 516–533. doi:10.1007/s12119-016-9402-x

Sikweyiya, Y., Addo-Lartey, A. A., Alangea, D. O., Dako-Gyeke, P., Chirwa, E. D., Coker-Appiah, D., Adanu, R. M. K., & Jewkes, R. (2020). Patriarchy and gender-inequitable attitudes as drivers of intimate partner violence against women in the central region of Ghana. *BMC Public Health, 20*, 682. doi:10.1186/s12889-020-08825-z

Social Institutions and Gender Index. (2015). *Ghana country sheet*. http://genderindex.org/sites/default/files/datasheets/GH.pdf

Straus, M. A. (2004). Prevalence of violence against dating partners by male and female university students worldwide. *Violence Against Women, 10* (7), 790–811. doi:10.1177/1077801204265552

Tavrow, P., Withers, M., Obbuyi, A., Omollo, V., & Wu, E. (2013). Rape myth attitudes in rural Kenya: Toward the development of a culturally relevant attitude scale and "Blame Index". *Journal of Interpersonal Violence, 28*, 2156–2178. doi:10.1177/0886260512471086

Tenkorang, E.Y. (2019). Intimate partner violence and the sexual and reproductive health outcomes of women in Ghana. *Health Education & Behavior, 46* (6), 969–980. doi:10.1177/1090198119859420

Tenkorang, E. Y., Owusu, A. Y., & Kundhi, G. (2018). Help-seeking behavior of female victims of intimate partner violence in Ghana: The role of trust and perceived risk of injury. *Journal of Family Violence, 33*, 341–353. doi:10.1007/s10896-018-9959-2

Tharp, A. T., DeGue, S., Valle, L. A., Brookmeyer, K. A., Massetti, G. M., & Matjasko, J. L. (2012). A systematic qualitative review of risk and protective factors for sexual violence perpetration. *Trauma, Violence, & Abuse, 14* (2), 133–167. doi:10.1177/1524838012470031

United Nations Ghana. (2020, April). *COVID-19 impact on gender-based violence.* Briefing Note #2. https://ghana.un.org/sites/default/files/2020-04/COVID-19_UN%20Ghana%20Briefing%20Notes_No.2_2020_04_14.pdf

Voith, L. A., Anderson, R. E., & Cahill, S. P. (2017). Extending the ACEs framework: Examining the relations between childhood abuse and later victimization and perpetration with college men. *Journal of Interpersonal Violence, 35* (17–18), 3487–3512. doi:10.1177/0886260517708406

World Health Organization. (2014a). *Gender, climate change and health.* Geneva: World Health Organization. www.who.int/globalchange/publications/reports/gender_climate_change/en/

World Health Organization. (2014b). *Global status report on violence prevention 2014.* Geneva: World Health Organization. www.who.int/violence_injury_prevention/violence/status_report/2014/en/

World Health Organization. (2021). *Violence against women prevalence estimates, 2018: Global, regional, and national prevalence estimates for intimate partner violence against women and global and regional prevalence estimates for non-partner sexual violence against women.* Geneva: World Health Organization. www.who.int/publications/i/item/9789240026681

Zagurny, E. S. F., Compton, S. D., Dzomeku, V., Cannon, L. M., Omollo, T., & Munro-Kramer, M. L. (2021). Understanding stalking among university students in Ghana: A mixed methods study. *Journal of Interpersonal Violence.* doi:10.1177/08862605211001485

20

DOMESTIC VIOLENCE, HUMAN RIGHTS, AND REFORM IN MAURITANIA

Nabil Ouassini and Anwar Ouassini

Introduction

Domestic violence is a universal problem with far-reaching physical, emotional, psychological, and spiritual effects on men, women, children, and families. In sub-Saharan Africa, domestic violence is an unfortunately pervasive human rights violation and public health issue affecting 36% of the population (McCloskey et al., 2016). A United Nations Women Report (2018) reveals 22.3% of sub-Saharan women between the ages of 15 and 49 experience physical/sexual violence by an intimate partner (IPV). A meta-analysis of 58 studies on gender-based violence in sub-Saharan Africa reported that 44% of women aged 15–49 experience IPV with the highest rates in (29.4%) emotional, (25.87%) physical, and (18.75%) sexual violence (Muluneh et al., 2020). Numerous factors contribute to domestic violence in sub-Saharan Africa: socio-economic conditions, cultural practices and norms, misinterpretation of religious teachings, and attitudes toward gender relations (Uthman, Lawoko, & Moradi, 2009). Most of these studies on sub-Saharan Africa overlook data and other sources of information from the West African country of Mauritania. The following chapter will explore domestic violence in Mauritania, address the current gaps, and contribute knowledge to the ever-growing literature from sub-Saharan Africa.

Mauritania is an Islamic Republic with about 4.6 million citizens (U.N. World Population, 2020). Bordering Morocco and Algeria in the north, Mali in the east, and Senegal in the south, the country consists of close to 400,000 square miles, most of it in the Sahara Desert. Like other countries in the Maghreb, Arabic is the official language, with French as a secondary language. Nearly all Mauritanians are Muslim with diverse ethnic identities comprising ethnic Beydane and Haratine Moors and numerous others of Halpulaar, Fulani, Soninke, Wolof, and Bambara descent (Central Intelligence Agency, 2020). After independence from the French in 1960, Mauritania's legal system combined French civil law with the country's traditional Maliki form of Islamic law. The legal system has been regrettably subservient to Mauritania's political affairs as the country became renowned for consecutive military coups. From 1984 to 2005, Mu'awiya Ould Taya ruled Mauritania after an army coup 1984–2005 until his regime was overthrown by Mohamed Ould Abdelaziz in a 2009 coup. President Abdelaziz ruled Mauritania for ten years until a peaceful political transition to President Mohamed Ould Ghazouani in 2019, the first elected president in Mauritania's history. Each coup and change of government regimes reveal the rampant corruption at all levels of the Mauritanian government. Transparency International (2019) ranked Mauritania as the 137th most corrupt country in the world out of the 180 countries with a score of 28/100.

DOI: 10.4324/9781003264040-24

A report by the NGO Sherpa (2017, p. 14) called *Corruption in Mauritania* describes Mauritania as "one of the most corrupt countries in the world" and documents corruption in cases at the presidential level that includes an $11 million payment to the former president's son in a bid to construct a power plant through a French subsidiary of a Finnish company. The high levels of corruption reveal how a country that is one of the largest producers in Africa of iron ores, fisheries, and so many other extractive resources remains one of the poorest nations on earth. For example, the United Nations Development Program (2019) reported Mauritania 161st out of 188 countries in the Human Development Indicator rankings.

Excessive corruption and poverty harm Mauritania's administration of justice. According to the U.S. Department of State (2018), the Mauritanian legal and criminal justice systems are "under-resourced, poorly coordinated both domestically and regionally, and has a weak institutional foundation." The State Department further describes the system as reactive rather than proactive with rampant corruption, distrust, and abuse of power. The World Justice Project (2021) ranked Mauritania 133 out of 139 countries when measuring the framework for the rule of law that includes factors such as constraints on government powers, absence of corruption, open government, fundamental rights, order and security, regulatory enforcement, civil justice, and criminal justice. The judiciary lacks any form of independence as the president remains the center of the government to appoint judges at each level of the government unilaterally and upholds a disturbing capability to retaliate against judges that render any rulings against the regime (Freedom House, 2020). The power over the judiciary has prompted numerous arbitrary arrests of students, academics, activists, journalists, and any other persons that voice an opinion against the government.

The discussion on domestic violence, human rights, and reform in Mauritania must also address the country's legacy of slavery. In 1981, Mauritania became the last country to abolish slavery and only criminalizing the practice in 2007. As of 2019, Mauritania has an estimated 90,000 modern slaves or 21.43 victims per 1000 people in the general population (Global Slavery Index, 2019). Under significant international pressure, the government has passed numerous anti-slavery laws and amendments to address the issue better. The U.S. Department of State (2019) reports that President Ghazouani has created the General Delegation for National Solidarity and the Fight against Exclusion or Taazour to eliminate slavery/slavery-like practices and implement plans to improve the living conditions of the marginalized Haratine communities. Unfortunately, the government's attempts have fallen relatively short. Human Rights Watch mentions that, in 2019, the government investigated a mere four cases, with only nine other cases from previous years pending an appeal in the anti-slavery courts.

Mauritania's Legislative Framework

According to Make Every Woman Count (MEWC), an African woman-led non-government organization, Mauritania has signed most international conventions related to women's rights but remains deeply discriminatory against women. Mauritania, for example, ratified the Convention on the Elimination of All Forms of Discrimination against Women (CEDAW) in May of 2001. In 2005, Mauritania ratified the Protocol to the African Charter on Human and Peoples' Rights on the Rights of Women in Africa or the Maputo Protocol. Within Mauritania, a Personal Status Code was adopted in 2001, with subsequent legal reforms addressing local gender concerns (U.N. 2014). One of the essential legislations is the 2016 draft bill supported by the government on gender-based violence that has yet to be passed. Although the proposed law falls short of international standards, it would improve legal and support services for victims and decisively define various types of sexual violence absent in the current laws (Human Rights Watch, 2018). The government has passed laws in 2017 regarding reproductive health while maintaining the ban on abortion in Article 293 of the Penal Code, a relic of French colonial rule (Hessini, 2007).

Despite these laws and a National Action Plan on Gender-Based Violence (U.N. Women, 2014), there remain numerous concerns in the progress of women's rights, especially in domestic violence. A 2007 CEDAW report mentions Mauritania's entrenched patriarchal ideology and cultural norms as a significant source of violence against women (Serge, 2009). Another report from the Mauritanian National Office of Statistics (2014) cited in Musawah (2017) found that 27% of women between the ages of 15 and 49 believed that a husband is justified in physically beating a wife if she leaves the house without permission, neglects her children, argues with her spouse, and/or burns his food. International media has also reported domestic violence cases that were perceived as an attestation of pride and love for Mauritanian women (Mint Zeidane, 2017). Cases of domestic violence remain underreported and according to the U.S. Department of State (2019) ineffective law enforcement; monetary compensation; the possibility of arrest for intercourse outside of marriage; and the reliance on families, non-governmental organizations in civil society, and others are some of the reasons that victims were discouraged from reporting domestic violence. The latter has contributed to the evasion of arrests and prosecutions of perpetrators. A National Human Rights Commission (2017, p. 21) report adds the "inadequacy of existing implementation measures … women's poverty and low literacy rates, the lack of knowledge of their right[s]" as some of the additional factors that impede the progress of women's rights in Mauritania.

Contemporary Gender Issues

Human Rights Watch (2020) reported several concerns surrounding gender-based violence and human rights in Mauritania. These issues stem from Mauritania's regressive laws that lag far behind international standards. For example, there are currently no laws against sexual harassment, although the problem is rampant and shared in many Mauritanian work environments (U.S. Department of State, 2019). The U.N. High Commissioner for Refugees (2005) has defined sexual harassment as unsolicited sexual advances, verbal and physical sexual conduct, requests for sexual favors, or any other behavior of a sexual nature that reasonably offends or humiliates another with either male or female offenders and victims. Sexual harassment is a crime that is universal and Mauritanian law must address crimes of this nature due to the physical and psychological impacts on victims. Scholars confirm that sexual harassment can cause shame, depression, fear, and anxiety with long-term effects on an individual's mental and physical well-being and health (Hutagalung & Ishak, 2012; Luthar & Luthar, 2002). Even the severe forms of gender-based violence remain legally under-defined. In rape cases, convictions are rare due to ambiguous laws and definitions of crimes, and the heavy burden of securing a confession from the rapist or finding four eyewitnesses to the crime of rape (Haddad, 2017). A more disturbing legal trend occurred when women who reported their cases to police were incarcerated under the charge of sex outside of marriage and forced to serve sentences of two to five years. Nearly 40% of incarcerated women in Mauritania are serving time for the crime of having sex outside of marriage (Peyton, 2018). This legal phenomenon is delicately documented in a Human Rights Watch (2018) report called "'They Told Me to Keep Quiet': Obstacles to Justice and Remedy for Sexual Assault Survivors in Mauritania." Victims of sexual violence have a grueling experience reporting sexual assault to government officials that openly suspect, mistreat, and question their moral character. The report further details the problems with law enforcement's investigative procedures and the limited resources available to survivors. One case described the story of a 15-year-old that fled from her sexually abusive father to an older man that locked and drugged her for gang rapes. The young girl was arrested and sent to prison on charges that she engaged in sexual relations outside of marriage despite her horrific ordeal. These laws have discouraged survivors from filing any complaints against rapists for fear of facing prosecution from officials. This environment has unfortunately made Mauritania a regional destination for human traffickers. According to the U.S. Department of State (2019), countless West African women and girls have become exploited victims of sex trafficking and forced prostitution in Nouakchott, Nouadhibou, and Russo, with others recruited for Middle Eastern, North African, and European countries.

Gender-based violence is commonly attributed to the substantial legal inequalities that exist between the genders. The U.N. Women Global Database on Violence against Women (2016) ranks Mauritania at 147th in gender inequality and 129th in the gender gap. There are no specific laws that criminalize or punish for involving in domestic violence or marital rape. However, there are sporadic physical or sexual violence cases where general crimes in the criminal penal code are applied (Musawah, 2017). Like many other nations, Mauritania perceives domestic violence as a private family matter rather than a social problem that families should handle through the formal legal system (Punitha, 2019). This perception is regrettably common in societies that distinguish domestic violence from other forms of assault. These proponents assume that domestic violence is a private family dilemma that authority figures in the government should not meddle into with arrests, prosecutions, and the courts. Abusers in these instances can use the reluctance to intervene to continue their abuse while arguing that the problem is private.

Although domestic violence is traditionally associated with battered spouses and children in physically, sexually, and mentally abusive relationships, in the Mauritanian context, domestic violence takes on other distinctive forms. The most apparent forms of domestic violence persist in the institution/laws of marriage and their reinforcement by the justice system. Legally, both the bride and the groom must consent to a marriage (Article 26 of Personal Code 2001). However, a 2015 survey estimated that 23,000 or 53% of marriages were forced (Musawah, 2017) and typically occurred when girls forcibly marry their cousins, girls from low-income families to marry for financial reasons, or girls forced into a polygamous marriage (Immigration and Refugee Board of Canada, 2012). Polygamy is legal in Mauritania, with around 8% of men marrying more than one wife (Musawah, 2017). The law enables a man to marry up to four women without any permission of a court or that of the existing wife/wives (Article 45 of Personal Code 2001). The legal age of marriage is 18, yet child marriages are widespread, with 37% of girls marrying before the age of 18 and 18% of girls marrying before the age of 15, ranking Mauritania as the 20th most prevalent country with child marriages in the world (Girls Not Brides, 2020). According to Nour (2006), child marriage is a human rights violation of young girls' mental and physical health. Child marriages are usually driven by poverty and prevent young girls from education, psychological maturity, and the freedom to choose a spouse. The pervasiveness of child marriages has generated the phenomenon of forced feedings called *leblouh* (Hassaniya Arabic) or *gavage* (French) as a form of domestic violence directed at women's health for the benefit of men. Since obesity is a sign of cultural beauty, families force-feed girls at a very early age with high fattening foods, steroids, and growth hormones to increase their marriage prospects. In a study by Ouldzeidoune et al. (2013), the researchers found that the phenomenon was predominantly practiced by Mauritanian Arabs, with 23% of women experiencing forced feedings as children. The same study found that 29% of men and 32% of women supported and encouraged the practice of forced feeding.

Mauritania also is one of the countries that has continued the practice of female genital mutilation or (FGM). The cultural practice involves the partial or complete removal of the external genitals of a female. Mauritanian law has criminalized FGM, but it remains widespread, especially in the rural deserts in the country (Human Rights Watch, 2020). According to Ouldzeidoune et al. (2013), the prevalence of FGM is at a high 77% as the majority of both males, 70%, and females, 64%, support its continuation. FGM is usually a rite of passage to womanhood in some cultures. The practice can result in severe injury or pain, infection, urine retention, shock, hemorrhage, and death with long-term physical, psychological, and sexual complications (World Health Organization, 1998). Cetorelli et al. (2020) found that the 2005 law that criminalized FGM did not significantly reduce the practice and that simply passing laws was an insufficient approach. In each of the various forms of domestic violence, the Mauritanian government is deficient in its laws, and the current laws are overwhelmingly violated, ignored, or even challenged by large segments of Mauritanian society.

COVID-19 and Climate Change

There is also a concern for COVID-19 and its long-term effects on gender-based violence. Globally, the quarantine and stay-at-home instructions increased the reported cases of domestic violence as the crackdown amplified unemployment through the decimation of major industries (Kofman & Garfin, 2020). On the 13th of March 2020, Nouakchott reported the first case of COVID-19. The government implemented the necessary preventative control measures to suppress the spread of COVID-19. Internationally, Mauritania closed its borders from foreign countries. However, locally, the government applied curfews, closed markets, businesses, mosques, and schools as the pandemic tested the fragile health system. Scholars have highlighted the connection between COVID-19 and the high risk of gender-based violence (Evans, Lindauer, & Farrell, 2020; Viero et al., 2020). According to the African Union Commission (2020), domestic violence has increased by around 10% in Mauritania, and about 15 million cases occur in the continent every three months. The inaccessibility to services and resources is an issue that victims of domestic violence have to deal with in every country. There is a genuine concern that the pandemic will reverse many of the advancements made in the past few decades in the realm of women's rights and gender equality. The U.N. Population Fund (2020) estimates that over 13 million preventable child marriages and 2 million FGMs will occur in the next ten years due to the pandemic. The protection of women from domestic violence should be a priority in any government's response. The U.N. Women (2020) suggests that governments respond to COVID-19 by providing services that address domestic violence (hotlines, shelters, and counseling), urge police agencies to enforce the laws, and support victims by all possible means. Although Mauritanian data on domestic violence during the pandemic is practically nonexistent, scholars should explore and further research the types/forms of violence, the risk factors, and the possible state services, policies, and responses needed to confront this proliferation.

Both climate change and the COVID-19 pandemic aggravate the issue of gender-based violence. According to the Intergovernmental Panel on Climate Change (IPCC) Report, Mauritania and other neighboring states are the most vulnerable regions for climate-related disasters (Olsson et al., 2019). Climate change will undoubtedly affect numerous livelihoods, particularly in agriculture and pastoralism. As temperatures rise, food insecurity will increase droughts and floods throughout the region. Thomas and Nigam (2018) describe how desertification has intensified and will expand toward fertile lands and homes in the Sahel. An even calamitous scenario is water scarcity from climate change and the drying of water sources. The described effects of climate change that will ensue from such a catastrophe could produce displaced climate migrants, political instability, and various forms of civil unrest. Women under these stressful circumstances will feel the full brunt of climate change. The current studies on gender-based violence and climate change are scarce; however, some researchers found that gender-based violence does intensify in the aftermath of disasters (Parkinson & Zara, 2013; Sety, James, & Breckenridge, 2014; Yoshihama et al., 2019). An even bigger problem for the region is the growth of religious extremism and armed conflict as security disintegrates. In Mauritania, future policies and programs should position women at the forefront of climate change and the compounded financial, economic, political, and social pressures they will likely experience.

Domestic Violence Reform

In the review and analysis of domestic violence in Mauritania, numerous institutions require effective reform. The government needs to pass the 2016 draft law pending in parliament that would define various forms of domestic and gender-based violence, create special courts to process cases, and permit non-governmental organizations from civil society to present cases for victims (Human Rights Watch, 2020). Furthermore, the government must strengthen legal institutions to review and overhaul laws that contribute to domestic violence. Members of parliament should further legislate laws that defend the human rights of its citizens, criminalize all forms of violence against women, and include measures that protect victims from further ill-treatment by the state. As previously mentioned, the Penal Code criminalizes rape while neglecting an unequivocal definition of the crime. Human Rights Watch (2018) reports that the hazy legal definition of rape has allowed judges to convict rape victims of sex outside of marriage without addressing whether the act was non-consensual.

Along with the lack of domestic violence laws, a noticeable gap exists between the ideals of current laws and actual practice. In the reports on domestic violence in Mauritania, individuals find different ways to circumvent the legal system. In cases of rape, the U.S. Department of State (2019) recounts the practice of perpetrators agreeing with the family of rape victims on monetary compensations. A similar account exists in FGM crimes, child marriages, and the sexual exploitation of children where the law punishes offenders with imprisonment and heavy fines but is rarely enforced due to prevailing social attitudes and inadequate procedural laws (Cetorelli et al., 2020; U.S. Department of State, 2019).

The role of government actors is fundamental to domestic violence reform. Politicians should recognize the need for a comprehensive approach to legislating laws that criminalize different forms of domestic violence, offering the necessary support and facilities for victims, and providing resources for law enforcement and the judicial system (U.N. Women, 2012). Law enforcement officers, prosecutors, and judges are responsible for revising the procedures on domestic violence. Domestic violence is already one of the universally underreported crimes in the justice system, and Mauritanian law enforcement has to work better in the enforcement of codes, investigation of reported cases, the assistance of victims, and the accountability of offenders. Some of the reasons that dissuaded Mauritanian victims from reporting domestic violence to law enforcement cited were law enforcement's treatment of victims and refusal to investigate cases (U.S. Department of State, 2019). Police should have standardized training courses like many departments in the developed world to understand the dynamics of domestic violence. These training programs specialize in exercising new techniques to identify victims, improve the interactions and abilities in treating victims, and prevent future cases. In the judicial system, Human Rights Watch (2019) has also advocated for specialized prosecutorial units trained for domestic and sexual violence cases that treated victims with compassion rather than as offenders with the burden of proving their innocence to judicial authorities.

In the reform of domestic violence, the function of civil society and non-governmental organizations are vital to Mauritania's success. A comprehensive approach to the problem of domestic violence will involve civil society organizations that will provide alternative points of access to support and assistance outside of the formal legal system. Human Rights Watch (2020) documents the tremendous work that non-governmental organizations provide in the legal services by helping victims file reports to governments and health services through shelters and therapy for victims. These organizations in civil society have actively defended the rights of victims and can continuously evaluate laws, monitor domestic violence programs, and provide training for government actors. If the government permits, civil society organizations can contribute resources to prosecuting domestic violence and introduce innovative rehabilitation initiatives to help abusers with treatment after serving time for their crimes. Civil society organizations can also mobilize communities in Mauritania with campaigns and awareness-building experiences worldwide. Mauritania's cultural perceptions, attitudes, pressures, and stigmas shape the offenders' crimes, victims' reactions, and the government actors' interpretation of the laws. The role of civil society in the upcoming years will be the development of educational outreach programs on domestic violence that challenge the social norms, values, and perceptions; educate the public; and help modify behaviors. In the Mauritanian context, Islamic scholars and other famous cultural personalities will be pivotal in domestic violence awareness.

This chapter explored the issue of domestic violence in Mauritania and found that the legislative framework is far behind international standards. Although Mauritania has signed most international conventions, its national laws on domestic violence necessitate revision. Some of the contemporary gender issues emanate from laws that are either regressive or too ambiguous for application. The chapter discusses the reforms required for domestic violence in Mauritania. To move forward, the government must strengthen legal institutions to overhaul domestic violence laws. In the laws that meet international standards, the justice system must narrow the substantial gap between the written laws and actual application. Furthermore, the Mauritanian government has to be more transparent with official information regarding domestic violence and other criminal justice issues. The real facts and figures in domestic violence remain vague. An open approach to domestic violence will bring attention to the issue and allow for multiple researchers, non-governmental organizations, and scholars to address the problem head-on. Domestic violence reform will need to involve politicians, law enforcement officers, legal actors, and members of civil society to build the initiative that improves the condition of domestic violence victims.

References

African Union Commission. (2020). Gender-Based Violence in Africa during the COVID-19 Pandemic. Retrieved from: https://africa.unwomen.org/en/digital-library/publications/2020/12/gbv-in-africa-during-covid-19-pandemic

Central Intelligence Agency. (2020). Mauritania. *In the World Factbook*. Retrieved from: www.cia.gov/library/publications/the-world-factbook/geos/mr.html

Cetorelli, V., Wilson, B., Batyra, E., & Coast, E. (2020). Female genital mutilation/cutting in Mali and Mauritania: understanding trends and evaluating policies. *Studies in Family Planning*, *51* (1), 51–69.

Evans, M. L., Lindauer, M., & Farrell, M. E. (2020). A pandemic within a pandemic—Intimate partner violence during Covid-19. *New England Journal of Medicine*, *383* (24), 2302–2304.

Freedom House. (2020). Mauritania. Retrieved from: https://freedomhouse.org/country/mauritania/freedom-world/2020

Girls Not Brides. (2020). Mauritania. Retrieved from: www.girlsnotbrides.org/child-marriage/mauritania/

Global Slavery Index. (2019). Africa. Retrieved from: www.globalslaveryindex.org/2018/findings/regional-analysis/africa/

Haddad, M. (2017). Victims of rape and law: How the Arab World laws protect the rapist not the victim. *Jurist*. Retrieved from: www.jurist.org/commentary/2017/05/Mais-Haddad-arab-world-laws-protect-the-rapist-not-the-victim/

Hessini, L. (2007). Abortion and Islam: Policies and practice in the Middle East and North Africa. *Reproductive Health Matters*, *15* (29), 75–84.

Human Rights Watch. (2018, September 5). "They told me to keep quiet." Obstacles to justice and remedy for sexual assault survivors in Mauritania. Retrieved from: www.hrw.org/report/2018/09/05/they-told-me-keep-quiet/obstacles-justice-and-remedy-sexual-assault-survivors#_ftn1

Human Rights Watch. (2019, October 15). Mauritania: Take key steps for women's rights. Retrieved from: https://www.hrw.org/news/2019/10/15/mauritania-take-key-steps-womens-rights

Human Rights Watch. (2020). Mauritania Events of 2019. Retrieved from: www.hrw.org/world-report/2020/country-chapters/mauritania#d91ede

Hutagalung, F., & Ishak, Z. (2012). Sexual harassment: A predictor to job satisfaction and work stress among women employees. *Procedia—Social and Behavioral Sciences, 65*, 723–730.

Immigration and Refugee Board of Canada. (2012, June 27). Mauritania: Prevalence of forced marriage; information on legal status, including state protection; ability of women to refuse a forced marriage. Retrieved from: http://www.refworld.org/docid/5035f2ea2.html

Kofman, Y. B., & Garfin, D. R. (2020). Home is not always a haven: The domestic violence crisis amid the COVID-19 pandemic. *Psychological Trauma: Theory, Research, Practice, and Policy, 12* (S1), S199–S201.

Luthar, V., K., & Luthar, H., K. (2002). Using Hofstede's cultural dimensions to explain sexually harassing behaviours in an international context. *The International Journal of Human Resource Management, 13* (2), 268–284. https://doi.org/10.1080/09585190110102378

Mauritanian National Office of Statistics. (2014). Mauritania monitoring the situation of women and children: Cluster Survey with Multiple Indicators 2011. Retrieved from: https://mics-surveys-prod.s3.amazonaws.com/MICS4/West%20and%20Central%20Africa/Mauritania/2011/Final/Mauritania%202011%20MICS_French.pdf

McCloskey, L. A., Boonzaier, F., Steinbrenner, S. Y., & Hunter, T. (2016). Determinants of intimate partner violence in sub-Saharan Africa: a review of prevention and intervention programs. *Partner Abuse, 7* (3), 277–315.

Mint Zeidane, N. (2017, February 25). 'It must be love': Wife-beating a source of pride for some in Mauritania. Retrieved from: www.reuters.com/article/us-mauritania-women/it-must-be-love-wife-beating-a-source-of-pride-for-some-in-mauritania-idUSKBN1640B9

Muluneh, M. D., Stulz, V., Francis, L., & Agho, K. (2020). Gender based violence against women in sub-Saharan Africa: A systematic review and meta-analysis of cross-sectional studies. *International Journal of Environmental Research and Public Health, 17* (3), 903.

Musawah. (2017, May 31). Mauritania Overview of Family Laws & Practices Retrieved from: www.musawah.org/wp-content/uploads/2019/03/Mauritania-Overview-Table.pdf

National Human Rights Commission (2017) Thematic Report on Women's Rights in Mauritania. Retrieved from: www.cndh.mr/images/rapport_thematique_de_la_cndh_sur_les_droits_des_femme_2017.pdf

Nour, N. M. (2006). Health consequences of child marriage in Africa. Emerging Infectious *Diseases, 12* (11), 1644.

Ouldzeidoune, N., Keating, J., Bertrand, J., & Rice, J. (2013). A description of female genital mutilation and force-feeding practices in Mauritania: Implications for the protection of child rights and health. *PLoS One, 8* (4), e60594.

Olsson, L., Barbosa, H., Bhadwal, S., Cowie, A., Delusca, K., Flores-Renteria, D., Hermans, K., Jobbagy, E., Kurz, W., Li, D. (2019). Land degradation: IPCC special report on climate change, desertification, land degradation, sustainable land management, food security, and greenhouse gas fluxes in terrestrial ecosystems. Intergovernmental Panel on Climate Change Report. Retrieved from: https://www.ipcc.ch/srccl/

Parkinson, D., & Zara, C. (2013). The hidden disaster: Domestic violence in the aftermath of natural disaster. *Australian Journal of Emergency Management, 28* (2), 28–35.

Peyton, N. (2018, October 30). Mauritanian Women Imprisoned for Being Raped Are Now Fighting Back. Retrieved from: www.globalcitizen.org/en/content/mauritania-violence-against-women/

Punitha, S. P. (2019). Preventing Gender-Based Violence through Safety and Security Mechanism. In K. R. Murugan. (Ed.), *Safety and Security for Women* (pp. 213–222). Chennai: MJP Publisher.

Serge, N. Z. (2009). Law and Legal Systems in Mauritania. Retrieved from: www.nyulawglobal.org/globalex/Mauritania1.html

Sety, M., James, K., & Breckenridge, J. (2014). Understanding the risk of domestic violence during and post natural disasters: Literature review. *Issues of Gender and Sexual Orientation in Humanitarian Emergencies* (pp. 99–111). Switzerland: Springer.

Sherpa. (2017). Corruption in Mauritania. Retrieved from: www.asso-sherpa.org/wp-content/uploads/2017/09/Sherpa-Corruption-in-Mauritania_A-gigagntic-evaporation-system-2017-1.pdf

Thomas, N., & Nigam, S. (2018). Twentieth-century climate change over Africa: Seasonal hydroclimate trends and Sahara desert expansion. *Journal of Climate, 31* (9), 3349–3370.

Transparency International. (2019). Mauritania. Retrieved from: www.transparency.org/en/countries/mauritania#

U.N. Development Program. (2019). Mauritania. Retrieved from: http://hdr.undp.org/en/countries/profiles/mrt

U.N. High Commissioner for Refugees. (2005). UNHCR's policy on harassment, sexual harassment, and abuse of authority. Retrieved from: www.un.org/womenwatch/osagi/UN_system_policies/ (UNHCR) policy_on_harassment.pdf

U.N. Population Fund. (2020). Impact of the COVID-19 Pandemic on Family Planning and Ending Gender-based Violence, Female Genital Mutilation and Child Marriage. Technical Note, 27. Retrieved from: www.unfpa.org/resources/impact-covid-19-pandemic-family-planning-and-ending-gender-based-violence-female-genital

U.N. Women. (2012). *Handbook for Legislation on Violence against Women*. New York, U.S.A.: U.N. Women. Retrieved from: www.unwomen.org/-/media/headquarters/attachments/sections/library/publications/2012/12/unw_legislation-handbook%20pdf.pdf?la=en&vs=1502

U.N. Women. (2014). *National Action Plan on Gender-Based Violence*. Nouakchott, Mauritania: U.N. Women. Retrieved from: https://evaw-global-database.unwomen.org/en/countries/africa/mauritania/2014/plan-daction-national-sur-les-violences-basees-sur-le-genre

U.N. Women. (2016). Global Database on Violence against Women. U.N. Women. Retrieved from: https://evaw-global-database.unwomen.org/en/countries/africa/mauritania

U.N. Women. (2018). Turning promises into action: Gender equality in the 2030 Agenda for Sustainable Development. U.N. Women. Retrieved from: www.unwomen.org/-/media/headquarters/attachments/sections/library/publications/2018/sdg-report-fact-sheet-sub-saharan-africa-en.pdf?la=en&vs=3558

U.N. Women. (2020). COVID-19 and Essential Services Provision for Survivors of Violence Against Women and Girls. Retrieved from: www.unwomen.org/en/digital-library/ publications/2020/04/brief-covid-19-and-essential-services-provision-for-survivors-of-violence-against-women-and-girls

U.N. World Population. (2020). Mauritania. Retrieved from: https://worldpopulationreview.com/countries/mauritania-population

U.S. Department of State. (2018). Mauritania. Retrieved from: www.state.gov/mauritania/

U.S. Department of State. (2019). Human Rights Practices: Mauritania. Retrieved from: www.state.gov/reports/2019-country-reports-on-human-rights-practices/mauritania/

Uthman, O. A., Lawoko, S., & Moradi, T. (2009). Factors associated with attitudes towards intimate partner violence against women: A comparative analysis of 17 sub-Saharan countries. *BMC International Health and Human Rights*, *9* (1), 14.

Viero, A., Barbara, G., Montisci, M., Kustermann, K., & Cattaneo, C. (2020). Violence against women in the Covid-19 pandemic: A review of the literature and a call for shared strategies to tackle health and social emergencies. *Forensic Science International*, *319*, 110650.

World Health Organization. (1998). *Female Genital Mutilation: An Overview*. Geneva: World Health Organization.

World Justice Project. (2021). Mauritania ranked 133 out of 139 countries on rule of law. Retrieved from: https://worldjusticeproject.org/sites/default/files/documents/Mauritania_2021%20WJP%20Rule%20of%20Law%20Index%20Country%20Press%20Release.pdf

Yoshihama, M., Yunomae, T., Tsuge, A., Ikeda, K., & Masai, R. (2019). Violence against women and children following the 2011 Great East Japan Disaster: Making the invisible visible through research. *Violence against Women*, *25* (7), 862–881.

SECTION FOUR

Perpetrators and Victims (Intersectionality: Race/Ethnicity, Gender, Migrant, and Refugee Populations)

21

RESPONDING TO INTIMATE PARTNER VIOLENCE AGAINST WOMEN IN SPAIN

Perpetrators' Accounts as a New Variable to the Ecological Approach Model

Mostafa Boieblan

Introduction

The family sphere is the most unsafe societal context for women because they are more likely to be abused and killed by someone they know than by a stranger (United Nations Office on Drugs, & Crime, 2018, 2019). In marriage, for instance, recourse to violence against wives for "disciplinary" purposes was a mainstream norm (Counts, Brown, & Campbell, 1992; McLean, 2002; Walker, 1989) which had been viewed as a personal dispute till the late 19th century and, as such, did not legitimize legal intervention except in extreme cases wherein the victims were murdered or seriously injured (Renzetti & Adair, 2018). In view of the insidious effects, this epidemic exerts on their integrity, modern societies have long become conscious of the dire necessity to intervene (Corradi et al., 2016; Vives-Cases et al., 2016; WHO, 2016), but a criminal justice response was out of place because, to legislate against this phenomenon, it had been necessary to first implement a conceptual shift that recognized the problem as a public health, social, legal, and human rights issue.

Spain witnessed this transition in its fight against this phenomenon inasmuch as this drastic shift gradually occurred due to nationwide social movements ensuing the murder of Ana Orantes, who was burnt alive by her ex-husband on December 17, 1997. The resulting conceptual frame, which was institutionally coined as Intimate Partner Violence Against Women (IPVAW), made a major break with the traditional one, first, by establishing a legal framework that enabled policymakers to devise a penal code according to which offenders now were held accountable for their aggression and legally sanctioned (Organic Act 1/2004 of 28 December on Integrated Protection Measures against Gender Violence) and second, by collecting and classifying data regarding different types of violence against women through a national statistical system (Instituto Nacional de Estadística) to comprehend the sheer scale of IPVAW.

Though eliciting a criminal justice response signaled the potential for eradicating IPVAW, a corollary of this conceptual transition was that by criminalizing it, the criminal justice system became the main source of institutional response—more incidence, more laws (Corvo & Johnson, 2003, p. 272; Goodmark, 2018). In this respect, Brenner (2013, p. 301) warns against the adverse effects of focusing on one single approach by stating that "… many of the existing laws, policies, and practices tend to impose a '*one size fits all*' solution to a problem that is incredibly complex".

Additionally, casting IPVAW as a criminal practice runs counter to framing it as a social construct, primarily acquired and reproduced within the family sphere because crimes are usually seen as random, spontaneous, and deviant acts. This means that IPVAW was now readily believed

DOI: 10.4324/9781003264040-26

to thrive in disadvantaged settings, e.g., low-income backgrounds (Bonomi, et al., 2014; Gondolf, 1995; Schwab-Reese et al., 2016) and to be correlated with other illegal practices, e.g., drug abuse (Frye et al., 2014; Galvani, 2006; Gilchrist et al., 2003).

Likewise, academic research used to adopt a single-factor theory to explore IPVAW: each discipline contended with the phenomenon based on its theoretical and experimental practices because they were the ones that produced valid and reliable findings (Heise, 1998). Psychology, for instance, regards IPVAW as primarily about male's self-esteem, stress, etc. (Heise, p. 262). Sociology, by contrast, seeks to answer the question of how gender asymmetry (Dobash & Dobash, 2015), lower socioeconomic status, and poor education (Bosch & Ferrer, 2012) potentially lead to women victimization in intimate partnership.

Nonetheless, a body of research attempts to surmount these disciplinary biases by accounting for IPVAW as an interplay of myriad factors at a multilevel layer—i.e., Ecological Approach (EA) (Crowell & Burgess, 1996; Ferrer & Bosch, 2017; Heise, 1998). This holistic approach seeks to bring together what is known and theorized across various disciplines to advance hybrid practices to fight IPVAW on several fronts. Accordingly, intervention and prevention methods managed to widen their areas of interest, one of which has been to gain insights into offenders' justifications and rationales for committing violent acts (Loinaz, 2014). For instance, Ptacek (1988) conducted a survey on 18 perpetrators and found that common themes across the participants were frustration, alcohol, and loss of control as main triggers of their violence. Yllö and Bograd (1988), Anderson and Umberson (2001), and Borochowitz (2008) undertook similar studies and all concluded that offenders' justification was that the victims did not rise up to their expectations of what a wife should be (see also Cavanagh, Dobash, Dobash, & Lewis, 2001; Dobash, Dobash, Cavanagh, & Lewis, 2004).

In this vein, after presenting an overview of nature and prevalence of IPVAW in Spain and their trends under the impact of the COVID-19, this chapter will aim to extend this knowledge through exploring the conceptual systems that characterize the perpetrators' accounts[1] of their aggressions. Qualitative data consisting of testimonies of perpetrators who accepted their responsibility for their violence has been collected from four mainstream Spanish news outlets from 2003 to 2020 ("El País", "El Mundo", "El Periódico", and "ABC"). The purpose is to examine how these perpetrators (n=13) construe their relationships with their victims. These accounts, which took place either during a court trial or a press interview ensuing acts of violence during or after an intimate partnership, will be analyzed from a cognitive linguistic approach, paying special attention to conceptual metaphor. Finally, the chapter will highlight the importance of findings in the realm of preventing and responding to IPVAW taking an ecological approach (EA).

Nature and Prevalence of IPVAW in Spain and Their Trends under the Impact of COVID-19

The European Institute for Gender Equality (EIGE) defines intimate partner violence (IPV) as any physical, sexual, psychological, or economic violence among current or former intimate partners, whether or not they cohabit (EIGE, 2017, pp. 44–46). Miguel-Luken (2015) further elaborates on these types of violence when the victim is female by highlighting that physical violence can be perpetrated through slapping, pushing, and the like. Sexual violence may consist of forcing the victim to have sex against her will or to perform any (humiliating) sexual practice. Psychological violence takes various forms too but, in general, falls into two categories: coercive control consisting of exercising continued vigilance about the victim's schedules and behavior or posing obstacles so that the victim cannot freely see her friends or family. The second category, emotional abuse, may include insults, contempt, etc. Finally, economic violence is inflicted in different ways too, some of which strive to restrict the victim's access to family income as well as systematically deny her economic independence.

All in all, though victimization patterns differ, they serve one primary purpose—to maintain male's "power and status" (Walker, 1989, p, 697; see also United Nations Office on Drugs, & Crime, 2018, 2019). The same holds true for sexual assault, which also seeks the victim's submission to male power and not just sheer pleasure (Koss, 1990). Furthermore, rather than being random or spontaneous, acts of violence against women are usually experienced as a "continuum", from mild to severe violence often leading up to the murder of the victim (Manjoo, 2012, p. 15; see also Dobash & Dobash, 2001). This systematicity has been also extensively reported in the literature pointing out that perpetrators who have been in different intimate relationships *did* inflict violence against a former partner (Dobash & Dobash, 2011; Dobash et al., 2004).

Consistent with the experience of other EU countries, Spain does not seem to curb IPVAW despite the increasing enactment of legislation for men and women equality and the conducting of continuous awareness campaigns. A nationwide survey on prevalence of IPVAW in Spain was undertaken in 2015 by the Government Delegation for Gender Violence with the collaboration of the Center for Sociological Research (CIS, from Spanish, Centro de Investigaciones Sociológicas) (study number 3,027), in which female participants (n=10,171) aged 16 or older answered whether they suffered any of the above-mentioned types of violence by a current or former intimate partner. Overall, 12.5% reported having been victims of sexual and/or physical violence, 10.3% victims of physical violence, and 8.1% victims of sexual violence (Miguel-Luken, 2015, p. 9). To fully understand these results, it is necessary to bear in mind that 60.2% of participants had only had one partner the time they were interviewed.

Overall, a woman's murder by an intimate partner remains the most repulsive manifestation of this hidden epidemic. Lethal victimization is the most tragic toll that gender-based violence takes on women, their family, and society. As of December 28, 2020, 1076 women have been killed due to gender-related violence since 2003, the year this crime started to be on record as gender-related killing. In 2019, the victimization rate, 55 victims, closed with a rebound for the third consecutive year: 49 victims in 2016, 50 in 2017, and 51 in 2018. These figures show a downward trend compared to 2015, the year which recorded a peak with 60 victims. The survey further disclosed that the age with the highest risk of this crime ranges from 41 to 50, representing 27.8% of the victims and aggressors, though its occurrence is reported across a larger age span for both—from 21 to 84.

Nevertheless, the outbreak of the COVID-19 in Spain exacerbated the vulnerability of the victims of IPVAW because the very measures with which the government aimed to combat the virus such as lockdowns and social distancing are those that further isolate the victims from their social support networks while obliging them to cohabit with their aggressors. Even so, the COVID-19 quarantine, from March 14 to April 28, 2020, recorded a significant fall in the complaints rate. This trend does not imply a de-escalation of violence though, but it seems that victims decided as a last resort to phone the police to seek protection instead of filing complaints because of the potential risk they would face in trying to do so while cohabiting with their aggressors. This downward trend may also be due to the fact that violations of restraining orders significantly decreased during confinement or because women who lived with their abuser were reluctant to report their victimization because they were being continuously controlled by the aggressor (Paleo, 2020). Accordingly, phone calls to Helpline 016, the number for the victims of violence against women to call for information and legal advice, have registered a historical peak since 2007, only exceeded once in 2016 with 9.916, whereas in April of 2020, in the midst of quarantine, it reached 8.692 (Delegación de Gobierno contra la Violencia de Género, 2020). Similarly, while the average of reporting victimization since 2010 on the same date stands at 7.8% of cases (11 out of 141), during the quarantine, it rose to 25% of cases. In a health emergency situation such as this and with the little room for maneuver that the virus leaves, the government's response system is being put to the test because its infrastructures for filing against the aggressors and requesting protection continue to be operational during the lockdown.

Metaphor Use in the Perpetrators' Accounts

Given the power of conceptual metaphor in constructing social reality, this figure of speech has become a crucial analytical tool within the field of Cognitive Linguistics for exploring embedded meanings in a wide range of discourses, including politics (Musolff, 2004), economy (Herrera-Soler & White, 2012), and social psychology (Landau, 2016). It has gained this status because, being an integrated part of our conceptual systems, it shapes how we reason, act, and interact in society (Lakoff & Johnson, 1980; Thibodeau & Boroditsky, 2011). Therefore, analyzing its use in the perpetrators' accounts of their violent acts against their intimate partners would offer deep insights into how they reason, act, and relate to their victims—the more detailed insights we gain regarding risk factors, the better the prevention and response programs will be. Before dealing deeply with this issue, first it is necessary to outline what it means for a concept to be metaphorically understood and how this may shape our reason and social behavior.

Two concepts—aka conceptual domains within Cognitive Linguistics—constitute a metaphor when one of them (target domain) is understood in terms of the other (source domain) (e.g., Lakoff & Johnson, 1980). For instance, following these scholars, the conceptual domain ARGUMENT[2] is construed via WAR and the corresponding conceptual metaphor is identified as ARGUMENT IS WAR. Notice that this conceptual metaphor is made manifest in linguistic expressions such as:

> Your claims are *indefensible.*
> He *attacked every weak point in* my argument. His criticisms were *right on target.*
> I *demolished* his argument....
>
> *Lakoff and Johnson, p. 5*

It is worth noting that mapping source and target domains in conceptual metaphor such as in the examples above yields certain inferences that constitute a conceptual system which characterizes our understanding of and reasoning about a particular phenomenon. To illustrate, in ARGUMENT IS WAR, the underlying conceptual systems comprise inferences such as an opponent in a debate is viewed as an enemy in a war, arguing as fighting, ideas as territories to defend or attack. What is important about these systems for the study of IPVAW is that they not only shape our reasoning system but also the way we behave. That is, construing a debate through ARGUMENT IS WAR *does* induce the necessity to develop best strategies to attack the opponent's weak positions to win an argument. In contrast, mapping ARGUMENT onto another domain would probably elicit different conceptual systems and spur different actions (Chilton, 1996; Semino, 2008, pp. 5–6).

Therefore, the importance of analyzing metaphor in the perpetrators' accounts rests on its potential for providing insights into the conceptual systems operating in their construal of an intimate partnership. That is, identifying and analyzing the conceptual metaphors in the IPVAW perpetrators' accounts of their violent acts will contribute to a better understanding of potential risk factors. For space limit, the focus will fall on the most common metaphors,[3] one of which is RELATIONSHIP IS OWNERSHIP, (e.g., ... *there comes time, in the first year of marriage that I am afraid of losing her* ...). Mapping intimate PARTNERSHIP onto OWNERSHIP is so entrenched in our conceptual system in that this conceptual metaphor goes unnoticed (e.g., "you are mine", "I am yours") (see also Adams, 2007; Polk, 1994). The domain OWNERSHIP is based on prototypical relations between the possessor and the possessed in which the former is a human being, who is rational, superior, and legitimate to control and use inanimate beings. The possessed, conversely, is an object, which is an inferior, selfless, and irrational being. Taylor (1995, pp. 202–206) highlights more inherent concepts to this domain such as proximity, exclusiveness, one-to-one, and long-term bonds between the possessor and the possessed. The question then becomes one of seeking to understand how mapping intimate PARTNERSHIP onto OWNERSHIP is important for exploring the etiology of IPVAW.

Conceptual metaphor, as argued before, shapes our reasoning system and social behavior. As the perpetrators employ intimate PARTNERSHIP IS OWNERSHIP to conceptualize their victims and their interaction with them, their construal of INTIMATE PARTNERSHIP allows viewing the victim as a selfless, irrational, and inferior being. These entailments closely fit into the sociological theories that sustain that IPVAW is rooted in the conceptualization of marriage as a patriarchal institution, in which women were viewed as property (e.g., Walker & Conte, 2018, p. 398). Accordingly, the victims are not legitimate to end the relationship, but if they attempt to do so, the perpetrators can resort to corrective actions.

This conceptualization is further strengthened through FEMALE PARTNER IS COMMODITY (e.g., "… *I used to tell her, you are worth nothing except for cleaning* …."). This mapping builds up on the inferences drawn from the previous metaphor to degrade and humiliate the victim by associating her personal worth to a domestic chore. Similarly, MALE PARTNER IS UP/FEMALE PARTNER IS DOWN (e.g., "*I used to feel above her* …") reveals certain inferences that offer valuable insights into how perpetrators conceptualize their victims, which can be summarized in the metaphors BEING UP IS HAVING POWER and BEING DOWN IS BEING SUBJECTED TO IT.

The analysis of the data thus far has focused on how the perpetrators perceive their victims. The following metaphors concern the perpetrators' accounts of their aggressions against intimate partners, which show a common cognitive pattern: using conceptual metaphor in which they resort to different uncontrollable phenomena as source domains to rationalize their drive for violence. The focus here will be on three facets of this pattern. First, PSYCHOLOGICAL TRAITS ARE INHERITABLE POSSESSIONS (e.g., *I inherited my father's impulsiveness.*) allows the perpetrator to attribute his aggressions to his inherited psychological traits. As he is unconscious of the process of acquiring these traits, he is not aware of how he became violent. Indeed, some of the perpetrators in the data argue that they did not know they were violent till they committed injurious actions for which they were arrested (e.g., *And a light came on for me, as if a veil had been removed*).

The second is IDEAS ARE VIRUS (e.g., *It is like a virus that infiltrates in your way of being, little by little you become used to behaving in that violent or fearful way*). To employ VIRUS as source domain to conceptualize their changing orientations toward their victims, the perpetrators aim to rationalize that this experience is identical to that of a computer system which has been infected by malicious software causing its total dysfunction. As is the case for the computer system, the perpetrators' attitudes were "healthy" and functional, but their aggressions stemmed out of an infection from a strange and malicious agent.

The third is THINKING IS MOVING/MOTION, (e.g., *You start getting into a wheel, you forgive yourself again, you betray it and you start falling into a spiral, and each time the circle between an episode of violence and forgiveness is getting smaller*). The perpetrators use MOTION to construe their changing attitudes via a prototypical *motion schema*, in which the following elements are identified: *source* (starting point of the motion), *path* (trajectory), and *goal* (destination) (Talmy, 2000, pp. 226–230). Nonetheless, this schema deviates from the usual scenario because, by mapping "wheel" and "spiral" from MOTION, the goal of the schema becomes unclear, foregrounding in this manner the uncontrollability and unintentionality of the motion. This loss of control, extensively reported in the literature to be one of the causes of IPVAW, enmeshed the perpetrators in a set of repeated and undesired events. Similar findings have been confirmed by Rakovec-Felser (2014) and Seligman (1972), who use "the theory of cyclic abuse" to postulate that men abusing women in an intimate partnership can be captured through recurrent episodes of violence and forgiveness.

In sum, resorting to uncontrollable phenomena as source domains for such metaphors is significant in that the perpetrators construct a cognitive foundation according to which they should not be held accountable for these acts inasmuch as they are not responsible for their predisposition to inflict violence. Indeed, taken together, these three conceptual metaphors reveal that the perpetrators of IPVAW conceptualize themselves too being victims in that they are influenced by an external power such as a virus (see also Seidler, 1999) or also as the data indicates, as an uncontrollable internal power such as anger.

Conclusion and Implications of this Study

This study aims to increase knowledge about the ways perpetrators of IPVAW construe their relationships with their victims and the dynamics of their aggression—the more information we gain regarding risk factors, the better our response can be. The metaphors analyzed above reflect certain conceptual systems according to which the perpetrators conceptualize their partners and reason about their interaction with them, including why they inflicted violence against them. These systems, and probably more could have been found if a larger database was available, are an impermeable barrier against intervention and prevention methods if they are not addressed adequately. Criminal justice sanctions or their substitutions with community service do not tackle the root cause of perpetrators' orientations toward intimate partnership—more sanctions do not challenge nor change conceptualizing female intimate partners as objects.

These insights should be brought to the process of devising response measures to transcend this barrier. As argued before, the EA to IPVAW stems from the fact that this phenomenon is complex and necessitates hybrid responses. First, it is necessary to identify and challenge these systems not only in the perpetrators' accounts but also across a wider cultural context of gender relationships. Acts of IPVAW, as mentioned earlier, are not spontaneous or deviant but have an underlying cognitive foundation which is probably shaped, embedded, and reinforced through different social practices. To illustrate, sex buying or sex workers, being based on conceptual systems which are endorsed through the objectification and commoditization of women (e.g., see INTIMATE PARTNERSHIP IS OWNERSHIP above), are a social sphere that warrants major governmental policies to be disrupted. That is, tracking and cognitively restructuring the conceptual systems that legitimate these social constructions of female identity is a massive step toward abolishing IPVAW.

Another major area for responding to IPVAW may concern the public media. Again, in this arena, the aim may be to identify and challenge the contents that promulgate the conceptual systems that enhance social roles based on gender and adapt them to a more equal representation of women and men. Targeting women when commercials concern selling cleaning products and man when selling cars, for instance, further reinforces the superiority of men within and outside the family sphere.

Notes

1 These accounts were published as perpetrators' direct quotations.
2 Throughout the text, words written in small capital letters represent conceptual domains.
3 These metaphors are manifested through various linguistic expressions in the data but only one linguistic expression for each is explored in the data analysis.

References

Adams, D. (2007). *Why do they kill?: Men who murder their intimate partners*. Nashville, TN: Vanderbilt University Press.

Anderson, K. L., & Umberson, D. (2001). Gendering violence: Masculinity and power in men's accounts of domestic violence. *Gender & Society, 15* (3), 358–380.

Bonomi, A. E., Trabert, B., Anderson, M. L., Kernic, M. A., & Holt, V. L. (2014). Intimate partner violence and neighborhood income: A longitudinal analysis. *Violence against Women, 20* (1), 42–58.

Borochowitz, D.Y. (2008). The taming of the shrew: Batterers' constructions of their wives' narratives. *Violence against Women, 14* (10), 1166–1180.

Bosch-Fiol, E., & Ferrer-Pérez, V. A. (2012). Nuevo mapa de los mitos sobre la violencia de género en el siglo XXI. *Psicothema, 24* (4), 548–554.

Brenner, H. (2013). Transcending the criminal law's one size fits all response to domestic violence. *William & Mary Journal of Women and the Law, 19*, 301.

Cavanagh, K., Dobash, R. E., Dobash, R. P., & Lewis, R. (2001). 'Remedial work': Men's strategic responses to their violence against intimate female partners. *Sociology, 35* (3), 695–714.

Chilton, P. (1996). *Security metaphors: Cold war discourse from containment to common house*. New York: Peter Lang.

Corradi, C., Marcuello-Servos, C., Weil, S. & Boira, S. (2016) 'Theories of femicide and their significance for social research'. *Current Sociology, 64* (7), 975–995.

Corvo, K., & Johnson, P. J. (2003). Vilification of the "batterer": How blame shapes domestic violence policy and interventions. *Aggression and Violent Behavior, 8* (3), 259–281.

Counts, D. A., & Brown, J. K. (1992). *Sanctions and sanctuary: Cultural perspectives on the beating of wives*. Boulder, CO: Westview Press.

Crowell, N. A., & Burgess, A. W. (Eds.). (1996) *Understanding violence against women*. Washington, DC: National Academy Press.

Delegación de Gobierno contra la Violencia de Género. (2020, Octubre) Boletín estadístico mensual – Octubre 2020 Retrieved from https://violenciagenero.igualdad.gob.es/violenciaEnCifras/boletines/boletinMensual/

Dobash, R. E., & Dobash, R. P.. (2001). "Domestic violence: Sociological perspectives." In N. J. Smelser & P. B. Baltes (Eds.), *International Encyclopedia of the Social & Behavioral Sciences* (pp. 3830–3834). Oxford: Elsevier.

Dobash, R. E., & Dobash, R. P. (2011). What were they thinking? Men who murder an intimate partner. *Violence against Women, 17*, 111–134.

Dobash, R. E., & Dobash, R. P. (2015). *When men murder women*. USA: Oxford University Press.

Dobash, R. E, Dobash, R. P., Cavanagh, K., & Lewis, R. (2004). Not an ordinary killer—just an ordinary guy: When men murder an intimate woman partner. *Violence against Women, 10*, 577–605.

EIGE. (2017). Glossary of definitions of rape, femicide, and intimate partner violence; 2017. Retrieved from https://eige.europa.eu/rdc/eige-publications/glossarydefinitions-rape-femicide-and-intimate-partner-violence

Ferrer-Pérez, V., & Bosch-Fiol, E. (2017). Levels of prevention of intimate partner violence against women analysed from the multi-causal-ecological pyramidal model: The case of Spain. In D. Peterson, & J. Schroeder, (Eds.), *Domestic Violence in International Context*. New York: Routledge, 74–89.

Frye, V., Blaney, S., Cerdá, M., Vlahov, D., Galea, S., & Ompad, D. C. (2014). Neighborhood characteristics and sexual intimate partner violence against women among low-income, drug-involved New York City residents: Results from the IMPACT studies. Violence against *Women, 20* (7), 799–824.

Galvani, S. (2006). Alcohol and domestic violence: Women's views. *Violence against Women, 12* (7), 641–662.

Gilchrist, E., Johnson, R., Takriti, R., Weston, S., Beech, A., & Kebbell, M. (2003). *Domestic violence offenders: Characteristics and offending related needs*. London: Home Office. Research, Development and Statistics Directorate.

Gondolf, E. W. (1995). Alcohol abuse, wife assault, and power needs. *Social Service Review, 69* (2), 274–284.

Goodmark, L. (2018). *Decriminalizing domestic violence: A balanced policy approach to intimate partner violence*. California: University of California Press.

Heise, L. L. (1998). Violence against women: An integrated, ecological framework. Violence against *Women, 4* (3), 262–290.

Herrera-Soler, H., & White, M. (Eds.). (2012). *Metaphor and mills: Figurative language in business and economics* (Vol. 19). Berlin: Walter de Gruyter.

Koss, M. P. (1990). The women's mental health research agenda: Violence against women. *American Psychologist, 45* (3), 374.
Lakoff, G., & Johnson, M. (1980). *Metaphors we live by*. Chicago: University of Chicago press.
Landau, M. J. (2016). *Conceptual metaphor in social psychology: The poetics of everyday life*. New York: Routledge.
Loinaz, I. (2014). Distorsiones cognitivas en agresores de pareja: análisis de una herramienta de evaluación. *Terapia psicológica, 32* (1), 5–17.
Manjoo, R., (2012). Report of the Special Rapporteur on violence against women, its causes and consequences. UN General Assembly, Twentieth session.
McLean, L. (2002). "Deserving" Wives and "Drunken" Husbands: Wife Beating, Marital Conduct, and the Law in Ontario, 1850–1910. Histoire sociale/Social History.
Miguel-Luken, V. (2015). *Macroencuesta de violencia contra la mujer 2015*. Ministerio de Sanidad, Servicios Sociales e Igualdad. Retrieved from https://violenciagenero.igualdad.gob.es/violenciaEnCifras/estudios/colecciones/pdf/Libro_22_Macroencuesta2015.pdf
Musolff, A. (2004). *Metaphor and political discourse: Analogical Reasoning in Debates about Europe*. New York: Palgrave Macmillan.
Paleo, N. (2020, August 26). *Feminicidios y otros asesinatos de mujeres en España durante la cuarentena por COVID-19*. Retrieved from https://feminicidio.net/feminicidios-y-otros-asesinatos-de-mujeres-en-espana-durante-la-cuarentena-por-covid-19/
Polk, K. (1994). *When men kill: Scenarios of masculine violence*. Cambridge: Cambridge University Press.
Ptacek, J. (1988). "Why do men batter their wives?" In Kersti Yllo & Michele Bograd (Eds.), *Feminist perspectives on wife abuse* (pp. 133–157). Newbury Park, CA: Sage.
Rakovec-Felser, Z. (2014). Domestic violence and abuse in intimate relationship from public health perspective. *Health Psychology Research, 2* (3), 62–67.
Renzetti, C., & Adair, A. (2018). Family violence. In A. Treviño (Ed.), *The Cambridge Handbook of Social Problems* (pp. 327–344). Cambridge: Cambridge University Press.
Schwab-Reese, L. M., Peek-Asa, C., & Parker, E. (2016). Associations of financial stressors and physical intimate partner violence perpetration. *Injury Epidemiology, 3* (1), 6.
Seidler, V. (1999). Men, power, control and violence. In J. Wild (Ed.), *Working with men for change* (pp. 141–153). London, England: UCL Press.
Seligman, M. E. (1972). Learned helplessness. *Annual Review of Medicine, 23* (1), 407–412.
Semino, E. (2008). *Metaphor in discourse*. Cambridge: Cambridge University Press.
Talmy, L. (2000). *Toward a cognitive semantics* (Vol. 2). Cambridge: The MIT press.
Taylor, J. R. (1995). *Linguistic categorization: Prototypes in linguistic theory*. Oxford: Clarendon Press.
Thibodeau, P. H., & Boroditsky, L. (2011). Metaphors we think with: The role of metaphor in reasoning. *PloS One, 6* (2), 1–11
United Nations Office on Drugs, & Crime. (2018, 2019). *Global study on homicide gender related killing of women and girls*. Vienna: United Nations Publications.
Vives-Cases, C., Goicolea, I., Hernández, A., Sanz-Barbero, B., Gill, A. K., Baldry, A. C., ... & Stoeckl, H. (2016). Expert opinions on improving femicide data collection across Europe: a concept mapping study. *PloS One, 11* (2), e0148364.
Walker, L. E. (1989). Psychology and violence against women. *American Psychologist, 44* (4), 695–702.
Walker, L. E., & Conte, C. B. (2018). Description of the problem. In V. B. Van Hasselt, & M. I., Bourke (Eds.), *Handbook of behavioral criminology: Contemporary strategies and issues* (pp. 113–138). New York: Springer.
WHO (2016) Women's health and well-being in Europe: beyond the mortality advantage. Retrieved from https://apps.who.int/iris/bitstream/handle/10665/332324/9789289051910-eng.pdf
Yllö, K. E., & Bograd, M. E. (1988). Feminist perspectives on wife abuse. In *National conference for family violence researchers, 2nd, 1984, U of New Hampshire, NH, US*. Sage Publications, Inc.

22

WHY DOMESTIC VIOLENCE REMAINS UNDER-REPORTED WITHIN MIGRANT COMMUNITIES IN GERMANY

Fiza Lee-Winter

Introduction

As a globally pervasive issue, domestic violence (DV) still remains to be part of many women's daily lives, regardless of their socioeconomic status or education level, with greater physical and sexual violence faced by victims of migrant backgrounds (German Federal Ministry for Family Affairs, Senior Citizens, Women and Youth [BMFSFJ], 2017). In Germany, DV, or better known as "*häusliche Gewalt*", along with gender-based violence (GBV) and violence against women (VAW) remains a pressing issue, as highlighted by the Committee on the Elimination of Discrimination Against Women (CEDAW Committee) in the "*Concluding observations on the combined seventh and eighth periodic reports of Germany*" in March 2017 (UN Doc CEDAW/C/DEU/CO/7-8). These figures have also been rising in recent years (Deutsche Presse-Agentur [DPA]/The Local, 2020), with the Covid-19 pandemic further exacerbating matters (Brady, 2020).

According to a 2009 analysis that the BMFSFJ carried out on the health and violent situation of women with and without migrant backgrounds, more women with migrant backgrounds experience domestic, sexual, and psychological violence as compared to other women in Germany. Overall, 46% of women with migrant backgrounds experienced physical or sexual violence from a current partner as compared to only 13% of women of German origin (p. 14). In a slightly more recent survey published by European Union Agency for Fundamental Rights (FRA) in 2014, 35% of women in Germany have experienced physical violence or threats by a partner or a non-partner since the age of 15 (European Agency for Fundamental Rights [FRA], 2014, p. 24). Overall, 22% of the women surveyed in Germany stated that their perpetrators were either their current and/or previous partners (ibid., p. 28), with 3% having experienced physical and/or sexual violence by their current and/or previous partners in the preceding 12 months before the interview (ibid., p. 34)—statistics all in line with those of the BMFSFJ nation-wide study.

Unfortunately, new data purely on numbers of victims show a disturbing trend—"[i]n total, more than 114,000 women were victims of domestic violence, threats, stalking or coercion by their partners or ex-partners in 2018. Of these victims, 122 were killed that year—one every three days" (Deutsche Welle [DW], 2019). In early 2020, particularly during the months where lockdowns and contact restrictions were the strictest, as a safety measure against the spread of the Coronavirus, the German Interior Minister reported at a news conference on crime statistics in Berlin that "there was a rise in reported domestic violence mainly against women, but did not give any figures as the

DOI: 10.4324/9781003264040-27

data was incomplete" (Reuters, 2021). Discouragingly, Seehofer also mentioned that the reported incidents "were most likely only a fraction of the real numbers" (ibid.).

Within the German context, immigrants often come from a "patriarchal society" where men are viewed as aggressive and macho. These men often feel that they are entitled to discipline their wives who often have less autonomy, and this level of violence is considered "normal" (Grafe & Hagemann-White, 2015, p. 14). Many of these women have also faced DV and GBV from their country of origin, and the abuse continued with them along their way while escaping and many are still facing DV and GBV whilst in refuge in Germany, even though actual numbers still remain unknown (Schmollack, 2017, p. 248). An investigation in Berlin's refugee camps showed that women in the camps face "grossly inadequate protection from sexual and gender-based violence", with many of them living in constant fear of attack, prompting accusations that Germany has failed female refugees due to the lack of legal protection (The Local, 2017; see also Atmaca, 2017, p. 14).

As a state party to both the Convention on the Elimination of Discrimination Against Women (CEDAW) and also recently to the Council of Europe (CoE) Convention on preventing and combating VAW and DV, also known as the Istanbul Convention, Germany has a legal obligation to prevent GBV and VAW, which includes DV (United Nations [UN] Treaty Collection; see also CoE Istanbul Convention, n.d.). Despite not having a legal definition of DV (Thomson Reuters Foundation et al., 2013, p. 124, see also German Violence Protection Act, *Gewaltschutzgesetz-GewSchG*), Germany has set up a comprehensive federal action plan (BMFSFJ, 2007), accompanied by awareness raising activities to encourage victims to come forward to seek help, as well as increased funding support (DPA/The Local, 2020)—all of which provide for a positive outlook; however, the problem still persists due to the inherent gaps between policy and actual implementation (Grafe & Hagemann-White, 2015).

This chapter aims to contribute to the ongoing discussion of DV by highlighting the gaps and dissonance between policy and reality within the context of migrant communities in Germany. This chapter is also an adapted version of my master's thesis where the main goal of the research was to understand why DV remains under-reported within the migrant communities in Germany, even despite having the necessary prevention and intervention strategies and tools set in place. Mirroring the structure of the original thesis, it is pertinent that in order to answer the question of why DV remains under-reported in general, but especially more so within the migrant communities in Germany, one needs to understand reporting behaviors as well as the drivers behind them, especially bearing in mind the cultural difference and the complexity of DV as a crime. In the thesis, a further analysis of local laws as well as its implementation highlighted the system's shortcomings and factors which influence victims' reporting behaviors, reflected in existing available research—one example is the Cultural Encounters in Intervention Against Violence [CEINAV] project (for German context by Grafe & Hagemann-White, 2015). These findings were further supported and confirmed by anecdotal evidence, collected through semi-formal interviews, provided by three subjects who have had first-hand experiences in their interactions with the legal and intervention system in Germany. As such, the following sections of this chapter will touch upon the core factors which contribute to negative reporting behavior in DV victims. Relevant substantive areas have been updated to reflect recent developments, particularly those stemming from the Covid-19 pandemic toward DV/SGBV policy-making in Germany. Additionally, since the climate crisis will fuel more migration in the future (Podesta, 2019), it is important that the protection framework is improved following culturally sensitive approaches.

What Makes DV So Under-Reported?

The answer to the research question "why does DV remain under-reported, especially within the migrant population in Germany?" can be explained through an understanding of the factors which encourage or discourage victims' reporting behaviors. Why does it matter? Simply, without understanding these factors, as well as the impacts of current intervention approaches, which includes the legal system, we end up blindsided as to the extent and severity of the issue. Compounding this would be further developments of *incompatible* or *inappropriate* responses and intervention strategies, something that will adversely affect the overall efficiency of such responses. This can further result in victims' distrust in the system all together (BMFSFJ, 2017, p. 6).

DV—An Insidious Crime

A good starting point is to rediscover and find out what DV really is, what forms of violence it entails, what its definition truly is, and why it is so important to understand in depth. DV or sometimes known as Intimate Partner Violence (IPV) is violence involving a former/current spouse or partner in an intimate relationship setting, or in some cases even Family Violence (*häusliche Gewalt* in the German language), with acts of violence perpetrated against family members, children, parents, and the elderly. It is an ongoing worldwide epidemic that does not discriminate against gender, race, color, religion, and culture; affects people across various socioeconomic classes; and reaches far across oceans to every corner of the world (United Nations Women, n.d.). It can happen to anyone and the vicious cycle of victimization prevents victims from easily getting out of the situation (Walker, 2009, p. 91).

DV victims normally go through a continuum of violence at the hands of their known aggressors, which is what differentiates DV greatly from criminal incidents where the victim and perpetrator are strangers to each other, such as stranger rape and murder. A "regular" assault occurs once, but an assault in a DV setting occurs multiple times, with the perpetrator aiming to achieve control over the victim usually through a pattern of repeated behaviors and tactics selectively chose by the perpetrator himself. This continuum experienced by the victims is also what makes it extremely insidious, with one episode building upon past episodes and setting the stage for future ones (Ganley, 1995, p. 62). Forms of violence in DV that are inflicted upon the "weaker" partner by the "stronger" partner include physical, sexual, psychological, and even economic abuse. These acts of violence range from threats, intimidation, physical, and verbal humiliation, to being slapped, beaten up, raped, or even killed. According to Tuerkheimer (2004), these behaviors vary widely in range and intensity with some leading to actual physical injury, while others do not, making it extremely difficult to criminalize (p. 966). However, cumulatively, all behaviors are psychologically damaging to the victim (ibid.). There is, however, no causative behavior in victims that cause DV incidents (ibid., p. 73).

There are several theories explaining the phenomenon. One of the long-standing theories is the "Cycle Theory of Violence", which was first developed by Lenore E. Walker in 1979. This theory depicts three very distinct phases that occur in a DV cycle (pp. 91–95). In a 2010 multi-agency guidelines for staff responding to DV/VAW in the highlands in United Kingdom (UK), another tool which further highlights the complex nature of DV is called the "Six Stages", identified by Liz Kelly. It describes not only the stages of DV from the victims' point of view but also stresses the need for varying intervention strategies, which depend on the stage that the victim is in within the ordeal (p. 6). Experiencing such abuse in the long-term can have adverse impacts to the victims' mental health, even though many victims eventually recover. The guidelines also urge staff members to be patient when assisting victims and remember the context and challenges that the victims have faced, in order to facilitate victims' disclosure (p. 5).

Some common characteristics of DV victims include (but are not limited to) suffering from extremely low self-esteem, having poor self-confidence, and negative self-image (Walker, 2009, pp. 154–155), as well as having emotional dependency issues (ibid., p. 209). It is not unusual for them to accept responsibility for the violence they have experienced (BMFSFJ, 2004, p. 31), often staying in the relationship. Additionally, in line with the "learned helplessness" theory, victims who remain in such violent relationships eventually stop believing that they can escape their perpetrators so that they can develop coping strategies for themselves to stay alive and minimize their suffering (Walker, 2009, pp. 8–9).

The Problem with The Lack of Legal Clarity

Despite its insidious nature, in Germany, DV is not defined under the German Violence Protection Act, or Gewaltschutzgesetz (*GewSchG*) (Thomson Reuters Foundation et al., 2013, p. 124, see also *GewSchG*). The *GewSchG* was enacted as part of the "Act to Improve Civil Jurisdictional Protection against Violent Acts and Stalking and to Ease the Abandonment of the Marital Home in Cases of Separation" (ibid., p. 126). It contains only four sections outlining protection mechanisms and the rights available to victims of "violence". The provisions enable the victim the right to seek protection from the perpetrator, similar to court issued interim protection measures such as legal protection orders or restraining orders in various jurisdictions worldwide. The validity of the court order is limited but can be extended and includes protection measures such as prohibiting the perpetrator from contacting the victim, bringing about a meeting with the victim, and appearing at places where the victim often frequents, in order to maintain physical distance between the victim and the perpetrator (*GewSchG*, Section 1). Penalties for criminal manifestations of DV are covered under the German Criminal Code (*Strafgesetzbuch-StGB*); however, since there is no express legal definition for DV, the acts are criminalized as manifestations of violence and not under any particular context. This causes an added challenge for DV cases by placing the burden of proof on the victim, which can discourage victims from reporting DV incidences since not all DV manifestations are punishable crimes.

In section 1, paragraph 1 of the *GewSchG*, the only given phrase, presumably to define an act of violence (without any context), written as "If a person intentionally violates another person's body, health, and freedom unlawfully, ..." can be loosely interpreted or even misinterpreted due to a lack of clarity. Similarly, this lack of clarity is also exhibited in the German Civil Code (*Bürgerliches Gesetzbuch—BGB*), "If the spouse against whom the application is directed has unlawfully and intentionally injured the body, health or liberty of the other spouse or unlawfully threatened such an injury or injury to life,..." (para. 1361b). Even though a supplementary document has been drawn up by the BMFSFJ, which provided more information along with the definition of the term "violence", while explicit and written, presumably in the context of DV, it is unfortunately not legally binding.

> Violence within the meaning of the Act on Protection against Violence means any unlawful physical assault, impairment to the health of or encroachment on the freedom of another with intent, regardless of whether the acts take place within or outside the context of a joint household. Psychological violence is also covered by the Act on Protection against Violence: explicitly in the case of threats and unreasonable harassment, and indirectly when it has led to psychological or physical impairment to the health of another person.
>
> *BMFSFJ, 2017, p. 11*

If an interpretation of the above were to be made, one can assume that DV is included in the phrase "*regardless of whether the acts take place within or outside the context of a joint household*". While the above definition covers some manifestations of psychological and physical abuse, the actions perpetrated must lead to injury of the body, health, or personal freedom of the victim, which shows that proof must exist, and must be manifested "*with intent*", which is very hard to prove. In any case, bodily injury can be defined as any "unlawful physical assault", psychological abuse can include "threat or unreasonable harassment", and violence can also include "encroachment on the freedom of another".

There is, however, no explicit mention of other manifestations of DV such as sexual violence or economic violence, or even the term "domestic violence". Although such a document can be useful to victims in providing information, regardless of how comprehensive it is, it only acts as a document which provides answers to questions and doubts any person might have regarding the topic of DV, similar to that of a "Q & A" publication. Additionally, elaborations and clarifications can be said to be of procedural in nature. Any interpretation or definition provided in the document is also not legally binding. While soft law publications are considered to be non-legally binding, they can have the potential to aspire standards to become hard law at a later stage. However, as a document that is neither hard—nor soft—law, it has no legal application, except for informational purposes.

This lack of clarity in terminology, especially in legislation, can have adverse legal ramifications, which can be a contributing factor to victims' reporting behaviors. In Frankfurt, in 2019, a 35-year-old woman was reported to have been stabbed 18 times by her former partner, who was later charged with murder and sentenced to life imprisonment (Goldenberg, 2020). While this might be a hoped-for outcome, especially where a DV victim has lost her life, such a verdict is rare. Unfortunately, in many other cases, "German courts are more lenient, passing a verdict for voluntary manslaughter, which carries a sentence of up to ten years". Even though all circumstances are taken into account when deciding a case, judges see the "perpetrators distress as a mitigating circumstance" and often refer back to a 2008 landmark federal case where the court "overturned a lower court's murder verdict and ruled that the defendant had not been malicious in his actions" due to the perceived absence of *mens rea* (motive or criminal intent) for a murder sentence (ibid.).

Burden of Proof as an Obstacle

There are three main routes with a recently available fourth new route in which victims of DV can take in order to enter the intervention system in Germany. The first one begins by the victim actively seeking assistance through a nearest local women's shelter (*Frauenhaus*) or women's counseling center (*Beratungsstelle*). The second route begins when the police is contacted and called to the residence. The third route begins when the victim is actively seeking ways to escape the violence. And finally, the fourth new route begins by having either the victim, or someone concerned about the victim, contacting the 24-hour Telephone Helpline which was recently established by federal law and went into service in March 2013 (Grafe & Hagemann-White, 2015, pp. 2–4). Unfortunately, all routes mentioned above place a high level of responsibility from the victim to come forward herself in order to stop the cycle and liberate herself and her children (if any) from the ordeal (ibid., p. 8). As clarified above in the section explaining how insidious DV truly is, this is not always possible because not all victims will feel empowered to do so, with many preferring to suffer in silence out of fear. Also, many do not know that what they are facing is indeed DV and this level of "normal" violence is further perpetuated in migrant cultures (ibid., pp. 11–15).

Also, in accordance to the *GewSchG*, perpetrators have to leave when the police are called to the residence and violence was found to have occurred. Due to their duty to protect, the police can be viewed as "door openers to the help system" (ibid., p. 7). Police can issue a civil "go-order" to the perpetrator, which becomes a criminal issue once breached (Kury & Smart, 2006, p. 398). However, professional dilemmas arise for the police officers called, due to the uncertainty of whether what had happened was indeed DV or whether they would cause unnecessary disturbance to the family by issuing the "go-order". Further repercussions, both positive and negative, also have to be considered before issuing the "go-order", bearing in mind the safety of the victim and the children, if any (Grafe & Hagemann-White, 2015, p. 16). Additionally, the length and level of enforcement of the "go-order" varies regionally in the different *Bundesländer* (states) in the country (ibid., p. 7), making for an unstandardized protection mechanism for victims.

For the valid and more serious DV cases, criminal prosecution, however, is not always possible due to the lack of evidence or the unwillingness of the victim to testify (ibid., p. 21). This route also places the added pressure on the victims, requiring their further cooperation to go through the justice system which can take a long time from start to finish. Additionally, prosecution also almost always only ends up in monetary penalties, often at the cost of the victim where she ends up paying for the violence, gets back with her perpetrator, and the cycle begins again (ibid., p. 23).

Unsustainable Network of Systems

In Germany, there is a heavy reliance on a national network of organizations in providing aid as laid out in the National Action Plan II to combat DV/GBV, with more than 130 measures in various areas (ibid., p. 5). However, due to the multiple lines of coordination, reporting structures have become "lost" and it becomes no longer clear who or which organization or authority is responsible for the upkeep and functioning of these support providers (Office of the United Nations High Commissioner for Human Rights [OHCHR], 2017), making these intervention systems unsustainable and unmanageable in the long-run due to the high dependency on the building and maintenance of these system of networks (Grafe & Hagemann-White, 2015, p. 6).

Germany was commended for achieving legislative progress through the amendment of section of the German Criminal Code (*Strafgesetzbuch—StGB*) and for improvement efforts in eliminating discrimination against women through the creation of the "*Hilfetelefon – Gewalt gegen Frauen*" a national VAW support telephone hotline in 2013 (UN Doc CEDAW/C/DEU/CO/7-8, 2017, Paras. 4a, 5e). More recently, in order to address the rising numbers in DV cases, further exacerbated by the Covid-19 pandemic, a website was created to increase awareness and provide online resources and support to victims (Brady, 2020). However, as mentioned in the above section, the system places a high burden on the victim to come forward and to prove that she was indeed a victim of DV.

In situations where victims (and her children, if any) engage in the intervention system through counseling and manages to escape to a shelter, logistical challenges emerge. For instance, the victim's location must be kept hidden in order to protect her. However, some institutional processes and procedures have unfortunately left paper-trails, allowing her to be located and at risk for further violence by her perpetrator (Grafe & Hagemann-White, 2015, p. 17). Counselors and social workers are also faced with the dilemma in their approach to empowering the victims because of the direct risk to the victims' safety in the event the perpetrators discover that assistance has been provided in cases where a victim has been put in touch with a counselor (ibid., p. 20).

Often, if a DV victim has suffered bodily injuries, she will go to the hospital or a doctor to seek some form of medical treatment. This normally would theoretically enable health-care professionals to intervene. However, due to the code of confidentiality being extremely strong in the area of health care, victims might only be provided with information and encouraged to seek help, if the hospital belongs to a network referral system. However, if the hospital is not part of such a system, victims will only be treated of their injuries and no other forms of assistance outside the line of health care will be provided (ibid., pp. 4–5). Other times, some health-care professionals decline to even ask the victims out of their own personal reservations (Ibid., p. 20).

Despite the severe need, many women's shelters (*Frauenhäuser*) in Germany still remain underfunded with bed shortages (OHCHR, 2017), resulting in many women victims being rejected due to a lack of space. According to the previous German Family Minister Franziska

Giffey, as of 2019, there are only 350 women's shelter nationwide, further announcing that the "government will spend €30 million each year over the next four years toward increasing the capacity of women's refuge shelters" (DW, 2019). Seeking refuge at a women's shelter is considered to be one of the oldest and often, the only route for many DV victims (Grafe & Hagemann-White, 2015, p. 4), making the continued existence and upkeep of these shelters not only out of necessity, but also a legal obligation, as highlighted in the Report of the Special Rapporteur on VAW (UN Doc A/HRC/35/30, 2017, para. 19).

As mentioned, the 24-hour Telephone Helpline went into service in March 2013. It is "an around-the clock, multilingual and anonymous advisory service that helps callers to find local support facilities". This process involves the caller, who can be the victim herself, or her family, friends, and can even be organizations who the victim has been directly turning to and confiding in, making the call. The caller "will be given advice and referred to appropriate sources of help in the area where they live" (Grafe & Hagemann-White, 2015, p. 4). This has been reportedly "well received by victims of violence, their friends and relatives, and professionals" (UN Doc CEDAW/C/DEU/Q/7-8/Add.1, 2017, Para. 47). However, it was highlighted that violence is not stopped just by making one anonymous phone call since the central responsibility still lies on the victim to seek intervention and follow through with the recommendations provided. The BMFSFJ also launched the "*Stärker als Gewalt*" (Stronger than Violence) website in November 2019, first and foremost to provide information and support to the affected, in hopes of empowering victims. Nonetheless, further impacts remain to be seen.

Migrant Community—A Community Left Behind?

According to the CEDAW Committee report titled "*Consideration of reports submitted by States parties under article 18 of the Convention seventh and eighth periodic reports of States parties due in 2014 Germany*," "...many migrant women do not appear to benefit from measures against domestic violence or to receive information about possible protection..." (UN Doc CEDAW/C/DEU/7-8, 2015, para. 129). DV victims coming from migrant backgrounds face several added challenges. Some of the basic challenges include language barriers, not knowing what their rights are whilst in Germany, and a lack of familiarity in understanding the German legal system. They are also unfamiliar with the existing intervention and support systems, causing many of them to resort to suffering in silence because DV is also considered the norm in their culture. Aside from the "regular" integration courses, the Federal Government funds special low threshold courses (women courses) directed toward migrant women who have a permanent residence title as part of the National Action Plan II. These courses aim to empower migrant women "to fulfill their function as bridges between their families and society" by addressing DV protection and prevention topics; however, due to their sensitive nature, an "atmosphere of trust" is needed, an environment that takes years to build, a component that is missing despite trainers being fully trained and qualified (ibid., paras. 191 192).

Additional to the basic challenges, migrant victims really have their hands tied. In accordance with Article 78 (2) of the Istanbul Convention, a State Party is legally allowed to make reservations to certain provisions of the Convention. Of relevance specifically to the migrant DV victims, making a reservation not to apply Article 59, paragraphs 2 and 3 (Council of Europe [CoE], n.d.), can be interpreted as the possibility that these DV victims can be expelled from Germany if the women have been married for less than three years to their perpetrator husbands. Due to the difference in German law between obtaining residence permits for family reasons and humanitarian grounds, the burden of proof also rests on the woman to prove that she needs to stay in the country on humanitarian grounds (Atmaca, 2017, pp. 20–21). Unfortunately, through these reservations, migrant DV victims are presented with very limited choices, mostly ending up with them staying with their perpetrator husbands and to tolerate the situation until the three-year marriage rule has been met.

This is further aggravated by the fact that violence is considered "normal" in their *home* culture. Because DV acts often occur inside of the home, the lack of witnesses and substantial proof also contribute to law enforcement officers' refusal to get involved, and especially in cases where migrant communities are involved, they are viewed as a waste of time since such behaviors are inherently part of their culture which they have brought with them (Menjívar & Salcido, 2002, p. 901).

DV during Covid-19

The ongoing pandemic has had far-reaching consequences and its effects have permeated all levels of society. In the context of DV and SGBV in Germany, the lockdown measures—which can be argued to have lasted for quite a significant amount of time (from a hard lockdown in the beginning of the crisis, to lockdown light over some months in 2020, and later to reimpose restrictions again post-Christmas 2020)—have led to local shelters and counseling centers voicing their fears of increased DV, pointing toward "stressful circumstances in the home" contributed by loss of income and working from home as the cause (Brady, 2020). In a 2020 quantitative study led by Dr. Janina Steinert, Professor of Global Health at the Technical University of Munich (TUM) and Dr. Cara Ebert of the RWI, Leibniz Institute for Economic Research,

> around 3 percent of women in Germany were subject to physical violence at home during the strict lockdown period and 3.6 percent were raped by their partner... In cases where women were in quarantine or families suffered from financial insecurity, the figures were significantly higher. Only a very small percentage of the women concerned made use of support services.
>
> *TUM, 2020*

The study also highlighted financial insecurity as a top risk factor, further trapping DV victims with their abuser. For refugees and asylum seekers, violence can be further amplified during Covid-19; coupled with immigration uncertainty, these women are often isolated and at increased risk of becoming DV victims.

Concluding Remarks

Explicit legal protection is imperative to safeguard the human rights of DV victims. However, the "weakening" of legislation can not only hamper the application of any provision at the time of implementation but also negatively impact reporting behaviors. Additionally, while civic remedies and actors play an important role in combating DV, any disconnect or disorganization within the network system, as well as unresolved practical challenges can also lead to negative reporting behaviors. For DV victims of migrant backgrounds, especially when violence is considered "normal", the stakes are much higher.

Throughout the sections, one constant remains—there is a profound need to empower the DV victims themselves in order to seek assistance since the "help system" relies on them actively seeking it in order for them to be protected. However, due to the complexed nature of DV, victims are often not always easily empowered. Many have extremely low self-esteem and for victims of migrant communities, adding the element of culture further complicates the issue, contributing to existing negative reporting behaviors. Along with legal and practical challenges, as examined in the previous sections, victims of migrant communities may have less incentive to seek help through civic means, let alone institutional means.

There is much improvement needed for Germany within the DV space, beginning with the legal framework. Unfortunately, there seems to still be a gap in implementation which leads to negative reporting behavior. By looking at all aspects and facets of DV, it is now understood that this is a crime which requires an interdisciplinary lens. This is especially important in cases of DV within the migrant communities where culture plays a huge role in creating a DV conducive environment, which distorts the reality for many DV victims, an aspect which this chapter has intentionally left out due to space constraints, and more importantly, it deserves an entire chapter alone. From the legal perspective, not having an express legal definition leads to subjective interpretations, misinterpretations, and high threshold to prosecute DV cases. From a civic intervention perspective, the network of system is unmanageable, unsustainable, and not "friendly" enough to empower survivors.

Just like a domino effect, it leads to negative reporting behavior, which leads to low reporting rates, because DV victims simply do not have enough confidence in the existing system, legal and civic support alike. Through an in-depth analysis of existing national laws, prevention and civic intervention programs, as well as the operationalization and implementation of both laws and intervention programs, a clearer picture has been painted. DV victims of migrant communities continue to face various challenges which ultimately led to negative reporting behaviors. From this point on, moving forward, any updates to the framework, legal or otherwise, need to be designed with the goal of promoting positive reporting behavior since the aspects that promoted negative reporting behavior have thus been established.

According to a 2018 World Bank report, it is "estimated that three regions (Latin America, sub-Saharan Africa, and Southeast Asia) will generate 143 million more climate migrants by 2050". Even though climate change and DV/SGBV may not be directly related, the climate-migration nexus is real. This would mean that DV/SGBV the protection framework has to be improved and adapted to be culturally sensitive in order to prevent negative reporting behavior especially from DV victims of migrant backgrounds. Further research is also recommended to understand civic populations' perceptions of DV, particularly those with migrant backgrounds, paving way for better long-term prevention and intervention strategies.

References

Atmaca, D. (2017, November 25). *Eröffnungsrede der Vorsitzenden Dr. Delal Atmaca: Migrantinnen* auch! Nein zu Gewalt an Migrantinnen* und geflüchteten Frauen*!* in DaMigra #MITOO Conference on International Abolishing Violence Against Women Day (Frankfurt am Main, Germany). Retrieved 20 June 2020 from www.damigra.de/publikationen/.

BMFSFJ. (n.d.). *Stärker als Gewalt.* https://staerker-als-gewalt.de/.

BMFSFJ. (2004). *Health, Well Being and Personal Safety of Women – A Representative Study of Violence against Women in Germany.* (Berlin, Summer 2004, reprint November 2006). Retrieved 18 June 2020 from www.bmfsfj.de/blob/93906/9c0076fc66b1be6d0eb28258fe0aa569/frauenstudie-englisch gewalt-gegen-frauen-data.pdf.

BMFSFJ. (2007, November 28). *Second Action Plan of the Federal Government to Combat Violence Against Women.* Retrieved 18 June 2020 from www.bmfsfj.de/blob/93226/82b46beb83664de4234c49a05cd89132/aktionsplan-ii-gewalt-gegen-frauen-englisch-data.pdf.

BMFSFJ. (2017, August). *Greater Protection in Cases of Domestic Violence – Information on the Act on Protection Against Violence.* (Berlin, last updated April 2019, 5th Edition), Retrieved 18 June 2020 from www.bmfsfj.de/blob/121760/b227b8b02448a576045c444efe81b792/mehr-schutz-bei-haeuslicher-gewalt-englisch-data.pdf.

Brady, K. (2020, March 19). Coronavirus: Fears of domestic violence, child abuse rise. *Deutsche Welle*. Retrieved 19 June 2020 from www.dw.com/en/coronavirus-fears-of-domestic-violence-child-abuse-rise/a-52847759.

Bundesministerium für Familie, Senioren, Frauen und Jugend (BMFSFJ – German Federal Ministry for Family Affairs, Senior Citizens, Women and Youth). (2009, July). *Gesundheit – Gewalt – Migration – Kurzfassung' in 'Gesundheit-Gewalt-Migration: Eine vergleichende Sekundäranalyse zur gesundheitlichen und Gewaltsituation von Frauen mit und ohne Migrationshintergrund in Deutschland*. Retrieved 18 June 2020 from www.bmfsfj.de/blob/93964/588d6d5da075d2803f8696dfbbe3d35c/gesundheit-gewalt-migration-langfassung-studie-data.pdf.

Bürgerliches Gesetzbuch (BGB). (1896). www.gesetze-im-internet.de/bgb/BGB.pdf.

Council of Europe (CoE). (n.d.). *Reservations and Declarations for Treaty No.210–Council of Europe Convention on Preventing and Combating Violence against Women and Domestic Violence*. Retrieved 17 June 2020 from www.coe.int/en/web/conventions/full-list/-/conventions/treaty/210/declarations?p_auth=JpC28t4f.

Deutsche-Presse Agentur (DPA) & The Local DE. (2020, November 25). Domestic violence on the rise in Germany with one woman killed every three days. *The Local DE*. Retrieved 19 June 2020 from www.thelocal.de/20191125/domestic-violence-against-women-increasing-in-germany.

Deutsche Welle (DW). (2019, November 25). Germany: 1 woman per hour is victim of domestic violence. *DW*. Retrieved 14 October 2021 from www.dw.com/en/germany-1-woman-per-hour-is-victim-of-domestic-violence/a-51396638.

European Agency for Fundamental Rights (FRA). (2014, April). *Violence Against Women: An EU-wide Survey*. Retrieved 24 June 2018 from http://fra.europa.eu/en/publication/2014/violence-against-women-eu-wide-survey-main-results-report.

Ganley, A. L. (1995). *Understanding Domestic Violence: Preparatory Reading for Participants* in Domestic Violence: A National Curriculum for Family Preservation Practitioners, Family Violence Prevention Fund. Retrieved 18 June 2020 from https://andvsa.org/wp-content/uploads/2009/12/60-ganely-general-dv-article.pdf.

Gesetz zum zivilrechtlichen Schutz vor Gewalttaten und Nachstellungen (Gewaltschutzgesetz – GewSchG). (2001). www.gesetze-im-internet.de/gewschg/GewSchG.pdf.

Goldenberg, R. (2020, November 25). Germany sees high numbers in femicide. *Deutsche Welle (DW)*. Retrieved 14 October 2021 from www.dw.com/en/germany-sees-high-numbers-in-femicide/a-55555702.

Grafe, B. & Hagemann-White, C. (2015, January). *Working Paper on Intervention Against Domestic Violence in Germany, from the Research Project "Cultural Encounters in Intervention Against Violence" (CEINAV)*. Retrieved 17 June 2020 from www.londonmet.ac.uk/media/london-metropolitan-university/london-met-documents/faculties/faculty-of-social-sciences-and-humanities/research/child-and-woman-abuse-studies-unit/ceinav/DV-working-paper-DE-final.pdf.

Kury, H. & Smartt, U. (2006). Domestic violence: Recent developments in German and English legislation and law enforcement. *European Journal of Crime, Criminal Law and Criminal Justice*. 14 (4). 382–407. Retrieved 18 June 2020 from http://ursulasmartt.com/pdf/Kury-Smartt.Dom.Viol.EurJourn.Dec06.pdf.

Lee-Winter, F. (2017). *Why Domestic Violence Remains Under-Reported: A Case for Migrant Communities in Germany* (Master's thesis, Ruhr-Universität Bochum, Global Campus Europe-EMA). Global Campus Open Knowledge Repository. https://doi.org/20.500.11825/891.

Menjívar, C. & Salcido, O. (2002). Immigrant women and domestic violence: Common experiences in different countries. *Gender & Society*. 16 (6), 898–920.

Podesta, J. (2019, July 25). The climate crisis, migration, and refugees. *Brookings*. Retrieved 14 October 2021 from www.brookings.edu/research/the-climate-crisis-migration-and-refugees/.

Reuters. (2021, April 15). Pandemic deters thieves, fuels domestic violence, German police say. *Reuters*. Retrieved 14 October 2021 from www.reuters.com/world/europe/pandemic-deters-thieves-fuels-domestic-violence-german-police-say-2021-04-15/.

Schmollack, S. (2017). *Und er wird es wider tun: Gewalt in her Partnerschaft*. Frankfurt-am-Main, Westend Publishing, 248.

Strafgesetzbuch (StGB). (1871). www.gesetze-im-internet.de/stgb/StGB.pdf.

Technische Universität München. (2020, June 3). Domestic violence during the coronavirus pandemic. *Research-in-Germany*. Retrieved 14 October 2021 from www.research-in-germany.org/news/2020/6/2020-06-03_Domestic_violence_during_the_coronavirus_pandemic.html.

The Highland Council. (2010, August). *Responding to Violence Against Women – Multi-Agency Guidelines for Staff Highland Community Planning Partnership*. Retrieved 19 June 2020 from www.womenssupportproject.co.uk/userfiles/file/VAW%20Multi-Agency%20Guidance.doc.

The Local DE. (2017, May 11). Germany 'grossly' failing female refugees on sexual violence: report. *The Local DE*. Retrieved 18 June 2020 from www.thelocal.de/20170511/report-finds-wide-spread-sexual-violence-against-refugee-women-in-berlin.

Thomson Reuters Foundation et al. (2013, December). *A Landscape Analysis of Domestic Violence Laws*. Retrieved 19 June 2020 from www.trust.org/contentAsset/raw-data/02bf55c6-0d6b-4799-b9ba-eab57c5b93a9/file.

Tuerkheimer, D. (2004). Recognizing and remedying the harm of battering: A call to criminalize domestic violence. *Journal of Criminal Law and Criminology*. 94 (4), 959–1032.

UN CEDAW Committee. (2015, October 21). *Consideration of Reports Submitted by States Parties under Article 18 of the Convention Seventh and Eighth Periodic Reports of States Parties due in 2014 Germany*. UN Doc CEDAW/C/DEU/7-8.

UN CEDAW Committee. (2017, January 11). *List of Issues and Questions in Relation to the Combined Seventh and Eighth 151 Periodic Reports of Germany – Addendum, Replies of Germany*. UN Doc CEDAW/C/DEU/Q/7-8/Add.1.

UN Human Rights Council (UNHRC). (2017, June 13). *Report of the Special Rapporteur on Violence against Women, Its Causes and Consequences*. 35th 166 Session, Item No. 3. UN Doc A/HRC/35/30.

United Nations Committee for the Elimination of All Forms of Discrimination against Women (UN CEDAW Committee). (2017, March 9). *Concluding Observations on the Combined Seventh and Eighth Periodic Reports of Germany*. UN Doc CEDAW/C/DEU/CO/7-8.

United Nations Office of the High Commissioner (OHCHR). (n.d.). Retrieved 20 June 2020 from https://tbinternet.ohchr.org/_layouts/15/TreatyBodyExternal/Countries.aspx?%20CountryCode=DEU&Lang=EN.

UN OHCHR. (2017, February 20). *CEDAW Discusses Situation of Women in Germany, Sri Lanka, Rwanda and Micronesia with Civil Society Representatives*. Retrieved 18 June 2020 from www.ohchr.org/en/NewsEvents/Pages/DisplayNews.aspx?NewsID=21208&LangID=E.

United Nations Treaty Collections (UNTC). Retrieved 14 May 2020 from https://treaties.un.org/Pages/Treaties.aspx?id=4&subid=A&clang=_en.

United Nations Women. (n.d.). Facts and figures: Ending violence against women various forms of violence. *UN Women Website*. Retrieved 12 May 2020 from www.unwomen.org/en/what-we-do/ending-violence-against-women/facts-and-figures.

Walker, L. (2009). *The Battered Woman Syndrome*. 3rd Edition, New York, Springer Publishing Company.

23

RITUALIZED EXPERIENCES OF PAIN

Love and Domestic Violence among Transgender Women in Brazil

Thiago de Lima Oliveira and Verônica Alcântara Guerra

Introduction

Sited in a plastic chair outside the salon where she worked, Michelle said: "perhaps love isn't like in a soap opera, huh? I guess things are more complicated at home and in everyday life, especially for people like us". The conversation happened two years after we met, and it was the very first time she felt comfortable to talk about her family relationship. After a long description of life in the community where she came from, she said that and concluded: "family is such a complicated thing, there is a lot of love involved in hurt".

Like many trans women, Michelle left her parents' home at a very young age. As used to say, she was not expelled home but did not felt welcome. At the time, she used to be assaulted, humiliated and harassed. When left home, she was 16, uncompleted elementary school and had no professional experience. Living with her family was conflictive. Because of her being "sissy" and "effeminate", she had the long black hair cut by her siblings in public. Despite describing it as a humiliating situation, she told the story in a joking tone, even laughing in certain parts of it. The situation was not different from boyfriends and male partners she lived with. Passion and pain mixed into abusive and turbulent relationships combining what could be described as violent and caring.

In this text, we shall reflect on Brazilian response to domestic violence. The perspective of analysis is on the protective mechanisms as they are experienced by trans women. We aim to glimpse how the protective mechanisms were developed and how they establish inclusion and exclusion relations based on forms of categorization involving the understanding of what it is to be a woman.

It is used trans women as a category to circumscribe transgender women and travestis, that is, people who identify with a female gender identity despite an arbitrary social signing. In Brazil, cisgenerity and transgenerity work as markers to think about the relationships between forms of gender and body perception. So, it is a grammar that organizes meanings related to design of bodies, gender identity and social notions of personhood. Cisgender people are those who recognize themselves in a relationship of continuity and conformity with the body, gender and social identity that has been socially assigned to them since birth. Transgender people are those who do not recognize themselves within this grammar and trigger another social and gender identity, eventually performing forms of body intervention. Due to the complex class stratification, trans women can recognize themselves as travesti or transsexuals (Kulick, 1998).

The data presented come from experiences of ethnographic research in two contexts: the Amazonian border and the Brazilian northeast coast collected between 2010 and 2018. It is

DOI: 10.4324/9781003264040-28

presented here considering theories on gender, social suffering and domestic violence. In the first part of the text, we present the trajectories of two subjects. After we describe the responses built by the Brazilian state to deal with domestic violence against women. In the end, we argue how these responses relate to transgender women.

On Love and Pain

When we met, Suzy was 23 and lived in a small rented house a few meters away from her parents, in a small town on the northeast coast of Brazil. She worked at night, as a sex worker in a federal highway that crosses the city where she lived in. Her partner was a season construction worker, and Suzy was responsible for the domestic finances. Fights were usual in her life, besides verbal assaults, and a jealous behavior she described as proof of how much he loved her. Living together by three years, the situation became to a point she had no friends or used to visit the family anymore due to her partner restrictions. His jealous attitudes came to a point he threw a brick at her during a fight, injuring her at her arms and breast.

After being assaulted Suzy stay at home for one week. When we finally met, she told about the story laughing, as it was part of a joke. We asked her if she went to the police station to report her partner, which she answered no. Suzy had been in police stations a few times before, usually for conflicts created with clients. She knew that the police station was a hostile environment for "people like me", that is, trans women, especially black and poor. So, we inquired her "but do you know about your rights? About Maria da Penha law and that you can report any aggression, don't you?". To that she said only "that is for women, not for us".

Suzy was a black trans woman and was expelled from home at the age of 17. After that, she was received by other trans friends who sheltered her and gave her food. After that, she started to work as a prostitute to make some money and rented a small house in a poor area of the municipality, close to her parents. The relation with her family started to be better since she used to give them gifts and pay some bills for them. Violence and dependence were part of Suzy perception of love. Once she said: "as a family, we need to be kind and support each other, even with our differences".

Situations like Michelles' story tells about how domestic violence is entangled to gender violence. The experiences of being humiliated, abused or assaulted at home or by people someone live with are part of the same process. As a result, it creates a complex environment where affects, pain and dependence constitute the ideas of love, pain, home and relatives. State's responses need to cope with these layers of meaning framing the experience of domestic violence and its subtle differentiation among each woman context.

Domestic violence is a broad category operating as a way of describing experiences of oppression and, as well, as a legal category to typify crimes. The international definition adopted by the World Health Organization and by the Istanbul Convention guide that domestic violence should be understood as a form of violation of the dignity and personality of persons subjected to domestic coexistence. It is assumed that, in their multiplicity of forms, such violence is organized mainly based on gender and generational factors. In this respect, most of the victims of domestic violence are women and girls (WHO, 2013).

However, the correlation between domestic violence and gender tends to conceal how gender relates to other categories of social differentiation. In cases like Brazil's, violence and precariousness are structured from a very long colonial history that has its effects on the lives of women and men. This internal differentiation of gender is hardly considered in the legal system or by policymakers (Crenshaw, 1991), especially to fixed forms of identity as the standard of legal form (Butler, 1999). The correlation between forms of organization of meanings that compose subjects is central and should include a reflection on class, race, sexuality, body and gender identity to understand how violence is structured (Collins, 2017) and lived in everyday life (Kilomba, 2008).

The intersectional analysis is an important tool for understanding how forms of violence and mechanisms of oppression are articulated, and likewise for evaluating instruments of confrontation (Collins & Bilge, 2016).

The contemporary context on gender violence struggles with two major aspects. On one hand, it is necessary to consider the intersectional dimensions in which violence is experienced and elaborated. On other hand, given the environmental catastrophe we are living in, it is important to have an agenda of research and political intervention in order to understand the intimate relations between domestic violence and climate change. Nowadays, the public response on domestic violence is guided by legal principles as well as the emphasis on education as a critical project of social justice. That said, domestic violence as understood today corresponds to a large number of processes during the colonization process regarding to the practices of owning and controlling between the colonizers and the colonized. In other words, the effect of such a complex process must be understood as an effect of the attempt to control certain bodies as well certain environments.

If, as Butler (2006) points out, precariousness is part of our human condition but differently distributed between different classes of people, the effects of colonization and climate change in contemporary societies are quite different too. Neoliberal and modern practices of development make women in developing countries more vulnerable to certain conditions in a context where the environment and the gendered body are under appreciation. Given the slavery heritage and white supremacy ideologies, this appreciation condemns racialized, gendered bodies as well as LGBTQIAP+ subjectivities differently when compared to white straight men used to be. These other bodies are subject to the violence in its many forms since verbal insults to the effects of climate changes in the daily life. Domestic violence is both the result of conflictive gender and sexuality relations, as suggested by the histories above, and the result of systemic injustices over time.

Death is the ultimate experience in the broad and complex cycle of suffering. This cycle includes the experience of affection followed by humiliation, verbal assaults, financial dependence, harassment, blackmailing and other forms of female isolation. According to data from the Brazilian Ministry of Health, 67% of the cases of physical violence registered in 2017 victimized women. Women account for only 8% of homicide cases but were victims in 89% of rape cases (IPEA, 2018). Even though women are a small percentage of the victims of homicide, there is an increasing rate of feminicide in the general context of the homicide of women. According to the Brazilian Forum of Public Security, in 2017, it was 23.6% and 29.4% in 2018. Most of these crimes happened in a domestic context (65.5%) and were committed by partners (88.8%) as analyzed by Pereira et al (2020). This general experience is a showcase of the inequality structure that organizes women and men experiences of suffering and violence.

If men and women have different relations with violence in Brazil, this is even more complex when considered transgender women and men. Life expectation of trans women in Brazil is about 35 years, while among cisgender people it is around 76. As pointed by Amparo (2019), there is a general situation of invisibility in the accountability of data related to violence against LGBTQIAP+ people. It affects especially trans women due to the continuous exposition to violence and death throughout their life. Most of the murder crimes against trans women are not identified as "feminicide" neither "homophobia", which are the legal categories available in the Brazilian law. Overall, 54% of the victims were black trans women, and 49% had been assaulted at their own home. So, the questions are: what is the Brazilian response to domestic violence against women and how trans women relate to this?

Brazilian Response to Domestic Violence against Women

The Brazilian State's response to domestic violence against women is based on laws protecting children and the actions of organized feminist groups. The debates that led to the formulation of such policies have as their main recent milestone the process of redemocratization at the end of the 1980s and take its current form in the early 1990s with laws protecting the sexual abuse of girls and children. In the 2000s, domestic violence was characterized as a crime in the Penal Code, and in the following years, legal forms were produced to curb and punish gender-based violence against women.

The responses offered by government actions have two particularities that must be explored. The first is that they were established from local experiences of relative success. The second is the articulation with forms of women's organization in social movements and non-governmental organizations in the context of the fight against gender violence. There is also a third aspect that connects both instances, which is the history of almost five decades of research on gender and violence in Brazil (see Grossi, 2006; Pontes, 2018).

Regarded to the first particularity, it is necessary to emphasize that the model of Women's Police Station (so-called DEAM or DDM in Portuguese, henceforth WPS) was developed in local contexts before becoming a policy in all the states of the federation. The first WPS were created in 1985 in the federated state of São Paulo. At that time, there was 6 WPS across the state of São Paulo. In the same year, other 5 WPS were created in other capitals (Belo Horizonte, Curitiba, Recife, Cuiabá and Florianopolis), and more 14 in 1986. However, it should be noted that in the context of police stations, Brazil registers an enormous disparity of conditions. Currently, 36% of the WPS are in the state of São Paulo. In many federated states, the volume WPS is insufficient to attend to the population, and many of them have problems of functioning and structure. In 2006, the law 11.340 was published and the police districts became part of a broader structure with the Courts of Domestic and Family Violence against Women. Only in 2010 was a protocol established to standardize the police stations, through a technical standard edited by the Ministry of Justice (Brazil, 2010).

WPS constitutes one of the main axes of confrontation to domestic violence against women. It is the result of the junction between state debates and the pressures placed by the feminist movement and organized civil society. In this sense, it is highlighted the action of important political players, especially NGO, such as SOS Corpo, SOS Mulher, Instituto Patrícia Galvão and others that have action linked to the different regional contexts (Bonetti, 2007).

The creation of the Secretariat of Policies for Women was important for the consolidation of policies to confront domestic violence against women. This Secretariat was created in 2003 as a special area within the Ministry of Justice responsible for the formulation and application of policies on gender equity and combating violence. Through the secretariat was established a closer dialogue between States and civil society including from women's movements and NGOs in policy formulation. It was also from it that the National Policy to Combat Violence against Women was established in 2003, and forms of interlocution that were guided by the proximity between society and the State, such as the Conference on Women's Policy, held for the first time in 2003.

Legislation concerning to domestic violence against women was published only after 2006 in Brazil. Before that, crimes used to be persecuted with no consideration to gender specificities, except in cases like rape and child abuse. After the 2003, other legal measures were formulated and adopted, such as the compulsory notification of physical assaults in public health services in cases of violence against women (Law 10.788/2004). However, only in 2004, domestic violence is categorized as crime in the Brazilian penal code (Law 10.886/2004). According to the new text, domestic violence is considered "injury to an ascendant, descendant, brother, spouse or partner, or to those who live or have lived with, or the agent of domestic relations, cohabitation or hospitality prevails" (Brazil, 2004).

Currently, two major legal tools to combat domestic violence against women are the Maria da Penha law (published in 2006) and the law of feminicide (published in 2015). Both aims to provide definitions of what should be considered a crime establish responsibilities and penalties to the aggressor.

The so-called Maria da Penha law creates the measure to combat domestic and familial violence against women. It is based on three main assumptions: (a) the relation between gender-based and domestic violence; (b) violence against women is a violation of human rights; and (c) the concept of violence itself. It conceptualizes violence as any form of assault, psychological, moral, sexual, patrimonial and physical damage committed against women. It also expands the relational context of violence considering people who shared a commonplace, even if seasonal, and family as an affect-based relation, not only those of consanguinity. In that sense, there is a redefinition on how to prosecute cases of domestic violence against women considering the gender-based specificities and the very reason of what should be understood as "domestic" and "familiar".

The results observed in the application of the Maria da Penha law were positive, at least in the first years (Pasinato, 2010). They offered a legal attendance and prescription for crimes and punishments. However, during its implementation, gaps and problems were observed. These gaps were related to issues that the law did not consider by not analyzing social reality in its most complex dimension (relations between gender and class, for example). And in turn, the deficient structure of the state, such as the lack of training of police officers to receive and deal with victims of violence (Lins, 2014; Melo, 2008).

The feminicide law was published in 2015 to correct the gaps identified in the Maria da Penha Law. According to the new law, feminicide must be understood as the homicide against women because of her gender. It is considered when the context includes expression of hate against women or domestic and familial violence. Thus, it seeks to establish stricter forms of punishment for hate crimes or those motivated by gender.

Silence and Jokes: Coping with the Pain

The main responses adopted by the Brazilian state aimed at the adoption of punitive measures. This occurs by establishing criminal types and forms of punishment that are important for the confrontation of domestic violence against women. Nevertheless, in its execution, it is perceptible that the first and main instance of reception is still oppressive for women. The police station is not an inviting space, and part of this may be related to the masculine basic aspect that involves police work and illustrated by continuous reports of bad reception to victims of violence. It is especially oppressive for trans women who need to face the institutional sexism and transphobia by the police officers.

Moreover, there is uncertainty if the measures available will be adopted in her cases. As Suzy argued, the law seems not fit "for us". In this sense, it is important to note that in contemporary Brazil many of the laws to protect the trans community came not from the legislative, but Supreme Court. In June of 2019, for example, the Supreme Court considered homophobia and transphobia as varieties of the crime of racism. The decision was made considering the omission of the legislative to analyze projects regarded to the criminalization of homophobia and transphobia. Still in this context, in 2019, the National Forum of Judges of Domestic and Family Violence against Women (FONAVID) decided that the Maria da Penha law should be applied to trans women, even if they had not undergone procedures of genital reassignment or civil name change (CNJ, 2019).

Despite recommendations such as that of FONAVID, the decision is not binding and used to be subject to individual decisions on a case-by-case basis until April 2022, when the Court decided that, as legal device, Maria da Penha law must be applied to all women, no matter their sexuality or gender identity. Since the enactment of the Maria da Penha and feminicide laws, cases of greater prominence have eventually recorded the characterization of crimes from these measures. In most cases, the decision remains by silencing, or by general characterization as a homicide.

The result of this silencing or omission in law enforcement is a ritual of suffering. Michelle, in telling us how she deals with family aggressions, describes it with the expression "one day at a time", an expression also found in Suzy's response. There is a ritualized experience of suffering that begins with the aggressions and is perpetuated in institutional spaces. Suzy does not feel good about having to go to the police station for the experiences of mistreatment she had in previous situations. She prefers the omission to have to deal with a new layer of pain.

As Das (2007) recalls, violence tensions the very frontier of language and the human. There are deep silences that separate who can claim to be human and under what conditions. In the case of Suzy and Michelle, this is done not only through silence, but also through play. There are circumstances in which laughter allows the daily experience of communicating pain. There are others where the senses of affection cannot go beyond silence. In both cases, there is a temporality in which the pain persists and continues.

Michelle and Suzy's experiences traduce how pain is legible and verbalized only under certain way. Due to most of their narratives came from intimate relations with relatives, intimate partners and friends, the experiences of pain are ritualized in both silencing and joking spaces since it is not allowed to code as "violence". As argued by Das (2007) in her ethnographic account on critical events, the silence is a way to cope with the continued exposition to pain, danger and death people experienced. Among trans women, to transform pain into jokes and comic stories is a way to share information about critical situations. Through these strategies, there is the idea that love is something to considerate when conceptualizing if an experience is "violence" or not. Moreover, violent-conceptualized experiences need to face the bureaucratic and embarrassing institutional trajectories in which their gender identity and narratives are suspicious. These ritualized experiences of pain are continued bureaucratic, institutional and intimate relations that entangle suffering and gender in transgender women's daily life.

Locked Down in Pain

Surveys conducted since the beginning of the pandemic point to a direct increase in cases of domestic violence. It is a result not only of the greater coexistence among people who make up the domestic nucleus, by the increase in emotional tensions that isolation produces, but also fundamentally because sexism functions as an organizing language of social structures. In Brazil, this situation repeated. The resulting situations of vulnerability take two forms. The first marks the overload of domestic work and the care of others, exposing women and girls to micro aggressions and violence. These situations are common especially in the context of extended families sharing the same space due to financial constraints. A second case is the inability to access channels of support and care, or even the cultivation of interpersonal relationships due to exogamous marriage patterns, where there is a distance between partners and former families.

When it comes to transgender women, these dynamics have other forms. In the first case, micro aggressions are the result of financial constraints due to the reduction of work, as Michelle told us in a conversation in the first months of the pandemic. Access to public services was already a problem. According to her, situation became worse since the lack of work, reduction of income and the family regroup activated pre-existing conflicts. Broadly, it is illustrated by statistical increase of violence against the trans community. Between March and April 2020, there were 26 cases of homicides, and 25 in May and June. It was 89 deaths in total just at the first semester of 2020, representing a 39% increase over the previous year. In the same period, were registered 14 cases of suicide, according to the National Association of Transgender and Travestis (ANTRA, 2020).

The Brazilian government's responses to the health crisis were not enough resulting in its position in the podium of death cases by covid-19. If the health and social welfare system were remarkable and strong until the mid-2010s, since 2016 it has been weakened due to political instabilities and neoliberal projects. As a result, the communities most vulnerable by the pandemic were those most in contact with the demand for public health and shelter services. Michelle and Suzy both received BRL 600 in support from the federal government that allowed for subsistence and food maintenance. Besides the payment being less than half a salary, it was paid only to two persons living in the same registered address, thus producing what Suzy described as "a fight to see who needed it more". Pain and death were always lurking in their lives as transgender women in a country known for its brutal treatment of its community. However, before there was the possibility of running. In September 2020, while hospitalized with covid-19, Suzy summarized the situation as follows: "you have to decide whether to get beaten up at home or hurt yourself in the street. It feels like we are back in our teens".

Conclusion

The increasing rates of violence against women are historical evidence of gender inequality in Brazil. Based on female and feminist social movements actions, in the last 15 years, Brazilian legislation increased and improved the legal devices to prevent and restrain multiple forms of violence against women. It included the creation of specialized police districts, legislation, supporting services and investments in the production of statistics and other public policies. Besides this context, there are some important elements in the discussion of domestic and gender violence in Brazil still under discussion. To understand the connections between gender and violence is necessary to take into consideration the overlapping between gender and other forms of social differentiation, like class, race and ethnicity. Even though there are some improvements in terms of intersectional analysis, accounts on how cisgender and transgender women are differently affected by violence are lacking. In Brazil, transgender women have life trajectories marked by being expelled from their home, few job opportunities, low schooling and high lethality. Also, they are not protected by protective laws designed to cisgender women, such as Maria da Penha and the law against feminicide. In a certain way, these cases demonstrate that what is under stake is the actual concept of gender and how it could be manipulated in the production of politics. In this chapter, are discussed some of these disputes considering the perspective of the transgender women about domestic violence.

References

Amparo, T. (2019). Desvendando o mapa da invisibilidade da violência contra LGBTI+. In: S. Bueno & R.S Lima (Eds.). *Anuário Brasileiro da Segurança Pública 2019* (pp. 90–106). São Paulo: Fórum Brasileiro de Segurança Pública.

ANTRA. (2020). *Boletim 003: Violência contra travestis e transexuais*. São Paulo: Associação Nacional de Travestis e Transexuais.

Bonetti, A. (2007). Etnografia, gênero e poder: antropologia feminista em ação. *Mediações 14 (2),* 105–122. Retrieved from www.uel.br/revistas/uel/index.php/mediacoes/article/view/4509

Brazil. (2004). Law 10866, published on June 17th 2004 – aims to define and characterize the crime of domestic violence. Brasília: Ministry of Justice.

Brazil (2006). Law 11340, published on August 7th, 2006 – aims to create measures to combat domestic and familiar violence against women. Brasilia: Ministry of Justice.

Brazil. (2010). *Norma Técnica de Padronização das Delegacias Especializadas de Atendimento às Mulheres – DEAMs*. Updated edition. Brasília: Ministry of Justice, Special Secretariat of Policy for Women.

Brazil. (2015). Law 13104, published on March 9th, 2015 – on feminicide. Brasília: Ministry of Justice.

Butler, J. (1999). *Gender Trouble: Feminism and the Subversion of Identity*. 2nd ed. New York: Routledge.

Butler, J. (2006). *Precarious Life: The Powers of Mourning and Violence*. New York: Verso.

CNJ – Brazilian Board of Justice. (2019). *Enunciados*. Brasília: FONAVID/CNJ.

Collins, P. H. (2017). On violence, intersectionality and transversal politics. *Ethnic and Racial Studies, 40 (9)*, 1460–1473. DOI 10.1080/01419870.2017.1317827
Collins, P.H. & Bilge, S. (2016). *Intersectionality*. Cambridge: Polity.
Crenshaw, K. (1991). Mapping the Margins: Intersectionality, Identity Politics, and Violence against Women of Color. *Stanford Law Review, 43 (6)*, 1241–1299. DOI 10.2307/1229039
Das, V. (2007). *Life and Words: Violence and the Descent of the Ordinary*. Berkley: University of California press.
Grossi, M. (2006). Ajudando a iluminar o caminho das pesquisas sobre gênero e violência. In: M. Grossi, L. Minella & J. Losso (Eds.). *Gênero e violência*: pesquisas acadêmicas brasileiras (pp. 9–14). Florianópolis: Editora Mulheres.
IPEA. (2018). *Atlas da violência* 2018 . Brasília: Applied Economics Research Institute.
Kilomba, G. (2008). *Plantation Memories: Episodes of Everyday Racism*. Toronto: Between the lines.
Kulick, D. (1998). *Travestis: Sex, Gender, and Culture among Brazilian Transgendered Prostitutes*. Chicago: Chicago University Press.
Lins, B.A. (2014). "'A lei ficou louca': a Lei Maria da Penha e os efeitos da incondicionalidade da lesão corporal no trabalho policial em duas DDM de São Paulo. In: *Cadernos de Campo, 22*, 289–300. DOI 10.11606/issn.2316-9133.v22i22p289-300
Melo, F.C. (2008). Delicta factis permanentis: marcas de um delito invisível. 251p. Master's thesis in Social Anthropology. State University of Campinas.
Pasinato, W. (2010). Final Report – *Condições para aplicação da Lei 11.340/2006 (Lei Maria da Penha) nas Delegacias Especializadas de Atendimento à Mulher (DEAMS) e nos Juizados de Violência Doméstica e Familiar nas capitais e no Distrito Federal*. Brasília: Observe.
Pereira, Carolina; et al. 2020. Feminicídios no Brasil. In: S. Bueno & R.S. Lima. (Eds.). *Anuário Brasileiro da Segurança Pública 2019* (pp. 116–145). São Paulo: Fórum Brasileiro de Segurança Pública.
Pontes, H. (2018). From "Death in the Family" to "Freud's nanny": a homage to Mariza Corrêa. In: *Cadernos Pagu, 54*, 1–15. DOI 10.1590/18094449201800540003
WHO. 2013. *Global and Regional Estimates of Violence against Women*. New York: United Nations Edition.

24

SOCIO-LEGAL RESPONSES TO IMMIGRANT AND REFUGEE MALE BATTERERS IN THE EU AND MENA REGIONS

Chuka Emezue

Introduction

Approximately 3.5 percent or 272 million of the world's population are migrants or foreign-born people living in a host nation (IOM, 2020). This number is expanding exponentially given rising population growth in some parts of the world, rising inequality, persistent conflicts, and climate change. In 2020, migrants outnumbered expected predictions for 2050 (272 million vs. 230 million predicted) (IOM, 2020). Similarly, refugees-including asylum seekers and internally displaced persons (IDPs-comprise 25.9 million and 41.3 million in 2018, respectively (IOM, 2020). While men make up the majority of global migrants (52 percent), more than half of the world's refugees are under 18 (about 52 percent; IOM, 2020). Canada was the largest refugee resettlement country in 2018.

Recent migration and displacement (forced or voluntary) have been influenced by several push-pull factors. Given the Middle East and North Africa (or MENA region) is a popular host to the largest population of *refugees* globally, and the European Union (EU) is a known destination for most immigrants, this chapter reviews socio-legal responses targeting immigrant men who are abusive in both regions. We specifically explore social, criminal, and civil policies and procedures for engaging with immigrant and refugee batterers who perpetrate violence against women (VAW), particularly domestic abuse. In addition, this chapter examines government, community, and service provider responses in the EU and MENA regions, acknowledging that each region possesses distinct socio-legal frameworks and hosts diverse migrant populations. Finally, we discuss emerging threats to socio-legal responses, such as the COVID-19 pandemic, climate change, and the mobilization of far-right political factions in Europe, and how these issues have influenced socio-legal responses to domestic violence (DV) and batterer intervention programs (BIPs) in the EU and MENA regions.

Prevalence of Refugee—and Immigrant-Specific DV

Despite acknowledged difficulties in acquiring robust data on DV and VAW in some countries, lifetime physical or sexual violence rates for immigrant and refugee women range from 15 to 71 percent (Gonçalves & Matos, 2016). Depending on who you ask, population-based lifetime partner violence victimization rates for immigrant women are as high as 70.5 percent in some non-representative samples (Lee & Hadeed, 2009), or at comparable or higher past-year victimization

DOI: 10.4324/9781003264040-29

rates compared to non-immigrant women in the same host country (Gonçalves & Matos, 2016). Marriage is often a contributory factor to victimization. Married immigrant women experience higher and severer forms of victimization (including multi-perpetrator violence from in-laws in the home) compared to unmarried immigrant women (59.5 vs. 49.8 percent) (Gonçalves & Matos, 2016). Still, victimization estimates often suffer from data aggregation and contradictory evidence. Immigrants, as well as asylees, refugees, and other migrating peoples, are predictably placed into one monolithic category based on nationality, gender, age, and abilities. Prevalence notwithstanding, being an immigrant remains an independent risk factor for partner violence (Madden et al., 2016). Crenshaw (1990) refers to this as the "double subordination" that migrant women and girls face as a result of immigration stressors and add-on relationship abuse in immigrant contexts.

Immigrant men, on the other hand, report a wide range of partner violence perpetration rates, ranging from 25 to 80 percent, according to self- and validated reports (Fulu et al., 2013). However, prevalence rates remain conflicting and context-specific. For example, in a national sample of 15,733 foreign-born people, Latin American immigrants had a higher likelihood of past-year DV perpetration (8.99 percent) than all other immigrant groups studied, according to Vaughn et al. (2015). From the same study, Asian (5.7 percent), African (3.51 percent), and European (3.3 percent) immigrants had a lower risk of DV perpetration than non-immigrant Americans (7.3 percent). It is worth noting immigrant perpetrators (like general partner abusers) were much more likely to meet criteria for both comorbid mental health and substance use issues (p. 1898). In other contexts, when assessing lifetime perpetration rates, immigrants appeared to have lower perpetration rates than non-immigrant persons. Overall, Gupta et al. (2010) suggest acculturative factors, such as time spent in the host nation, have an impact on perpetration rates. For instance, in a community sample of 1,668 immigrant and non-immigrant men, Gupta et al. (2010) found DV perpetration among only 16 percent of immigrant men who had lived in the United States for less than six years (i.e., recent migrants), compared to non-recent immigrant men who had lived in the United States for more than six years (23.9 percent). However, both immigrant groups perpetrated less DV than non-immigrant men in general (26 percent) (Gupta et al., 2010). Still, the "immigrant paradox" is rich-as suggested by Vaughn et al. (2013), immigrants are no more likely than non-immigrant men to commit generally criminal violent actions, undocumented immigrants have substantially lower rates of crime compared to both US citizens and legal immigrants. However, Vaughn et al, (2015) found immigrant men remain more likely than non-immigrant men to perpetrate IPV, driven significantly by Latin American immigrants, and attributed to co-morbid mental health and substance use disorders; while African, European, and Asian immigrants were less likely than native-born Americans to perpetrate IPV (p. 1900). Although, we caution, this data comes from the 2005 National Epidemiologic Survey on Alcohol and Related Conditions (NESARC). These finding clearly allude to the high heterogeneity and rich diversity of immigrant men. Acculturative and hold-over factors such inherited patriarchal ideology from the home country, restrictive gender standards, levels of poverty and unemployment, heavy alcohol consumption, social isolation, and political violence may be more relevant predictors of IPV among immigrant and refugee groups (Gupta et al., 2010; Vaughn et al., 2013, 2015).

In addition to the abovementioned reasons, local definitions of DV and the problematic grouping of *all* migrants, asylee, internally displaced, and refugee groups in surveillance data compromise prevalence reporting. Likewise, the specificity and sensitivity of outcome measures and non-representative sampling of documented immigrants (over undocumented persons) contribute to a lack of clarity regarding DV prevalence. A little considered reason for these discrepancies lies in the inability of westernized researchers from developed countries with *etic* knowledge to capture DV dynamics among historically marginalized groups, with an *emic* understanding of dynamics of DV that impact them. Underreporting is another cause of this discrepancy. Immigrant and refugee families may weigh the perceived repercussions of disclosing violence more heavily, and as a result, DV events are underreported. Hence, a violence-deterring effect occurs, fueled by fear of sanctions (e.g., detention, deportation, threats to residency/citizenship, loss of child custody) balanced against the newly realized empowerment and expanded rights of immigrant women in host countries. Economic difficulties and host-country discrimination may also cause familial stress, which can lead to unnoticed DV and conflict. These characteristics not only impede surveillance of immigrant-specific DV, but they also influence socio-legal responses to DV responses, largely harming women and girls and limiting the efficiency of programs designed to hold abusers accountable.

Programs Designed to Rehabilitate Abusive Men

Often described as Partner Abuse Intervention Program (PAIP) or BIPs, these programs utilize various standardized and state-endorsed curricula to facilitate group and individual counseling for abusive men. There are at least 2,500 BIPs in the United States and approximately 500 in the EU (Ferrer-Perez & Bosch-Fiol, 2016)—although, no reliable count of BIPs in the MENA region. Nevertheless, male perpetrators comprise up to 90 percent of BIP enrollments. After therapy, and even with mandatory sentencing to attend program, between 21 and 35 percent of abusive men recidivate in the first three months, with program drop-out rates ranging from 25 to 65 percent (Arias, Arce, & Vilario, 2013). These frustrating statistics point to treatment gaps and therapeutic disparities replete in the literature and policy hurdles in the host country. At the family level, however, scholars agree foreign-born perpetrators draw from diverse sociocultural schemas of masculinities that impact their openness to treatment, program adherence, and gender equity intentions.

For example, *machismo* (or the conception of toxic masculinity) and *caballerismo* (positive masculinity) among Latinx/Hispanic immigrants, Islamic laws in MENA countries, and patriarchal *Confucianism* in East Asian culture help institutionalize female subordination within the family, community and society (Ozaki & Otis, 2017). These cultural beliefs also govern masculine and feminine conduct, and set the stage for abuser culpability, negative attribution for using violence, and violence-tolerant attitudes toward women and girls (Ozaki & Otis, 2017). Given these cultural schemas, immigrant males frequently exhibit a sort of protest masculinity in host-country rehabilitation programs, especially when required to complete seemingly moralizing and prescriptive programs that contradict how they have always known to be men. Fearing a loss of both their masculine and cultural identity, immigrant male batterers remain resistant to westernized Anglocentric rehabilitation models they describe as one-dimensional. Moreover, these programs ignore abuser psychodynamics, situational risk factors, culture-care needs, and trauma histories (Waller, 2016). Therefore, program philosophies must reflect these local contexts and inherited cultural practices. We discuss some ways to go about doing this in a later section.

Socio-Legal Responses in the EU

As of 2019, over 82 million international migrants lived in the EU. This number increased by 10 percent since a 2015 estimate of 75 million (IOM, 2020) coming mainly from Africa, Asia, Latin America, and the Caribbean. According to Amnesty International, 33 percent of EU women (61 of 185 million) have experienced physical or sexual violence, or both, since age 15, and over 1 in 20 women have been raped since age 15, with migrant and refugee women reporting slightly higher prevalence of physical and sexual violence (Morten, 2014). Siloed responses to VAW, led to the establishment of The Istanbul Convention (or the Council of Europe Convention on preventing and combating VAW and DV)-a superseding socio-legal and regional treaty to prevent and combat

VAW and DV, providing social protections for groups vulnerable to all forms of gender-based violence (GBV).

By June 2019, almost all EU Member States had ratified the legally binding Istanbul Convention, while some non-members had signed but not ratified the agreement. The Convention establishes basic standards (supplementing national socio-legal frameworks) for assisting survivors, prosecuting abusers, and teaching the public on gender equality, sexuality, and healthy relationships. However, its ratification and implementation are beset with complications. Actual enactments vary, and some governments have withdrawn (Turkey withdrew in March 2021, although one of the first countries to sign in 2011). Other have threatened to withdraw (Poland, Slovakia, Hungary, and Bulgaria) from the pact, alleging its threat to "traditional family values" in calling for the inclusion of LGBT+ rights—even though the Convention does not specifically include same-sex recommendation. The Convention, however, in its anti-discrimination clause (i.e., Article 4 of the Convention), encourages guidance on underserved groups, including specific provisions for refugee and migrant women and girls facing abuse. Furthermore, countries like Malta, Iceland, Croatia, Greece, Sweden, and Denmark have recently changed their legislation to guarantee rape is defined as *sex without consent*, as required by the Convention. Consequently, convictions for DV-related offenses have also increased in Sweden.

Still, across the EU, police and court systems take a narrow or overly broad approach to defining DV and enforcing legislation to hold abusers accountable. Some countries only acknowledge "forcible rape," placing an overwhelming burden of proof on female victims to prove forcible rape or sex without consent as rape. In the absence of evidence of violence, threats, or coercion, perpetrators are frequently charged with a lesser charge of sexual abuse. The "Wolf Pack" case in Spain is a prime example, in which five men (including a police officer) were found guilty of "sexually assaulting" an 18-year-old woman in 2016, receiving 9-year sentences each rather than the 20–25-year sentences sought by the prosecution for the more serious charge of gang rape, having repeatedly penetrated her orally, vaginally, and anally—even though they videotaped their attack and boasted about it online. After three years of regional protests and global outrage, the Supreme Court revised their sentences from 9 to 15 years in prison each and promised changes to Spain's rape statute.

Similarly, legal definitions of rape and other forms of DV (such as stalking, harassment, and online abuse) remain imprecise. Hence, their surveillance and prosecutions differ between the Member States. Notably, some countries focus on criminalizing DV as codified in criminal statutes, establishing criteria for penalizing abusers, and putting in place various laws and compliance measures to safeguard victims. It is worth mentioning, however, in certain EU regions, a legal culture of DV tolerance, or in the least, apathy, often aligns with local norms, guaranteeing DV is downplayed and categorized as a misdemeanor charge.

Over the decades, migrant-friendly global pacts, such as the Istanbul Convention, the Convention on the Elimination of all Forms of Discrimination against Women (CEDAW), and, more recently, the UN 2030 Agenda for Sustainable Development Goals (SDG) have remained arbiters of women empowerment and gender justice. However, considering the substantial increases in GBV in various EU and MENA regions, these initiatives may not represent immigrant survivors' lived reality and needs (Mojahed et al., 2020). To their merit, these agreements aid in the development of provincial "minimum standards" in response to VAW and have an indirect influence on batterer programs by setting operational and strategic benchmarks for success, rehabilitation, and reintegration into society. Euro-specific charters, such as the European Convention on Human Rights (ECHR), the Victims' Rights Directive, and the European Pact for Gender Equality (2011–2020), also play a key role in determining the EU's socio-legal responses to VAW, however, with a focus on victim support.

Another critical socio-legal instrument is the European Protective Order (or EPO), commonly recognized across the Member States. The EPO offers continuous and synchronized protection for victims moving across EU borders. However, like most strategies at the supranational level, EPOs have variations in their use and prominence. For example, some member states may criminalize violation of an EPO (by the threat of a fine). Others may offer short- and long-term imprisonment for protection orders violations (up to five years in Denmark). Some EU countries, however, continue to be anti-violence pioneers. Italy, for example, increased its use of mandatory arrests (describing this as *flagrante delicto* or "a blazing offence"), as well as the irrevocability of stalking complaints, and rapid deportation of abusers. Based on a National Anti-Violence Plan, Italy has also established processes to expedite residency permits for immigrant victims of DV. However, as we will see, some of these provisions have come under threat given COVID-19 restrictions.

Batterer Intervention Programs in the EU

Some batterer programs in the EU report up to half of their clientele are migrants and refugees (Fernández-Montalvo et al., 2011). In addition, EU programs differ in terms of the type of clientele they serve (which includes both court-referred and self-referred clients). They also differ in their financing sources, program delivery, and cultural competency strategies. However, program sizes vary greatly, from individual to group sessions—with well-known disparities in access to and utilization of batterer services. Nonetheless, the ultimate task of program execution remains a regional responsibility. Given complex legal acrobatics threatening the full implementation of the Istanbul Convention, Member States strive to uphold victim-facing laws, while holding abusers accountable through a combination of criminal and civil (soft law) measures that differ by country.

An EU-wide review of 54 batterer programs across 19 countries found current EU programs replicated programs in North America in their direct (or derived use) of the Duluth Model—first developed by the Domestic Abuse Intervention Project (DAIP) (Hamilton, Koehler, & Lösel, 2012). With its growing diversity and cultural ecosystems, batterer programs in the EU experiment with the Duluth model approach or use hybridized programs mixing cognitive-behavioral, psychodynamic, and pro-feminist modalities. Like those in North America, EU programs prioritize victim safety through coordinated community responses (CCR; another feature of US-based models). Thus, multi-agency strategic partnerships are formed across the board without clearly favoring pro-prosecution and pro-punishment policies. However, these partnerships infrequently address violence against migrant and refugee women. On the flip side, low-income, uneducated migrants—especially Migrants of Color—remain prime targets of regular and forceful sanctions. In this way, minority perpetrators are overrepresented in local crime statistics—signaling an interplay of racism, xenophobia, classism, and anti-migration sentiments (Flood, 2018).

Like programs in North America, EU programs report minimal to moderate program effectiveness. Treatment effects are small and seldom statistically significant (Akoensi, Koehler, Lösel, & Humphreys, 2012). While several programs for non-institutionalized males are community-based, in several EU countries (e.g., Spain), BIPs are administered both inside and outside of prisons, albeit focusing on "treatment" (Ferrer-Perez & Bosch-Fiol, 2016). Most EU perpetrator programs are government-funded with various levels of oversight and political involvement, making socio-legal responses to migrant-specific DV reflective of local sentiments and policies (Hamilton, Koehler, & Lösel, 2012).

A shortcoming of EU programs is their lack of disaggregated data based on gender, nationality, and immigration status, making it difficult to map out migrant-specific socio-legal responses (Ferrer-Perez & Bosch-Fiol, 2016). Programs also report high attrition rates and variations in success rates (between 23.8 and 93.5 percent, see Ferrer-Perez & Bosch-Fiol, 2016). Inconsistencies in treatment focus (e.g., cognitive/emotional skills vs. recidivist behaviors vs. socioecological risk factors) and logistical challenges with following up with migrant and unstably housed clients after their intake are other critical issues of concern in EU programs. Canales and colleagues (2015) found over 20 percent of programs had no program evaluative components or plans to gauge their success at preventing violence. Fortunately, programs like the European Network for the Work with Perpetrators of Domestic Violence (with over 64 members active throughout 32 European countries) support evidence-based practices in working with perpetrators and have driven innovations in this area. Simultaneously, programs like the European Family Justice Center Alliance (EFJCA, with over 40 members in 22 European countries) help victims of GBV, DV, child abuse, and sexual violence with select services for perpetrators via Family Justice Centers (FJC). These organizations span multiple EU countries and represent a foremost collaborative of networked agencies working on GBV, DV, child abuse, sexual violence issues.

Socio-Legal Responses in the MENA Region

The MENA region hosts half of all the world's IDPs and 57.5 percent of all refugees in the world. The Arab world is a racially and ethnically diverse society, with 22 countries in the MENA and over 423 million geopolitically distinct people living in countries like Bahrain, Kuwait, Oman, Qatar, Saudi Arabia, and the United Arab Emirates (UAE), Jordan, and Lebanon, and spread out to Western Asia, North Africa, the Horn of Africa, and Western Indian Ocean islands (Mojahed et al., 2020). At the time of this writing, all MENA countries (except Iran, Sudan, Somalia) have ratified or acceded to the CEDAW—a vital treaty for the rights of women at home and in society, ratified or recognized by most countries in the MENA region.

However, representative prevalence data on GBV in this region is insufficient and unreliable. Likewise, available data are more representative of DV more than other forms of GBV (broader forms of VAW, such as female genital mutilation, child marriage, and "honor killings"). A recent meta-analysis (41 studies from ten Arab countries) indicates high pooled prevalence estimates of lifetime partner violence (73.3 percent), psychological abuse (49.8 percent), physical violence (35.6 percent), and sexual violence (22 percent) ion the MENA region (Hawcroft et al., 2019). Between 40 and 60 percent of EU women report experiencing sexual harassment by 31–64 percent of EU men (primarily young, educated men, with adverse childhood experiences). Although, with limited population-based data, DV statistics do not fully capture prevalence in this region. Most studies on the prevalence of DV in the Arab context favor reports on documented immigrant households in North America (e.g., Arab Canadian and Arab-American families) while ignoring refugees and IDP populations. Accordingly, there is little discourse on socio-legal responses to abusive immigrant male batterers in both of these contexts.

Recent improvements in female education and health (improved female life expectancy, fertility, and maternal mortality) in some MENA countries are a welcome development. For instance, Jordon, Egypt, Tunisia, Morocco, and Lebanon recently repealed "marry-your-rapist" norm-based laws supporting honor-based marriages to *save face* after rape. A Promundo study in Egypt, Lebanon, Morocco, and Palestine found only a small fraction of men (25 percent) still hold gender-equitable views and behave accordingly by engaging in housework and supporting their wife's decision to start a business or join the workforce (El Feki, Heilman, & Barker, 2017). However, norm-based and religious laws in the MENA region, such as the "*Obedience in return for maintenance*" law (or financial support in return for complete and utter obedience), still depict wives as passive commodities and diminish the effects of these gains on the ground (Mojahed et al., 2020).

Women and girls still contend with patriarchal discrimination and face inequalities in marriage, divorce, family life, employment, reproductive health, political participation, and prejudices under religious law (i.e., Shari'a). For instance, Islamic laws in countries like Sudan, Iran, Pakistan, Saudi Arabia, Indonesia, the UAE, and Nigeria enforce the concept of *Zina* (i.e., adultery or fornication between two consenting adults). Thus, infidelity is usually defined in the same way as rape (or *Zina* without consent). Making *rape* and *adultery* conflated incidents, with the burden of proof resting on the female victim to prove her rape and lack of consent. Not being able to prove this means adultery is punishable by death for married women or a beating for unmarried women, with the interpretation of the same Islam laws differing across countries (Mojahed et al., 2020).

The MENA region, Western Asia, and sub-Saharan Africa have more countries without DV laws protecting women and girls than any other region in the world (Garcia-Moreno et al., 2013). Most jurisdictions have yet to legislate DV, allowing men convicted of rape to evade the law. Legal definitions for rape (marital rape or otherwise) remain ambiguous. In some instances, perpetrator sentences are weakened by lenient penal codes for violence against an *unfaithful wife*, for marriage-by-rape laws, for so-called crimes of passion, and for violence in defense of family honor. It does not help that around 20–50 percent of women in MENA countries endorse accepting attitudes of IPV (Mojahed et al., 2020; Tran et al., 2016). Several women justify using GBV *under certain situations* (El Feki, Heilman, & Barker, 2017). Consequently, there are few support services for victims and even fewer formal batterer programs to curtail violence and hold abusers accountable (Mojahed et al., 2020).

In some countries, the constitution stipulates anti-DV laws prohibiting family and partner violence. However, some MENA countries have no criminal or penal codes for perpetration (including marital rape). For example, the constitution in Iraq prohibits "all forms of violence and abuse in the family," while permitting wife-beating and corporal punishment of children *within the law's limits*. In addition, patrilineal family honor and reputation keeping justify "honor killings," thus preventing abuse disclosure and the prosecution of abusive husbands and in-laws. Violence-forgiving norms further restrict help-seeking behaviors and restrain the self-determination and rights of women and girls. Attitudes aside, cultural and moral sensitivities impede data gathering on socio-legal responses to immigrant male batterers in some MENA countries. Other issues in the MENA region, such as security concerns, diversity of political and cultural realities, community resistance, and high rates of forced migration, for instance, in Syria, Turkey, Yemen, Iraq, Lebanon, and Jordan, undermine efforts to map socio-legal responses.

Where present, socio-legal responses to DV are civil or administrative and offer only temporary relief. With disjointed and mixed governmental support, much is left to international non-profit organizations (or NGOs) who tackle DV using primary and secondary prevention strategies (e.g., changing oppressive gender attitudes). Competency training of religious leaders, police departments, and agency staff funded by external donors are standard strategies for changing patriarchal attitudes that disadvantage women and girls. In addition, non-profit programs offer emotional and material support (i.e., microfinance, job skills, crisis counseling, and legal aid), even as most of these services are contingent on residency or citizenship. However, refugee families in crisis avoid using these services where their irregular or undocumented status may jeopardize their resettlement.

Programs for refugee batterers are hardly described in the MENA literature. However, there are growing reports of male-centered programs to engage boys and men as allies and targets of anti-violence prevention among immigrants in general. Programs like Promundo's *Program H* in the Middle East (recognized by WHO and UNICEF), the *White Ribbon Campaign*, and *MenEngage* are exemplary international programs with vital partnerships between migrant communities and non-government organizations (Flood, 2018). These programs are pioneering in using non-curricular and region-specific strategies to engage men and boys in dismantling rigid gender norms in low-income local communities. Non-curricular approaches leverage pedagogic experiences in informal spaces where boys and men regularly meet, such as the workplace, sport/recreation clubs, health centers, and community hotspots (Flood, 2018). These programs deliver group psychoeducation using customizable toolkits, youth-led, male-facing social campaigns, and "bottom-up" community mobilization, invariably addressing partner violence at all socioecological levels (Flood, 2018).

Where Do We Go from Here?

For decades, there has been an ostensible desire to make BIPs "culturally competent" and to differentiate programs around the world. In fact, this is usually a matter of practicality. BIPs are hesitant to apply these modifications because of the significant expense of updating program models and training personnel, as well as the time and financial consequences of implementing ideas from out-of-touch academic experts, not to mention the difficulty in quantifying post-program efficacy. Moreover, the ample intersectional identities of immigrant clients complicate current efforts. Our best efforts are diminished by regional variations in program clientele. Foremost critiques of immigrant-facing programs highlight their one-size-fits-all approach, high attrition rates, program resistance, inadequate funding, cultural insensitivity, theoretical illiteracy, methodological disparities, and a characteristic lack of therapeutic alliance (Ferrer-Perez & Bosch-Fiol, 2016). Still, several scholars espouse the benefits of culture congruent programs (Healey et al. 1998; Waller, 2016; Williams & Becker, 1994).

While programs continue to do their best, anti-migrant sentiments bolstered by populist, anti-feminist, and nationalist views have given rise to fast-growing far-right political groups in the EU (such as the Vox in Spain, Northern League in Italy, The National Rally in France, the Danish People's Party, The Party for Freedom in the Netherlands, and Alternative for Germany, to name a few). As members of these groups win elections, they continue to incite hatred and fuel overt racism, islamophobia, the subordination of women's rights, and, most significantly, antagonistic beliefs toward immigrants, particularly Muslim immigrants (Duina & Carson, 2020). Legislatively, dubbed the "fastest-growing party family in Europe" (Duina & Carson, 2020, citing Golder, 2016, p. 477), these factions continue to conscript crucial policymaking roles to fit their propaganda while simultaneously harboring bogus pseudo-progressive beliefs. For optics and to garner wider support, they recruit women, minorities, and LGBTQ+ supporters who share their views, and epitomize a "whataboutism" stance (Duina & Carson, 2020). This pathologizing of immigration as a social and political burden threatens socio-legal responses, insofar as male migrants and refugees continue to be portrayed as hypersexual, aggressive, and criminally minded (Arsenijević et al., 2018; Flood, 2018)—even as studies show immigrants are less likely to be criminally violent than non-immigrant Americans (Wright & Benson, 2010)

Sensitization Programs: Engaging Men and Boys as Allies

Several EU Member States have re-focused these negative stereotypes by setting up acculturating education programs like *movemen*[1] in Germany. These programs educate and speed up the sensitization of newly arrived migrant and refugee men and boys, specifically on sexual norms and legal codes, sexual health education, bystander training, language/cultural integration, gender equality, and anti-radicalization pedagogy. Whether government-run or not, these projects are usually mandatory in some communities and can be a pre-requisite for full involvement in society. For example, in Spain, these acculturation classes are grouped by gender to promote active participation in reception centers and destigmatize specific topics. However, the focus here is on acclimatization, often at the expense of long-held protective values within cultures, such as social support networks, spirituality, communal support, empowerment, positive coping, and culturally responsive approaches for addressing DV (Sabri, Simonet, & Campbell, 2018). Importantly, even when well-intended, this strategic acculturation often plays up Western ethnocentrism—what Volpp (2000) refers to as our propensity to *blame culture for bad behavior.*

However, we must engage immigrant men and boys as allies in VAW prevention. According to Flood (2018), "we must start with men wherever they are" (p. 155). I argue for a position of negotiating cultural schemas of masculinity. Because the masculine identity is a prized and privileged identity for most men, expecting immigrant male batterers to easily renounce the only way they have learned to be men can be a futile if not arduous undertaking. We must begin to examine their relationships to power, dominant masculinity, host country masculinity, and, most significantly, their relationships to the immigrant and non-immigrant women in their lives. Efforts to rehabilitate abusive men must begin from here to restructure damaging stereotypes and violence-tolerant attitudes without pedestalizing these men as "bad men" or their cultures as violence-tolerant.

Whole-Family Approaches (WFA)

The family unit (where one exists) remains a practical location for preventing the start and interrupting the transmission of gender norms. It is possibly the single most influential petri-dish for generating, testing, and sustaining gender norms and attitudes (Morris et al., 2008). Thus, local and national programs must include immigrant and refugee men (and women) as co-planners on teams tasked with designing rehabilitation programs. In this way, a family justice model centers on *whole-family* violence prevention.

Co-designing whole-family programs with immigrant users (or graduates of such programs) will foster community buy-in, ownership, intent-to-use, and engagement. Importantly, whole-family strategies are optimized where they emphasize the same ideals immigrant families hold in high esteem. Family preservation, positive parenthood, spirituality/religiosity, ethnic pride, and negotiated masculinity and femininity are values identified in a recent literature review describing how immigrant male batterers fare in foreign programs (Emezue, Williams, & Bloom, 2019). Few programs are designed for the family-as-a-unit. There are well-founded pragmatic, ethical, and logistical reasons for this. Whole-family programs, for example, are frequently construed as *restorative justice* programs, which have been criticized for their antiquated focus on family preservation, forced forgiveness, toxic positivity, and anti-divorce bias—all of which are detrimental to the victim's safety and the well-being of their children, while undermining the restorative justice praxis (Stith & McCollum, 2011).

However, family-based programs operate in social work contexts that emphasize family support, healthy family functioning, and parental self-efficacy—ideals which may not always be attainable (Morris et al., 2008). Therefore, WFA robustly support the family as a "whole" where one exists (Morris et al., 2008). Another criticism of WFA is that these programs assume normative depictions of what characterizes a *family* and are maladaptive to non-normative family types (Morris et al., 2008). Today, family formations are progressively non-normative. However, most immigrant families are traditionally *heteronormative* as a function of culture and social norms in their country of origin, and so, stand to benefit from whole-family strategies.

The Goal of Sustained Rehabilitation

The minimization and justification of VAW must be constructively challenged at the offender, family, and community level. We must re-focus rehabilitation programs from merely computing DV outcomes (e.g., re-abuse, re-arrest) and move beyond bare-bones attempts at cultural congruency (e.g., bilingual programing). This calls for evidence-based rehabilitation models that center rehabilitation principles, offender cultural beliefs, client-centered approaches (e.g., Motivational

Interviewing), and self-directed goal settings (Cannon et al., 2016; Waller, 2016). Examples of rehabilitation models include the Risk-Need-Responsivity (RNR) model for offender rehabilitation focused on reducing dynamic risk factors, meeting criminogenic needs, and responding to risk levels (see Andrews & Bonta, 2010), and the Good Lives Model (GLM; see Willis & Ward, 2013)—a strength-based, positive psychology, and restorative approach. Whereas the GLM attempts to use assets in the offender's community, crucial skills, and self-directed beliefs, to encourage behavior change and better living, the RNR model focuses on pragmatic problem identification and risk assessment. Even as scholars debate the soundness of one over the other, I believe both models play vital functions. However, incorporating these models presents a challenge to program adoption for various reasons, including a lack of familiarity with these models, logistical issues with maintaining fidelity to these models, stringent state regulations centered on the Duluth Model, and other forms of cognitive-behavioral therapies, and the worrying emergence of for-profit BIPs.

While programs for immigrant batterers demand an infusion of much-needed novelty, they must also address contextual and situational risk factors and non-criminogenic needs that precipitate and sustain their use of violence, including economic and social stressors. Notably, the concept of welfare for immigrants (e.g., structured financial assistance) is frequently a contentious issue, owing to anti-immigrant sentiments and the growing wealth gap in host countries, making government assistance and life skills training for non-citizens—a proven strategy to mitigate DV—problematic for citizens. Receiving countries, on the other hand, must design policies that address non-criminogenic requirements considering pre- and post-migration risk (and protective) factors. In addition, we must provide immigrant male offenders (and their service providers) with wrap-around resources (e.g., mental health services, employment, fatherhood, and substance use treatment) and skills for sustained reformation (Ward & Maruna, 2007; Ward & Salmon, 2009). The period after program completion is a critical window of opportunity for developing a continuing care and "service-extending" modality to build on skills obtained in the program.

We must also address the diversity of typologies and more radical forms of abuse, such as acid attacks, honor killings, forced marriage, female genital mutilation/cutting practices, sex selection, female infanticide, human trafficking, and child labor practices, that make their way to the host country (Babcock, Green, & Robie, 2004; Mojahed et al., 2020; Waller, 2016). In the absence of these actions, immigrant and refugee men and boys who use violence will remain disinclined to help-seeking, as they presume rehabilitation programs to be stigmatizing and marginalizing, reflecting broader social discrimination (Waller, 2016).

Another promising practice is engaging men and boys in violence early prevention (before the fact) using an intersectional and social justice approach centering race/ethnicity, class, sexuality, age, and other social exclusion categories that foment systemic oppression. This stance does not nullify but augments feminist intersectional frameworks on partner violence affecting minority female survivors. However, comprehensive guidelines for working with abusive men and boys are needed and must reflect the needs of newly arrived families and their lived experiences.

The COVID-19 Pandemic and DV Responses in the EU and MENA Region

As if these socio-legal responses to DV were not already challenging enough, the novel coronavirus (COVID-19) pandemic has worsened existing disparities and fragilities, including gender inequalities, mostly harming women and girls at home, in the workplace, and on the frontlines of the pandemic response. Specifically, several community-based agencies now report disruptions to the usual channels for victim support and systems for perpetrator accountability (Emezue, 2020). In addition, fear of cross-border virus transmission also exacerbated migration restrictions and impacted agency, medical, and humanitarian efforts, as well as the reliability of essential services such as shelter programs, rape-crisis centers and sexual violence referral centers, migration paper renewal centers, and court processing times for DV offenders, to name a few.

Notably, countries like the United States, India, Russia, the United Kingdom, France, Brazil, and Turkey are reporting the highest case and death rates from COVID-19 rates in—at the time of writing (Català et al., 2021). MENA countries like Iran, Turkey, and Egypt are also reporting high case rates from the virus. Consequently, with stay-at-home mandates, work, and family stressors, unemployment, infection fears, and so on, there have been exponential spikes in GBV worldwide (Emezue, 2020; Piquero et al., 2021). DV has been dubbed a "*shadow pandemic*" by the United Nations Director-General (UN). Women and girls in the EU and MENA region continue to contend with stricter gender roles in lockdown and barriers to economic opportunities. According to World Health Organization, emergency calls in numerous European countries have increased by up to 60 percent compared to previous year. A rapid gender analysis conducted by CARE International, migrant domestic workers, adolescent boys, and young men are other distinct groups reporting increases in DV (Phelps, 2020).

On the other hand, disruptions in the supply of sexual and reproductive health services, rollbacks to gains realized in women's participation in the labor force, fractured testing and vaccination services continue to threaten recent gains for women and girls in the region in the COVID era. Furthermore, lockdowns and social isolation have influenced support programs for women and girls in the MENA region while increasing women's unpaid care duties, exposing survivors to greater domestic abuse, and slowing prosecutorial services for immigrant male offenders. Furthermore, the pandemic has provided an opportunity for abusers to utilize novel techniques, such as infection threats as a control tactic and to limit their partner's freedoms, as well as round-the-clock monitoring of at-home technologies (phone, browsing history, and internet tracking) (Emezue, 2020). Countries in the EU (especially Italy and Spain) and in the MENA region (Saudi Arabia, Jordan, and Lebanon) with stricter lockdown and stay-at-home mandates—at the time of this writing—have struggled to curtail the spread of this pandemic. Food insecurity, water scarcity, densely populated IDP camps, poorly coordinated COVID-19 testing, and vaccination campaigns, as well as ongoing conflicts and forced migration in Syria, Yemen, Iraq, Libya, Palestine, and Afghanistan, are just a few issues that have exacerbated DV for migrant groups during this pandemic. However, several MENA governments are increasingly adopting a gender- and equity-focused approach to their COVID-19 responses, including offering government support to survivors' organizations, NGOs, and advocacy groups.

In the EU, the European Network for the Work with Perpetrators of Domestic Violence (WWP EN) promptly created and distributed the "*European Network Guidelines for Working Responsibly with Perpetrators of Domestic Violence During the COVID-19 Pandemic*." Recommendations for working with abusive men included modifications to center evidence-based therapeutic techniques to support men's recovery in treatment (emphasizing coping skills, emotional regulation, self-management, psychoeducation, and strategies for preventing COVID-19 transmission). Furthermore, a shift to technology-based services (online, web, and phone) ensures that program and court processes are uninterrupted.

However, these approaches are not without drawbacks. First, a digital divide prevents full participation in online sessions for immigrant men in programs requiring low- and high-data platforms like Skype, WhatsApp, Facebook Messenger, Google Hangouts, and Zoom. Not to mention language barrier concerns. Second, as clients juggle family duties during a global pandemic, providers report frequent service interruptions, court no-shows, and delayed supervisory visits. Third, logistically, some batterer programs cannot afford to upgrade their technologies to meet this new reality; in addition, the learning curve service providers must overcome to use these "socially distant" strategies in a trauma-informed and culture-responsive manner is an impediment. Lastly, I want to point out that a recent review of hate speech online suggests likely increases in hate speech often follow a black swan event, like a natural disaster, terrorist attack, and now a pandemic (Calderón et al., 2020). As a result of unverified claims that the COVID-19 virus originated in Wuhan, China, anti-Asian violence is on the rise. Natural calamities like this aggravate anti-immigrant sentiment. As a result, we should expect the inevitable undermining of socio-legal responses to serious issues like DV in communities where the negative impacts of DV and the prevalence of family violence are construed as *justified* and driven by culture.

Climate Change and DV

Given the MENA region is a hotbed climate-related issues, such as rising sea levels, droughts, extreme temperatures, threats to crop yields, and climate change, I will be remiss not to mention how climate change poses a threat to DV socio-legal responses. While it may appear to be a stretch of the imagination, the link between climate change and GBV is a reality and a significant concern. Already, the UN has warned unabated global warming—above 1.5°C—and "sudden onset" weather events will significantly increase the risk of species extinction, resulting in warmer and infertile oceans, degraded ecosystems, crop loss, environmental disasters (drought, floods, cyclones, wildfires), climate refugees and migration, and other consequences.

According to recent displacement data, Syria and Turkey were the origin and destination of the greatest number of global refugees, with 6.7 million and 3.7 million, respectively (IOM, 2020). Climate change has the potential to amplify and accelerate the displacement of women and girls in areas where a climate-related disaster not only threatens livelihoods (e.g., agricultural losses and poor livestock production) but also puts them at high risk of GBV. Women who travel long distances in drought-stricken areas are also vulnerable to in-transit sexual assault. Women and daughters must fend for themselves when their husbands are away seeking seasonal work (male migrant workers exceeded female migrant workers by 28 million in 2017, 58 vs. 42 percent) or engaged in farm work in their traditional position as providers. In some circumstances, they are compelled to barter sex in exchange for food and necessities. Climate change would aggravate regional competition for food, water, and other valuable resources, particularly in the MENA (Northwest Africa) and sub-Saharan African regions.

With climate migration on the rise, internal and external displacements will lead to climate and environmental refugees. As their numbers grow, the international community will find it increasingly challenging to respond to climatic emergencies and the climate refugees they will generate. It remains to be seen how the climate crises will affect socio-legal responses to DV perpetration, but this impact is inescapable. Strong global and state-level leadership is required to increase victims' access to support services while also establishing avenues to rehabilitate abusive immigrant men, whose use of violence may be linked to their power and control attribution, as well as their experiences escaping a climate crisis, adverse childhood experiences, and histories of trauma.

Conclusion

Overall, NGOs, traditional shelters, criminal justice systems, immigration, health, and social service providers continue to be central and essential for immigrant families (Simmons et al., 2016). However, most of these services are geared toward survivors, with assistance for perpetrators designed as an ancillary criminal justice response, calling for overdue innovation in the content and deployment of services designed to rehabilitate men. As Flood (2018) points out, immigrant and refugee men are no more violent than non-immigrant men in the host countries, even as they show higher likelihood of perpetrating IPV in some samples. However, this link is not as linear as it appears (see Vaughn et al., 2015). I advocate for nuanced, client-centered, and intersectional approaches to rehabilitating abusive immigrant men. Recognizing anti-immigrant sentiments remains a daily and persistent stressor in these men's lives should be a central consideration of program core curricula. The intent should not be rote program completion. Instead, we must ensure reasons these men use to justify VAW are constructively challenged. To generate realistic and useful answers to the daily challenges that trigger or worsen DV, the principles of humane rehabilitation we choose to utilize must transcend academic performativity and theorizations. Importantly, grassroots programs must have the full support of governments as they deal with staffing shortages, community distrust, funding cuts, punitive legislation, and other logistical issues. Governments must devote essential resources to ensuring programs, which are frequently the first responders to family violence, are equipped and supported to address the intersectional needs of newly arrived immigrants, asylum seekers, and refugees.

Note

1 https://movemen.org/en/

Reference list

Akoensi, T. D., Koehler, J. A., Lösel, F., & Humphreys, D. K. (2012). Domestic violence perpetrator programs in Europe, part II. *International Journal of Offender Therapy and Comparative Criminology*, *57* (10), 1206–1225. doi:10.1177/0306624x12468110

Andrews, D. A., & Bonta, J. (2010). *The psychology of criminal conduct*. New York: Routledge.

Arias, E., Arce, R., & Vilariño, M. (2013). Batterer intervention programs: A meta-analytic review of effectiveness. *Psychosocial Intervention*, *22*, 153–160. doi:10.5093/in2013a18

Arsenijević, J., Burtscher, D., Ponthieu, A., Severy, N., Contenta, A., Moissaing, S., ... & Venables, E. (2018). "I feel like I am less than other people": Health-related vulnerabilities of male migrants travelling alone on their journey to Europe. *Social Science & Medicine*, *209*, 86–94.

Babcock, J. C., Green, C. E., & Robie, C. (2004). Does batterers' treatment work? A meta-analytic review of domestic violence treatment. *Clinical Psychology Review*, *23* (8), 1023–1053.

Calderón, C. A., de la Vega, G., & Herrero, D. B. (2020). Topic modeling and characterization of hate speech against immigrants on Twitter around the emergence of a far-right party in Spain. *Social Sciences*, *9* (11), 188.

Canales, O. G., Geldschläger, H., Nax, D., & Ponce, A. (2015). European perpetrator programmes: A survey on day-to-day outcome measurement. *Studia Humanistyczne AGH*, *14* (2), 33–52.

Cannon, C., Hamel, J., Buttell, F., & Ferreira, R. J. (2016). A survey of domestic violence perpetrator programs in the United States and Canada: Findings and implications for policy and intervention. *Partner Abuse*, 7 (3), 226–276.

Català, M., Pino, D., Marchena, M., Palacios, P., Urdiales, T., Cardona, P. J., ... & Alvarez-Lacalle, E. (2021). Robust estimation of diagnostic rate and real incidence of COVID-19 for European policymakers. *PLoS One*, *16* (1), e0243701.

Crenshaw, K. (1990). Mapping the margins: Intersectionality, identity politics, and violence against women of color. *Stanford Law Review*, *43*, 1241.

Duina, F., & Carson, D. (2020). Not so right after all? Making sense of the progressive rhetoric of Europe's far-right parties. *International Sociology*, *35* (1), 3–21.

Echauri, J. A., Fernández-Montalvo, J., Martínez, M., & Azkarate, J. M. (2013). Effectiveness of a treatment program for immigrants who committed gender-based violence against their partners. *Psicothema*, *25* (1), 49–54.

El Feki, S., Heilman, B., & Barker, G., Eds. (2017). *Understanding masculinities: Results from the International Men and Gender Equality Survey (IMAGES) – Middle East and North Africa*. Cairo and Washington, DC: UN Women and Promundo-US.

Emezue C. N. (2020). Digital or digitally delivered responses to domestic and intimate partner violence during COVID-19. *JMIR Public Health Surveill, 6* (3), e19831 URL: http://publichealth.jmir.org/2020/3/e19831/ doi: 10.2196/19831

Emezue C. N., Williams, O. J., & Bloom, T. L. (2019). Culturally differentiated batterer intervention programs for immigrant male batterers: An integrative review. *Journal of Aggression, Maltreatment & Trauma*. doi:10.1080/10926771.2019.1685042

Fernández-Montalvo, J., Echauri, J., Martínez, M., & Azcárate, J. M. (2011). Violencia de género e inmigración: un estudio exploratorio del perfi l diferencial de hombres maltratadores nacionales e inmigrantes [Gender-based violence and immigration: An exploratory study of the differential profile of citizen and immigrant male perpetrators]. *Behavioral Psychology/Psicología Conductual, 19*, 439–452.

Ferrer-Perez, V. A., & Bosch-Fiol, E. (2016). Batterer intervention programs in Spain: An analysis of their effectiveness. *International Journal of Offender Therapy and Comparative Criminology, 62* (4), 885–897. doi:10.1177/0306624x16672455

Flood, M. (2018). *Engaging men and boys in violence prevention*. New York: Springer.

Fulu, E., Jewkes, R., Roselli, T., & Garcia-Moreno, C. (2013). Prevalence of and factors associated with male perpetration of intimate partner violence: Findings from the UN Multi-country Cross-sectional Study on Men and Violence in Asia and the Pacific. *The Lancet Global Health, 1* (4), e187–e207.

García-Moreno, C., Pallitto, C., Devries, K., Stöckl, H., Watts, C., & Abrahams, N. (2013). *Global and regional estimates of violence against women: Prevalence and health effects of intimate partner violence and non-partner sexual violence*. Geneva, Switzerland: World Health Organization.

Golder, M. (2016). Far right parties in Europe. *Annual Review of Political Science, 19*, 477–497.

Gonçalves, M., & Matos, M. (2016). Prevalence of violence against immigrant women: A systematic review of the literature. *Journal of Family Violence, 31* (6), 697–710.

Gupta, J., Acevedo-Garcia, D., Hemenway, D., Decker, M. R., Raj, A., & Silverman, J. G. (2010). Intimate partner violence perpetration, immigration status, and disparities in a community health center-based sample of men. *Public Health Reports, 125* (1), 79–87.

Hamilton, L., Koehler, J. A., & Lösel, F. A. (2012). Domestic violence perpetrator programs in Europe, part I. *International Journal of Offender Therapy and Comparative Criminology, 57* (10), 1189–1205. doi:10.1177/0306624x12469506

Hawcroft, C., Hughes, R., Shaheen, A., Usta, J., Elkadi, H., Dalton, T., ... & Feder, G. (2019). Prevalence and health outcomes of domestic violence amongst clinical populations in Arab countries: A systematic review and meta-analysis. *BMC Public Health, 19* (1), 315.

Healey, K., Smith, C., & O'Sullivan, C. (1998). *Batterer intervention: Program approaches and criminal justice strategies*. Washington, DC: National Institute of Justice.

IOM. (2020). *World migration report, 2020*. Geneva: International Organization for Migration.

Lee, Y. S., & Hadeed, L. (2009). Intimate partner violence among Asian immigrant communities: Health/mental health consequences, help-seeking behaviors, and service utilization. *Trauma, Violence, & Abuse, 10* (2), 143–170.

Madden, K., Scott, T., Sholapur, N., & Bhandari, M. (2016). Prevalence of intimate partner violence among South Asian women living in Southern Ontario. *Journal of Immigrant and Minority Health, 18* (4), 913–920.

Mojahed, A., Alaidarous, N., Shabta, H., Hegewald, J., & Garthus-Niegel, S. (2020). Intimate partner violence against women in the Arab countries: A systematic review of risk factors. *Trauma, Violence, & Abuse, 23* (2), 390–407. doi:10.1177/1524838020953099.

Morris, K., Hughes, N., Clarke, H., Tew, J., Mason, P., Galvani, S., Lewis, A. and Loveless, L. with Becker, S. and Burford, G. (2008). *Think family: A literature review of whole family approaches*. London: Cabinet Office.

Morten, K. (2014). *Violence against women: An EU-wide survey*. Luxembourg: Publications Office of the European Union.

Ozaki, R., & Otis, M. D. (2017). Gender equality, patriarchal cultural norms, and perpetration of intimate partner violence: Comparison of male university students in Asian and European cultural contexts. *Violence Against Women, 23* (9), 1076–1099.

Phelps, C. (2020). *COVID-19 Rapid Gender Analysis in the Middle East and North Africa Summary*. CARE International. https://reliefweb.int/sites/reliefweb.int/files/resources/CARE-MENA-COVID-19-RGA-200720201.pdf

Piquero, A. R., Jennings, W. G., Jemison, E., Kaukinen, C., & Knaul, F. M. (2021). Domestic violence during the COVID-19 pandemic—evidence from a systematic review and meta-analysis. *Journal of Criminal Justice, 74*, 1–10. doi:10.1016/j.jcrimjus.2021.101806

Sabri, B., Simonet, M., & Campbell, J. C. (2018). Risk and protective factors of intimate partner violence among South Asian immigrant women and perceived need for services. *Cultural Diversity and Ethnic Minority Psychology, 24* (3), 442.

Simmons, C. A., Howell, K. H., Duke, M. R., & Beck, J. G. (2016). Enhancing the impact of Family Justice Centers via motivational interviewing: An integrated review. *Trauma, Violence, & Abuse, 17* (5), 532–541.

Stith, S. M., & McCollum, E. E. (2011). Conjoint treatment of couples who have experienced intimate partner violence. *Aggression and Violent Behavior, 16* (4), 312–318. https://doi.org/10.1016/j.avb.2011.04.012

Tran, T. D., Nguyen, H., Fisher, J. (2016). Attitudes towards intimate partner violence against women among women and men in 39 low- and middle-income countries. *PLOS ONE, 11* (11), Article e0167438. 10.1371/journal.pone.0167438

Vaughn, M. G., Salas-Wright, C. P., Cooper-Sadlo, S., Maynard, B. R., & Larson, M. (2015). Are immigrants more likely than native-born Americans to perpetrate intimate partner violence?. *Journal of Interpersonal Violence, 30* (11), 1888–1904. doi:10.1177/0886260514549053

Vaughn, M. G., Salas-Wright, C. P., DeLisi, M., & Maynard, B. R. (2013). The immigrant paradox: Immigrants are less antisocial than native-born Americans. *Social Psychiatry and Psychiatric Epidemiology, 49* (7), 1129–1137. doi:10.1007/s00127-013-0799-3

Volpp, L. (2000). Blaming culture for bad behavior. *Yale Journal of Law & the Humanities, 12*. Available at: https://digitalcommons.law.yale.edu/yjlh/vol12/iss1/3

Waller, B. (2016). Broken fixes: A systematic analysis of the effectiveness of modern and postmodern interventions utilized to decrease IPV perpetration among Black males remanded to treatment. *Aggression and Violent Behavior, 27*, 42–49. doi:10.1016/j.avb.2016.02.003

Ward, T., & Maruna, S. (2007). Rehabilitation: Beyond the risk paradigm. Routledge. London. https://doi.org/10.4324/9780203962176.

Ward, T., & Salmon, K. (2009). The ethics of punishment: Correctional practice implications. *Aggression and Violent Behavior, 14* (4), 239–247.

Williams, O. J., & Becker, R. L. (1994). Domestic partner abuse treatment programs and cultural competence: The results of a national survey. *Violence and Victims, 9* (3), 287–296.

Willis, G. M., Prescott, D. S., & Yates, P. M. (2013). The Good Lives Model (GLM) in theory and practice. *Sexual Abuse in Australia and New Zealand, 5* (1), 3–9.

World Health Organization. (2003). *Intervening with perpetrators of intimate partner violence: A global perspective* / Emily F. Rothman, Alexander Butchart, Magdalena Cerdá. World Health Organization. Geneva, Switzerland https://apps.who.int/iris/handle/10665/42647

Wright, E. M., & Benson, M. L. (2010). Immigration and intimate partner violence: Exploring the immigrant paradox. *Social Problems, 57* (3), 480–503.

APPENDIX I: IPES GLOBAL MEETINGS

	COUNTRY	THEME	HOST
1994	Switzerland	Police Challenges and Strategies	Canton Police, Geneva, Switzerland
1995	Spain	Challenges of Policing Democracies	International Institute of the Sociology of Law, Basque Country, Spain
1996	Japan	Organized Crime	Kanagawa University
1997	Austria	International Police Cooperation	Federal Police in Vienna, Austria
1998	The Netherlands	Crime Prevention	Dutch Police, Europol
1999	India	Policing of Public Order	Andhra Pradesh Police, Hyderabad, India
2000	Evanston, Illinois, USA	Traffic Policing	Northwestern University, Center for Public Safety
2001	Poland	Corruption: A Threat to World Order	Police of Poland
2002	Turkey	Police Education and Training	Turkish National Police
2003	Bahrain	Police and Community	Kingdom of Bahrain
2004	Canada	Criminal Exploitation of Women and Children	Abbotsford Police Department Canadian Police College, Royal Canadian Mounted Police, University College of the Fraser Valley, Vancouver Police Department
2005	The Czech Republic	Challenges of Policing in the 21st Century: A Global Assessment	The Czech Police Academy, The Ministry of the Interior, The Czech Republic
2006	Turkey	Local Linkages to Global Security and Crime: Thinking Locally and Acting Globally	Turkish National Police
2007	Dubai	Urbanization and Security	Dubai Police
2008	USA, Ohio	Police Without Borders: The Fading Distinction Between Local and Global	Cincinnati Police Department and Ohio Association of Chiefs of Police

	COUNTRY	*THEME*	*HOST*
2009	FYR Macedonia	Policing, the Private Sector, Economic Development and Social Change: Contemporary Global Trends	Ministry of Interior, Republic of Macedonia
2010	Malta	Tourism, Strategic Locations and Major Events: Policing in an Age of Mobility, Mass Movement and Migration	Commissioner John Rizzo and Malta Police
2010	India	Community Policing: Theoretical Problems and Operational Issues	Government of Kerala and the Kerala Police Department
2011	Argentina	Policing Violence, Crime, Disorder, and Discontent: International Perspectives	IPES
2011	Sweden	Contemporary Issues in Public Safety and Security	The Blekinge Institute of Technology and the Swedish Police
2012	USA, New York	Economic Development, Armed Violence and Public Safety	In Cooperation with the United Nations Dept. of Economic and Social Affairs NGO Branch
2013	Hungary	Global Issues in Contemporary Policing	The Ministry of Interior and The Hungarian National Police
2014	India	Policing by Consent: Theoretical Challenges and Operational Issues	Kerala Police Department
2014	Bulgaria	Crime Prevention and Community Resilience: Police Role with Victims, Youth, Ethnic Minorities, and Other Partners	IPES and the Bulgarian Ministry of Interior
2015	Thailand	Police Governance and Human Trafficking: Promoting Preventative and Comprehensive Strategies	The Royal Thai Police Association, The Royal Thai Police, and Shinawatra University
2016	USA, Washington DC	Urban Security: Challenges for 21st Century Global Cities	The George Washington University
2017	England	Organized Crime and Terrorism: Policing Challenges for Local to International Level	Liverpool John Moores University
2018	Austria	International Police Cooperation	United Nations Office on Drugs and Crime
2019	Serbia	Contemporary Police Challenges in Light of a New World and New Knowledge	IPES
2022	Albany, New York, USA	Integrating Science, Technology, and Higher Education into Policing: Interdisciplinary and International Perspectives	IPES and University of Albany (Criminal Justice School)

APPENDIX II: IPES PUBLICATIONS

A. Advances in Police Theory and Practice—Routledge

1. *Exploring Contemporary Police Challenges: A Global Perspective*
   - Sanja Kutnjak Ivković
   - Jon Maskály
   - Christopher M. Donner
   - Irena Cajner Mraović
   - Dilip Das
2. *Translational Criminology in Policing*
   - The George Mason police research
   - David Weisburd
3. *Police Behavior, Hiring, and Crime Fighting: An International View*
   - John A. Eterno
   - Ben Stickle
   - Diana Scharff Peterson
   - Dilip K. Das
4. *Women in Policing around the World: Doing Gender and Policing in a Gendered Organization*
   - Vanessa Garcia
5. *Policing in France*
   - Jacques de Maillard
   - Wesley G. Skogan
6. *Policing and Mentally Ill: International Perspectives*
   - Duncan Chappell
7. *Civilian Oversight of Police: Advancing Accountability in Law Enforcement*
   - Tim Prenzler
   - Garth den Heyer
8. *Cold Cases: Evaluation Models with Follow-Up Strategies for Investigators*, Second Edition
   - James M. Adcock
   - Sarah L. Stein

9. *Collaborative Policing: Police, Academics, Professionals, and Communities Working Together for Education, Training, and Program Implementation*
   - Peter C. Kratcoski
   - Maximilian Edelbacher
10. *Community Policing: International Patterns and Comparative Perspectives*
    - Dominique Wisler
    - Ihekwoaba D. Onwudiwe
11. *Community Policing and Peacekeeping*
    - Peter Grabosky
12. *Crime Linkage: Theory, Research, and Practice*
    - Jessica Woodhams
    - Craig Bennell
13. *Delivering Police Services Effectively*
    - Garth den Heyer
14. *Ethics for Police Translators and Interpreters*
    - Sedat Mulayim
    - Miranda Lai
15. *Honor-Based Violence: Policing and Prevention*
    - Karl Anton Roberts
    - Gerry Campbell
    - Glen Lloyd
16. *Los Angeles Police Department Meltdown: The Fall of the Professional-Reform Model of Policing*
    - James Lasley
17. *Police Corruption: Preventing Misconduct and Maintaining Integrity*
    - Tim Prenzler
18. *Police Integrity Management in Australia: Global Lessons for Combating Police Misconduct*
    - Louise Porter
    - Tim Prenzler
19. *Police Investigative Interviews and Interpreting: Context, Challenges and Strategies*
    - Sedat Mulayim
    - Miranda Lai
    - Caroline Norma
20. *Police Performance Appraisals: A Comparative Perspective*
    - Serdar Kenan Gul
    - Paul O'Connell
21. *Police Organized Crime: Intelligence Strategy Implementation*
    - Petter Gottschalk
22. *Policing Terrorism: Research Studies into Police Counterterrorism Investigations*
    - David Lowe
23. *Policing White-Collar Crime: Characteristics of White-Collar Criminals*
    - Petter Gottschalk
24. *Policing in Hong Kong: History and Reform*
    - Kam C. Wong
25. *Policing in Israel: Studying Crime Control, Community, and Counterterrorism*
    - Tal Jonathan-Zamir
    - David Weisburd
    - Badi Hasisi

26. *Security Governance, Policing, and Local Capacity*
    - Jan Froestad
    - Clifford Shearing
27. *The International Trafficking of Human Organs: A Multidisciplinary Perspective*
    - Leonard Territo
    - Rande Matteson
28. *Police and Society in Brazil*
    - Vicente Riccio
    - Wesley G. Skogan
29. *Police Reform in China*
    - Kam C. Wong
30. *Cold Cases: An Evaluation Model with Follow-Up Strategies for Investigators*
    - James M. Adcock
    - Sarah L. Stein
31. *The Crime Numbers Game: Management by Manipulation*
    - John A. Eterno
    - Eli B. Silverman
32. *Mission-Based Policing*
    - John P. Crank
    - Dawn M. Irlbeck
    - Rebecca K. Murray
    - Mark Sundermeier
33. *The New Khaki: The Evolving Nature of Policing in India*
    - Arvind Verma

B. Co-Publications—Routledge/Taylor & Francis

34. *Change and Reform in Law Enforcement: Old and New Efforts from across the Globe*
    - Scott W. Phillips
    - Dilip K. Das
35. *Contemporary Issues in Law Enforcement and Policing*
    - Andrew Millie
    - Dilip K. Das
36. *Criminal Abuse of Women and Children: An International Perspective*
    - Obi N.I. Ebbe
    - Dilip K. Das
37. *Economic Development, Crime, and Policing: Global Perspectives*
    - Frederic Lemieux
    - Garth den Heyer
    - Dilip K. Das
38. *Effective Crime Reduction Strategies: International Perspectives*
    - James F. Albrecht
    - Dilip K. Das
39. *Examining Political Violence: Studies of Terrorism, Counterterrorism, and International War*
    - David Lowe
    - Austin Turk
    - Dilip K. Das

40. *Global Community Policing: Problems and Challenges*
    - Arvind Verma
    - Dilip K. Das
    - Manoj Abraham
41. *Global Environment of Policing*
    - Darren Palmer
    - Michal M. Berlin
    - Dilip K. Das
42. *Global Issues in Contemporary Policing*
    - John Eterno
    - Arvind Verma
    - Aiedeo Mintie Das
    - Dilip K. Das
43. *Global Perspectives on Crime Prevention and Community Resilience*
    - Diana Scharff Peterson
    - Dilip K. Das
44. *Global Trafficking in Women and Children*
    - Obi N.I. Ebbe
    - Dilip K. Das
45. *Police without Borders: The Fading Distinction between Local and Global*
    - Cliff Roberson
    - Dilip K. Das
    - Jennie K. Singer
46. *Policing Global Movement: Tourism, Migration, Human Trafficking and Terrorism*
    - S. Caroline Taylor
    - Daniel Joseph Torpy
    - Dilip K. Das
47. *The Evolution of Policing: Worldwide Innovations and Insights*
    - Melchor C. de Guzman
    - Aiedeo Mintie Das
    - Dilip K. Das
48. *Urbanization, Policing and Security: Global Perspectives*
    - Gary Cordner
    - AnnMarie Cordner
    - Dilip K. Das
49. *Policing Major Events: Perspectives from Around the World*
    - James F. Albrecht
    - Martha Christine Dow
    - Darryl Plecas
    - Dilip K. Das
50. *Strategies and Responses to Crime: Thinking Locally, Acting Globally*
    - Melchor de Guzman
    - Aiedeo Mintie Das
    - Dilip K. Das

C. Interviews with Global Leaders in Policing, Courts and Prisons—Routledge

51. *Trends in the Judiciary: Interviews with Judges across the Globe*, Volume Four
    - Wendell C. Wallace
    - Michael M. Berlin
    - Dilip K. Das
52. *Trends in Policing: Interviews with Police Leaders across the Globe*, Volume Six
    - Bruce F. Baker
    - Dilip K. Das
53. *Trends in Corrections: Interviews with Corrections Leaders around the World*, Volume Two
    - Martha Henderson Hurley
    - Dilip K. Das
54. *Trends in Corrections: Interviews with Corrections Leaders around the World*, Volume One
    - Jennie K. Singer
    - Dilip K. Das
    - Eileen Ahlin
55. *Trends in Legal Advocacy: Interviews with Prosecutors and Criminal Defense Lawyers across the Globe*, Volume One
    - Jane Goodman-Delahunty
    - Dilip K. Das
56. *Trends in Policing: Interviews with Police Leaders across the Globe*, Volume Five
    - Bruce F. Baker
    - Dilip K. Das
57. *Trends in Policing: Interviews with Police Leaders across the Globe*, Volume Four
    - Bruce F. Baker
    - Dilip K. Das
58. *Trends in the Judiciary: Interviews with Judges across the Globe*, Volume One
    - Dilip K. Das
    - Cliff Roberson
59. *Trends in the Judiciary: Interviews with Judges across the Globe*, Volume Three
    - David Lowe
    - Dilip K. Das
60. *Trends in the Judiciary: Interviews with Judges across the Globe*, Volume Two
    - David Lowe
    - Dilip K. Das
61. *Trends in Corrections: Interviews with Corrections Leaders around the World*, Volume Three
    - Dilip K. Das
    - Philip Birch
62. *Trends in Policing: Interviews with Police Leaders across the Globe*, Volume Two
    - Dilip K. Das
    - Otwin Marenin
63. s*Trends in Policing: Interviews with Police Leaders across the Globe*, Volume Three
    - Otwin Marenin
    - Dilip K. Das

INDEX

Note: Page numbers in **bold** and *italics* represents tables and figures, respectively.

For Product Safety Concerns and Information please contact our EU representative GPSR@taylorandfrancis.com Taylor & Francis Verlag GmbH, Kaufingerstraße 24, 80331 München, Germany